MW01140294

Beyond Rationality

Egon Brunswik. A revolutionary thinker in psychology and an underappreciated man who was a century ahead of his time. (Reprinted courtesy of the Department of Psychology, University of California, Berkeley.)

Beyond Rationality

The Search for Wisdom
in a Troubled Time

Kenneth R. Hammond

UNIVERSITY PRESS

2007

OXFORD
UNIVERSITY PRESS

Oxford University Press, Inc., publishes works that further
Oxford University's objective of excellence
in research, scholarship, and education.

Oxford   New York
Auckland   Cape Town   Dar es Salaam   Hong Kong   Karachi
Kuala Lumpur   Madrid   Melbourne   Mexico City   Nairobi
New Delhi   Shanghai   Taipei   Toronto

With offices in
Argentina   Austria   Brazil   Chile   Czech Republic   France   Greece
Guatemala   Hungary   Italy   Japan   Poland   Portugal   Singapore
South Korea   Switzerland   Thailand   Turkey   Ukraine   Vietnam

Published by Oxford University Press, Inc.
198 Madison Avenue, New York, New York 10016

www.oup.com

Oxford is a registered trademark of Oxford University Press

Library of Congress Cataloging-in-Publication Data
Hammond, Kenneth R.
Beyond rationality : the search for wisdom
in a troubled time /
Kenneth R. Hammond.
   p. cm.
ISBN-13 978-0-19-531174-7
ISBN 0-19-531174-4
1. Judgment.   2. Decision making.   I. Title.
BF447.H36 2007
153.4'6—dc22   2006010277

9 8 7 6 5 4 3 2 1

Printed in the United States of America
on acid-free paper

Preface

This book concerns the search for wisdom in the twentieth century. No one book can tell that story in its entirety; this book will focus on the efforts of cognitive psychologists who introduced the study of human judgment in the middle of that century, not only because that is what the author knows best, but also because the work that has evolved from it, and will evolve from it, is the most likely source of wisdom in the twenty-first century.

I need not belabor the importance of the topic. Our previous mistakes (such as wars and pollution) have laid ruin to too much of the planet, and now it has become evident that our mistakes could be irrevocable: it is within our power to make the world uninhabitable. There may be many ways to prevent future mistakes, but one stands out for me, and that is the achievement of the wisdom to avoid them. And it will take wisdom, for it is now clear that our dependence on rationality and intuition is no longer sufficient. The purpose of this book is to make the achievement of wisdom more likely by creating a new way of organizing our knowledge of judgment and decision making.

In the attempt to achieve this goal, I first explain the nature of human judgment and the nature of the research that has been undertaken to study it. Second, I put forward a theory of human judgment that will serve to organize the content and form of the information provided. Third, I address the question of "what good is all this to the lay reader" by offering eight case studies that show how the theory can be applied. Finally, I address the question of what wisdom consists of and offer examples of persons who have achieved it and those who have not, and have left ruin in their wake. Possibly the small step toward achieving wisdom that this book tries to take will contribute to slowing the march toward what now seems to be inevitable: catastrophic events due to human folly. But even if it does nothing more than encourage more young scientists to engage in the study of judgment and decision making, and thus to produce the knowledge and skill we need to head off the catastrophes that seem to await us, I will be satisfied.

Note to the Layperson Reader

The intended audience for this book includes the layperson whose interest in judgment and decision making runs deeper than merely learning a few simple rules. I know, however, from much personal experience as a teacher, consultant, and researcher that most people, including most professional people, are romantics, not rationalists, with regard to behavioral science. So I shall address the place of the romantic approach. Although most people are willing to accept that the physical universe is under the control of physical laws, that these laws are objective and universal, and that they have always been so, their belief does not extend to the matter of our judgment and decision making—far from it. Nearly everyone believes that free will applies here, and it is the essence of our freedom that we can think, and form our judgments, in whatever manner we choose, and that no researcher knows any more about how we do that than we ourselves do. And so the author of a book that purports to tell the unconvinced that in fact a great deal is known about human judgment faces a difficult problem.

I have explained this because I want the reader to know that I am guessing that the reader is more of a romanticist than I, and I am accepting that this barrier exists between us. Yet I hope and believe that it is a permeable barrier, and that we will come to agree on the utility of much of what I have to say. It is for this reason that I have included eight case studies in which I demonstrate the explicit relevance of the material in this book to the social and political context in which we live. Finally, I hope that my effort to link modern cognitive psychology, history, and current events will succeed in enticing readers to pursue these topics themselves.

Throughout this book I will use material drawn mainly from the everyday problems of political and social life, rather than exclusively from scientific and technical papers and books, as illustrations and examples. Newspapers, magazines, and mid-level, nontechnical books, will be among the principal sources cited, and references to technical material will be held to a minimum. Although I will move the discussion away from technicalities, abstractions, and esoteric knowledge, that does not mean that I have written a "how to" book. An additional goal to those listed above is to inform interested citizens about the growth of knowledge about one of the most important activities of their lives as human beings and citizens—exercising their judgment, individually, and with others, in the creation of social policy.

Acknowledgments

Thanks go to Len Adelman, Peter Armbruster, Michael Doherty, Philip Dunwoody, Jack Dowie, Bo Earle, Gerd Gigerenzer, Dick Joyce, Alex Kirlik, Donald MacQuarrie, Kathy Mosier, Hedy Page, Court Peterson, Thomas Stewart, the Sunday Morning Breakfast Club, Claudia Tebaldi, Peter Todd, Elise Weaver, and James Wolf, for advice and criticism. Stephen Holtje provided developmental editing for Oxford University Press. I especially want to thank Jennifer Rappaport and Christine Dahlin of Oxford University Press for their unfailing assistance in the production of the book.

Special thanks to my two daughters, Pam Hammond and Kathy Armbruster, for their strong support and valuable critical comments on numerous drafts of the manuscript. Special thanks also to Bob Bateman for his many critical readings, many good suggestions for improving the manuscript, and those good Friday morning discussions.

This book is dedicated to my daughters, Pamela Hammond and Kathleen Hammond.

Contents

Introduction

Judgment and decision making became the object of serious, systematic inquiry in the twentieth century. Much progress has been made, but there are still considerable divisions in the field, and what has been learned has not, in general, been disseminated either to the general public or to policymakers, although certainly there have been some efforts made in the latter direction. It is hoped that this book can be another step in that dissemination by showing what the problems inherent in judgment and decision making are, what we have learned about the processes we apply to the task, which strategies work when and why, and what new modes of thought will need to be applied for future progress. By breaking the field down into specific topics and then taking what we have learned regarding them and applying it to case studies of famous circumstances of judgment and decision making, we will provide an overview of the field while examining real-life applications. Our case studies are on a macro scale, but the general principles involved can be applied on any scale, from the most personal to the grandest.

Uncertainty

The greatest barrier to the competence of our judgment, and thus to wisdom, is uncertainty—not the subjective uncertainty we feel when we exercise our judgment, but the uncertainty in the world to which our judgments apply. And, unfortunately, there are very few circumstances where such uncertainty is absent, and so we are left with getting it right sometimes and getting it wrong sometimes, without a clue as to why it is one or the other. And when that happens, it's hard to know where the trouble lies. Our inherent limitations? Simply faulty knowledge? Our emotions or passions? Perhaps all of these. But the view taken here is that it's the uncertainty "out there" that obstructs and divides us. So we will first examine uncertainty, a topic that has always been significant in our lives and the lives of our forebears. And now that terrorism is also a significant part of our lives, uncertainty will be prominent (look at any airport!), for terrorism thrives on it. But if uncertainty evokes and demands yet our judgment, and if judgment is such an integral part of our cognitive activity, surely we have developed ways of coping with it—and indeed we have, when we don't turn our backs on it. The most prominent method of coping, the method that has achieved the most respect, is to turn to the cognitive process of "rationality."

Combating Uncertainty with Rationality

No discussion of human judgment is complete without a consideration of rationality, for rationality is the modern tool we use to combat uncertainty. Rationality is a concept that has served us well in this battle, but we badly need a better idea, because after at least 5,000 years of vigorous discourse, rationality remains a concept whose interpretation is susceptible to personal preference, idiosyncratic explication, and popular misunderstanding, and, therefore, has produced countless varieties of meaning. As a result, at the beginning of the twenty-first century, there is no universal agreement on what it means to be rational. A proliferation of meanings makes it necessary for responsible authors to say exactly what they mean by rationality.

Here is a current and important example. Amartya Sen is a world-renowned scholar and a winner of a Nobel Prize in economics who recently wrote *Rationality and Freedom*. From an author such as this, we expect a clear definition and exposition of what "rationality" entails, and we do get both. But Sen introduces it to the reader by writing that "rationality is interpreted *here*, broadly, as the discipline of subjecting one's choices—of actions as well as of objectives, values and priorities—to reasoned scrutiny" (italics mine).[1] My purpose is not to quarrel with Sen's interpretation, but to ask, Why "here"? Because Sen expects rationality to be defined differently by different authors, and indeed it is. Sen says that "it is important to reclaim for humanity the ground that has been taken from it by various arbitrarily narrow formulations of the demands of rationality."[2] There are two things to learn from Sen's interpretation of the meaning of rationality. First, rationality has lost its status as a criterion with a uniform standard; second, that loss has occurred because that standard has been too narrow. In short, it is now recognized that something better is needed.

The need for "something better" became startlingly clear recently when Rex Brown, a distinguished practitioner of decision analysis and a long-term consultant to high levels of both industry and government, wrote an article titled "The Operation Was a Success but the Patient Died: Aider Priorities Influence Decision Aid Usefulness."[3] Brown drew the surprising conclusion that (quantitative) decision analysis did not drive out all nonreational features of decision making, for much depends on the interaction between the "aider" and the "decider." His quotations from leading persons in the field reach the level of "shocking." For example, Stephen Watson, the coauthor of a decision analysis text, wrote to Brown that "a reason for non use of [decision analysis] is the general flight from analysis. . . . Much of modern management writing talks about intuition and management craft, rather than analysis. . . . Intuition is always necessary—and may be better in the end than extensive analysis."[4] That sentence would have drawn a sneer from decision analysts as far back as the 1970s and might well have been used in a decision analysis text from then on as a horrid example of what happens when the benefits of decision analysis are ignored. Brown's article shows how far we have come from the days when analytical thought was considered to be the unimpeachable standard that trumped all other varieties of cognition and when intuition was scorned. Now we find that there has been a retreat from that position from those who were its most ardent advocates.

But that article wasn't enough for Brown. When invited to present the keynote address at the International Conference on Creativity and Innovation in Decision Making and Decision Support at the London School of Economics and Political Science on June 30, 2006, he went so far as to acknowledge that major corporations have cut back on decision analysis and that numerous authorities have disparaged it. Even Harvard, where it had all begun, has dropped study of decision analysis as an MBA requirement. Brown has acknowledged that "the decision analysis course [he] now teach[es] . . . is designed to educate the *intuition* of would-be deciders, not to have them rely on formal models when they come to make real professional choices."[5]

The struggle between analysis and intuition isn't a new one; it goes back in history. For example, Elizabeth Kolbert noted that Max Weber, the famous originator of sociological inquiry, was found to include in his oft-cited *The Protestant Ethic and the Spirit of Capitalism* (1904–1905) "sixteen different senses of 'rational' . . . among them 'systematic,' 'impersonal,' 'sober,' 'scrupulous,' and 'efficacious.' "[6] Isaiah Berlin, perhaps the twentieth century's foremost historian of ideas, takes us back a bit further. He compared the views on rationality of six famous seventeenth- and eighteenth-century philosophers and found that they all had something different to say about rationality, or different ways of employing "reason." According to Berlin, Rousseau, one of the most famous eighteenth-century philosophers, "speaks like any other . . . philosopher, and says 'we must employ our reason.' " But Berlin finds that he does so in a strange manner:

> [Rousseau] uses deductive reasoning, sometimes very cogent, very lucid and extremely well-expressed, for reaching his conclusions. But in

reality what happens is that this deductive reasoning is like a strait-jacket of logic which he claps upon the inner, burning, almost lunatic vision within; it is this extraordinary combination of this insane inner vision with the cold rigorous strait-jacket of a kind of Calvinistic logic which really gives his prose its powerful enchantment and its hypnotic effect. You appear to be reading logical argument which distinguishes between concepts and draws conclusions in a valid manner from prem-ises, when all the time something very violent is being said to you. A vision is being imposed on you; somebody is trying to dominate you by means of a very coherent, although often a very deranged, vision of life, to bind a spell, not to argue, despite the cool and collected way in which he appears to be talking.[7]

Berlin also notes that Kant, another famous philosopher, "did talk a great deal about how important it is to emphasize the element of rationality (though what he meant by that has always been very far from clear)."[8]

It would not be difficult to go on at length; entire books have been written about the disorderly life of the concept of rationality. But that exposition would be a digression. The critical question is: Why is it important for students of hu-man judgment to have a clear, consistent conception of what rationality means, and what it requires? Because one of the first questions a judgment will meet is, is it a rational judgment? If there is no clear, well-accepted conception of the meaning of rationality, we can't answer that question. In short, this book will go beyond rationality because we need to, and we need to because rationality has not rid itself of the ambiguity it has acquired over the millennia and, as a result, it remains dependent on idiosyncratic preferences. But where should we go when we go beyond rationality? We will search for wisdom, because this is the term we have for the cognitive activity we employ that we believe is better—somehow—than rationality.

The attack on the failure of rationality has been two-pronged. One concerns its failure as a description of human judgment (the psychologists are enthusiastic about this); the other is rationality's failure as a prescription for human judgment (the psychologists lead the way here also, but many others have joined them). In later chapters I will describe how rationality has been found wanting as a de-scription, a representation, of how people make their judgments, decisions, and choices, and also how rationality has failed as a guide to the proper way to make those judgments, decisions, and choices. Here I will add only that this topic is not restricted to ivory tower academics with their heads buried in books. Deputy Secretary of Defense Paul Wolfowitz sharply disputed the army's estimate that several hundred thousand troops would be needed in postwar Iraq. At a congressional hearing he said,

> We have no idea what we will need until we get there on the
> ground. . . . Every time we get a briefing on the war plan, it immediately goes down six different branches . . . If we costed each and every
> one the costs would range from 10 billion to 100 billion.

Thus, Mr. Wolfowitz was telling us, there was no point in trying to ascertain the cost of each and every one because the variation in the results would render the operation useless. So we should ask: Was Mr. Wolfowitz being irrational by not pursuing the costs on each of the branches—each, that is, of the various possible roads that the war might take? Well, yes, he was, if you insist on the standard logic that is held up to us as a necessary condition for the rationality of a judgment. But not if you listen to the researchers in judgment and decision making, for they have found that Mr. Wolfowitz's method is exactly the method implicitly used by all of us nearly all, if not all, of the time. It's called "bounded rationality," meaning being satisfied with pursuing logical branches only a small part of the way and being satisfied with the result. Actually, Mr. Wolfowitz seemed to be satisfied with *no* pursuit of the branches until "we get there on the ground" which, of course, means after the decision to go to war is made and one of the six branches is chosen and cannot be un-chosen.

Judgment: The Cognitive Process by Which We Are Judged

I must now say something about judgment, also a concept with its own baggage about rationality. If you are old enough to be aware of the critical role of judgment in your life, you will be curious about just how it works. You will also be keenly aware that any matter of importance will require your judgment, however it works. But just exactly how to make those judgments about important matters is a challenge in itself, and has been since we developed the capacity to reflect about our judgments. The intention to analyze our judgment processes was one of the boldest and most significant events in human history, and because judgment is the cognitive process that you—and everybody else—understands least, it is the central topic of this book.

One's judgment has long been the core cognitive process by which we are judged by others. And it is our judgment that we value highly, perhaps most of all. Rarely do we take kindly to the criticism that we "lack good judgment." In the seventeenth century, a very keen observer of human behavior, François, Duc de La Rochefoucauld, wrote, "Everyone complains of his memory, and no one complains of his judgment."[9] He saw that errors of memory were easily forgiven, but an admission of errors of judgment would cast doubt on a person's wisdom. Since one's wisdom defines one's value and status, the wise person gets respect from almost everyone; the fool from no one. Thus, everyone wants to be protective—and proud—of their judgments. And, of course, mistaken judgments give rise to major problems—war, for example, as I will show below. First, however, we will have to agree on just what a mistaken judgment is, or how we will recognize a mistake when it happens.

The Two Standards for Evaluating Judgment

There are two general ways we evaluate another person's judgments. One is to ask if they are empirically correct: When someone judges this tree to be ten feet tall, will a yardstick prove that she is right? Another way is to ask if they are logically correct: When someone says that a belief they hold is true, does it contradict some other belief they also assert is true? The first is called correspondence competence because it evaluates the correspondence between the judgment and the empirical fact that is the object of the judgment. (Was the tree actually ten feet tall?) The second is called coherence competence because it evaluates the consistency of the elements of the person's judgment. (Did the person making the judgment make contradictory statements in justifying his or her judgment?) Rationality is ordinarily of little importance in relation to correspondence competence; you don't turn to logic to prove that the tree you see over there is larger than the one over here, or that one person over there is taller than another. But sometimes there is no "tree," that is, no criterion to allow us to evaluate the competence of the judgment. In that case, we call upon rationality for evaluating the competence of the judgment. For example, a story told by someone usually offers no empirical criterion for its truth. Then, we can evaluate it by referring to the coherence of the story, that is, its rationality. It is always important that a story "makes sense," that it does not contain contradictions; that is all we can do when an empirical criterion is not available.

So it will be important for the reader to learn about these two very different ways of evaluating judgments; most people know nothing whatever about them, although, of course, they employ them all the time. I will have a great deal to say below about both of these ways of evaluating a person's judgments. Most important, I will explain how and why the concept of rationality no longer plays such a commanding role in the evaluation of the coherence of a person's judgment, and why such judgments as those by Wolfowitz (described above) are becoming more acceptable, despite their apparent lack of rationality.

Explaining Coherence

The concept of correspondence needs little explanation, for we frequently compare judgments with the empirical object or state of affairs judged, especially when the judgment is a prediction of a future event (did the prediction of the weather correspond to the weather that occurred?) The concept of coherence is not a familiar concept, however. So I explain this idea a bit more fully.

Webster's Third International defines coherence as "a systematic or methodical connectedness or interrelatedness, especially when governed by logical principles." That is really all we need for our purposes. But Webster's further definition helps because it speaks directly to our interests: "Coherence theory: the theory that the ultimate criterion of truth is the coherence of all its separate parts with one another and with experience—contrasted with correspondence theory."

Now we need an example of coherence theory at work. Consider the case of air traffic control. On days when the weather creates delays, the delays can back up much of the system. For example, if planes aren't leaving San Francisco because destinations in the Midwest are blocked or shut down because of snow or tornados, then planes headed for San Francisco cannot leave their locations because there are no empty gates in San Francisco for the arriving planes to discharge their passengers. So the planes for San Francisco can't depart from wherever they are, but not because of any difficulty on their part; it is the weather in the Midwest that keeps the San Francisco-headed planes from departing. So, because planes can't leave *from* San Francisco, planes can't leave *for* San Francisco. In short, traffic halts and a disaster due to a traffic jam is avoided. Thus, we see that the performance of each piece of the system—each plane—depends on the performance of each of the others. That interrelationship is what makes a system coherent. And that coherence is what makes the system work, and, as I shall show later, is also the Achilles' heel of the system.

A more cogent example is given by the economist Richard Parker in relation to the coherence of a part of the economic system. In his effort to show the regrettable effect of one of Ronald Reagan's policies, Parker states,

> The banks and S&L's tested their new freedom [given to them by
> Reagan] by raising the interest rates they paid on deposits in order to
> lure back the billions that had been siphoned off by money market
> funds, that Nixon-era invention which, free of federal regulations and
> insurance, had exploded in popularity and cash deposits. But this
> meant the banks needed to make high return loans in order to pay depositors the same rates as their new competitors, and that in turn
> meant—as it has with Third World lending—going after riskier loan
> customers, with what turned out to the same disastrous results.[10]

Tension between Correspondence and Coherence

We can see examples of the tension between the correspondence and coherence strategies for seeking truth in the newspapers every day. As I write, the United States is gripped with fear over the appearance of "mad cow disease." The future course of this disease is a topic of enormous interest in the newspapers, and *The New York Times* carried a column on January 2, 2004, by Eric Schlosser (an author of food-related books). Schlosser, after noting that "Japan tests every cow and steer that people are going to eat," included this paragraph:

> Instead of testing American cattle the government has relied heavily on work by the Harvard Center for Risk Analysis to determine how much of a threat mad cow disease poses to the United States. For the past week the Agriculture Department has emphasized the reassuring findings of these Harvard studies, but a closer examination of them is not comforting.

Why are these Harvard studies not comforting? Because "they are based on computer models of how mad cow disease might spread." In short, the conclusions they produce are justified by their coherence only. Schlosser quotes the Harvard report that acknowledges, "Our model is not amenable to formal validation . . . because there are no controlled experiments in which the introduction and consequences of [mad cow disease] to a country [have] been monitored and measured."[11] In short, the studies are "not comforting" because there are no corresponding empirical facts associated with them. That is a common objection to all coherence-based models.

But correspondence is the wrong criterion to apply to the justification of a coherence-based conclusion; the authors of the Harvard report knew that there were no new empirical facts available before they began their work. So they sought coherence among the facts they had. The correct criterion is the quality of the scientific information that went into the model and the logic of the model. When you don't have new empirical facts, you rely on the coherence of your representation of what knowledge you do have. (Trial lawyers have an old saying to illustrate the difference between coherence and correspondence: "If the facts are against you, pound the law. If the law is against you, pound the facts. If both the facts and the law are against you, pound the table." In other words, if you can't achieve correspondence, try urging coherence. If coherence is against you, try urging the facts. If both are against you, your cause is probably lost, but try vehemence.) The point of these examples is to provide a contrast of the coherence strategy with the correspondence strategy. It is easy to see the difference between the judgment that is directed toward coherence—"make it all fit together"—and one that is directed toward the correspondence between a judgment and a fact.

Throughout Western history there has been a long, tortured philosophical discourse about these two strategies for making judgments and their relative value as roads to "truth." But though these two judgment strategies are in constant use, few have ever made this distinction among their judgments, and nearly all—including our most respected intellectuals and political leaders—confuse them, to their detriment. As I will show in the case studies, one of our most gifted and intelligent secretaries of the treasury displayed his ignorance of these two strategies in a way that shows that he really didn't understand how he made his decisions. In short, understanding the strengths and weaknesses of these strategies and in which situations they are best suited for use is of critical importance, not only with respect to making judgments but also for evaluating the wisdom of the judgments of others.

Our Conception of Human Judgment Changed in the Twentieth Century

The difference lies in the fact that in the latter half of the twentieth century, students of human judgment began performing experiments in the effort to learn about the role of coherence and correspondence competence in the critical cognitive activity of judgment and decision making. That is, instead of merely arguing about their ideas, or justifying them by claiming coherence with some grand principle, psychologists began to test their ideas empirically. In short, they tested the correspondence between their ideas and the facts of behavior in experiments. And the results of these experiments have enabled us to learn a great deal.[12]

It is now apparent that the twenty-first century will bring forward new and more sophisticated research to enlighten us about human judgment. Even better, that research will take us to the next step beyond rationality; it will enlighten us about wisdom, which is what we have always been after. Although today few study wisdom empirically (I discuss two of the most prominent authors below), more will be undertaking that in the twenty-first century. And that is how things are different. We can now make some progress in understanding this most important feature of ourselves, and most important, perhaps discover why it is that human beings still find it necessary to seek out fellow human beings who live on other continents, and whom they have never seen, and never will see—and slaughter them and destroy everything they hold dear.

Undertaking Research in Human Judgment Marked a New Step

The most interesting and significant aspect of the empirical research on human judgment is the fact of its existence. All of us are jealous of our judgment, and we do not care to have others explain our mistakes in judgment to us. One psychologist, whose courage outran his abilities, did manage in the 1950s to convince a president of the United States that the president did have something to learn from him about wisdom, only to get a lecture from the president (Eisenhower).[13] As a result of general skepticism that such a complex topic could be studied empirically, even in the 1960s, the National Science Foundation in the United States looked askance at the idea of researching human judgment, refused to fund it, and left it to the Office of Naval Research to initiate the support of this research (under the rubric of "engineering psychology"). Thus it was that, despite all the skepticism, in the middle of the twentieth century, psychologists, and researchers in many other disciplines, for the first time took empirically based steps to the study of human judgment. That meant progress might well occur. And it has. As I will show in the following pages, we now know a great deal more about human judgment than we did a half century ago when this work began. (It is important to realize that this progress was not a foregone conclusion. Philosophers have done important work on this topic for centuries, but the shift from intellectual analysis to empirical study is a profound one. The interested reader can pursue philosophers' views of this topic by reading the recently published *Walking the Tightrope of Reason: The Precarious Life of a Rational Animal* by a philosopher, Robert Fogelin, who sees the many sides of rationality.)[14]

The Future

The next half century will bring changes in the way we think about human judgment and how we do the research that will enlighten us about it. That next half century will finish the break with the model of psychological science derived from physics that began in the late twentieth century and will see the adoption of a model derived from biology—surely the science of the twenty-first century. The views of these biologically oriented researchers will be of great interest, for they have, perhaps decisively, provided empirical data that has led them not only to lose faith in the value of reason but also to question our unaided ability to reason. And although their arguments differ, many researchers are asking whether the standards of reasoning that developed over the millennia are too rigid, too demanding, and too artificial to be useful. They have, in short, made a next step—a profoundly interesting one—necessary.

So, in its pursuit of the question of wisdom, this book will describe the new phase of our understanding of our most prized cognitive activity—our reason— and why that new phase developed. I have written this book for the reader who wants to know more about that. This situation holds with regard to intuition as well as reason. Again, the views of current scholars will be of interest, because they will be found to be different from those in the past that have proved to be of so little help to us that nearly all the old ideas about intuition have been abandoned. My contribution will be to offer an evolutionary view of intuition, one that has been largely missing so far. We will see what has happened to these two ideas—reason and intuition—in the twentieth century, why they do not satisfy us, and why the researchers of the twenty-first century will turn to a more powerful and ambitious endeavor: finding the character and determinants of wisdom.[15]

The New Challenge to Reason

Many scientists during the last half of the twentieth century have been empirically examining human judgment and reason and not only saw their conception of the reasoning process change but also had their faith in our ability to reason diminished. If this seems shocking or disturbing, I must remind the reader that this is not the first time in our history that reason, or rationality, has been challenged, both in terms of our capacity to be rational and in terms of the desirability of rationality itself. Irritation and impatience with analytical work has been commonplace. More than 150 years ago, the great enthusiast of rationality, John Stuart Mill, had to admit that his own thoroughgoing rational life was a personally unhappy one. In his *Autobiography* he describes how his father carefully tutored him in childhood, taught him Greek and Latin at age three (or so we are told), and led him to cultivate an enthusiasm for reason, rationality, and analysis to the exclusion of other processes. But as an adult he suddenly found that without "feelings," life becomes meaningless. He attributes this loss to his exclusive focus on reason and finds that "the habit of analysis has a tendency to wear away the feelings." He then slipped into a lengthy and profound depression. Fortunately, he recovered from that situation by finding that "the maintenance of a due balance among the faculties, now seemed . . . to be of primary importance," and he entered a new phase of life in which "the cultivation of the feelings became one of the cardinal points in [his] ethical and philosophical creed."[16] It is hard to find a better description of why a person might turn away from rational analysis toward "feelings" written by someone so well versed in what "analysis" signifies. Mill ends this episode by describing his new interest in poetry (an interest Darwin also developed at the end of a life devoted to rational analysis).[17] In short, the loss of faith in reason is not an unusual occurrence in human history.

Opposition to the desirability of reason became prominent in the seventeenth century in what became known as the Counter-Enlightenment, and is symbolized by the writings of Jean Jacques Rousseau (1712–1778), whom I introduced earlier. But if the reader is impatient for some current indications of the rejection of rationality, today's newspapers carry many examples. Corporate CEOs often proudly reject reason, as can be seen in those who will claim that important decisions came "straight from the gut." George W. Bush, president of the world's most powerful nation, described his thought processes by saying to Bob Woodward, "I just think it's instinctive. I'm not a textbook player. I'm a gut player."[18] And when Condoleezza Rice, one of Bush's closest advisors, was the national security advisor, she said her job was to "translate President Bush's instincts into policy."[19] Another indication of Bush's faith in the inexplicable is suggested by a remark he made, after his meeting with Vladimir Putin, in which he said he trusted him because he, Bush, can "see" another man's "soul" by peering into his eyes. (A few years later, when his relations with Mr. Putin became somewhat frosty, Bush would begin to doubt his initial trust.) Soon the press began focusing on Bush's decision making. As Bush was about to address the 2004 Republican convention, *The Washington Post* carried an article that included a number of answers on both sides of this question. The answer given by Fred Greenstein, a Princeton University political scientist and authority on presidential leadership styles, was this: "Bush's clarity of purpose reduces the tendency in government to let matters drift but too often 'results in a vision that may be simplistic or insufficiently examined, or something that undermines itself.' "[20] On the other hand, David Brooks, a prominent commentator on PBS and a *New York Times* columnist, demonstrated his enthusiasm for Mr. Bush's style by complaining that there wasn't enough use of instinctive judgment in forming foreign policy.

The regress from the seventeenth-century "Age of Reason" to the instinctive style of the American president is paralleled—and magnified—by the superstitions of today's terrorists, and came as a surprise to all those who thought the twenty-first century was beyond such reversions. Few expected the Counter-Enlightenment exhibited by those terrorists to reappear in such force, and with terrifying consequences. Evidently, despite all that we have heard about the glories of the Age of Reason, romanticism never disappeared or lost its attractions.

A New Component in the Challenge to Rationality

The earlier challenges to rationality were based on superstition and exhortation from religious authority. The Catholic Church took 300 years to accept Galileo, and many Protestant churches have fought against Darwin's revelations for decades; some do so—enthusiastically—even today. Now, however, the new and significant challenge to rationality comes from a new source: researchers in the field of judgment and decision making—experimenting psychologists, together with (some) experimenting economists and (some) experimenting lawyers. Thus, for the first time in history, the premier status of rationality itself is being tested on an empirical basis and—much to everyone's surprise, and to the dismay of many—found wanting. The current challenge to the idea that we are a reasoning species poses a grand paradox; are we using reason to deny that we are capable of reasoning? Yet there are also many psychologists who reject this new empirical examination of reason, and they have much on their side. In short, disarray prevails.

We will see how this situation is now being played out, not only by psychologists but also by some of our most prominent legal theorists and economists, and why three prominent researchers in this field have been awarded Nobel Prizes for their work. We need to know what these researchers have found and what they have to say about it. Should we or should we not rely on our reason? And if not reason, then what? Faith? Whose faith? Faith in what? But we all know that faith had its turn before the Enlightenment. The massacres and attendant cruelty it produced were appalling, and there is every reason to believe that they would be repeated, as the events in Ireland, the Middle East, Southeast Asia, and elsewhere show us. So the new science of human judgment will not advocate faith; it relies completely on scientific standards, and scientific standards do not employ savagery in their defense, as religious ones do. Instead, scientific practices will be used to seek wisdom.

What This Book Doesn't Cover

This book is incomplete; it is not a "theory about everything" or even a complete theory about judgment and decision making. It omits at least three important topics related to that process: the role of emotions, explication of the philosophical aspects of the process, and references to politics.

Emotions: I do not apologize for omitting discussion of the role of emotions in judgment and decision making, for two reasons: that topic has been vastly overworked to little avail in the professional and amateur literature, and I explained my views in detail in my *Judgments under Stress*. I stand by those views, which come down to this: The primary task for students of judgment and decision making is to discover the relation between the properties of the task and the properties of the cognitive system of the judge. More specifically, we should be able to predict the cognitive consequences of a *change* in task properties. I explain why, and how, this is done in that book.

Philosophical aspects: It took some courage on my part to make use of the terms *correspondence* and *coherence*, indeed, to make them cornerstones of my general theory. After all, these are terms that philosophers have used for centuries. In that sense, they *belong* to philosophers, and philosophers will surely be critical of my way of using them, for I have used them somewhat loosely; that is, I have not explained the various ways in which they have been used by philosophers. Nevertheless, I found that these concepts were fundamental to my topic and were badly needed in my discipline. So, I appropriated them, and I am glad I did, because they made it possible to organize my thoughts in a new way, as I did in *Human Judgment and Social Policy*. The reader will soon be well aware of the important place *correspondence* and *coherence* occupy in this book.

Political aspects: It was tempting throughout the writing of this book to make references to the cognitive style—and competence—of the White House's occupants at the time. By that I mean the president, vice president, and high-level members of the Bush administration. I have resisted that temptation, with the exception of my remarks about Colin Powell at the United Nations. I omitted reference to the others largely because I feared I would not have been able to escape the use of ridicule. But I respect Colin Powell and find his efforts to be worthy of criticism.[21]

PART I

The New Search for Wisdom

Clockwise from top left: **Daniel Kahneman, Amos Tversky, and Paul Slovic**. These three psychologists started a new field of research on judgment that earned Kahneman the Nobel Prize. (Photos reprinted with the permission of Daniel Kahneman, Barbara Tversky, and Paul Slovic.)

I

The Central Role of Human Judgment

Whenever the need for wisdom appears, one finds it is not merely the uneducated or poorly informed who prefer to rely on myths rather than scientific knowledge about human judgment. The search for the university president, the chief operating officer of the corporation, or the pope will begin with the formation of a committee that was itself constructed following a search for people who demonstrated what others thought to be acts of wisdom. All of these searchers will be victims of the myth that wisdom can be found only in a nominating process that buries the actual processes by which wisdom is exercised, because there is no alternative. (And the results of this mysterious process are, as might be expected, unreliable. It generally takes only five years for the carefully selected university president to be fired; CEOs fare about as well.)

Perhaps the clearest example of the belief of the educated in this process is offered to us by the great historian of ideas, Isaiah Berlin, who thought not only that we would never learn anything significant about human judgment but also that it wouldn't be a very good idea if we did, and that it might even be dangerous for all concerned. The myth that attracted Berlin was the myth of the "great man," the same myth that attracts the less fortunate: that the road to peace, justice, and success will be found by accepting the wisdom exhibited by someone who has already proven his wisdom.

For example, Berlin begins his inquiry into political judgment this way:

> What is it to have good judgment in politics? What is it to be politi-
> cally wise, or gifted, to be a political genius, or even no more than po-
> litically competent, to know how to get things done? Perhaps one way
> of looking for the answer is by considering what we are saying when
> we denounce statesmen, or pity them, for not possessing these quali-
> ties. We sometimes complain that they are blinded by prejudice or pas-
> sion, but blinded to what? We say that they don't understand the times
> they live in, or that they are resisting something called "the logic of
> the facts," or "trying to put the clock back," or that history is against
> them, or that they are ignorant or incapable of learning, or else [are]
> impractical idealists, visionaries, Utopians, hypnotized by the dream
> of some fabulous past or some unrealized future. All such expressions
> and metaphors seem to presuppose that there is something to know
> (of which the critic has some notion) which these unfortunate persons
> have somehow not managed to grasp.[1]

Berlin makes clear his disdain for a scientific approach to understanding
good judgment when he asks, "What is this knowledge that statesmen and
others fail to grasp? Is it knowledge of a science?" He thinks there is none. Yet
he has a clear idea of what good political judgment consists of, so we should
listen to him. "The quality I am attempting to describe is that special understanding of public life (or for that matter private life) which successful statesmen have, whether they are wicked or virtuous." And he points to certain
statesmen, who, he claims are "politician[s] endowed with considerable political judgment [such as] Franklin Roosevelt . . . which is conspicuously lacking
in men of more purely theoretical genius such as Newton or Einstein or Russell,
or even Freud."[2] We see from these remarks that Berlin is willing to argue that
at least some people have the capacity for good judgment (although these
might not be the ones respected for their brilliant contributions in other matters). Good judgment is clearly not simply a matter of IQ; it is a "special understanding," a gift that is granted to only a few. In short, he subscribes to the
"great man" theory of judgment.

Berlin's view comes down to the folk belief that although we can't say exactly what good judgment is, some people clearly have it, and some clearly don't,
and it's a mysterious gift, whatever it is. Widespread as that opinion might be—
even among scholars, as Berlin's remarks show us—it is precisely that belief that
science—and this book—challenges; the view taken here is that Berlin's folk belief is exactly wrong, and this book explains why.

Popular Nomination of the Wise

When we don't quite understand a concept—much as we don't understand just what the concept of wisdom entails—it is natural to look for examples of what we mean, and examples of their opposites, and work from there. So let me begin with a clear negative example: was Adolf Hitler a wise man? No. But why not? After all, millions of educated, twentieth-century Germans adored him, believed in his wisdom, and demonstrated their unquestionable willingness to die for him and his ideas. If we were operating on the assumption that we should study persons deemed wise by their peers or their followers (as the psychologists Baltes and Sternberg do) then—if we were studying this problem in the 1930s—we could defend our choice of Hitler as a wise man because millions of German citizens in the 1930s and 1940s venerated him. The same would be of true of Stalin and Mao, who were worshipped by millions of well-educated Russians, Chinese, and others in the United States, Europe, and the rest of the world.

Yet, now these men are more apt to be despised for their wanton cruelty and mindless destruction than venerated for their wisdom by the vast majority of the people who have heard of them. And no serious student of cognition would nominate them for their display of wisdom, however defined. But if we can point to men famous for their lack of wisdom, can we point to anyone famous for their possession of wisdom? Yes: Abraham Lincoln, a man acclaimed for his wisdom by the educated and uneducated alike for more than a century, will come to mind at once. (Note that the famous statue of Lincoln in Washington, D.C., portrays him sitting down, thinking, in sharp contrast to the countless portrayals of national heroes straddling white chargers, or standing with their sword pointing to the sky.)

Popular judgment aside, can we attribute wisdom to Lincoln using the theory of cognition presented here? And does the theory explain his achievement? Yes, and that account will follow. But I will be changing the criterion for apparent wisdom from peer nomination to evaluation in terms of a psychological theory of cognition. That requires some explanation.

Psychology Provides the Criteria for Wisdom

Peer nomination offers little ground for choice as a standard when pursuing academic rather than applied science; after all, why should we choose to abide by the nominations of persons who have given little thought to the problem, and in any event, would not know how to think about it if they were asked? Who knows what content and process would go into creating those nominations? What sort of defense of the choice would be offered? These questions make me skeptical toward previous work on wisdom that was based on peer nomination. Yet peer nominations do have a sociological value; it is clearly of interest to discover what sort of people are admired by their peers for their wisdom in any given place or period in history, because the characteristics of such persons will inform us about the society that nominated them. We could have learned, and possibly did learn, much about German (and Russian and Chinese) society and other societies by observing their choice of leader. But that information would tell us nothing about the psychological—particularly cognitive—processes that *produce* wisdom. It will take a theory of cognition—or better, of judgment—to do that.

But if we do not wish to rely on peer judgments of wisdom, where do we turn?

Turning to a New Discipline

Clearly, the mystique of human judgment remains, and it remains a barrier to problem solving. It is true that the scientific community has only recently pursued it, and it is also true that only a handful of experts on the subject can be found even now; just a half-century ago, there were none. Nevertheless, much has been learned, and there are now many technical and professional books available on the topic. What are they based on? On empirical research and mathematical statistics; essays are few and far between. And that is what made the difference. Instead of relying on long arguments to persuade one another of what we believe to be true about wisdom, we now point to the empirical data of experiments about human judgment. And that made it possible to progress in the latter part of the twentieth century.

Regrettably, however, little of that hard-won knowledge has been conveyed to the public at large. It is surely unfortunate because human judgment is a major operator—perhaps the major operator—in our lives. For too long, explanations and descriptions of behavior have relentlessly focused on people's motives; complex motivational theories (Freud's, for example) and restricted "reinforcement" theories fully occupy our attention. Even since the horrifying events of the twentieth century, the bloodiest century in history, there has been sharp scrutiny of the motives and personal histories of the major actors involved, but there has been scarcely any scientific study of the cognitive processes of the major actors. Yet, all those bloody battles and all those inhumane practices were—and still are—carried out as a result of someone's judgment that these were and are good things to do. Astonishing as it may be, at the beginning of the twenty-first century, the U.S. Senate finds itself discussing exactly how much torture should be practiced in prisoner interrogations.

Do cognitive scientists really know more about human judgment than the public knows? Yes. But is what they know useful? Yes. Scientific progress is being made. One goal of this book is to enable the reader to participate in, and perhaps contribute to, the understanding of that progress. And although this book will not offer a recitation of scientific studies, it is the results of scientific work that form the foundation of what will be discussed here. There is no other choice; all else is myth and misinformation, of which there is already far too much surrounding this all-important topic. Searching for the wise man, or woman, who somehow will bring his or her mysterious powers to bear on such matters is hardly a solution.

Focusing the Effort

We now have hundreds if not thousands of cognitive scientists—and cognitive neuroscientists—who are working very hard to understand our cognitive machinery, and training others to be just like them, so confident are they that finding better judgment lies, first, in gaining a scientific understanding of the human cognitive system, and, second, in discovering how to improve it. One of the reasons we focus on the cognitive processes is that is where psychology has always placed its focus—on the internal forces that drive the organism. This one-sidedness is gradually being recognized but not nearly quickly enough. And it is most important that it be recognized in the field of judgment and decision making. This field urgently needs a theory of tasks in the environment and a theory of cognitive systems—what I refer to as "ecological psychology." And psychologists' increasing interest in the ecological approach is now being matched by economists' interest in it; even Nobel Prize winners in economics are advocating an "ecological" approach.[3]

Therefore, the approach I will advocate for removing the mystery of human judgment is called the "ecological approach," and that means providing a theory of judgment tasks, and a theory of human judgment. V. O. Key gave a nice example of the environment's role in voter behavior when he said,

> The voice of the people is but an echo. The output of an echo chamber bears an inevitable relation to the input. . . . The electorate behaves about as rationally and responsibly as we should expect, given the clarity of the alternatives presented to it and the character of the information available to it.[4]

Thus, we address the problem of uncertainty in the environment, for it is that uncertainty that forces us to study judgment and decision making, since without uncertainty we would simply be talking about logic and reason and rationality. But it is uncertainty that causes—and has always caused—the greatest trouble for most of us, most of the time. And it is uncertainty that creates the drive for wisdom, for it is when we are uncertain about what to think, what to do, whom to trust, that we yearn for someone with wisdom—although we may not know exactly what wisdom is—to exercise their judgment, make the right decision for us, and tell us what to do.

Modern researchers who study judgment and decision making try to discover just how we, and other animals, cope with the uncertainty of the natural world—the world untouched by humankind. And they try to extend their work to include the unnatural world, the world of artifacts and artifactual tasks created by this same species—us. These two worlds largely overlap in terms of the judgment tasks they present.

Current Attempts at Managing Uncertainty

All of us manage uncertainty as a normal part of our existence. Generally, we pay little attention to uncertainty, and we cope with it in ways we are hardly conscious of. In these circumstances, we are not bothered by any sense of incompetence. But as the stakes become higher, and we become increasingly conscious of the uncertainty facing us, our incompetence becomes apparent to us, and we slow down and try to think. That is, we try to figure out how to use whatever information the task offers us. Unless we are trained as statisticians, however, this period doesn't last very long, for the simple reason that we don't know what to think about; that is, we don't know how to make use of the uncertain information we have. So we simply make a guess as to the correct action to take—in short, the correct judgment to make. That's all very well if we don't have to answer to anyone and are prepared to suffer the consequences of a mistake. But if we must explain ourselves to someone, then we have to figure out a way of defending our judgments; that is to say, explaining how we manage our uncertainty. That situation will drive us to think further, to become more analytical, and that will result in our becoming more aware of uncertainty and how we are managing it. Without education and training, it is doubtful that you will reach a satisfactory solution. But 9/11 led to an increase in the demand for a defensible method of dealing with uncertainty on a large scale. One way that many people found acceptable for coping with uncertainty was to employ "maximizing"; undoubtedly, you have been subject to this method many times and have always found it disagreeable. What is "maximizing"?

Maximizing: A "Brute Force" Solution to Managing Uncertainty

Let me give an example from experience with air travel. Before you board the airplane, you have to stand in line and go through a metal detector. Everyone does. No matter how unlikely it appears that a given person (a "little old lady," a tottering old man, a child) has weapons, everyone must go through the screening. The fact that everyone gets searched is society's way of managing uncertainty, and no doubt you have heard people complaint that it's obviously stupid and a waste of time. The name for the procedure that results in everyone being searched is "maximizing"; it refers to maximizing the number of correct detections of weapons. If you have taken a course in statistics, you have heard this term, because statisticians refer to the process of applying a rule to everyone as "maximizing": applying the rule to everyone maximizes the chance of success under irreducible uncertainty. It is justified, for not only is there a mathematical demonstration of the value of maximizing but there is a behavioral one as well.

Logical as maximizing may be, there is no doubt that it is an irritating way of doing things, from the perspective of those screened: it wastes a lot of time and produces many ridiculous errors. That is because searching everyone, no matter how improbable it is that they will be carrying a weapon, is a form of problem solving by "brute force"—and no one likes that, except those responsible for security and desperate for a solution.

The Duality of Error

The tactic of managing uncertainty by maximizing has obviously increased considerably in the Western world since September 11, 2001. The use of a brute force solution is excused because it is the most rational and effective means for coping with irreducible uncertainty.[5] All of us have been affected by this change in ways we generally consider unpleasant, the lines and the time wasted at airports being only one example. Every agency that is responsible for security knows that because the judgments of its screeners—any screeners—cannot eliminate the uncertainty in its efforts to detect terrorists, it must therefore treat everyone as a possible terrorist—that is the "brute force" aspect—even though they know that this tactic will result in numerous false positives. A *false positive* is a general term for someone declared guilty when in fact he or she is innocent. (A *false negative* refers to someone declared innocent when in fact he or she is guilty.)

Maximizing is a public acknowledgment of the failure of human judgment to solve the problem because human judgment produces too many errors. Human judgment as to who might be a terrorist was rejected as too weak a tool because it would produce too many false negatives, and therefore too many terrorist victories with too many innocent victims. Although the maximizing occasionally arouses outrage because of the numerous false positives, the agency practicing it knows that it takes only one false negative to create a disaster; false negatives carry far more dangerous consequences than false positives—at the airport, at least. Thus, because false negatives are often dreaded, the inconveniences produced by the false positives that brute force tactics yield are tolerated. Of course, the brute force technique does not guarantee that no false-negative errors will be made; that will also depend on the judgments of the human operatives: they are the backup. For example, despite maximizing, there were 19 false negatives—19 guilty hijackers were judged innocent by the airport screeners—and these false negatives resulted in the World Trade Center and Pentagon catastrophes on September 11, 2001.

Clearly, one faces difficulties when trying to detect dangerous persons; for example, any technique will be susceptible to both false positives and false negatives. The duality of error is a problem that any detection system coping with uncertainty must try to manage. And one of the most awkward features of systems that produce duality of error is that the errors are linked; that is, changing one error will have the opposite effect on the other: reducing false positives will increase false negatives, and vice versa. As a result, the manager of uncertainty will have to choose which one of the two errors is to be minimized. That choice will be determined by the managers' values. Introducing values has the consequence of obscuring the reason for the choice; rarely is the choice made explicit, and even less often is the value system that determined the choice made explicit and defended; most managers of uncertainty don't even know the choice exists.

Although I have discussed primarily the duality of error in relation to terrorism, it plays an equally important role in relation to social policy. In developing environment protection policy, for example, there is considerable uncertainty about the future of any ecology (the species and the environment that supports them). Therefore, any action taken to control or protect the ecology runs the risk of doing too much or not doing enough—that is, committing too many false positives or too many false negatives, overprotecting (with, for instance, negative economic effects) or underprotecting (in the worst cases, causing the extinction of species).

But not everyone has been oblivious to the implications of this significant idea. Jared Diamond, for example, in his acclaimed book *Collapse: How Societies Choose to Fail or Succeed*, understands the central role of the duality of error. In his discussion of the errors of judgment that environmentalists have made, he notes that the complaint "about some environmentalist predictions proving wrong boils down to a complaint about false alarms." He then places false alarms in the context of fire alarms: "Only if false alarms become an inordinate proportion of all fire alarms do we feel that something is wrong." But, he notes, as few have, "A very low frequency of false alarms proves that too many homeowners are being too cautious, waiting too long to call the fire department, and consequently losing their homes."[6]

Diamond extends this reasoning about uncertainty and the duality of error in a new, different, and significant way in relation to environmental judgments: "By the same reasoning, we must expect some environmentalist warnings to turn out to be false alarms, otherwise we would know that our environmentalist warning systems were much too conservative." This statement is truly revolutionary; it shows not only the frank acceptance of irreducible uncertainty but also a welcoming attitude toward error that is possibly the first of its kind. Indeed, he urges the courage to *make* errors of judgment that could have hardly been imagined in the early twentieth century. Thus, Diamond introduces a new kind of reasoning in relation to human judgment and social policy regarding environmental disputes. The importance of these remarks can hardly be overestimated.[7]

In short, the duality of error makes managing uncertainty far from the simple matter it appears to be. And now that the fear of terror is widespread and maximizing is widely used, we should ask: is maximizing a good idea? Is the achievement of rationality sufficient justification? Should false negatives never be tolerated? Maximizing may be rational, but will its practice be wise?

Recognizing the Duality of Error

Recognizing the duality of error in judgment was certainly a step forward, for that recognition opened up complexities in errors not previously recognized. Maximizing is surely rational in those circumstances in which we cannot allow a single false negative when the consequences of that error are terrible and intolerable. In these circumstances, it will be hard to think of a false positive in which the consequences of inconvenience and cost will match the inconvenience and cost of allowing the error. That is the case at the airport, and that is why I chose that example.

But although the error of assuming someone to be innocent when they are in fact guilty (the false negative) may well be intolerable at the airport, it will not always and everywhere be intolerable. A false negative must always be evaluated in terms of both the consequences of making that error and the consequences of making a false-positive error. For example, it would be easy to explain the consequences of violating the law against carrying weapons on an airplane because these consequences were observed in the disaster on 9/11; but it could be harder to explain the consequences of not permitting weapons on the plane (from the point of view of American society), because there would be none. But how should we think about denying authorities permission to search your home (thus creating conditions for a false negative)? Prior to the search, you would know that you were not hiding weapons, but of course the authorities would not know. Should you defy the authorities, your action would be praised—and justified— by those who value the Constitution. We presume that they are prepared to suffer the consequences of a false negative, that is, deaths and disaster. But the authorities responsible for security are not so prepared. Thus, being wise in these circumstances of irreducible uncertainty entails not only being rational but also evaluating the consequences of two types of errors in terms of social values in specific circumstances: that makes wisdom rare.

So, it is easy to see that if you are a bureaucrat with many people vying for your attention, and you want to be as accurate as possible, you will favor maximizing, for it maximizes the number of accurate predictions. But if you are wrongly accused, you will say, "That is unfair; I'm different. Everyone should be treated as an individual!" Of course, from this perspective, that statement is right. But the bureaucrat will have an answer:

> This is not a perfect world; I cannot afford to make all the errors I
> would make if I were to try to make a judgment for each individual.
> At the end of the day, I will have made more mistakes than if I had
> not tried to deal with individuals. And my boss—the citizens—won't
> stand for that.

Indeed, the bureaucrat will declare—correctly—that he or she is simply being rational. And isn't that the best thing to do?

Thus, maximization is a brute force tactic that is justified (by its users) by its rationality, for it maximizes accuracy. As a result, maximizing in the face of irreducible uncertainty is widespread. But when circumstances allow us to evaluate the consequences of different errors, then wisdom often leads us to deny maximizing.

Professionals can provide a professional justification for maximizing, at least some of the time. But maximizing is also often performed by people who are unwise, who are utterly callous and indifferent to an individual's suffering from a false positive. So the practice of maximizing should always be challenged by asking what the ethical or moral consequences of a false negative are, or are predicted to be, in relation to a false positive.[8]

The negative aspects of maximizing can be also be seen in the widespread resentment against "mandatory sentencing," the practice of making it mandatory for judges to sentence persons found guilty of certain crimes according to the crime and regardless of mitigating circumstances.[9] In short, the rational practice of maximizing often begins to look unwise when considering the larger context.

We will see this criticism of rationality being made again and again and being increasingly accepted emotionally, if not always logically. But it is such criticisms of rationality that lead to the search for something better, namely, wisdom.

In short, maximizing is a useful way of combating uncertainty that can serve humanity well in that it returns benefits for a lower cost. Yet it will become—and has become—not only offensive to the recipients of maximizing, but unacceptable as a moral, and political, principle. It may well have been the resentment of maximizing—the product of rationality—that led famed eighteenth-century Irish politician Edmund Burke to write, "Politics ought to be adjusted, not to human reasonings, but to human nature, of which reason is but a part, and by no means the greatest part." We will see the wisdom in Burke's remarks as we proceed, and find that uncertainty can be a friend as well as an enemy.

The Duality of Error Reveals Social Attitudes

Before discussing the value of uncertainty as a friend, we need to consider how a person's choice of error—false positives or false negatives—can reveal his or her social and political attitudes. Let me begin with an example I uncovered as a graduate student in 1947. I developed what I called an "information test," which it was, except that the answers I offered to the information questions were wrong. No right answer to any question was offered on the "information test." The answers were errors that were wrong in equal and opposite directions. So, for example, if the question asked about how many strikes had occurred last year, and if the correct answer was 500, the answers offered would be 250 or 750. And since there were a number of questions, the issue was whether the person taking the test made a systematic choice of a wrong answer. I found that people did indeed make systematic errors; moreover, they made the systematic error choices that their professional associations would lead you to expect. In the above example, members of trade unions made systematic errors that put the trade union in a favorable light, whereas members of business associations made systematic errors that put trade unions in an unfavorable light. (Several domains were employed with similar results, and no one ever complained about the nature of the "information test."[10])

But now we can be more sophisticated in the way we think about error, beginning with the fact that under uncertainty, two different types of errors can appear—thus, the duality of error. We now know that the duality of error is a general phenomenon, and that reducing the likelihood of one error only increases the likelihood of the other, and that it is our value system that leads us to prefer one type of error over the other. For example, if we consider the matter of civil liberties, we can readily hypothesize (I know of no research on the topic) that if we know someone is a political conservative, he or she will prefer the false-positive error in the justice system, whereas if someone is a liberal, we can anticipate that she or he will prefer to make the false-negative error.

It is also a useful way to think. Policymakers will often find themselves trying to define the advantages and disadvantages of a certain proposal. This often leads to two lists of value-laden attributes on the blackboard—a move that seldom reduces the dispute because it does not reveal the choice that is separating people, and that is the implicit choice of error.

The 19 false negatives of September 11, 2001, will never be forgotten. That memory, coupled with the awkwardness of the infinite number of false positives, means that there will be a demand for something better than the brute force approach. In short, we need to find a better way to cope with the more general problem of combating uncertainty. That better way will be found when we give up our myths and develop a greater understanding of the role of human judgment in combating irreducible uncertainty.

2

Combating Uncertainty

It has often been pointed out "we live in a sea of bacteria" (or viruses). But for those of us who are concerned with how we think, it would be equally appropriate to say "we live in a sea of uncertainty," for it is uncertainty that envelops our (almost) every judgment. All that is very general, but the pains of uncertainty can be very specific, and in retrospect very uncomfortable indeed. The report of the 9/11 Commission states that although in 1941 the United States "had excellent intelligence that a Japanese attack was coming . . . these were the days of 'excruciating uncertainty.'"[1] In *Roget's Thesaurus of English Words and Phrases* (1994) there are 282 entries for "uncertainty." Armed with that list of synonyms and related terms, any anthropologist who discovers us a few thousand years from now will be quick to point out how our language indicated a society mired in uncertainty, against which we have to pit our judgment.

If we are awash in uncertainty, what does the English language have to say about "judgment"? We are as surrounded by "judgment" as we are by "uncertainty," for there are 262 entries for judgment. That near-match (282–262) is to be expected, because "judgment" is the cognitive process evoked by uncertainty; uncertainty forces us to exercise our judgment.

Uncertainty and its close friend, probability, have become so widespread that more and more topics are being explicitly treated in gambling terms. For example, it is now possible, in England, to "make book" on the next big scientific discovery. Ladbrokes, a British bookmaker, is (at the time of writing) taking bets on "whether the biggest physics experiments in the world will come good before 2010." And they are willing to take bets on more mundane matters. As the *New Scientist* tells us: "Ladbrokes reckon the odds of finding the Loch Ness monster alive and well are 66–1, so anyone betting $1 would win $66 if it turned up."[2]

That "sea of uncertainty" engulfs those at the highest levels of decision making. In November 2003, James Fallows, a national correspondent for *The Atlantic Monthly,* interviewed Douglas Feith, the undersecretary of defense for policy in the second Bush administration. According to Fallows: "The limits of future knowledge, Feith said, were of special importance to [Secretary of Defense] Rumsfeld, 'who is death to predictions.' 'His big strategic theme is uncertainty,' Feith said. 'The need to deal strategically with uncertainty. The inability to predict the future. The limits on our knowledge and the limits on our intelligence.' "[3]

Seldom do we see policymakers make such frank admissions about the frustration that uncertainty causes. Uncertainty that is irreducible—that can't be reduced or eliminated—tends to create anxiety (some would say "stress"), and that creates the need for judgment and the drive for wisdom.

We know, however, that this is hardly a new state of affairs; our ancestors of 50,000 or perhaps 100,000 years ago would understand our frustration; they faced a lot of it. So we can assume that our long-past ancestors relied heavily on the judgment process, just as our leaders do now. They were always more or less uncertain where their predators were and what they might do, uncertain where food might be found and how much would be there when they found it, and uncertain what the weather might bring. Our ancestors relied on signs and signals from numerous sources, signs from the sky in the form of thunder and lightning, wind and storms, and signs from whatever artifacts were present, such as cracks in the bones of animals roasted over the fire, and the arrangement of animals' entrails. Aborigines still use many of these methods today.

Surprising as it may be in these days of extraterrestrial exploration, astrological forecasts—a mystical system from antiquity and utterly ridiculous from the point of view of modern science—still appear daily in many of our newspapers; such forecasts are relics that demonstrate the persistent dependence on myth. And astrology is not just for the uneducated; it reportedly influenced the behavior of prominent and powerful persons (U.S. president Ronald Reagan and French president François Mitterrand). Apparently, right from the beginning, we have been a species so eager to reduce our uncertainty that we are prone to accept almost anything that promises certainty. Expertise (even if bogus) in interpreting esoteric information has apparently always been highly valued and continues to be, often in the most unexpected places, such as in high government offices, in boardrooms, and even on Wall Street.

Whether irreducible uncertainty is friend or foe depends on whether the uncertainty resides in us or in our enemies. We prefer that it reside in our enemies. We can see how deep that runs when we learn from studies of chimpanzees that males are apt to kill infants they believe are not theirs. But if multiple males mate with a female in heat, and males are uncertain about paternity, the infant is less apt to be killed; inexplicably, those potentially lethal males seem to recognize the uncertainty of paternity, and in these circumstances, uncertainty is surely a friend of the infant and its mother. And uncertainty of origin has surely saved many humans from ethnic and racial murder; the ability to "pass" is valued among persecuted minorities. In this case, uncertainty—your enemy's uncertainty—becomes your friend.

But uncertainty in our enemies may also be disastrous; they may resort to brute force techniques such as maximizing to reduce their uncertainty. It was precisely that procedure that produced the concentration camp. "Kill (or imprison) them all" is the preferred procedure; errors (false positives) are ignored.

Even reducing uncertainty about unwelcome events is generally comforting; "at least we now know what we are up against" is our response. There are very, very few people of stature or prominence who have publicly welcomed their own uncertainty. But the famous Supreme Court Justice Oliver Wendell Holmes, Jr., is one who did; he plainly and explicitly expressed his aversion to certainty, or *certitude*, as he put it.[4]

Holmes has often been described as the most respected justice ever to sit on the court—which he did for 30 years, until the age of 91. But it was his experience as a soldier in the Union army in the Civil War, in which he was wounded three times, that led to his stance against certainty. Louis Menand describes this well: "The lesson Holmes took from the war can be put in a sentence. It is that certitude leads to violence." That is a thought to which I shall return.

While a 20-year-old student at Harvard, and a keen supporter of the abolition of slavery, Holmes was eager to enlist, and did, as soon as possible. But after witnessing at close range the carnage of the Civil War, Holmes made it a cardinal principle never again to become driven to violence by abstractions or belief. And Holmes disdained certainty as much in other people as in himself: "I detest a man who knows that he knows," he wrote to a friend. It was the complete capitulation to an ironclad form of thinking that Holmes would not accept: "When you know that you know, persecution comes easy. It is as well that some of us don't know that we know anything."[5]

That last remark by Holmes may have a familiar ring to readers of the classics, for it is close to a similar expression by Socrates "[who] knows that his wisdom is in truth worth nothing."[6] Holmes probably knew about Socrates' remark, for he was a close student of the classics.[7] Later, we will see that this reaction by Holmes evolved into his very thoughtful and profound view of how we think and how we make our judgments about the nature of the society we prefer.

Holmes's disdain for certitude would have found much application in today's political analyses. He surely would have been revolted by the emotionally derived religious certitude that drives the terrorists of the twenty-first century and others, and he would not have been afraid to say so. He would have been equally disdainful of the rationally derived political judgments of both Left and Right. Holmes might well have expressed reservations about President George W. Bush's administration's certitude about weapons of mass destruction in Iraq, reflected in Bush's February 8, 2004, interview with Tim Russert on *Meet the Press*. The excerpts from *The New York Times* included this passage:

> Russert stated, "Mr. President, the director of the C.I.A. said that his briefings had qualifiers and caveats. But when you spoke to the country, you said there is no doubt. When Vice President Cheney spoke to the country, he said it's no doubt. Secretary Powell: 'No doubt.' Secretary Rumsfeld: 'No doubt. We know where the weapons are.' You said, quote: 'The Iraqi regime is a threat of unique urgency. Saddam Hussein is a threat that we must deal with as quickly as possible.' "[8]

So the president received a full dose of certitude from his advisors about Saddam Hussein's possession of weapons of mass destruction, all of which turned out to be wrong. (Holmes might well have been smug about that.)

There are modern thinkers who share Holmes's dim view of certitude, today usually expressed in terms of antipathy toward socialism or other forms of rationalized systems of government. Roughly a hundred years after Holmes expressed his views, the distinguished philosopher Isaiah Berlin put forward the same aversion to certitude:

> Few things have done more harm than the belief on the part of individuals or groups (or tribes or states or nations or churches) that he or she or they are in sole possession of the truth; . . . & that those who differ from them are not merely mistaken, but wicked or mad: and need restraining or suppressing. It is a terrible and dangerous arrogance to believe that you alone are right: have a magical eye which sees the truth: and that others cannot be right if they disagree.[9]

Although a romantic view of the world can provide the comforts of certitude, the rational, analytical argument also carried danger. And that feeling of certainty, the feeling that "you know that you know," disturbed both Holmes and Berlin and led them to distrust and warn against narrow views and the certainty that accompanies them. Both men would distance themselves from the certitude that is allied with deep emotions.

It is striking that Holmes and Berlin arrived at the same aversion to certainty, for they were as different as any two men could be, and the same could be said of the sources of their beliefs. Although Holmes was a well-educated justice of the Supreme Court and an intellectual, he hardly thought of himself in that role, despite his origins as a Boston "Brahmin," a member of the New England upper class. He coined the term "jobbism" to explain his philosophy, meaning that he saw himself merely as a person who had a job to do and was doing it to the best of his ability. When he reached a decision, he did so as part of his job, which he saw to be interpretation of the U.S. Constitution in a manner entirely independent of his personal beliefs. And he never forgot his military service in the cause of abolition. But he had left his devotion to abstractions on the battlefield. When others looked askance at his indifference to such worthy abstractions as "abolition," he would show his critics his two Civil War uniforms, kept in a closet in his office at the Supreme Court, and point out to them that the blood on them was his. In short, he had paid his dues to a worthy cause, and that blood was the evidence. Few of his visitors could say the same.

Berlin, on the other hand, reached his antipathy toward certainty not as a result of searing personal experience, but as a result of prodigious reading of the history of ideas, the study of Russian philosophers in particular. He was born to Jewish parents in Latvia, attended a Hebrew school as a child, and then, after years with his family in Russia and in England, eventually became a member of the faculty at Oxford and soon became recognized as an outstanding scholar. During World War II, the British government sent him to the United States to observe what was going on there and to keep the British government apprised of what he learned. His reports were soon recognized as brilliant, and Churchill prized them. After the war, Berlin resumed the life of a scholar and became known as one of the most learned men in the world. He made his antipathy toward certitude the centerpiece of his philosophy when he introduced his notion of pluralism, the idea that there could be several competing and equally justified values but no resolution of differences.[10]

I mention Holmes's and Berlin's negative views toward certitude because they are unusual; indeed, the negative view of uncertainty is so general, and the positive view of certainty so widespread among professionals and academics— and most obviously among today's politicians—that Holmes's and Berlin's views will seem odd and perhaps incomprehensible. (I will say more about this in the discussion of the "cognitive continuum" on p. 119.)

How Isaac Newton's Success Impeded
Research on Uncertainty

With Sir Isaac Newton's discoveries of the nature of the physical world at the end of the seventeenth century, there was a great shift in the attitude toward Nature's unpredictability, at least among the educated. Newton had found order among natural phenomena, and his laws of mechanics and motion and gravitation and optometry demonstrated Nature's predictability and order. Order and certainty thus became expected; there were no probability clauses in any of Newton's laws. (These did not appear until the twentieth-century particle physicists found need for them.) In the seventeenth century, science and religion saw eye to eye on the order in God's handiwork. Alexander Pope made the point in his usual pithy manner:

> Nature and Nature's laws lay hid in night
> God said: Let Newton be! And all was light.

But not quite "all." Newton's laws enlightened us about that part of physical Nature that runs on a determinate basis, and, no doubt, it is an important part of Nature; the laws he discovered made possible the landing of people on the moon and robots on Mars, and permitted civilization to develop. But that part of Nature that includes the properties and behavior of living organisms runs on a different basis; it runs on an indeterminate basis and requires us to learn about probabilities. So it was a mistake for the psychologists studying learning in the first three quarters of the twentieth century to think that Newton's determinate universe included the behavior of living organisms. Because it doesn't, and because part of Nature is controlled by uncertainty, we need to recognize that difference if we are to succeed in endeavors other than physical science.

Because of Newton's success, the idea that behavior strictly followed laws was taken for granted in psychology; after all, everything else in science was done in search of laws, so the determinate nature of the anticipated laws of learning was hardly questioned until Egon Brunswik introduced the idea of uncertainty into that research in the 1940s.

Brunswik was able to show that, although "all was light" in physics, in the field of psychology considerable darkness prevailed and was stubbornly resisting the light. Brunswik tried hard to point out the difference between the physical, the natural, and the behavioral worlds to his colleagues in the 1940s and 1950s, to little avail. Clark Hull and Kurt Lewin, the most prestigious psychologists of the day, although differing sharply from one another, agreed strongly that Brunswik's ecological psychology, which insisted upon including the study of uncertainty, did not deserve to be part of scientific psychology. As a result, proper study of the nature of behavior in a world governed by uncertainty was long postponed. Current students of judgment and decision making, however, are pursuing the study of our cognitive activity under uncertainty because that is the psychological activity that must cope with the uncertain world in which we live.

When Uncertainty Is Encountered

One of the reasons for our dislike of uncertainty in the environment is that it induces a corresponding uncertainty in us. And it is that induced uncertainty— together with objective uncertainty—that creates the need for judgment, and thus wisdom. If the objective world lacked uncertainty, if we could be certain about the occurrence and nonoccurrence of every event, then our need for judgment would be greatly reduced; wisdom would come much more easily. Long ago, researchers (primarily Berndt Brehmer) found that the degree of uncertainty in a task would be closely matched by uncertainty in the person facing it. Another way of saying this is that objective uncertainty is matched by subjective uncertainty.

In modern times, uncertainty remains one of our most central concerns; achieving command of our economy, for example, is a constant worry. Reporting to the U.S. Senate in January 2001, Alan Greenspan, then chairman of the Federal Reserve Board, whose hand was on the throttle of the growth engine of the U.S. economy, indicated his uncertainty by referring to "the tentativeness of our projections." He then asked, "What if, for example, the forces driving the surge in the tax revenues in recent years began to dissipate or reverse in ways we do not now foresee?" Radical Muslims' attacks on New York City and the Pentagon in September 2001 have increased the level of everyday uncertainty considerably and have extended that uncertainty to everyday places, events, and people. Is this building going to be bombed? Is this person a terrorist? Will bio-terror attacks come via a suitcase bomb, or a missile, or some device we don't yet know about? Will the economy recover? When? Will international trade recover? As a result of recent large-scale corporate fraud and deception by traders, accountants, and CEOs in the United States, the uncertainty of these people's honesty reached a point where new steps had to be taken to monitor their actions. Surely, farmers in Mesopotamia were similarly driven by uncertainty to say things like, "What if the benevolence of the gods driving the surge in the flood waters begins to dissipate or reverse in ways we do not now foresee?" There is nothing new in the way that irreducible uncertainty induces the same anxiety in the twenty-first century; it surely did in the fifth, tenth, or fiftieth centuries BCE as well. Irreducible uncertainty about our natural environment is matched by uncertainty about our enemies, their character, their intentions, and their methods. But a new level of uncertainty has become a part of the lives of people in the United States and worldwide; tens of millions of people live with a new, significantly increased, uncertainty.

Coping with Uncertainty

Medical doctors have no doubt about whether uncertainty is a friend or an enemy—it is always an enemy. Atul Gawande, a surgical resident whose intriguing articles about medical practice appear in *The New Yorker*, makes his enmity for uncertainty plain: "The core predicament of medicine—the thing that makes being a patient so wrenching, being a doctor so difficult, and being a part of a society that pays the bills they run up so vexing—is uncertainty." It is significant that Gawande adds, "And wisdom—for both patients and doctors—is defined by how one copes with it."[11] Gawande is exactly right on both points.

The response to one's uncertainty has always been to seek more information. That is certainly the case with doctors, but it is true of almost everybody. So the information explosion is no accident; it is what we have always wanted. Now we have extraordinary means of acquiring more information than we can process. The increase in the amount and complexity of information coming at us creates joy as we revel in the power of being able to almost instantly get information previously out of reach, but creates a sense of tyranny in those who are expected to somehow make use of it all, or else be seen as failing in their duties. If the new and better technology provides us with more information more efficiently, more accurately, more rapidly, then what excuse do we have for not being able to use it effectively?

Do we not use it effectively? The evidence in both directions is merely anecdotal. But it is certainly timely to attempt to make the nature of information more understandable, make the process of human judgment more intelligible, increase our control over this situation, and thus increase the layperson's power to cope with it.

Passive Use of Information

The increase in the availability of information has led directly to an increase in the number of passive observers of information, those who have to separate all the interlocking and contradictory pieces of (uncertain) information in our heads, so to speak, in contrast to actively separating them in an experiment. Few rarely have the opportunity to carry out actual experiments—as scientists do—and thus become active observers.

The most difficult task for a passive observer is to disentangle various causes of the events he or she is observing just by looking at them, or better, observing and then thinking about them. For in the natural world, or especially in the social world in which we live, that increase in information means that we will find that there is almost always more than one cause of any event we observe. And, indeed, almost any cause, or set of causes, gives rise to more than one event. Scientists refer to this situation as "causal ambiguity." For example, the room in which you are sitting is heated from a variety of sources: the building's heating system, other bodies in the room, rays from the sun, and so on. And the sun that heats the room also causes other locations to become warmer. If scientists want to separate out—disentangle—various causes and effects, they must resort to controlled experiments, and indeed, the word "control" refers to separating the various causes (or effects) that enter the experiment.

That task of disentanglement is forced upon us by the interconnectedness of events and information about them; worse still, the more information we have, the greater the likelihood of entanglements and contradictions inherent in it. Therefore, passive observers of information have a much more difficult task than scientists, who can take complicated and confusing bits of nature into the laboratory, disentangle them piece by piece, and reach a clear and convincing conclusion. Clear and convincing conclusions, however, are seldom the happy lot of the user of uncertain information who must—passively—use his or her best judgment to disentangle uncertain information. When Atul Gawande complains of uncertainty, he is referring to the fact that he is forced to make passive use of information about his patients; he cannot take the patient apart, manipulate variables, and test his ideas about the causes of the patient's symptoms one cause at a time. And, as we shall see, those in the highest places in a leadership position in society—any society—are also tied to the passive use of information and must passively cope with entangled, uncertain information.

Friend or Enemy?

If you are persuaded by the admonitions from Oliver Wendell Holmes and Isaiah Berlin against "certitude," you will welcome uncertainty. But then you must be prepared to live with it. Are you prepared to live with uncertainty about which values you hold most dear, which ethical principles you feel bound to follow, which political philosophy you will endorse? Are you prepared for harsh criticism about your "wimpish" behavior, for not holding to firm principles? No lecture about Holmes and Berlin will convince either your friends or your enemies. (I speak from experience.)

That's a tall order but only part of it, for that is just your subjective uncertainty, the uncertainty from within. When making judgments about another person, uncertainty is probably your friend, for it may keep you from making judgments too soon, and it may remind you of your fallibility. Uncertainty may well make your judgments more difficult but may also keep you from making serious mistakes. It should always give you pause and perhaps induce some deserved humility. It was the absence of subjective uncertainty that Holmes and Berlin found to be obnoxious, for it represented a form of arrogance they found to be objectionable. In short, uncertainty may serve a useful purpose when it is a characteristic of your judgment about important matters.

On the other hand, uncertainty in the outside world is rarely, if ever, a friend. It only increases your errors of judgment, and you may be forced to choose between the error of *false positives* and the error of *false negatives* (see chapter 1). No one likes such choices. They require a careful consideration of the relationship between your values and the consequences of error. That will require hard cognitive labor. But Drew Erdman, a U.S. official in Iraq, who considered certainty a reason for caution, told a writer for *The New Yorker* in November 2003 that he was "very cautious about dealing with anyone talking about Iraq who's absolutely sure one way or the other."[12] To that official, certainty was an enemy.

Recognizing Irreducible Uncertainty Changes One's View of Error—and the World

Uncertainty in the natural environment is almost always an enemy. That is why governments spend vast sums of money worldwide to remove or reduce it. This is most evident in the establishment and maintenance of public health, weather stations and weather bureaucracies, aids for air and marine navigation and traffic control, and police and fire departments. And the production of uncertainty is the central asset of terrorism; it is the uncertainty of where or when or how the terrorist will strike next that creates the fear of his or her deadly actions. So we seek—sometimes desperately—ways to reduce uncertainty in the outside world. The case studies will demonstrate that. At the very least, we must find ways to manage it. One way to manage it is to understand it, and understanding comes through research.

One product of research in the twentieth century is the discovery of the duality of error, as discussed in chapter 1. Recognizing the duality of error means that in a world of irreducible uncertainty, one must choose, if possible, which error to tolerate—the false positive or the false negative. And that means that one must be explicit about the differential costs—since by using the term "irreducible," we have acknowledged that one or the other error is inevitable. As the reader will immediately recognize, that makes the judgment and decision problem much more complex than it would be if we had only to fight the problem of error. Indeed, it leads to a situation where error—or a least one form of it—is welcomed. It is on this foundation that the new form of thought about error has been built, as laid out in the rest of this book.

PART II

Strategies of Human Judgment

Herbert Simon. A brilliant man of great scope who introduced the idea of "bounded rationality" that led to his being awarded the Nobel Prize. (Courtesy of Carnegie Mellon University.)

3

The Strategy of Seeking
Correspondence Competence

The first strategy to consider is the oldest one: using information for the purpose of making empirically accurate judgments about the natural world. As a result of natural selection, human beings are good at these natural judgments. For example, we are good at judging that this tree is very tall and hard to climb, this animal is further away than that one but is larger, and that mountain, although it looks smaller than this one, is larger but further away. Indeed, our ability to use visual perceptions to make empirically accurate judgments under good conditions is astonishingly good, although we can be fooled under peculiar conditions.

That ability is the product of hundreds of millions of years of natural selection for the visual and other senses with which we are endowed, and we are not the only ones with this remarkable ability; we share it with other animals, fish, birds, and even some insects, also selected for this ability. It requires no long dissertation to convey the idea that it would be almost impossible for us to survive, even now, without the ability to make empirically accurate judgments that correspond to real objects in the world in which we live. And this ability is not restricted to vision; all our perceptual senses (hearing, taste, etc.) are remarkably accurate and demonstrate the extraordinary phenomena of *constancy,* the ability to maintain the correct judgment despite changing conditions. For example, we see the shape of a dish as a dish even when we hold it in a variety of positions. It is only under poor, or strange, conditions that our accuracy diminishes.[1]

I refer to this sort of competence as *correspondence competence* because it concerns the correspondence between our judgments and the objective circumstances we are judging (for example, the height of a tree). Correspondence competence apparently was selected right from our beginning as a necessary requirement for the survival of our species, and we see it in the survival of other species as well.

Another sort of competence has come to be demanded of us as well—but this one is ours alone; as far as we know, we are the only organisms that possess *coherence competence*. This is the competence you exhibit when you do arithmetic, algebra, or other forms of mathematics. You also exhibit this type of competence when you detect an inconsistency or a contradiction in someone's story or argument or when they recite a syllogism, or engage in other forms of logical argument. In short, coherence competence is exhibited when you perform a logical operation, for in a logical operation all elements must fit together; there must be no contradictions, or your judgment will be refused as incompetent. I will explore coherence competence in chapter 5.

Our thirst for the information that enables us to make accurate empirical judgments will never change. We have always wanted, needed, and used such information, and like so many things we have become used to, it never occurs to us to think about how we do it. That thirst for information has deep evolutionary roots, for it was imperative for our ancient ancestors—the hunter–gatherer, the primitive farmer, the primitive trader–merchant—to make effective use of information about the weather, the movement of other animals, the location of the best roots and berries, the signs that indicated the current temper of the gods . . . or their neighbors! It was the natural selection of those people who were good "readers" of the environment (and the other people in it) for procreation—the opportunity to pass on their genes—that resulted in our current extraordinary ability to read our environment. Good readers lived longer and more often survived danger and hardship than did poor readers. That premise guides all that follows.

The modern farmer, the modern businessperson, and the CEO, and all the rest of us, continue to display the thirst for information and the means to assimilate it. That led to the technology that created the information explosion that slaked our thirst.

Multiple Fallible Indicators

In what form does that information come? A good theory should give us a very general term—a concept—that will cover a wide range of types of information. In the present theory, that concept is called "multiple fallible indicators."

Jeff Tietz provides an example of the presence of multiple fallible indicators, and our ability to make use of them, in his December 6, 2004, article in *The New Yorker,* titled "On the Border: To Track Someone, You Have to Learn to See Fine Disturbances." He writes, "In the Border Patrol, Trackers look for tread designs printed in the soil and any incidental turbulence from a foot or moving body. They notice the scuff insignia of hesitation at a fence and the sudden absence of spider webs between mesquite branches and the lugubrious residue of leaked moisture at the base of broken cactus spines."[2]

The indicators that Tietz is talking about in the natural world—and the similar ones our long-ago ancestors used in their tracking efforts—are almost always fallible, that is, not perfectly dependable, and thus, being frequently wrong, lead us to make inaccurate judgments some fraction of the time. That is why it is fortunate that in the natural environment, indicators generally appear in multiples; notice all the different indicators that Tietz's trackers pick up: "scuff insignia, absence of spider webs, leaked moisture." An increased number of indicators provides a greater opportunity for redundancy, and thus a greater opportunity for a poor indicator to be corrected by a better one, or a related indicator to be present in case one or more are missing. And redundancy leads to greater confidence in the accuracy of one's judgment (albeit sometimes misleadingly so, as is discussed below). But we humans spend a great deal of time, money, and intellectual capital trying to remove the fallibility from the natural world's indicators and thus to create infallible indicators for the unnatural, artifact-filled world in which we now live, a change—a reduction in fallibility—in character that is occurring at an ever-increasing rate. For example, we have been creating more and more road signs and thousands of other infallible directional indicators, as well as increasing the digital (that is, categorial, "yes–no") nature of our surrounding environment. And we create redundancy—or try to—whenever we find mistakes being made.

The importance of indicators in our lives has a long history, hundreds of thousands of years, and over time we have become quite sophisticated in their use, especially in warfare. When our ancestors developed the tools of warfare, a different set of indicators from those trackers relied on came into use. The military historian John Keegan tells us how, in the eighteenth century, Frederick the Great made use of "indices," that is, indicators, to "provide rough-and-ready real-time intelligence when the enemy was in view. Dust was an important indicator." He quotes Frederick the Great: "A generalized cloud of dust usually signified that the enemy foragers were about. The same kind of dust, without any sign of foraging parties, suggested that the sutlers and baggage were being sent to the rear and that the enemy was about to move. Dense and isolated towers of dust showed that the columns were already on the march." Keegan also notes that "there were other signs. The gleam of the sun, on a bright day, on swords and bayonets was open to interpretation at distances of up to a mile, . . . [and] if the rays are perpendicular, it means that the enemy is coming at you; if they are broken and infrequent, he is retreating."[3]

Of course, the numerous fallible indicators now used by modern intelligence analysts are different, but the concept remains the same. Understanding the use of fallible indicators remains as essential to modern intelligence analysts as it was to the trackers thousands, if not hundreds of thousands, of years ago, and to the soldiers of the eighteenth century. Soldiers of the twenty-first century have an even more complex set of fallible indicators with which to find their enemies. I will have more to say about that below.

Generality

Our reliance on multiple fallible indicators is not, of course, limited to the natural world or to the military world; such indicators are the basis of the correspondence strategy that is employed to combat uncertainty. Thus, it is a very general term; it can be used to describe indicators found both in nature and in the most unnatural places, such as in Congress; in the justice departments of cities, states, and the federal government; and, especially, on Wall Street. For example, in its July 18, 2001, edition, a *Washington Post* headline read, "Greenspan Leaves Door Open for More Cuts, Calls Indicators Mixed." No one would have any difficulty understanding what Greenspan meant by "indicators," nor would anyone have any difficulty understanding why he was depending on them for his judgment; they are all he had.

Although the term *indicator* is used in every newspaper every day, the term *multiple fallible indicators* is not used, because it is an academic, theoretical, technical term. The reason for calling these signs, signals, and cues indicators is that all of them indicate—that is, provide uncertain information about—something else, that is, point to something, give us a hint about a different entity, beyond the indicators themselves. The clouds are indicators because they give us a hint about something else: the weather; that noise is giving us a hint about something else: a nearby animal; Greenspan's indicators—unemployment statistics, retail sales—give us hints about the future of the economy. Each of these indicators is of value because it tells us something of greater importance than itself. Note that each indicator that we can see (e.g., the price of oil) indicates something about objects and events we cannot see (e.g., the future of the economy). Our ability to use indicators in this way shows that we possess—our brain can perform—a cognitive process, a knowledge process, of enormous importance. (Try to imagine living without such a cognitive process.)

The shift from the concept of *stimulus* (psychology's traditional term for describing some input to the organism) to the concept of an "indicator" is of critical importance to psychology because it heralds a shift in the foundation of this discipline. As long as psychology thought of itself as a discipline whose fundamental concepts were stimulus and response, it was operating within the physicalistic theme. Both stimuli and responses were originally defined in physical terms only, which made it easy to see responses as a function of certain stimuli. Pavlov's dog received a stimulus that always signaled food, and Pavlov knew the dog had learned what the stimulus meant when the dog always salivated upon being presented with that stimulus. That classic conditioning experiment understandably recalls the experiment you did in your high school or college physics lab: both certainly looked scientific, and they were.

An indicator, however, is far different from a stimulus. A stimulus is perceived by the skin (or some other sensory apparatus), and physiological activity travels from there into the organism. But an indicator is different; it is "out there." Thus, to base the new cognitive science on the study of indicators is to introduce a whole series of new assumptions, the most important of which is the assumption that the organism possesses a brain whose fundamental activity is to make inferences from an indicator to the thing indicated. That is why it is called "cognitive" science.

Once the concept of indicators became basic to cognitive science, it became necessary to consider the technical aspects of the presence and use of multiple fallible indicators.

Technical Features of Multiple Fallible Indicators

There are two different causes of indicators' fallibility: on the one hand, random, unpredictable, unsystematic factors; on the other, systematic factors. The difficulty is that the person making use of indicators to form a judgment usually doesn't know how much of either is present in any one indicator. Is that flush on the face of your friend caused by embarrassment at your remarks? Or is it from a random, momentary change in blood pressure due to unknown causes? Unfortunately, there is usually some random error in most indicators. For example, there is randomness and unpredictability in the relationship between clouds and rain, wind and rain, and virtually every other weather predictor. And the fallible indicators one normally observes are even worse at predicting human behavior, because humans are motivated organisms with a wide range of goals, organisms that are highly complex and capable of deception.

Thankfully, we don't have to worry about deliberate errors in weather forecasting and reporting. No weather forecaster or reporter is likely to deliberately mislead us about the weather; none ever says it is clear when it is raining in order to encourage us to go shopping. We shouldn't underestimate the importance of that dependable honesty; its practice is far from universal. In the Soviet Union's government, this sort of honesty was notoriously absent, a fact that became glaringly obvious when a nuclear plant blew up at Chernobyl and the Soviet government refused to acknowledge it for days after, even after it was known around the world. Unhappily, deliberate error has become pervasive in the U.S. financial sector, where it has become common to find large companies systematically distort their financial condition, and some stockbrokers systematically falsify information about companies whose stock they sell.

At the time of this writing, the question of whether there was deliberate "error" by the Bush administration in the intelligence it provided regarding weapons of mass destruction in Iraq is still unresolved and likely to remain so for years. But as most of the world knows, the last of many committees appointed by President Bush concluded that there were no weapons of mass destruction. Although much was made of the threat that such weapons posed, no weapons have been found: a source of keen embarrassment to the administration. Seymour Hersh, a well-respected journalist writing in the October 27, 2003, issue of *The New Yorker* (which has a strong reputation for fact checking), pursued the question of how such a gross error could have occurred and concluded that it was because standard checking procedures were not used that the erroneous judgment that Iraq actually possessed weapons of mass destruction was made. Others have simply chalked it up to incompetence at the CIA. (I discuss this further in chapter 19.)

Fallibility due to random and systematic error and deliberate distortion must be combated in any effort to make an accurate inference about a condition not immediately apparent. These two forms of error are almost always present to some degree. The absence of dishonest, biased information is a benefit that should never be taken for granted, because, in fact, multiple fallible indicators are everywhere, even in modern society. Consequently, their accuracy, and the source of error in them, whether systematic or random, greatly affects society and our personal behavior.

Degrees of Fallibility

Because indicators vary considerably in their fallibility—from complete fallibility to perfect infallibility—whether the fallibility is due to random or deliberate factors, it is essential that we be able to measure their degree of fallibility so that we can discriminate among them. Indeed, discovering which indicators can be relied upon and which should be ignored has attracted the interest of many researchers, and they have found a way to measure the fallibility of a number of indicators in various situations. These measures simply indicate, in one form or another, how often an observable indicator is associated with an observable fact, condition, or event.[4]

In this context, we are interested in how often a given indicator that one can see is associated with a fact, condition, or event that one cannot see but that can be ascertained in other ways. Although modern researchers can count and measure various indicators the way our ancestors could not, we can nevertheless be sure our forebears could rely on experience to form at least some idea of the degree of association between various palpable indicators and impalpable events. Experience is a hard teacher, however, for it often makes us pay a heavy—sometimes even "the ultimate"—price for being wrong. Therefore, considerable technological effort is being exerted to improve the accuracy (our correspondence competence) of our inferences based on multiple fallible indicators.

One way to improve our accuracy is to use technology to remove random error in the data we observe, as has been done at the international airport in Amsterdam. Here, the art of using multiple fallible indicators to infer the identity of a person has been raised to the highest level of accuracy yet. A machine scans the iris of the eye—that ring around the pupil—to detect some 250 specks to be matched with the image of your iris on a special identity card. If the specks on the scanner match the specks on the card, a gate at the airport opens and lets you proceed. Because the arrangement of specks is unique to you, fallibility is removed, and the gate can be programmed to open, because the card shows you are indeed you. That example illustrates a second point: when necessary, a way will be found to reduce or eliminate fallibility. In the case of Schiphol Airport, it became critically important to identify hijackers and other criminals. So the authorities replaced fallible indicators with highly technical—and infallible—indicators, as described above. That phenomenon is occurring around the world as the threat of in-flight crime becomes more serious. Recently, science has provided us with a way of identifying someone based on a single, virtually infallible cue: DNA. This discovery has had significant repercussions in the courts, which dread error. But the concept of error turns out to be far from simple, because there are two main types of error that we have to keep in mind.

Duality of Error—Again

In the last 50 years, statisticians have come to understand—and use—the concept of the duality of error, but it is uncertain just how far that concept—the exact meaning of false positives and false negatives—is understood by others. Some 40 years after its introduction, this topic is still being discussed in a less-than-professional manner by the press and people who should know better. For example, reports about the efficacy of medical screening (e.g., for breast cancer or prostate cancer) note that the screening is not perfect and that false positives (reports that cancer is present when it isn't) and false negatives (reports that cancer is not present when it is) occur. Numerous press releases have reported that current tests for prostate cancer "miss 15% of the cases" (deliver false negatives). But, too often, they forget the general principle that irreducible uncertainty means that decreasing one error inevitably increases another. This principle is rarely appreciated by nonspecialists. The only way in which both forms of error can be decreased simultaneously is by reducing the uncertainty in the test.

Unfortunately, this failure to recognize the duality of error occurs at a time when increased uncertainty and the suspicion of persons and events have risen to unprecedented heights. When a train engineer refuses to stop, to the utter consternation of frustrated passengers, at a station where an unattended bag has been found, or the physician warns the patient that a certain cancer test has made "many" mistakes and, therefore, an expensive and risky biopsy is the "wisest" course of action, we should inquire as to the cost of the other action (or nonaction). When the security administrator assures the public that "the new rules will always err on the side of caution," which side of caution is he or she talking about—the false positive or the false negative? What will be the price of the confusion that results? For example, when the director of Homeland Security and the Transportation Security Administration, who, of all people, should understand this concept, assured the public that his office would "err on the side of caution," did he mean that airport screeners would take care not to make the false-positive error—thus detaining too many innocent passengers? Or did he mean that he would warn them to not make the false-negative error—thus reducing the chance of another 9/11-type hijacking? The one thing the director did not do is assure the public that he would reduce both errors, because that would mean introducing an entirely new method of screening that would reduce the inevitable uncertainty in the process—and no such method has been presented.

Redundancy: Assets and Liabilities

If we have multiple indicators, we have to consider the relationships among them. The term "redundancy" is used to describe the situation in which several indicators provide the same information. Two indicators are said to be redundant if either one can be relied upon to provide the same information as the other. If I describe your height in only inches, then in feet, the information is redundant. If you describe your wealth in dollars and in quarters, that information is redundant. It is important to realize that the accuracy of our judgments is not improved if redundant information is provided, although our confidence may be raised (unjustifiably). But if several different signals point in the same direction—that is, permit the same inference—our confidence in our judgment legitimately grows. If your height is described by a measuring stick and by a surveyor's techniques, and the result is the same, we can be confident of our judgment of your size.

This means that we must be careful to distinguish between redundant indicators and independent, convergent indicators. Independence means that information from one indicator tells you nothing about what information you might expect from the other. Thus, there is strong evidence of truth when two indicators are independent of each other yet prompt the same conclusion. When that occurs, the two indicators are said to converge on the same answer. That is because two indicators that are independent of one another supply evidence from different sources and thus offer more information than would two redundant indicators. For example, identical reports from each of two different observers provide more information than do two identical (redundant) reports from the same observer. This distinction is the basis of navigation. The ship's navigator uses two lighthouses' light beams that converge on the position of the ship to thus indicate the ship's position. (This practice is called "triangulation.")

This is a general principle of information. If we receive information—any kind of information—from several sources, we must be certain to distinguish between those that are redundant sources and those that are convergent sources. We should not confuse redundant information with convergent information. We need to understand the difference between the two because many, if not most, of the natural and social environments we encounter are rich with more or less redundant indicators, and more or less convergent indicators. Worse still, it may be very difficult to discover which is which (a point I will come back to). In contrast with the natural environment, nearly all the engineered environments we encounter are rich with independent, convergent indicators. When we humans build an environment in which people are to make use of information, we try very hard to tell the user which signals are redundant and which are convergent. But navigation in a social environment—finding who is dominant to whom, who is partial to whom—is problematic because it requires that we function without knowledge of which indicators are redundant and which are convergent. We usually have to decide that for ourselves, and that will ordinarily be a difficult judgment. Frequently, we will mistake redundant information for convergent information and thus err in our judgment.

For example, you may receive a negative comment from George about Tom, and a further negative comment from Fred about Tom. Since you now have two negative comments about Tom, you are inclined to believe the comments. But

George may have received the negative information about Tom from Fred; thus his comment is redundant, and you have in fact only one negative comment about Tom. If, however, George does not know Fred, and there is no communication between them, then you have reason to believe that the information comes from independent sources, and thus is convergent information. If so, then your judgment about Tom is more credible.

It is because of the danger of such redundancies that those who evaluate job applications prefer to have candidate endorsements from independent sources. These human resource personnel are following the same principle as the navigator of a ship who is plying waters that contain lighthouses and buoys and other navigational aids does. The difference is that the ship's navigator is operating in an environment that has been created to avoid redundancies, whereas our social environment is a far more chaotic one that lacks the engineering that would eliminate that risk. Thus, increased confidence in a judgment requires convergent information from independent sources.

Natural and Engineered Environments

Homo sapiens have not accepted as immutable the rich disorder of the information natural environments provide. As archaeologists have shown us, the early members of our species made tools and other artifacts to cope with what the environment delivered, but they also built devices to bring order into the disorder of the information the natural environment provided. Natural environments are like Darwin's "entangled bank" (see chapter 15); the operating environment of an automobile, kitchen, or office, however, best illustrates a modern environment. The "entangled bank" allowed little predictability: one could forecast only that disorder (at least to the untutored eye) would prevail. Exactly what information the engineered environment of the modern automobile, kitchen, or office will present is highly predictable, and those environments make clear exactly what each (nearly) infallible indicator will tell you. The slightest disorder is anathema to the operator in these and other highly engineered environments. These operators dread spontaneous information coming from outside the engineered arrangement of information (e.g., noise, smoke), for it usually raises the specter of disaster. Aviation and space flight may have compelled humans to develop the most controlled organization of information ever achieved. Aviation and space flight, of course, exemplify the ultimate engineered environments and controlled information. When unexpected information appears, disaster is anticipated.

For example, note how R. Dittemore, the project manager for the space shuttle *Columbia*, which disintegrated on re-entry on February 1, 2003, describes the information that was sent to the space center in Houston. First, he describes the rise in temperature that the monitors noted on the left fuselage. Then he says, "At 7:59 A.M., we were over West Texas. Again, we see an increase in the roll trim as indicated by elevon motion, indicating that the vehicle was reacting to an increased drag on the left-hand side." Notice, first, that this is unwanted information; that is, it is outside the normal information anticipated during the flight, exactly the sort that pilots dread. Notice also that this is a double-level inference: (1) "elevon motion" indicates increase in "roll trim," which, in turn, indicates (2) reaction "to an increased drag on the left-hand side." Most important, we see that Dittemore is now limited in information to indications of what is happening to the shuttle as a result of the way the shuttle is behaving in response to unknown events. That is in contrast to the direct observations of data that he (and the monitors at Houston) had been receiving electronically that described how the shuttle was responding to known events (e.g., the activities of the crew, the increased gravity). The cognitive process that is operating here is the same as the one that has been with us since the beginning: palpable multiple fallible indicators being added (or averaged) into an inference about an impalpable state of affairs. In other words, fallible indicators can be seen ("roll trim") being organized into an inference about a state of affairs (the potential disintegration of the shuttle) that can't be seen—in short, a disaster.

Thus we see that engineered, that is, highly controlled, environments are extremely sensitive to unanticipated events, and the person who must make inferences from them may well be thrown back on primitive cognitive processes to cope with them.[5]

Multiple (Competing) Indicators

Because of the multiplicity of indicators in most situations, there will be some indicators leading to one inference that will appear simultaneously with others leading to a different inference. Thus, the clouds overhead may indicate rain, but the patch of blue sky over there indicates no rain today. Indeed, that multiplicity of fallible weather indicators, some contradicting others, is what accounts for our enormous interest in that confusing panorama of fallible indicators that challenge our inferences about tomorrow's weather and make the Weather Channel the most watched station on television.

Our social environment is also rife with competing indicators. No sooner do we get negative information about a friend, or a politician running for office, than we get positive information about the same person. Which to believe? Can the person in question actually be both a good person and a bad person? Unhappily for easy judgments, the answer turns out to be "yes." The existence of competing indicators is one more factor that makes drawing inferences about other people the hazard that it is. It adds to the uncertainty created by fallible indicators.

Thus, our social environments differ in a second way from the ship navigator's environment, and that concerns the uncertainty in the message itself. There is no uncertainty in the light from the lighthouse; that light comes from one and only one lighthouse; the lighthouse does not move its location, and the light does not flicker. Engineered environments, such as marine or air navigation maps, are carefully designed to provide certain, unequivocal information. Nor do lighthouse signals compete with one another. But the social environment in which people send signals to one another is filled with confusion among sources and the uncertainty of the truth of the message; indeed, even the intention of the message sender may be doubtful; deception is always a possibility. As we all know, traditional, culture-bound cues such as hugging and smiling and other obvious indicators of affection are particularly likely to be misleading, if not actually deceptive.

Small wonder that we make many errors in our social judgments, for our social environments are not designed for truth and accuracy. Indeed, many seem to be designed (or else develop) to prevent truth and accuracy from appearing. This "design" is apparent in social conventions that regulate behavior and thus diminish conflict. It may be observed in pristine form at the United Nations or in the U.S. Congress, where members refer to one another as "my friend the Senator from . . ." or "my esteemed colleague" despite being bitter enemies.

Assets and Liabilities of Redundant Multiple Fallible Indicators

Not only is it possible that multiple fallible indicators may be redundant, but it is likely, in a natural environment; as predictors of storms, clouds are redundant of rain, and rain of wind, though not perfectly so. But engineered environments may deliberately refrain from building in redundancy, because redundancy is expensive. Road signs are often redundant, but their second appearance is carefully calculated. Engineering a complex operating environment requires carefully calculating the need for redundancies.

There are degrees of redundancy, and therein lies one of the great assets of inductive inference—and one of its difficulties. Redundancies can be assets when they make it possible to survive in a world of causal ambiguity created by competing, convergent, and error-filled indicators. Redundancies offer us "second chances," as, for example, when highway engineers post signs on the highway. They almost invariably erect a second sign—just in case you missed the first one, as you often do. The same occurs in nature, but by functional interrelatedness rather than by design. A tracker, for example, looks for many redundant "clues," whether tracking an animal in the wild or a criminal in the city, because redundancies create confidence. Bent leaves or twigs or footprints are functionally related to one another on the trail in the woods, just as fingerprints, forgotten objects, and letters are in the city. All these are redundancies that support the search. They allow us to recover from mistakes in our judgments.

Redundant multiple fallible indicators have drawbacks in addition to advantages, however. And, of course, it isn't only the weather and other naturalistic features of our environment that provide interrelated multiple fallible indicators that prompt different and confusing inferences. Our social world is full of many varieties of interrelated fallible indicators.

Entangled Causality

In addition to entangled indicators, our environments, both natural and social, provide entangled causes. That is, two or more unobservable features of an environment may give rise to the same observable event. Two or more different bacteria may cause your temperature to rise; two different motives—kindness (a genuine urge to help others) and greed (the hope for payment)—may nudge one to help a stranger; lightning may cause a forest fire, and a half mile away arsonists may cause another. In some cases, one causal feature (lightning) may stimulate another causal feature (arson) to function, and both may then give rise to the same observable events: fires.

The Centers for Disease Control and Prevention's struggle to warn people appropriately about the appearance of anthrax exemplifies multiple causation. Anthrax's first symptoms are similar to, and easily confused with, those of influenza. Confusing these diseases is serious not only because one disease quickly leads to death, but also because the amount of anthrax vaccine is limited, and thus using it unnecessarily reduces its availability, which might also lead to deaths. Possibly confusing anthrax and the flu calls attention to the role of entangled causes and entangled diseases. But this is a judgment problem that is common in many medical diagnoses, and every doctor faces it several times a day. Entangled causality is not a rare event. Studies of judgment need to pursue this topic, despite its difficulty.

Social and medical situations are also rife with entangled causality in which several causal features may operate simultaneously to produce a singular event. For example, a young man who may be very jealous concerning his girlfriend may also be anxious to display his strength and fighting abilities and may also be in competition with another young man for a place in school politics; all of these may operate simultaneously to cause a single event, an attack on a second young man.

Similar examples can readily be found on other social occasions. Often, a number of causal systems are covertly related. For example, for many years, certain insurance companies were accused of charging poor blacks higher premiums for burial insurance than they charged whites. A class action lawsuit resulted in a 1999 settlement of $45–60 million in fines and compensation to black consumers. The insurance industry defended its higher charges on the grounds that blacks had shorter life spans than whites but now acknowledges that it is poverty rather than race that leads to shorter lives.[6]

Assets and Liabilities of Entangled Causality

Entangled causality may assist us in making accurate judgments for the same reason that redundant cues assist us; they help us make the correct judgment—to be right—but for the wrong reason. For example, it is easy to infer the wrong motive for an act—because the fallible indicators are fallible, that is, occasionally wrong. Yet, if the correct motive is related to the incorrect one, the ultimate prediction can be correct. In the above example, we may well assign the cause of the fight to jealousy when in fact it was because of an urge to demonstrate masculinity through fighting. Yet, if the two motives—jealousy and an urge to demonstrate masculinity—were closely related in the person fighting, then a prediction of a fight based on an (incorrect) inference of jealousy would lead us to believe we had made the correct inference about the cause, and perhaps, to congratulate ourselves on having once more predicted social behavior successfully. (Such "correct" inferences lead us to be overly confident about our inferences in redundantly rich environments.) So, to the extent entangled causality in the environment allows correct predictions for the wrong reason, it is an asset, provided that empirical accuracy is all we are interested in. But of course that is not always the case; on many occasions it will be important to be correct for the right reason.

In short, it is important to understand that the assets that entangled causality offers us—increased accuracy—come with a price: being right for the wrong reason. That "accuracy" misleads us about our competence, particularly in social environments.

The more obvious liability created by entanglement of causes is that it creates opportunities for incorrect judgments. If there are multiple causes of an act, then we must somehow exercise our judgment to decide which one actually controlled the observed behavior. Normally, our only recourse is to rely on multiple fallible indicators, but since the indicators are fallible, this situation creates uncertainty. If we cannot manipulate any aspect of the situation—if we remain passive observers rather than experimenters—then we are very likely to remain uncertain about which motive or motives controlled the behavior of the person we observed. Therefore, we try to become active observers, and to do so we often try to arrange circumstances so that we can eliminate alternative hypotheses about causality.

Inductive Inference: A Challenge That Has Always Been with Us

A cognitive activity of such importance as human judgment based on multiple fallible indicators was bound to come to the attention of philosophers over the centuries, and they have given it a name: inductive inference. That allows me to say, "Because of the clouds I saw, I inferred it was going to rain." Or we might emphasize the fallibility of someone's judgment by saying, "It is merely an inference." But living in an uncertain environment created puzzles and problems for exactly how we make inductive inferences: "Why is that I got it right that time, but missed the time before?" Or, "Can I really trust Niko's judgment after his last mistake? Still, he often gets it right." Much time and effort was spent on such questions—including very sophisticated forms of them—as soon as people developed a society that provided enough leisure (at least for the privileged) for long discussions. From about 500 BCE forward, the societies bordering the Mediterranean found ways (slavery, technology) to provide leisure, and when they did they turned to philosophical questions about thought and values, and about human judgment—why it was so often right, and so often wrong—and invented terms such as *deduction* and *induction*. And *chance*! These Mediterraneans were adept at raising questions, but the answer to the problem of how we make inductive inferences remained unsolved, and, indeed, the problem persisted through the Middle Ages, and into the Age of Enlightenment and the seventeenth century, and the discussion continues today.

Note the modern tone of a well-known philosopher, Cicero, when he discussed the problem of inductive inference 2,000 years ago:

> You ask, Carneades, why these things happen, or by what rules they
> may be understood? I confess that I do not know. "Chance" you say.
> But can that be true? Can anything be by chance which has all the
> marks of truth? . . . It is possible for paints flung on a surface to form
> the outlines of a face; but, surely, you do not think a chance throwing
> could produce the beauty of the Venus of Cos? . . . But, it is objected,
> some things predicted do not happen. But what art—and I mean an

art that involves conjecture and opinion—is not like this? Is not medicine considered an art? And how many mistakes it makes. Do not
pilots make mistakes? . . . Surely, the fact that so many illustrious captains and kings suffered shipwreck did not make piloting not an art?
And is military science nothing, because a very great general recently
lost his army and fled?

Substitute "fallible indicators" for "marks" and "human judgment" for "opinion"
and Cicero sounds quite modern. He concludes by saying that "art" (he is referring to human judgment)

misleads sometimes, but most often it leads to the truth; for it has
been repeated from all eternity, during which almost countless instances of the same things following the same antecedent signs have
been observed and noted, resulting in the art.[7]

Cicero's "antecedent signs" are our "fallible indicators"; Cicero is struggling with
the problem of inference under uncertainty.

James Franklin finds the same battle with uncertainty in a passage by René
Descartes in which he writes,

Since in everyday life we must often act without delay, it is a most certain truth that when it is not in our power to discern the truest opinions, we must follow the most probable. Even when no opinions appear more probable than any others, we must still adopt some; and
having done so we must then regard them not as doubtful, from a
practical point of view, but as most true and certain, on the grounds
that the reason which made us adopt them is true and certain.[8]

Again, substitute "judgments" for "opinions," and we see that Descartes' concerns are our concerns. The same argument is often used today by practitioners
of decision analysis when acting as consultants. Translated, it reads:

The decision reached by our use of decision analysis is by no means certain to be the correct one, but it should be accepted over all other decisions because our method of reaching it is the most rational method of
reaching a decision under uncertainty.

These two examples indicate that philosophers approached the problem
of inductive inference in much the same way it is approached today. But it was
David Hume who took the big step, for he made it clear that we must distinguish between the perception—or judgment—of a causal relationship between
two events, and the data upon which we base that judgment. And he emphasized

the point that the objective data themselves do not offer evidence of a causal relationship; all they give us is the fact that one event followed the other. When he did that, he provided us with the distinction that is at the core of most studies of human judgment. That is, the researcher manipulates the relationship between various events and examines the judgment of the subject about that relationship. Thus, Hume provided a theme that became the basis of psychological research on human judgment, and once the statistical methods for coping with uncertain—that is, irregular—relationships became available, psychologists could do their work. But that would have to wait until the nineteenth century, when Francis Galton invented the correlation coefficient. That made it possible to measure precisely the relationship between the occurrences of two events (how much one event changes when the other does). That would be all that the psychologist Egon Brunswik would need to undertake his studies, in the twentieth century, of judgments of the size of objects—for he simply measured the size of an object and compared it to the subject's judgment of that size by calculating Galton's correlation coefficient (later known as Pearson's) of the two. When Brunswik did that, the science of human judgment had found a new method, as explained in greater detail in chapter 15.

Current Significant Appearances of Multiple Fallible Indicators

We should pause here to take special note of the crucial role of multiple fallible indicators in the history of *Homo sapiens*. One of the most obvious and enduring motives for murder has been racial and ethnic difference. As I write this, humans are enthusiastically killing one another all over the world because of racial or ethnic differences. And if they are not actually killing racially or ethnically different persons, then they are discriminating against them in a wide variety of ways all too familiar to the reader. This matter of hatred of differences is based on multiple fallible indicators of differences that are visually obvious, those exhibited mainly in the head and face: hair color and texture, eye shape, nose size and shape, height of cheek bones, shape of mouth and lips, and of course, color of skin—all indicators that are easy to see. All of these highly visible features play a role in the inferences (judgments) human beings make about one another in relationship to the most fundamental characteristics that one cannot see: intelligence, honesty, trustworthiness, and suitability as a mate, colleague, or citizen; indeed, these inferences include whether the other person should continue to live.

Notice that all these indicators are fallible; that is, there is no factual evidence of any significantly functional link (what researchers call "ecological validity") between any of these indicators and the traits purportedly indicated. That fallibility is an idea developed primarily in the knowledge base of the Western world. Students who become educated—that is, who become acquainted with that knowledge base—are quick to accept the idea of the fallibility of these indicators. But such education does not reach everyone and, as a result, the knowledge of fallibility does not reach everyone, and it is still common to find such indicators used if they were infallible.

The fallibility of these ethnic and racial indicators has been demonstrated through scientific research in the social sciences, but the implications of the concept of fallible indicators have not yet reached the military.

Military Intelligence

Military intelligence has been sharply criticized in the past decade, both because of its historical record over the long term and because of its failure to properly use modern technology. The highly respected military historian John Keegan has been particularly critical of the value of such intelligence, and in an interview with Judith Miller in *The New York Times,* he recently said, "Decision in war is always the result of a fight, and in combat, willpower always counts for more than foreknowledge."[9] In short, Keegan thinks military intelligence isn't worth much. But Miller also reports:

> Bruce Hoffman, director of RAND's Washington office and a terrorism analyst, said that although Sir John [Keegan] analyzed the role of intelligence in countering Al Qaeda, most of his examples were drawn from eighteenth- to twentieth-century wars rather than twenty-first-century conflicts. "Keegan is largely right on the role of intelligence in conventional wars," Mr. Hoffman said, "but he is not right about counterinsurgencies in any century, when intelligence is the sine qua non of success. . . . You can no longer fight, much less win them, just with military strength."

The military experts on both sides of this dispute about the value of military intelligence fail to do justice to their topic, however, for they ignore the critical role of human judgment in the evaluation of military intelligence. They don't take into account the properties of military information or the nature of the judgment process. I have never seen any comparative data on the quality of intelligence from technological surveys versus human intelligence, or comparative data on various measures of the reliability or validity of various sources. Nor have I seen any reference to random versus systematic error.

But the most significant aspect of judgments based on military intelligence occurred when the administration of George W. Bush raised such intelligence to the status of a sufficient basis for invading another country. That is new. Heretofore, intelligence has not been a sufficient basis for the United States to attack another country; traditionally, invading another country has required strong proof of some observable activity of great threat (crossing a border, for example). And when, for example, Japan bombed Pearl Harbor in 1941 because their (faulty) intelligence led them to infer that the United States was about to attack, the outraged president Roosevelt referred to it as "a day that would live in infamy." The presence of weapons of mass destruction in the world makes it plausible to assume that preemptive attacks by the United States and others will continue. And the new possibility of a devastating attack against millions of people by a very small number of attackers—something heretofore not possible—amplifies the need for good intelligence.

Thus, preemptive attacks will be justified on the grounds that no post hoc effective defense is possible against such weapons when they are delivered clandestinely or by unannounced ballistic missiles. (The "blogs" of Gary Becker and Richard Posner on December 7, 2004, offered such justification.) Consequently, not only must each country raise the quality of its military intelligence to the best that it can afford and achieve, but each country must also control its military activity to the greatest degree possible, inasmuch as that activity will be the basis of the attackers' judgments. The potential for almost instantaneously delivering a weapon of mass destruction has changed the importance of the role of military (and political) intelligence, making its accuracy—its correspondence competence—essential. The correspondence competence of U.S. military intelligence in the Iraq war was so poor as to lead Congress to demand an investigation; following the investigation, the latter produced a highly critical report.

The mounting evidence of incompetence in judgments regarding military activity and aggressive intentions in other nations raises the question of whether the U.S. intelligence agencies are ready to take a science-based approach to the matter of human judgment in relation to military intelligence. One indication of the possibility that they have recognized a need for this but do not know where to turn is the Defense Intelligence Agency's republication of a 30-year-old essay by Cynthia Grabo, a much-respected intelligence analyst. Although the essay about the value of intelligence was undoubtedly valuable when initially published in 1972, its republication raises the question of what the Defense Intelligence Agency has learned since then; there is no science in Grabo's essay.[10]

Disinformation, Dishonesty, and Deviltry

Intelligence works both ways. Because each side is eager for information about the other, and each side knows that, there is a strong incentive for each side to deceive the other by feeding it false information (disinformation). Just as there is a constant struggle between building armor to overcome armament and concocting heavier armament to pierce the stronger armor, there is a constant struggle to gain information and a constant struggle to defeat that effort, which results in an equilibrium that is only occasionally upset (as it was in World War II when the United States broke both the German and Japanese secret codes). There is one big problem with disinformation, however, and that is that both your friends and your enemies receive it; thus you are deceiving your friends even as you are deceiving your enemies. And although you intend to deceive your enemies, and no one will consider that dishonorable, deceiving your friends is considered dishonorable, and they will punish you for the deceit. So when *The New York Times* reported, under the headline "Pentagon Weighs Use of Deception in a Broad Arena," that the United States was contemplating the use of disinformation, it also included a subhead that said "The Nation's Credibility Is at Risk, Military Critics Contend."[11] Clearly, this step is a big one, and not to be taken lightly.

Personal Inferences

As we all have been told, "appearances are deceiving" and "you can't tell a book by its cover," and we are thus advised about the fallibility of appearances as indicators of less-apparent but more-important aspects of personality. In the highly appearance-centered Western society, inferences based on clothing and style are rampant. The trend among people of all ages and ranks in Western society to be (comparatively) slovenly in appearance in the 1960s—which seemed so shocking— actually began at the time of the French Revolution. In Barzun's recent European history, he describes the change during the French Revolution; this is worth reading because it gives us an idea of how far we have come:

> Men's clothes started on their democratic simplification. Though not altogether colorless, they became subdued and gradually dropped such frills as wigs, powder in the hair, ribbons, knee breeches (hence *sans culottes*), garters and silk stockings, silver buckles on shoes, and felt hats.[12]

And it isn't merely clothing or hairstyle that can serve as an indicator of one's attitudes toward politics, or life in general, but also something that has come to be called "lifestyle."

But not all commentators on modern life use these indicators in the same way. Richard Posner, a federal judge and prolific writer, noted Barzun's use of these indicators but disagreed with the way he used them, and came to a different conclusion. Posner points out,

> If positions of authority were always assigned on the basis of merit alone, and if the performance of people occupying those positions were perfectly transparent or perfectly monitored, no one would care how they dressed or how they looked. A person in authority would not have to dress differently from his underlings in order to cement his authority.[13]

In short, Posner thinks all this change in appearances was to the good, because real, fundamental aspects of one's character now have a chance to become apparent, and we are less likely to be fooled by the artificial, highly fallible indicators of dress.

Although making our personal inferences—and judgments—based on others' appearance probably occupies a fairly large proportion of our time, we of course make many other inferences about many other things in a given day. As indicated above, multiple fallible indicators are everywhere and are used for almost every purpose. The surprising thing about all of this is that it has been found that the same general process appears to control all of these judgments. Give someone a set of fallible indicators about a company to invest in, a possible marriage partner, the weather, a vacation spot, a home to buy—it doesn't matter which—and the process for combining and using this information is roughly the same; agree on the indicators and then add them up. Judgment researchers know much more about this process than this simple rule, of course. They will know when this simple rule is not used, and when it is (more about this below). But the general reader will not be far wrong if she or he assumes that people use multiple fallible indicators very frequently, and when they do, they simply add them up.

Profiling

Police officers' perennial use of multiple fallible indicators has given rise to the concept of "profiling," which has been informally and formally raised to the level of a crime for which a police officer can be punished. (The term "profiling," it should be noted, is a term lifted from research on the subject of judgment that uses profiles of data to be judged.) Are the police engaging in what is loosely called "racial profiling," that is, using race as an indicator of past, present, or future criminal behavior? They are constantly making inductive inferences, judgments based on many different multiple fallible—very fallible—indicators, a perfectly natural thing to do and something we human beings will be doing forever. But it isn't the process of inductive inference—that is, using multiple fallible indicators (that can be seen) to infer characteristics (that can't be seen)—that people find objectionable, it is the use of racial and ethnic indicators as if they were infallible indicators of criminal intent or behavior that is inflammatory. ("Driving while black" is a phrase blacks use that springs from their resentment of racial profiling.) Obviously, profiling is unfair because black skin color is certainly not an infallible indicator of criminal behavior. Unfortunately, however, blackness is seen as a highly salient objective indicator that is correlated with criminal activity (far more blacks are in prison, proportionately, than whites). It can be (and is) argued, however, that this disproportion is merely a (fallible) indicator of the injustice, the unfairness, with which the police and the white community have historically treated blacks. Thus, we are at the mercy of fallible inductive inferences, the fallibility of which is exceedingly difficult to reduce to the satisfaction of all the constituents.[14]

So it is not difficult to find examples of police using racial and ethnic indicators. And in the days following 9/11, when fear and suspicion were high, it was common to see racial and ethnic indicators used in relation to Arabic men. For example, in a newspaper account of the arrest of two Indian men (who share some facial characteristics and skin color with Arabs) suspected of being associated with the terrorist attacks on the World Trade Center, it appeared that ethnic indicators created that suspicion. According to the newspaper report, "Both men were asleep when the train arrived in Fort Worth. . . . Once the police awakened them, an artery on Mr. Azmath's neck began 'visibly pulsating' and his forehead got sweaty, while Mr. Kahn's hands trembled."[15] Note that these policemen are observing the men's anxiety and using those visual indicators as to presume their guilt. But there was more. The article went on to note that the suspected men had received letters instructing them to shave the "excess hair from their bodies," that they had "bought their tickets at the last minute with cash," and that "they had receipts showing that they had recently received transfers of money." When the policemen made note of these events, however, they were no longer using direct visual indicators but intellective ones, that is, conceptual or abstract indicators. I point this out not only to show which specific fallible indicators were used but to show how readily we accept the range of multiple fallible indicators from visual to intellective functions in newspaper accounts of behavior related to judgments. Our ready acceptance of that range reaches from our ancestors, who relied entirely on visual (and other perceptual) indicators, to ourselves, who apply this process to intellective ones as well. In this case, the men were eventually released; all these indicators had led to the wrong conclusion. So these false positives resulted in little more than inconvenience, but false positives can have far different consequences, as, for example, when misjudgments concerning supposed weapons of mass destruction in Iraq were relied upon for military action that resulted in thousands of deaths (discussed in chapter 4).

The police should be criticized for their mistakes, but consider the task facing them. If the police are to prevent crime (and thus protect the public) and capture criminals after the crime is committed, they need to be reasonably accurate in their predictions of the future behavior of people, not only to protect others but also to protect themselves. And in the case of the two passengers on the train, the appearances (and certain behaviors) of these men were the only predictors the police had. The police will be far more afraid of a false negative (letting a guilty person go free) than a false positive (arresting an innocent person), for the latter is an act that can be corrected, albeit at some inconvenience to those arrested. Until society tells the police that it prefers the false-negative error to the false-positive error, the police will be apt to commit false-positive errors more frequently than false-negative ones, particularly in times of fear.

The Role of Multiple Fallible Indicators in Natural and Sexual Selection

Natural selection was Darwin's explanation of how the natural environment determines which species survive to pass on their genes. Sexual selection was his explanation of which individuals are chosen to participate in procreation, thus passing on their genes. In his famous *Origin of Species,* he concentrated on natural selection but at one point was moved to say "a few words" on what he called "Sexual Selection." (In 1871, he wrote a book on sexual selection.) His "few words" in 1859 were, "This form of selection depends, not on a struggle for existence in relation to other organic beings or to external conditions, but on a struggle between the individuals of one sex, generally the males, for the possession of the other sex. The result is not death to the unsuccessful competitor, but few or no offspring. Sexual selection is therefore less rigorous than natural selection."[16]

Reproduction, it must be noted, is as important in the long term for species as survival is; survival is merely a precondition for reproduction. Therefore, it is not surprising that about 20 years after introducing the idea of natural selection, Darwin set about writing his book on the sexual form of selection—and selection by the environment—that played a role in the evolution of *Homo sapiens.* The important point is that mating wasn't—and isn't—just a random, haphazard process. Rather, partners are selected, and selection occurs because some are judged by the opposite sex to be more desirable than others. The important point for us is that the same cognitive activity plays a role in both processes (although it is not the only factor): the application of the correspondence strategy that employs multiple fallible indicators.

Sexual selection is not restricted to *Homo sapiens*; it has become apparent in a variety of species from insects to whales, and the wonders of mating displays—elaborate dances, bright colors, songs—that create such interest are now provided nightly on televised "nature" shows.

Note that the individual's choice of a sexual partner is as important as nature's choice of which individual should survive. If men and women were to choose the "wrong," that is, unproductive, partners for mating, or the fathers turned out to be poor providers, or the mothers failed to care for their children, then the union would not be a successful one, in the sense that the progeny would not survive and would not reproduce themselves.

Although sexual selection is widely recognized, the cognitive basis of this selection process is rarely mentioned. That is because it is biologists, rather than psychologists, who are keenly interested in evolutionary processes, and because cognitive psychology is a fairly new science. The interesting topic—to cognitive psychologists—is the nature of the process that uses the indicators that are involved in sexual selection. The process used by organisms to select partners for sexual intercourse and thus reproduction is the same as the process used for survival in the natural world. Just as the organisms use fallible indicators to make accurate empirical judgments regarding physical objects in the natural world, the organisms' effective use of multiple fallible indicators make accurate judgments possible with respect to social objects (persons of the opposite sex). Moreover, it is the same cognitive process we can observe in operation in a wide variety of activities today. And because there is great deal known about the use of multiple fallible indicators under uncertainty—many hundreds of experiments have been done—we now know a great deal about this process.[17] It is called the "linear model" because it signifies that the organism simply adds (or averages) the information from the indicators. Man, the whale, the dog, and all other mammals use information in sexual selection in this way, just as Alan Greenspan used information to predict the course of the economy, and just as the statisticians use the information to put together the economic indicators to do the same thing. The generality of this simple process is astonishing. But a process that is so widely used would be expected to be robust and simple.

Although the natural environment's selection of humans may now be mitigated by the many precautions (such as public health measures) we have taken against it, sexual selection is still a vigorous process. When one considers the time and money spent on cosmetics and other methods of improving one's attractiveness and the time and money spent on clothing intended to beautify and thus increase attractiveness, it appears that possibly more time and energy is spent on the human sexual selection process than ever before. And it is apparent that this process is also based on the premise that the cognitive activity—judgment—of the potential partner will use these multiple fallible indicators.[18]

Differences between Natural and Sexual Selection

There are several similarities in the cognitive activity involved in natural and sexual selection. In both cases, the organism relies on the correspondence strategy, the use of multiple fallible indicators, and the cognitive tactic of intuitive inference (see chapter 5).

But there are important differences between inferences involving natural selection and those involving sexual selection. First, there is a sharp competence difference between our accuracy when judging objects and events in the physical environment and our accuracy judging objects and events in the social environment. Judgment of physical objects and events is normally very accurate; judgment of social objects and events is normally far less accurate. There are several good reasons for this important difference. One receives clear outcome feedback, at least a large part of the time, when judging events in the physical environment. If you judge that you are going to step over that rock in the path but miss, you learn that fact of misjudgment immediately. In short, your mistakes usually become quickly obvious. If, however, you mistakenly judge your friend to be honest, it may be years before you learn that he isn't; indeed, you may never learn that fact. And although learning with outcome feedback (knowledge of results) in relation to intuitive judgments under uncertainty is very slow, it is normally better than no feedback at all.

Second, when feedback from social objects and events does occur, it is generally far more unreliable and erratic, or long delayed, than feedback from the natural environment. (Think of how difficult it must have been for primitive people to make the connection between sexual intercourse and childbirth.) Worse still, feedback in social situations may be deliberately falsified; although deception does occur in nature, it is far more common in social affairs. The delay in feedback, together with its untrustworthy character, also plays a large role in the difficulties everyone—particularly policymakers—have learning what works and what doesn't. (I will have more to say about this in chapter 17 in connection with the problem of learning from history.)

Aside from the difference in feedback, the indicators of social objects and events necessary for a judgment may be absent or hard to find. As Geoffrey Miller points out, periods of ovulation are concealed among women; thus, men, eager to procreate and thus to pass on their genes, were—and usually are—ignorant of the likelihood of actually conceiving a child from any specific instance of copulation. And indicators of all kinds may even be intentionally misleading. This is particularly true among humans, but it occurs among insects and animals as well.[19]

In summary, for the foreseeable future, we will all be using multiple fallible indicators, largely unconsciously, to make our judgments, and we will continue to call this "intuition." There is certainly nothing wrong with that. But we do have to be aware of the nature of the process and the conditions in which we apply it. If we apply our intuition to tasks that demand logic rather than experience, it does not serve us as well, nor should we expect it to. But all too often we lack a logical, or scientific, model to apply to a logic- (or science-) demanding task, and therefore must treat it at least partly intuitively; that is, we must treat some of the information in the task as if it simply represented multiple fallible indicators. If we lack the model required, we have no alternative. And once we turn to multiple fallible indicators, we are susceptible to all the criticisms usually directed at intuition; it is defenseless against demands for explanations because it is a process that is largely unconscious. Frequently, however, there are times when there will be no criterion available against which to compare your judgment, and therefore you will have to rely on the logical force of your argument. Those conditions will evoke a different cognitive process, and we turn to that process next.

4

The (Mis)Judgments of Colin Powell

Before the UN Security Council on February 5, 2003, Colin Powell, then U.S. secretary of state, presented his judgment that Saddam Hussein's possession of weapons of mass destruction and Hussein's intention to use them against the United States called for the United Nations' approval of the invasion of Iraq. This was a highly significant international event; Powell's goal was to persuade the council members that his judgment that Saddam Hussein possessed such weapons was to be trusted and that they should act on it. He made it clear that his judgment was based on the authenticity of the information that he presented.

Yet, as the whole world was soon to learn, his judgment was completely wrong; Saddam did not possess weapons of mass destruction. That judgment was empirically tested, and tested again, yet it was never found to correspond with the facts. The consequences of Powell's erroneous judgment were significant, for although the council refused to accept his judgment that an invasion was warranted, the United States and Great Britain and a handful of other countries did accept the validity of his judgment and mounted an invasion, with considerable loss of life and property. At the time of this writing, the death and destruction continue, and no clear resolution of the conflict is in sight.

Powell's manner of presentation had made it clear that his was a persuasive effort, and he proceeded, as all persuaders do, by presenting his information as if it were based on proven facts that were empirically true, and that those "facts" corresponded to the "true" intentions of Saddam Hussein. However, his persuasion failed, and numerous countries eventually rejected his judgment about both Saddam's weapons and intentions. As it turned out, the world was right, and Colin Powell was wrong.

The decision not to sanction the invasion of Iraq was surely a critical moment in world history because it was clear, in that moment, that the potential for widespread death and destruction—and the vote of each member of the Security Council—rested on human judgment under uncertainty.

What attracts our attention here is that Powell presents his judgment (that military action is imperative) to a world organization, and his judgment is based on his inference about the *intentions* of another head of state. That is new. Other nations in recent history (Germany, Japan) have taken military action based on inferences about their adversary's intentions, but none have made plain that their justifications are based on human judgment, and none have laid out the basis—the fallible indicators—for that judgment in Powell's frank and open manner. Powell, and apparently everyone else, was aware of the fallibility of those indicators, and thus the uncertainty underlying his judgment, but no one seemed to notice that Powell's task, that of reducing uncertainty to near zero, was in fact intractable—by which I mean, impossible. Because of that uncertainty, neither he, nor anyone else, could have made a fully defensible judgment—reduced uncertainty to near zero—about Saddam's intentions. If that is true—and I believe that any professional student of judgment and decision making would believe that it is true—then it is not surprising that Powell was wrong. We should not give credit to his opponents for being right, either; for if the task was indeed intractable, we must conclude that his opponents were merely lucky in being right. We need to grasp that fact.

In what follows, I want to show that Powell's task was indeed insurmountable, and that the task of inferring the intentions of a potential adversary will remain so for the foreseeable future. That means that a preemptive war based on the inferred intentions of a presumed adversary (or friend) will be very risky indeed; there will often be both false positives (assuming aggressive intentions when none exist) and false negatives (not assuming aggressive intentions when they do exist).

Preemptive War Based on Judgment under Uncertainty

With a few exceptions, wars have been declared after disputes over territory, or property, go unresolved for some period—that is, after a nation or its land is invaded, or after some other unacceptable act eliminates or sharply reduces uncertainty about the adversary's intentions. Recent exceptions include Germany's preemptive strategy in 1914 to begin World War I (for a highly praised description of this action, see Tuchman's *The Guns of August*).[1] Germany's second preemptive action in 1939 began World War II, and Japan's preemptive attack on the United States in 1941 brought the United States into World War II. Irrespective of the relative frequency of the occurrence of preemptive and border-crossing wars, we can say with confidence that preemptive war is *always* based on information—indicators—about the inferred intentions of some other nation, or an organization such as al-Qaeda. Thus, judgments to engage in preemptive war (the two efforts by Germany and the one by Japan) are markedly different from judgments to engage in war based on conventional, directly observed border violations; it is the difference in certitude, as Oliver Wendell Holmes would put it, that makes these two circumstances significantly different. And that difference has consequences for death and destruction; it is irreducible uncertainty at the bottom of inferences about intentions that makes errors (of both kinds) inevitable in relation to preemptive war.

Uncertain Inferences about Intentions

Judgments about others' intentions are as different from objective judgments that a line has been crossed as judgments of beauty are from judgments of a line's length. And because Powell's speech consisted entirely of uncertain inferences, based on multiple fallible indicators of Saddam Hussein's intentions, it was not unexpected that a dispute would arise. Powell's uncertain inferences of Iraqi intentions are in clear contrast to the pronouncements he and others made based on the directly observed acts of Iraqi troops' crossing the border into Kuwait in 1991, an example of the traditional evidence used for hostilities. (In 1961, Adlai Stevenson presented aerial photographs of the Soviet missiles themselves—these were indeed weapons of mass destruction—in Cuba to the UN Security Council as evidence that the Soviet Union posed a "clear and present danger," to use Oliver Wendell Holmes's phrase; he did not have to rely on inferences based on photographs of trucks that were presumed to be servicing weapons of mass destruction. The Cuban photographs provided the direct observation of weapons of mass destruction and so left no need for uncertain inferences about intentions.)

Once Powell took the very significant step from direct observation to uncertain inference, scientists (and laypersons) interested in human judgment took note and raised questions about possible error. For example, scientists asked whether the methodological criteria used by scholars in this field would be used to evaluate Powell's crucial judgments. Future academics will ask that the duality of error in such judgments be acknowledged and the differential risks of false positives and false negatives be made explicit. It may even become unacceptable for declarations of war to rest on a list of unverified and obviously fallible—in Powell's case, later shown to be outright false—indicators of another nation's intentions to do harm. Future judgments of others' intentions may require that a third party authenticate the fallible indicators used. (The Security Council did not formally attempt this.) A neutral party may be asked to investigate the validity of indicators of intentions before quarreling nations resort to death and destruction. The UN of the future may demand a truly coherent presentation of indubitable facts indicating intention instead. The putative coherence of these facts would be determined by scholars. If not by scholars, then by whom? In short, shifting the basis for military intervention from the direct perception of a traditional offense, such as a border crossing, to the uncertain—and very dangerous—inference of another nation's intentions raises new questions, all related to the discipline of human judgment.

As indicated above, these questions have arisen from the criteria for credible judgments that judgment researchers have developed over the past half century. In the future, it will seem peculiar that the knowledge that undergraduate students are taught to apply to judgment is ignored by those making the most important judgments imaginable—presidents and other statesmen and women. Future students must also be prepared to learn that even the commentators in prestigious newspapers such as *The New York Times* wrote columns calling for politicians' intuition to replace "social science" in decision making. See, for example, David Brooks, who writes, "When it comes to understanding the world's thugs and menaces, I'd trust politicians, who, whatever their faults, have finely tuned antennae for the flow of events." He further wrote, "Individuals can use intuition, experience and a feel for the landscape of reality" (thus expressing a view, similar to that of Isaiah Berlin, that I described on p. 4. This is a view that can no longer be supported by any serious student).[2]

Powell's speech suggests that the world may soon be exposed to similar speeches; therefore, anticipation of these issues may be useful. Indeed, even scholars' post hoc reviews of his speech would be useful. Mr. Powell is regarded as one of the most trustworthy men—if not the most trustworthy man—in the world. Therefore, we will not entertain alternative hypotheses that include deception and dissembling.

Because of the failure to find the weapons of mass destruction that President Bush and his advisors, including Colin Powell, so confidently assured the public were in the hands of Saddam Hussein, Powell faced hard questions from reporters. *The New York Times* quoted Powell as saying, "Last year when I made my presentation [at the UN], it was based on the best intelligence that we had at the time." The article further quoted, "Now, I think their best judgment was correct with respect to intention, with respect to capability to develop such weapons, with respect to programs." But the newspaper noted Powell as asking how many stocks they had, if any: "And if they had any, where did they go? And if they didn't have any, then why wasn't that known beforehand?"[3] The reader will note that Powell *accepts* the intelligence agencies' advice about Saddam's intentions ("I think their best judgment was correct with respect to intention"), the very inference that carries the greatest uncertainty, but *questions* the advice about "stocks," the inference grounded in direct perception ("if they didn't have any, then why wasn't that known beforehand?"). This suggests that even men as experienced as Powell need to learn more about the nature of the judgments they are required to make.

Judgments of Intentions and the Duality of Error

Making a judgment under uncertainty requires an informed and responsible decision maker to face the problem of the duality of error: the false positive and the false negative. Facing this ever-present dilemma requires carefully explicating the consequences of each error, and that requires being explicit about the value of each error, that is to say, how much one dreads either error. The Bush administration did indicate that it considered the consequences of a false negative—not taking action against Iraq when it should have; both then National Security Advisor Condoleezza Rice and the president cautioned the public about "not waiting for a mushroom cloud." Both clearly expressed the danger of waiting until it was "too late." And in the age of missiles that can arrive without warning, no one doubts the wisdom of caution. In the case of Iraq, however, these warnings implied that Saddam Hussein had the nuclear capacity to make a nuclear bomb that could produce the "mushroom cloud," but later investigations showed that he did not; thus, a false-positive error occurred. Although the consequences of a false negative were made explicit, the risks—and consequences—of a false positive (taking action against Iraq when action should not have been taken) were never made public by the administration, as far as I know. They may never have been considered seriously.

Recognizing the continuum of ambiguity of perception, ranging from the crystal-clear case of physical invasion to the highly ambiguous case of uncertain inferences of intentions, raises questions about the Iraqi situation that do not arise in territorial disputes. The change from direct perception of empirical fact to human judgment about others' intentions—and that is what preemptive war involves—places the policymaker in a much riskier, uncertain situation.

It is precisely this situation that illustrates the utility of placing the judgment task on the surface–depth continuum. A person's intentions generally lie far along that continuum, toward the depth pole, because a person's intentions can be expressed in so many ways by so many fallible indicators; that is what it means to be abstract. For that reason, the proof of an intention to commit an act is difficult to establish, as Colin Powell discovered on the world stage at the UN.

Because of their abstract nature, judgments of intention fall squarely within the province of the academic field of judgment and decision making. In view of policymakers' past reluctance to rely on "social science" research, however, and the current disarray in the field of human judgment, it seems doubtful that the knowledge developed by the scientific research on this subject will soon be brought to bear on this critical matter. Yet, it is this sort of change that the intelligence community is beginning to recognize. David Kay, the former chief weapons investigator for the United States, shows the need for such change when he notes, "And, you know, almost in a perverse way, I wish [the error of judgment] had been undue [political] influence because we know how to correct that. We get rid of the people who in fact were exercising that. The fact that it wasn't, tells me that we've got a much more fundamental problem of understanding what went wrong. And we've got to figure out what was there. And that's what I call fundamental fault analysis."[4] Of course, "fundamental fault analysis" can best be carried out by students of human judgment.

There are many hypotheses offered by laypersons about where the fault for Powell's misjudgments is likely to be found. As Douglas Jehl and David Sanger reported in *The New York Times* on February 3, 2004, "In hindsight, both Dr. Kay and close allies of the White House say too much weight was given to untested sources of human intelligence, and too little credence given to the possibility that satellite photographs and intercepted communications might have benign interpretations." They further wrote, "A senior intelligence official said Saturday that American intelligence agencies 'continue to believe that, given the information available to us at the time, it is hard to see how analysts could reasonably have come to any other overall judgments than the ones they reached.' The official described as 'premature' any conclusion that the intelligence agencies' prewar judgments were 'all wrong' (as David Kay had described them)."

The question of the relative value of "human intelligence" and technological intelligence, such as that afforded by satellite photographs and overheard voice transmissions, came to the forefront when people asked why the CIA intelligence had been wrong. So, it should be pointed out that if it is the adversary's *intentions* that are to be determined, no satellite photograph is possible. In every case, an intention must be inferred from fallible indicators. That is part of what makes the task of inferring the intentions of the other intractable: there is no escape from the uncertainty generated by the fallibility of the indicators—and there will be many—of the other's intentions. But there are other parts of this task that add to its intractability, and these are illustrated by the appearance of tribal terrorists such as al-Qaeda.

Detecting the Intention to Deceive

Warfare and other forms of hostility afford an oft-encountered opportunity to learn about the intention to deceive. Ordinary communication frequently includes deception, sometimes benign—as between friends, sometimes vicious—as between enemies. Once it is assumed (or discovered) that one's friend or adversary intends to deceive, the learner will likely assume the enemy is employing the coherence strategy of judgment. That is because the learner seeks the rationale for the adversary's deception, and that goal drives the learner to use reason— Why are they doing this? What are they trying to do? Trying to find an answer to these questions will result in the search for coherence in the other's cognitive activity (i.e., What is their plan?).

The learner's assumptions involve risk, however. First, the learner will have several conjectures, several assumptions about the adversary, and that will require choosing among them, or assigning priorities for investigation. Such choices will be difficult, for the fallible information will likely evoke several plausible alternative conjectures. Finding the critical differences among them will entail coping with uncertainty again. Second, if the learner seeks the adversary's coherence strategy, he or she will be risking the construction of a highly incorrect assumption, for all rational, analytical cognitive efforts risk being wildly wrong although they may be exactly correct (see chapter 11 for more). In short, if the learner chooses to assume that the other is employing a coherence strategy, not only does the learner run the risk of being misled through deception (as the Germans were misled during World War II by Eisenhower, who offered them fake direct perceptual evidence about the port of embarkation for the invasion of Normandy), but the learner also runs the risk of making a huge error (again, illustrated by German gullibility). But if it is risky to assume that the other is using a coherence strategy, it is also risky to assume that the other is using a correspondence strategy.

First, the infrequency of terrorist events creates a serious problem because both bitter experience and statistical logic have taught us that highly infrequent events are almost impossible to predict. And infrequency means poor feedback, simply because the necessary data is absent. When something occurs infrequently and feedback is poor, it is close to impossible to learn.[5] Consequently, authorities will rely on maximizing, and that means treating *every* threat as credible. But although maximizing may work at the airport, it cannot work in all circumstances because of the costs of the searches and of false positives. The subway bombings in London on July 11, 2005, illustrate well how a singular event can lead to maximizing—with all of its faults. About two weeks after the London subway bombings, there was a move toward maximizing on the New York subways, when police began randomly searching bags, including purses. The dubious efficiency of this practice in those circumstances was obvious, but the inconvenience was considerable, and newspaper editors began immediately receiving letters protesting the policy.

A second reason that learning about terrorists' intentions is very difficult is that the ecological validities of the multiple fallible indicators of attack are (apparently) very low. Reports from infiltrators are unreliable (they may be double agents), and informants may simply be undependable or inaccurate in their reports. Nor will aggregating a series of indicators of unknown, or low, ecological validity necessarily result in accurate inferences under these circumstances. Neither quasi-rationality based on worthless (or deliberately deceptive) indicators nor any set of heuristics is likely to produce accurate predictions of an attack, as Colin Powell's experience demonstrates.

The Intractability of the Task of Learning about Another Party's Intentions

We can anticipate an increase in preemptive actions in the future. And because all preemptive war is based on *learning* about the intentions of the other, international relations faces new problems. The inevitable and inherent irreducible uncertainties make it impossible to learn about the other to the degree necessary to justify causing their death and destruction. (That has been demonstrated mathematically and empirically.) Therefore, the task is intractable, at least for the foreseeable future.

But experts in the field of international relations and those in related professions have not recognized this situation. For another example, consider Vice President Dick Cheney's speech to the Veterans of Foreign Wars, on August 26, 2002, in which he states, "There is no doubt that Saddam Hussein now has weapons of mass destruction [and] there is no doubt that he is amassing them to use against our friends, our allies, and against us." Our ability to learn about the intentions of others remains unquestioned, even in the most serious of circumstances; claims similar to Cheney's—claims of having learned of the intentions of others will, despite their falsehood, again be used to justify preemptive war. But the learning about intentions is a task that is not only fraught with uncertainty, but also in fact intractable, and that means that errors will be inevitable (as in the cases of Cheney and Powell). However, nations failing to grasp the fact of intractability risk falsely taking the path of death and destruction in the immediate future.

But such judgments are never simple.

Learning about al-Qaeda's Intentions

The problem Secretary Powell had ascertaining Saddam Hussein's intentions will seem minimal when compared with the problem of ascertaining al-Qaeda's intentions. The most pressing questions after the attack on the World Trade Center and the Pentagon were "what will happen next, and when?" Answering these questions requires learning about the other, just as answering questions about Saddam Hussein's intentions did. These were the same questions Powell had to address about Saddam, and that Kennedy and his executive committee had to address following the discovery of the Soviet atomic weapons in Cuba, and which they found so difficult to answer. Kennedy and his committee had the advantage of direct communication with their Soviet counterparts, however, whereas Bush and his advisors can communicate with their enemy, al-Qaeda, only through pronouncements, signs, and signals—that is, there were multiple fallible indicators on both sides. Additionally, Kennedy had only one adversary—Khrushchev—to learn about, whereas Bush has only a vague idea about the makeup of his enemy, which might consist of only one person, bin Laden, about whom he knows very little; might be a small group about whom he knows almost nothing; could be a highly decentralized arrangement; or might involve changing combinations of people. John Keegan, one of our most noted military historians, observed, "Al-Qaeda has no identifiable base and no territory. The size and composition of its membership is unknown, as is the identity of its leadership, a few self-declared though elusive figureheads apart, and the structure of its command system, if one exists; it is a strength of Al-Qaeda that it appears to be a coalition of like-minded but separate groups rather than a monolithic entity."[6]

These conditions are representative of the nature of tribal arrangements and make interpersonal learning extremely difficult, if not impossible. Nevertheless, al-Qaeda's intentions became the critical question that members of the American government and others had to address following al-Qaeda's clear demonstration of its intention to harm the United States, and the government would make numerous inferences about the group's intentions. What actions does al-Qaeda intend to take to inflict this harm? Where and when will those actions be taken? The demand for answers to those questions increased dramatically after the revelation that the White House (Clinton's and Bush's) had received a significant amount of information (intelligence) prior to September 11 regarding al-Qaeda's terror-related activities; the demand became even more acute after the London subway bombings on July 16, 2005, that killed 55 people and maimed hundreds.

The difficulty of learning about al-Qaeda's intentions was foreshadowed by Kennedy's experience with Khrushchev: it is hard to learn about someone who does not subscribe to the same form of rationality that you do. The case of al-Qaeda is made more difficult not only by its loose tribal organization but also by the highly indeterminate nature of the organization of its thought.

The usual difficulties created by the uncertain meaning of messages received from one's adversary is compounded by the fact that al-Qaeda, like any enemy, will use messages to mislead. For example, seeing a high volume of electronic messages between members of al-Qaeda would ordinarily be taken as a sign that the group was preparing for a terrorist activity. But since al-Qaeda members know that the Americans monitor their message traffic, al-Qaeda has only to increase message traffic in order to deceive the Americans into believing an attack is imminent, thus increasing uncertainty within the population and the security forces. Making message traffic a fallible indicator is a risk-free method for increasing fear and uncertainty in the enemy.

Although experts in decryption are familiar with attempts to deceive, the nature of this adversary makes decryption a formidable problem. The geniuses that broke the Japanese and German codes during World War II had enormous difficulties to overcome, but at least they had identifiable adversaries with familiar methods of operation.

Learning "Who"

The intractability of the interpersonal learning problem makes itself felt severely today by the murderous attacks on men, women, and children by bombers such as Timothy McVeigh, who killed 168 people in Oklahoma City; those who brought down the Twin Towers in New York and blew up the trains in Madrid and London; and perpetrators of other atrocities. Their motives—even the motives of the al-Qaeda group—have not been learned.

Here is the way Keegan describes the task for those who wish to "decrypt," or otherwise understand, al-Qaeda's intentions. He writes: "The challenge to the West's intelligence services is to find a way into the fundamentalist mind and to overcome it from within."[7] There are few platitudes to be found in Keegan's books, but this is one of them. For there is no operation by which the "West's in-telligence services" can "find a way into the fundamentalist mind."

Keegan is right to say that it is the "West" that seeks to learn how the funda-mentalist thinks, for it is not simply the United States or Great Britain that faces the problem of these anonymous bombers; attacks have occurred in many na-tions. But after the London subway bombings, in what was termed a major speech, British Prime Minister Tony Blair made it plain that he believed that mere security measures would not deter such bombers, when he said, "In the end, it is by the power of argument, debate, true religious faith and true legitimate politics that we will defeat this threat."[8] Is it possible that Mr. Blair really believes that it is through the "power of argument" that he will deter such acts? Does he really believe that people who are prepared—indeed, eager—to die for their beliefs can have those beliefs changed by an argument? Does he not realize that it is as diffi-cult for a Muslim to change his (coherent) fundamental beliefs as it is for Mr. Blair to change his? As for "true" religious faith, it is precisely because Muslims believe as firmly in the truth of their religious faith as Tony Blair believes in his that they do what they do. In their view, they are acting out the will of their God, just as George Bush believes he is acting out the will of his God through his own "true religious faith." And, of course, the bombers long ago rejected the use of "true legitimate politics," whatever that may mean. Mr. Blair's plea for "argu-ment, debate, true religious faith and true legitimate politics" as a means for de-terring the bombers is as likely to be realized as Mr. Keegan's plea for the intelli-gence services to "find a way into the fundamentalist mind." It is surprising that an experienced politician like Mr. Blair would make such remarks, his frustration notwithstanding.

But we must remember what he is up against. When the Irish Republican Army was killing and maiming innocent men, women, and children with their attacks in England, he at least knew what they wanted: they were Catholics who wanted the British out of Ireland. (Of course, this being a religious as much as a political war, there were Protestant Irish who did not want them out, and were also willing to kill and maim to keep the British there.)

But what do the Muslim bombers want? They have not told Mr. Blair (or anyone else). There seems little reason to think that it is merely the war in Iraq that motivates the bombers (see, for example, "It's Not Who We Are, It's What We Do" by Fred Kaplan in a *Slate* article posted July 20, 2005). The 9/11 attack on the Twin Towers preceded the Iraq war.

Yet it is not merely the bombers' failure to explain to Mr. Blair what they want that is so disturbing; there is also a lack of visual and verbal indicators of who the bombers are. That anonymity presents a grave difficulty for those who need to identify them before they bomb—thereby preventing future bombings—and adds to the puzzle of what these events signify, as Mr. Blair made plain when he said, "This is the battle not just about the terrorist methods, but their views. Not just about their barbaric acts . . . but what they *think and the thinking* they would impose on others" (italics mine).[9]

These remarks are significant: they indicate that Mr. Blair now understands that he can no longer identify bombers by their adherence to a creed or by any physical indicators—fallible or otherwise. Bombers can be identified with any degree of certainty only by their credo or propaganda.

Unfortunately, whatever they may be thinking is so firmly coherent that it is not susceptible to information not congruent with it; therefore, Mr. Blair's attempt to change it though his debate, faith, and legitimate politics will surely be useless. Indeed, Mr. Blair's remedies have already been acted upon, with dire consequences. A previous London police commissioner (Lord Stevens) had sent antiterrorism teams to train in Israel and other countries and came to the conclusion that "there is only one sure way to stop a suicide bomber determined to fulfill his mission; destroy his brain instantly, utterly."[10] Subsequently, a London police officer shot a suspected bomber in the head eight times in the London subway. The suspect proved to be innocent, but the officer could hardly be criticized for acting in good faith. For if the man had indeed been a bomber, there would have been no other way to stop his suicide mission other than to "destroy his brain instantly, utterly," according to what the police had already concluded after training in Israel.

Thus, Mr. Blair and Lord Stevens had agreed on the location of the problem (the brain of the suspect), but Mr. Blair's vague suggestions for changing the content of that brain were ignored. Insofar as the police were concerned—and it is the police who must take concrete action to prevent the next bombing, not the prime minister—Lord Stevens's approach was the only practical one. Is his method the future's only hope?

The future had actually arrived before Lord Stevens made his pronouncement, for on August 4, 2005, the International Asssociation of Chiefs of Police issued new guidelines, which had been published on July 8—two weeks before the innocent man mistaken for a suicide bomber was shot in the head by the London police.[11]

The important role of multiple fallible indicators can be readily seen in the "behavioral profile" the police provided. All the indicators in this profile are highly fallible, as is obvious from the killing of an innocent person. The police organization's behavioral profile notes this fallibility in its use of the word "might" in connection with each indicator, as the International Asssociation of Chiefs of Police guidelines note: "Such a person might exhibit 'multiple anomalies,' including wearing a heavy coat or jacket in warm weather or carrying a briefcase, duffle bag, or backpack with protrusions or visible wires. The person might display nervousness, an unwillingness to make eye contact, or excessive sweating. There might be chemical burns on the clothing or stains on the hands. The person might mumble prayers or be 'pacing back and forth in front of a venue.' "

Significantly, the guidelines also say the threat to officers does not have to be "imminent": "An officer just needs to have a 'reasonable basis' to believe that the suspect can detonate a bomb." An American police chief observed, "I can guarantee you that if we have, God forbid, a suicide bomber in a big city in the United States, 'shoot to kill' will be the inevitable policy. . . . It's not a policy we choose lightly, but it's the only policy."[12]

The relevance of the concepts of uncertainty, with its false positives and false negatives, thus makes itself quite clear in relation to modern survival and modern morality. Clarifying that relevance is one aim of this book. For it is extremely doubtful that the current leaders of nations and their cohorts are likely to be thinking in these terms; it may even be that some are incapable of doing so. Colin Powell's performance at the United Nations may turn out to be a classic example of innocent judgmental incompetence. For until someone makes clear that they recognize the degree of uncertainty in these situations, shows that they grasp the concept of false positives and false negatives, and specifies the differential values they place on these errors, in short, makes explicit their judgment policy in appropriate terms—until that is done, we are likely to wander back and forth in a wilderness of words and death and destruction.

Data Explosion

One consequence of the convergence of psychology and economics with the ecological model of science is that there may well be an explosion of data, much as we have already seen as a result of the technological revolution of the twentieth century.

No one will doubt that the technology of the twentieth century brought us a plethora of information. Granted that much of it is disorganized, false, or at least unreliable, and its sources are often unknown, nevertheless, the difference between the amount of useful information available to a citizen in 1900 and that available in 2000 is vast. And that vast difference can be seen in the new terms invented to describe this situation—"information overload" is now a common term; "data mining" is less familiar but has a specific methodological reference. It is now plain that our ability to *collect* information results in unbelievable amounts of data crammed on electronic disks, that is, in a very small amount of space. This technical achievement has far exceeded our ability to organize information in terms that make it usable; data mining amounts to "digging around" in the data in the hopes of finding something meaningful. What is missing are well-established tools for extracting meaning from what is "dug up." Although there are many online advertisements for such tools, they are generally algorithms that are highly specific, geared to a certain set of data.

Early in the twentieth century, the focus on getting information was so strong, and so little of the information was actually retrieved, that there was little emphasis on the nature of the cognitive activity employed to organize it, either in our mind or in our files—alphabetically seemed to be good enough. However, now that the emphasis has shifted radically to the question of how to make sense of all the data we have, there has been an increasing effort to find good and useful means of making order of the chaos in these mounds of data. At present this problem is largely in the hands of technicians, whose main focus is to develop statistical and mathematical algorithms for very specific tasks, without regard for the overall problem. Eventually, the problem of understanding this situation will fall on the doorstep of the science of judgment and decision making.

Policymakers' and Technicians' Data-Mining Strategies and Tactics

With its trendy sound, "data mining" appears to be a new way of doing things. It is not: It is an old and, for the most part, discredited technique.

The most important thing to keep in mind about data mining is that it is a post hoc procedure, and thus inevitably suffers from that fact. That is, data mining works on data that have *already* been accumulated, usually by means and methods unknown, or at least uncontrolled, without any regard for how the data might be used. One cannot support the conclusions based on attempts at organization and analysis of the data because these conclusions rely on unknown and unknowable factors. Data-mining enthusiasts believe that irrelevant and misleading causes will be swamped out of the data by the sheer volume of information in the "mine." Because compact disks can store and retrieve huge amounts of data, hundreds of thousand of items of information can be organized and ordered in countless ways according to innumerable mathematical combinations. And that is what is new. There will be occasions when that hope of finding a "pattern" will be justified, more or less. The real test of the truth of the hypothesis that arises from the mining of the data will require an empirical test of the conclusions, independent of the mining.

The history of data mining is best seen in the field of medicine, especially epidemiology, where data mining has been known for almost a century as *retrospective analysis* and is compared unfavorably with the procedure known as *prospective analysis*. For example, a study that used retrospective analysis would include in one group children who had watched television six hours a day or more for the preceding six months, and would compare their grades with a group of children who had watched television for less than six hours a day for the same time period. Should the grades differ in these two groups, one would infer that watching television affected their grades. However, there may have been many differences between the children in these two groups aside from television watching that led to the difference in their grades.

Such retrospective studies have been the bane of medical research because they are frequently anecdotal, seem reasonable to the uninitiated, and are easy to quote. Yet pharmaceutical companies are often stuck with undertaking such studies (for example, observing side effects of drugs in patients that have taken them for years; see publicity about Vioxx and similar drugs), because the problem of digging out ("mining for") other causes for the side effects can lead to long, bitter arguments; the corrective, prospective, random-assignment, clinical trials take years. But, in the meantime, the FDA must decide whether to keep the drug on the market. The controversy over whether cigarette smoking caused lung cancer derived from the fact that the early epidemiological studies were retrospective—that is, data-mining—studies. Steps can be taken to reduce the likelihood of a mistaken inference, and Doll and Peto took just such steps, but it was really the huge numbers of cases involved in these studies that gave them their credibility and left little doubt about the cancer-causing role of cigarette smoking.

As matters stand, the regulatory authorities take a dim view of retrospective studies but find it hard to dismiss them, given their intuitive appeal. (The same problem underlies the issue of learning from history, since historians do nothing but retrospective studies; see above on "learning from history.")

The Differences in Technicians' and Policymakers' Strategies

Policymakers find mounds of data overwhelming. As a result, they ignore it and make insupportable generalizations without looking at it. Analyzing it is simply too difficult and expensive. Much of our folklore about traffic, water use, and the like resulted because analysts felt defeated before they began.

But when technicians, statisticians, and mathematicians look at the masses of electronic data, they react like hungry horses looking at a haystack; for technicians, the masses of data are an opportunity and a challenge, not a bulwark against progress. The problems of retrospective analysis don't bother them (much) because they know they exist and because they believe they can overcome them with sophisticated algorithms; in any event, they are prepared to test their conclusions (most of the time) against empirical events.

It is the policymakers, however, who listen to and are guided by the data miners, who are our concern, because policymakers will likely never get a chance to *test* the accuracy of data miners' inferences. That means that the policymaker will not be able to employ the correspondence strategy of testing against empirical accuracy but will have to rely on the coherence strategy—the internal logic and consistency of the argument. The inference drawn from that process is, unfortunately, subject to catastrophic error, as the following example shows.

Colin Powell: Victim of Data Mining and the Coherence Strategy

Colin Powell's February 5, 2003, address to the Security Council was a historic event watched with keen interest around the world. I present a fragment of this speech to show how one leading U.S. government figure failed by virtue of his ignorance of a simple rule of inference—a rule he would have known had he been a student of judgment and decision making.

In his introductory remarks, Powell said, "My second purpose today is to provide you with additional information, to share with you what the United States knows about Iraq's weapons of mass destruction as well as Iraq's involvement in terrorism, which is also the subject of Resolution 1441 and other earlier resolutions."

He then described the data-mining effort (retrospective analysis) that produced the material for his speech, although he did not make his audience aware of the methods that were used to produce his evidence. In all likelihood, neither he nor his audience realized the implications of his methods. However, the readers of this book will.

Here is Powell's description of the data mining:

> The material I will present to you comes from a variety of sources.
> Some are U.S. sources. And some are those of other countries. Some
> of the sources are technical, such as intercepted telephone conversations and photos taken by satellites. Other sources are people who
> have risked their lives to let the world know what Saddam Hussein is
> really up to.

(The reader will recognize instantly the doubtful reliability of such material. Powell's audience apparently did, even as Powell himself apparently did not.)

Powell continued,

I cannot tell you everything that we know. But what I can share with
you, when combined with what all of us have learned over the years, is
deeply troubling.

What you will see is an accumulation of facts and disturbing pat-
terns of behavior. The facts on Iraqis' behavior—Iraq's behavior—
demonstrate that Saddam Hussein and his regime have made no effort—
no effort—to disarm as required by the international community. *Indeed, the facts and Iraq's behavior show that Saddam Hussein and his
regime are concealing their efforts to produce more weapons of mass destruction* (italics mine).

I italicized the last sentence because it is critical—and false. "Saddam Hussein
and his regime" could not have been concealing their efforts to produce *more*
weapons of mass destruction because, as became widely known, much to the embarrassment of Secretary Powell and the Bush administration, they did not have any
weapons of mass destruction. This critical sentence was an unfounded inference
produced by data mining; it is a perfect example of a flawed retrospective analysis.

Powell continued,

Let me begin by playing a tape for you. What you're about to hear is a
conversation that my government monitored. It takes place on November 26 of last year, on the day before United Nations teams resumed
inspections in Iraq. The conversation involves two senior officers, a colonel and a brigadier general, from Iraq's elite military unit, the Republican Guard.

Powell then played the mined tape. Here is a transcription of the first part;
it is sufficiently representative for the reader to be able to form an idea of the
kind of material Powell relied on. In any event, *all* of this material was discredited as evidence by virtue of the fact that no weapons of mass destruction were
ever found, despite extensive efforts. (Vice President Cheney's remarks that there
was "no doubt, no doubt" about their existence were also shown to be false.)

First, the senior officers acknowledge that our colleague, Mohamed El
Baradei, is coming, and they know what he's coming for, and they know
he's coming the next day. He's coming to look for things that are pro-
hibited. He is expecting these gentlemen to cooperate with him and
not hide things.

But they're worried. [The colonel says,] "We have this modified vehicle. What do we say if one of them sees it?"

What is their concern? Their concern is that it's something they
should not have, something that should not be seen.

[The general is incredulous and says,] "You didn't get a modified vehicle. You don't have one of those, do you?"

[Colonel:] "I have one."

[General:] "Which, from where?"

[Colonel:] "From the workshop, from the Al Kendi Company?"

[General:] "What?"

[Colonel:] "From Al Kendi."

[General:] "I'll come to see you in the morning. I'm worried. You all have something left."

[Colonel:] "We evacuated everything. We don't have anything left."

Note what he says: "We evacuated everything."

[Colonel:] "We didn't destroy it. We didn't line it up for inspection. We didn't turn it into the inspectors. We evacuated it to make sure it was not around when the inspectors showed up."

[General:] "I will come to you tomorrow."

Let me play another tape for you. As you will recall, the inspectors found 12 empty chemical warheads on January 16. On January 20, four days later, Iraq promised the inspectors it would search for more. You will now hear an officer from Republican Guard headquarters issuing an instruction to an officer in the field. Their conversation took place just last week on January 30.

[Powell cues an audiotape of someone speaking in Arabic.]

Let me pause again and review the elements of this message.

[Republican Guard Officer:] "They're inspecting the ammunition you have, yes."

[Field Officer:] "Yes."

[Republican Guard Officer:] "For the possibility there are forbidden ammo. . . . And we sent you a message yesterday to clean out all of the areas, the scrap areas, the abandoned areas. Make sure there is nothing there."

Remember the first message, evacuated.

This is all part of a system of hiding things and moving things out of the way and making sure they have left nothing behind.

Following the tape, Powell asked, "Why? Why?" making clear his commitment to a coherence strategy; he wants to answer the "why" question, show that the "facts fit together," so that he can claim a coherent argument. But it turned out that whatever these two Iraqis were talking about was irrelevant to Powell's assertions. The empirical base that is so important to the justification of technicians' data mining was missing in Powell's use of retrospective analysis.

It is this sort of thing that makes the coherence strategy of judgment so dangerous in relation to retrospective analysis, or data mining, or indeed learning from history. Learning *that* the generals said what they said is one thing, but learning *why* they said it, as Colin Powell so badly wanted, is quite another. Retrospective analysis is a dangerous method for policymakers to use to answer the "why" question. It always requires an independent source present confirmatory evidence of the inference's validity.

But if no one tells the Colin Powells of this world—and their political colleagues—of the dangers of retrospective analysis and other aspects of what we now know about judgment and decision making, how will they learn? Is it important that they learn? A look at Iraq in 2005 answers that question.

Why Data Mining and the National Security Agency Are Threats to U.S. Security

The prime function of the National Security Agency (NSA) is to seek information by reading or listening to enemies' electronic communications. This agency has the technical means to eavesdrop on telephone conversations and other forms of electronic communication globally. Because the number of these communications has risen to astronomical levels, this tactic has been called "data mining." James Risen writes in his recent book *State of War: The Secret History of the C.I.A. and the Bush Administration*: "Today, industry experts estimate that approximately nine trillion e-mails are sent in the United States each year. . . . Americans make nearly a billion cellphone calls and well over a billion landline calls each day." Digging into this mountain of calls surely deserves to be called data mining and retrospective analysis.

It is assumed that in this mountain of calls lies buried information of critical military value, and therefore it should be examined, read, or listened to. It was just such eavesdropping that produced the material that was the showpiece of Colin Powell's presentation to the Security Council when he pleaded for the council members to participate in the U.S. invasion of Iraq. That telephone conversation was captured through listening to countless conversations between Iraqis, which, on the face of it, seems a very good way to gain information about an enemy's intentions.

There are problems, however; the conversation Powell repeated to the council is a nice example of the prime problem—information that appears to be plausible later turns out to be extremely misleading. The sort of information Powell relied on misled because it was nothing but *retrospective analysis*—an examination of past events, of what one person said to another. Although these conversations in themselves are "bare facts," there is no means of ruling out alternative plausible explanations of those facts (i.e., the meanings of those conversations). Thus, had he been challenged, Powell could not have ruled out alternative plausible explanations for those phone conversations. Moreover, we now know there were *no* WMDs, while his explanation for the conversation (WMDs are present) turned out to be false. Nothing in the process of retrospective analysis could resolve this matter because the variety of alternative plausible explanations for those conversations is endless.

It is clear that Powell did not know he was presenting an explanation of bare facts that could be (and would be) refuted—an indefensible explanation that would result in the loss of thousands of lives, tens of thousands of dismemberments, and huge destruction of property. *Should* he have known? Probably not.

Given the Bush administration's negative attitude toward analytical methods, and President Bush's commitment to romantic goals, it is unlikely there would have been anyone willing to question Powell's use of retrospective analysis and face the resultant torrent of criticism. Retrospective analysis ("data mining") has now found a secure place among military intelligence practices, and the NSA budget for this tactic is in the billions. Regrettably, technological advances in data collection has brought with it a long discredited methodology that political and military operatives in our government may yet rely on for a long time to come.

Worse still, retrospective analysis is now used not only for international spying but for domestic surveillance, with the expected results. On January 17, 2006, a headline in *The New York Times* read "Spy Agency Data after Sept. 11 Led F.B.I. to Dead Ends." The lead paragraph read,

> In the anxious months after the Sept. 11 attack, the National Security Agency began sending a steady stream of telephone numbers, e-mail addresses and names to the F.B.I. in search of terrorists. The stream soon became a flood, requiring hundreds of agents to check out thousands of tips a month.
>
> But virtually all of them, current and former officials say, led to dead ends or innocent Americans, although "Vice President Dick Cheney has said it has saved thousands of lives."[13]

And of course, it was just this method that led Powell to urge the members of the Security Council to join the United States in an invasion of Iraq.

Although the use of this very weak method is often criticized for its doubtful moral and constitutional character, its weakness as a method and the strong likelihood of its producing errors—so well demonstrated by Colin Powell's UN speech—are never mentioned. Bishop and Trout's remarks are highly relevant to the absence of this feature of data mining:

> It is time for epistemology [the science of knowing] to take its rightful place alongside ethics as a discipline that offers practical, real-world recommendations for living. In our society, the powerful are at least sometimes asked to provide a moral justification for their actions. And there is at least sometimes a heavy price to be paid when a person, particularly an elected official, is caught engaging in immoral actions or defending clearly immoral policies. But our society hands out few sanctions to those who promote and defend policies supported by appallingly weak reasoning. Too often, condemnation is meted out only after the policies have been implemented and have led to horrible results: irresponsible war and spilt blood or the needless ruin of people's prospects and opportunities.[14]

5

The Coherence Strategy

Trying to Be Rational

Although we can be quite confident that we have possessed correspondence competence for millions of years, when coherence competence emerged is another matter. We certainly could have gotten along quite well without a coherent set of thoughts for the million years we lived as hominids. There was little or nothing in the natural environment that demanded a coherent judgment strategy from hominids and their immediate successors—no algebra, no Cartesian coordinates, and little if any social organization to demand coherent judgments, so far as we know. And since thoughts from prehistory are not preserved, we can only wonder how and why and when this type of cognition developed. I will offer speculation about these questions below.

Whatever precipitated the appearance of coherent cognition in *Homo sapiens* remains buried in our past. Yet this clearly was one of the great occasions in our cognitive history. So we are goaded to try to learn more about it. Indeed, it was the undeniable empirical fact of our coherent cognitive competence that drove Alfred Wallace away from Charles Darwin.

Wallace's simultaneous development of the idea of natural selection had made him famous and had put him right up there with Darwin, who was his hero. But Wallace abandoned the idea because he became convinced people were capable of coherent cognition, despite the apparent fact that coherent cognition had no survival value whatever; only cognition directed at empirically real objects—correspondence cognition—could have survival value, making one organism more fit than another. Wallace was so convinced that natural selection could not have been responsible for the appearance of coherent competence that he attributed this complexity to the intervention of some "intelligence." He asked,

> How were all or any of these faculties [mathematical reasoning, and geometrical spatial abilities, morality and ethical systems] first developed when they could have been of no possible use to man in his early stages of barbarism? How could natural selection, or survival of the fittest in the struggle for existence, at all favor the development of mental powers so entirely removed from the material necessities of savage men, and which, even now, with our comparatively high civilization, are, in the farthest developments, in advance of the age and appear to have relation rather to the future of the race than to its actual status?[1]

Darwin's biographer, Janet Browne, states that Wallace, after many years of supporting Darwin, "backtracked on his commitment to natural selection in 1869. He claimed that natural selection could not account for the mental attributes of modern humans." Thus Wallace came to claim that at some point during mankind's early history, physical evolution had stopped and some higher driving force or spirit had taken over. "Modern mankind," he wrote, "thus escaped the fierce scrutiny of natural selection. The development of human thought freed humanity from the inexorable laws of nature."[2]

Wallace's unease about the origins of human coherence competence was not born of mysticism (that developed later), nor was it completely arbitrary. Two puzzling features about the evolution of coherence competence stood out for him—and stand out for us: how and why was coherence competence selected by the environment? It seems clear that the natural environment selected correspondence-competent creatures for survival because those organisms were more empirically accurate in their judgments of objects and events in their surroundings. Competence in recognizing the appearance of a predator trying to eat you is surely a survival skill, and in chapter 3, I describe the important role of correspondence competence in sexual selection. But how does cognitive coherence contribute to fitness? Fitness to what? Are there coherent (well-designed) pieces of the environment to which our judgments should fit?

Questions like these seem particularly difficult to answer if we regard the world of even 50,000 years ago as devoid of demands for coherent explanations, while being full of critical demands for empirical correctness. The theory of evolution rests on natural selection, and natural selection—apparently—rests on *fitness,* that is, good, accurate empirical correctness. But how does coherence competence lead to fitness? What are the elements that require a fit? Such competence did get started, somehow, and it persisted. How, and why?

This is not the place to introduce the reader to Wallace's speculations about that "superior intelligence," inasmuch as they failed to capture the interest of his peers, Darwin explicitly rejected them, and they are they unrelated to our topic. (The interested reader should consult Shermer's *In Darwin's Shadow.*) But they won't go away. Darwin, however, clung to his idea that natural selection did apply to human cognition and conceived of the judgment process in a manner very similar to the way many modern psychologists conceive of it today. As he saw it, the fundamental process of judgment rests on the use of multiple fallible indicators, although Darwin never used these terms. Janet Browne says that he "depended on probabilities" and he "was inviting people to believe in a world run by irregular, unpredictable contingencies," and thus he anticipated the fundamental premise introduced by Egon Brunswik for the modern judgment and decision researcher.[3]

Unfortunately, however, Darwin did not distinguish between correspondence competence and coherence competence, nor did he address directly Wallace's problem. Therefore, he bypassed the problem that Wallace raised—why are we coherence competent?—and thus left an opening for modern religious fanatics, and also scholars, to introduce ideas such as "intelligent design." (Oddly, even modern psychologists such as Gerd Gigerenzer bypass Wallace's problem by denying the relevance of coherent cognition. Inexplicably, Daniel Kahneman, Cass Sunstein, and others bypass it by looking the other way, that is, by ignoring the glaring fact of correspondence competence, instead expending all their energy on coherence competence—and finding it wanting, all the while ignoring the process of correspondence competence!)

By the twenty-first century, however, we had learned more about human cognition than either Darwin or Wallace knew. Perhaps the move from correspondence to coherence isn't a leap but a few short, connected steps. There is a thought process that can be seen as a natural bridge between correspondence and coherence. When people see that a particular confluence of objects and/or events is followed regularly by the same or similar results, they may begin thinking about these things together and expecting these objects and/or events to be followed by these results. Some theorists would refer to this perception of the confluence as *pattern recognition*; others would call it *multiple probabilistic cues*. The basic point to consider is that this sort of perception can be considered a complex form of correspondence cognition but also has strong similarities to the correspondence strategy.

The correspondence aspect of pattern recognition is that just as we can identify individual objects and events in our environment through past experience, we can also recognize arrays of objects or events. We become aware that when we see a particular confluence of objects and/or events that in the past produced a certain result, there is a good probability that the reappearance of those objects and/or events heralds the reappearance of the same result they produced in past instances. From there, it is a short but significant step to looking for the pattern rather than the individual causes, and to adjusting one's thinking so that individual objects and events are fitted into the pattern. There are several significant activities and institutions that would then bolster the drive to further develop coherence competence. Among these are oral communication and language, narrative, and eventually written language; the shift from hunting and gathering to farming, which requires a systematic demonstration of tasks that presupposes at least a primitive understanding of cause and effect; larger societies that give rise to bureaucracy (which is linked to writing); mathematics, one of the most inherently coherence-oriented mental activities; domestication of animals; and technology. Many pages could be and have been written on the relationships between these activities and the application of coherence judgment, although because several of these activities have prehistoric origins and the surviving history of the origins of the others is spotty, what we may surmise or suppose about them must remain speculative.

The Drive for Coherence

We take it for granted that narratives have had a long existence; no primitive society has been found without them. And narratives had the important function of providing origin explanations—how people appeared on the Earth, for example, or the origins of certain species, snakes, birds, and so on. But once narratives started, there would be no holding them—or coherent cognition—back; Socrates (fourth century BCE) is the classic example of a willingness to die to preserve the integrity of his beliefs. And Pythagoras (sixth century BCE) is the classic example of the use of coherent thought using mathematics. Those who wanted to apply a logical approach to nature—the physicists and engineers—also began to employ the coherence strategy at about the same time or before. And they not only built houses and boats but also built the pyramids. All this demanded coherent cognition.

But the world would have to wait for Galileo (1564–1642) to create the circumstances that would make famous the motivating effect of coherent thought. For it was not the correspondence features, the empirical facts (the moons of

Jupiter, the less-than-smooth surface of our moon), of Galileo's discoveries that resulted in the Church's order for his house arrest and a brush with death. The Church could always avoid explaining these by using its coherent narratives. It was the clash of his coherent theory of the movement of the Earth that led Galileo to a confrontation with the Church's coherent, but different, supernatural, mystical origins theory. Galileo escaped death not by denying the empirical facts but by recanting his coherent theory and pretending that all he had discovered were some new empirical facts. Giordano Bruno (1548–1600), a defiant priest, was not so evasive, and paid a high price; he stuck with the coherent (heliocentric) theory of Copernicus and was dragged by his tongue to the stake where he was burned alive.

I mention the severity of the Church's confrontation with Galileo and Giordano Bruno to show the extraordinary motivating power of the need to maintain the truth of one's coherent thought against alternative coherent explanations. There was no middle ground for either side. The same powerful motivation to preserve the coherence of one's beliefs reappeared some 200 years later in the reaction to Darwin's theory of evolution. Darwin understood this motivation well; he kept his idea of natural selection secret for 20 years, fearful of what the Protestant church's response might be and made it public only when forced to do so by Wallace's letter indicating that he had independently developed the same idea. Darwin was certainly right when he anticipated the religious communities' strong negative emotional reactions to his theory, which continues to this day. These outstanding events in our intellectual history demonstrate humans' strong motivation to preserve coherence of thought. And these events (together with many similar ones) indicate that, however the coherence strategy—and its amazing competence—got started as a cognitive mechanism, it deserves our attention, for it has maintained a strong hold on human judgment from that day to this.

Bureaucracy as the Source of the Demand for Coherent Judgments

We turn now to an examination of four types of societies and how they may have affected their participants' cognitive activity. Jared Diamond presents a remarkable story of human history in his *Guns, Germs, and Steel: The Fates of Human Societies*.[4] That story is important for us because it throws some light on the cultivation of coherence competence. A brief overview (and simplification) of his classification allows us to see the relative demand on coherence competence that each type of society makes, and thus enables us to estimate the degree to which such competence flourished. Diamond describes each type of society as follows:

> Band: small numbers of people (dozens), nomadic, egalitarian government, no bureaucracy
>
> Tribe: hundreds of people, fixed residence (1 village), egalitarian (or "big-man") government, no bureaucracy
>
> Chiefdom: thousands of people, fixed residence (1 or more villages), centralized, hereditary government, no bureaucracy or 1 or 2 levels
>
> State: over 50,000 people, fixed residence, many villages and cities, centralized government, many levels of bureaucracy.[5]

Diamond recognizes the importance of differences in cognitive activity induced by these different societies by including decision making in his classification, as when he notes that in bands these processes are "egalitarian," in tribes they are "egalitarian or big-man," and so on.[6] Large, formal bureaucracies are present only in states. Thus, once the state appears and the concomitant increase in the complexity of social organization occurs, there are demands for the coherence of institutions, organizations, and rules to a degree unprecedented in previous social forms.

Let me take this further. The practices of bureaucracy and its demands for coherence competence apparently created the conditions for a new practice, and that is writing.[7] We can be sure that although writing can exist without bureaucracy, it would be very hard—but not impossible—to have a bureaucracy without writing. For if your words are not written down, there is no record, and you can always deny that you ever said them. (Everyone has heard the imperative "put that in writing!" and understands why this demand is so often made.) Once your words are written down, others can point to them and hold you accountable. That is, people can examine your written words, and if the examiners have the ability—the cognitive competence—to recognize inconsistencies, faulty logic, and incoherence, then they can challenge your rationality and your honor. For your writing makes your reasoning explicitly retraceable. Thus retraceability, the critical component of coherent, analytical cognition was made possible in a significant new way. And, of course, with writing, everything took longer.

Jack Goody sees a link between the appearance of writing and bureaucracy, as do I, and his reasoning is similar to mine. He writes: "The more complex the organization of the state and the economy, the greater the pressure toward graphic representation of speech."[8] Nevertheless, it must be acknowledged that bureaucracies, and even empires, existed and thrived without the advantages of writing. Diamond points out that the large Inca Empire of Peru lacked writing, as did others.[9]

But were there important differences between societies that had writing and those that did not? Goody has examined what he calls the "power of the written tradition" by comparing literate and nonliterate societies.[10] He makes an important point when he writes:

> When we speak of "changes in cognition," in modes of thought, as one of the implications of literacy, we are not thinking of a point at which the introduction of writing suddenly changed the totality of man's understanding of the universe. That would involve a notion of instant literacy, immediate changes in ways of life and thought following the introduction of writing.[11]

So, of course, he doesn't make that claim, and neither do I. But he does want us to see, and so do I, that although writing began as a primitive system and took a variety of forms that developed over a long period of time, it made an enormous difference. Nor is "the appearance of such logics (as Modus Tollens) [if p, then q] necessarily a quantum jump in logical operations, nor of course does it represent the discovery of logical thinking in any global sense."[12] Nevertheless, the appearance of these logical operations marks a beginning that is enhanced by writing.

Did Writing Encourage a Specific Form of Coherent Cognition?

One consequence of writing is that it causes words (and thus ideas) to appear sequentially, both in the construction of a message and in reading it. That is, it encourages a sequential and retraceable, and possibly cumulative, mode of cognition. Thus it could discourage, or even displace, the form of coherence cognition that a pictorial presentation of the same information will encourage. But if the appearance of writing did indeed encourage the employment of the (sequential and retraceable) analytical form of cognition, then it encouraged a specific analytical form of cognition that is different from one that demands coherence. For example, with writing one can look back and see a statement that is at odds with the statement one is currently examining. But would not writing (with its encouragement of the sequential analytical form of cognition) then have displaced the pictorial form of communication, which, because pictorial, also encouraged a coherent (holistic or Gestalt) form of cognition? The answer is no.

And it is no because there are two forms of coherence; one is the sequential (sometimes called "linear") form of analysis made explicit by writing (best seen in the "if this, then that," or "if p, then q" argument), and the other is the pictorial form in which coherence is implicitly induced by a wholistic arrangement (a circle, or a parallelogram)—a *pattern recognition.* So both forms persisted. Writing continued to make possible its analytical form of coherence by making contradictions explicit, and pictorial expressions continue to make possible its intuitive form of coherence by creating a sense of completeness, as the Gestalt psychologists demonstrated.

Mathematics and Coherence Competence

I haven't mentioned mathematics as a form of coherence: should it be linked with writing or pictorial expressions? The answer is both; mathematics and its inherent calculations are a form of linguistic expression in which its elements are not words but numbers or symbols. Manipulation of these is done strictly according to rules that demand coherence. And, of course, these symbols can be linked to empirical objects (as when we build bridges) and thus help us test the correspondence of our ideas and symbols and concepts to empirically real things. As we shall see below, some researchers make the coherence of these symbols their primary focus of interest; others focus on the judgment of the symbols' correspondence to empirically real objects.

If we accept the positive link between the growth and development of the state and bureaucracy to mathematics and accounting, that is, to writing and coherence competence, then we can ask whether the opposite occurs: does the putative shrinkage of the state diminish its contingencies? That is, if the state shrinks, will its bureaucracy also diminish? Probably. And will there be fewer members of the state's society who exhibit coherence competence in their judgments as well? That seems less certain but still plausible. As the need for coherence competence diminishes, the presence of that competence itself may also diminish. Is that happening in the world today? Or is the opposite the case?

Shifting from Hunting–Gathering Cognition to Farming Cognition

What does a hunter–gatherer do? Both hunters and gatherers *look* for a substance they will never see—*sustenance;* they will only see indicators of it. That is, they are passive cognizers: the hunter looks for indicators (tracks, movement, droppings, sounds, smells); he or she doesn't create them. These indicators are fallible signs—evidence—of the presence and activity of birds, animals, or fish. And that presence is exactly what the hunter is interested in. The gatherer looks for visible, fallible indicators (round, soft, sweet, easily accessible) of invisible life-sustaining material, thus using exactly the same cognitive process as the hunter to infer the presence of sustenance.

How do the hunters and gatherers organize these (visible) indicators into a judgment of the presence of (invisible) sustenance? Both use the same method; they add up (or average) the values ("fresh dung," "very sweet") and reach a judgment ("the prey is nearby," or "this stuff is good to eat"). Then, the hunters trail the game that left the high-value indicators, and the gatherer finds and eats the fruit or berry or nut that offers the best indication of sustenance.

But how do we know that they are using *this* process, this principle of organization, rather than some other? We know that this process—the adding or averaging of the values of multiple fallible indicators—is used because it has been documented—and challenged and tested—in hundreds of controlled studies in what is known as the representative design of experiments.[13] In these studies, participants are presented with several (multiple) indicators that have an imperfect (fallible) relation to a criterion variable. They are given many learning trials, and their performance is then examined. (There are variations of this, but this is the general model.)

Is the hunter–gatherers' cognitive organizing process different from the farmers'? Indeed it is. The hunter–gatherers employ the *correspondence* strategy because they are intent on empirical accuracy; they want to hit their prey with a rock or spear or arrows or, in the case of gatherers, pull it off the branches. Empirical accuracy is everything; if the hunter is accurate, he or she will obtain food. Inaccuracy means hunger. So hunters use the information—the multiple fallible indicators—they get in order to kill or capture their prey. The hunter–gatherer had little or no interest in formal explanations of empirical accuracy, that is to say, developing coherence competence.

The farmer, however, did have considerable interest in coherence competence because he or she cannot live by empirical accuracy alone; he or she needs to grasp, at least somewhat, *how things work*; that is, what the functional relationships among plant growth, water, sunshine, fertilizer, and soil conditions are, and thus the farmer becomes an active cognizer seeking coherence competence. But we must remember that it is a hunter–gatherer—a person immersed in the search for correspondence competence—that, once committed to farming, now is seeking *coherence* competence. And when he or she does seek that form of competence—trying to find the proper functional relationships among the variables in a system—it will be difficult.

In short, the "new" farmer's cognitive goal is much more than simple empirical accuracy. He or she will be seeking to understand how the system works—not such an easy cognitive task; our agricultural colleges are still exploring this today. Therefore, the shift from hunting and gathering to farming implies that farming, and also bureaucracy and writing, was evocative of coherence competence. And indeed, farming, bureaucracy, and writing all seem to have occurred in roughly the same place—the Fertile Crescent—at about the same time.

Feedback is a critical feature of any form of learning. There are two kinds of feedback: *outcome* feedback and *cognitive* feedback. Outcome feedback tells the learner the results (the outcome) of each attempt to achieve the goal, that is, success, failure, or something in between. Because learning refers to a change in behavior following observing the effects (the outcome) of attempts to achieve a goal, observing those effects is critical to learning. Any delay in feedback, however, is detrimental to such learning because the delay provides an opportunity for irrelevant events to occur and thus to mislead the learner. And, of course, a delay between the action taken and its outcome means that the learner will have to rely on his or her memory of what the action was that led to the outcome. So, it will come as no surprise that researchers have learned that feedback delay is an important detriment to learning.

The hunter–gatherer ordinarily experiences little delay between his or her observation of indicators and feedback on the correctness of the inference from the observation; that delay may range from seconds to minutes to as much as an hour, but it will seldom be as long as a week or a month. But for the farmer it will rarely be as short as a minute or an hour, and will often be as long as several days, a week, a month, or even a year. That difference is critical. Feedback delay differs according to circumstances, but it is surely a factor to be considered in the differential ability of the hunter–gatherer and the farmer to learn. But delay in feedback is intrinsic to farming and no doubt accounted for the long period it typically took for groups to adopt the practice.

Cognitive Feedback versus Outcome Feedback, and Hunting–Gathering versus Farming

Cognitive feedback refers to the situation in which one does not learn from outcomes but from instruction. That instruction can come in the form of information about the task (for example, being told which indicators are most important, or whether the indicators are linearly or curvilinearly related to the criterion). Sometimes, such information is called "feed-forward" because one is told beforehand what to look for and instructed in the relative importance of various indicators. So, although hunter–gatherers generally must try to learn from outcome feedback, even when they do have the opportunity to learn from an instructor's cognitive feedback, instruction still differs greatly from the instruction a farmer can get. For example, it is easy for an instructor to show a hunter–gatherer *which* fallible indicators to look for (e.g., droppings or footprints), identify which animal produced them, and thus educate him or her via cognitive feedback ("yes, these are deer droppings").

But the job of providing cognitive feedback or feed-forward to the farmer is much harder because the farming instructor will ordinarily be trying to explain how something *works*. For example, the plant needs water to grow, sunlight to thrive, and fertilizer to increase the size of the fruit ("see, this plant got too much; this plant got too little"), all of which illustrate a *functional* relationship. Thus, the farmer's instructor's task is not merely to show that this visible indicator means the presence of that invisible prey, as in the case of the hunter–gatherer. Once the hunter–gatherer is shown what to look for, he or she will follow the simple positive linear-relation principle, "the more of this the more of that" or "if a little is good, more is better," *without being told to do so,* and will thus develop correspondence competence.

The farmer, however, has much more complicated information to cope with. For example, the farmer's instructor 11,000 years ago would have had to explain to his student about the *tipping point*, a concept which has only recently been introduced to the masses in the twenty-first century by Malcolm Gladwell's best-seller *The Tipping Point.*[14] (The tipping point is the point in a line on a graph at which the line changes direction, say, from up to down, and is known to students of calculus as the *inflection point* of a curve.) The tipping point is always important in connection with nonlinear lines on a graph (it is sometimes called the *optimal point*).

For example, there will be a tipping point with regard to how much water a plant will need; that is, more water is better, up to a point, and then, as the line on the graph "tips," more is worse as the plant begins to drown. The same will be true with regard to fertilizer and other conditions: there will be an optimal amount. And that, of course is a far different matter than "if a little is good, more is better," which is the purely linear relationship. So while the hunter–gatherer can get through life with a simple cognitive rule, the farmer cannot. A farming environment will demand coherence rather than correspondence competence.

Just exactly how the would-be farmer learned those complex rules is a matter we know little about. Archaeologists can't dig up thoughts quite the way they can dig up utensils. So although we can't be specific about how farming practices evoked coherence competence, we can easily see how farming practices demanded it. And we can guess that the would-be farmer first learned some simple relationships from outcome feedback, although such learning which would be very slow and error-ridden. But as more complex knowledge was gained the hard way, cognitive feedback replaced outcome feedback and occurred within and across societies; coherence competence developed intermittently until its advantages accumulated, and then its users overcame those who remained tied to correspondence competence.

Once we understand these concepts and are thus able to see the hunter and gatherers' development of correspondence competence and the farmers' need for coherence competence, we can see how natural selection acts on coherence competence in relationship to both interpersonal learning and farming. Those individuals who were more competent in interpersonal learning (in learning from others) particularly with respect to new and more complex forms of inference, would be better fitted to agriculture because agriculture requires coherent thought, not merely inferences from the visible to the invisible. And those who could learn from delayed feedback and could learn curvilinear functions in addition to linear ones would be better fitted to agriculture. In short, the appearance of farming meant that natural selection might well be applicable to coherence competence, precisely as Darwin had hoped.

Hunting, Gathering, and the Romantic View of Life versus Domestication and Analytical Cognition Today

The above remarks, contrasting the hunter–gatherer's cognitive activity with the farmers' cognitive activity, were intended to be highly focused and closely connected to factual matters. However, I do not want to leave this matter without offering a hypothesis about contemporary events, one derived from comparing the hunter–gatherer's putative correspondence cognition with the farmer's more coherent cognition. My hypothesis is that there is a remnant of the hunter–gatherer in all of us (some much more than others, of course) and that this remnant plays a significant role in today's governments.

I will characterize moderns as *romantics* when they incorporate the hunter–gatherer cognitive style, and offer as my best examples two U.S. leaders, presidents Ronald Reagan and George W. Bush. I suggest the term *romantic* inasmuch as both men energetically chose to be symbolically representative of the hunter–gatherer style of the nomadic life, the unreflective life, and indeed, the uneducated life. These characteristics allow one to be "clear-headed" (simpleminded), that is, uninterested in the analysis of the issues, as for example, George W. Bush has declared himself to be on more than one occasion. No one would accuse either of these presidents of being "bookish," or even interested in reading about (let alone studying) any issue. Their judgments rested largely on abstractions provided by aides, and come down to questions of good and evil—both of which are immediately apparent, much like what happens in Westerns (of which both presidents were fans). (The opposite kind of cognitive activity comes to mind in relation to the former presidents Woodrow Wilson, John F. Kennedy, and Jimmy Carter.)

I offer my characterization of these forms of presidential leadership to illustrate two types of management based on cognitive activity. Just as the shift from hunting and gathering to farming presented a challenge to the longstanding cognitive strategy of correspondence to that of coherence, the threat to the planet from global warming and pollution offers a challenge of similar magnitude. As this threat becomes more apparent, and climate science becomes better understood, the cognitive style of the world's leaders will become more relevant to the search for solutions. World leaders who prefer to maintain their dependence on the correspondence strategy and remain romantically aloof and remote from the demands of a coherence strategy necessary for comprehending and coping with the complexities of climate change run the risk of being seen for what they are—a threat to humankind.

Differences in Cognitive Activities in Different Social Organizations

The suggestion that we should examine the differences in cognitive activities in the populations of tribal and state organizations is not a new one, but the research on judgment and decision making in the last half of the twentieth century will allow us to carry the examination further. For we can now examine differences in the thought processes—in the way people think about social and political matters, rather than what they think. Although differences in cognitive processes have often been suggested as a source of discord between ethnic and cultural groups, it is only recently that we have become able to examine these differences.

But first we should ask: is it proper to extend the concept of coherence to social organizations? Is it appropriate to declare that Western societies—state organizations—have achieved more (or less) coherence in the organization of their societies than tribal societies have? My answer is yes. If we begin with the idea that both cognitive activities and social organizations are to be thought of as systems, then it is easy to see that each can be described in terms of its coherence. What makes the comparison difficult is that there is no standard, accepted measure of the degree of a system's coherence, whether we are talking about a cognitive system or a sociopolitical system. Gross measures such as the number of inconsistencies or contradictions in an utterance or text are commonplace, but that helps us only in the case of gross differences in cognitive systems. Sociopolitical systems can be examined in somewhat more detail: the presence of a written constitution, specific rules and regulations governing the powers and duties of rulers, terms of office, the powers and duties of bureaucrats (if any), and the extent of the formal arrangement of public services (electric power grids, water-distribution systems, sewage systems, postal services) can make clear how large the differences are between Western societies and tribal societies in the extent to which have achieved coherence. But we do not have any standard method for combining those features (some are obviously more important than others) and so we make subjective judgments about the degree of coherence in a cognitive system or a sociopolitical one. These judgments allow us to ask: is the degree of coherence a mark of the longevity and power of a society, or an indication of its vulnerability? Seeking the answer to that question will lead us to ask whether the more coherent, highly organized societies will be undone by those that are less coherent and organized.

Which Shall Endure: The State or the Tribe?

In the beginning of the twenty-first century, something utterly unexpected happened: a tribe (or perhaps chiefdom) headed by Osama bin Laden challenged a state, the United States of America, and scared the hell out of the state by hijacking four commercial airplanes and ramming three of them—fully loaded with fuel—into the World Trade Center and the Pentagon. They killed more than 3,000 persons in the process, and seriously disrupted (and continue to disrupt) the U.S. economy and transportation system. The state quickly learned that it was its coherence—the rational, closely interwoven nature of its systems and their interdependence—that made it so vulnerable to such an attack. For when a single element of a tightly linked system is damaged or removed, the entire system falters and potentially fails.

Although the tribe's governmental support unit, the Taliban in Afghanistan, was destroyed militarily by the United States, it was the lack of coherence of the tribe (al-Qaeda) or chiefdom that made it so resistant to attack, retribution, or revenge. For after the demise of the Taliban, the tribe had no central location to bomb, no significant political or administrative bureaucracy to disrupt, and few, if any, military "assets" to destroy. So how could it be attacked by the enormous military power that had been created by the state to do all those things? It could not be, at least not very well, a fact almost immediately acknowledged—and endlessly repeated—by the state's leaders.

The electrical power system in the United States epitomizes the establishment of a coherent system. Duncan Watts, one of the leaders of the science of social networks, asserts,

> The electrical power system arguably is the most essential technological feature of the modern world. . . . Without power, pretty much everything we do, everything we use, and everything we consume

would be nonexistent, inaccessible, or vastly more expensive or incon-
venient.[15]

The awkwardness and near-helplessness of our highly organized state is
clearly described in the *9/11 Commission Report*.[16] Although there were repetitious
explanations of how the attack on the United States was "different," how the entire nation-state "would no longer be the same," there was little serious consideration for diminishing the strong demand for coherence that made the state so
vulnerable to attack by one very loosely organized tribe. There were no calls for
"decentralizing" government or industry. In fact, steps were taken to make the
bureaucratic system even more tightly organized; new rules were instated to control citizens' activities; new fences were built. And no one was suggesting that the
state should return to a tribal organization or chiefdom, consisting of little more
than small cells as organizational units. Indeed, it would occur to no one that the
coherence of a modern society should be relinquished to defend against a tribal
organization that focuses on destroying that coherence to wreak havoc.

It will be a long time before anyone can say how this situation will be resolved.
Will the state be so severely disrupted that it will have to protect itself against tribal
terrorism and so will no longer place such a high premium on coherence, will lose
faith in its constitutional liberties, and will become a pragmatic semi-state in which
the only criterion would be the success of an operation, not its logical arrangements
or its considerations of justice, as is the case for a tribe? Will the citizens of the state
lose interest in the civil liberties that are the society's core values?

Or will the state prevail over the tribe or chiefdom by wreaking physical havoc
on whatever primitive "assets" it can find, dispersing the tribe's military, killing its
leaders, crushing what little government it has, disrupting its financial networks, its
cells, and its status among nations? Will the tribe's venture into modernity (for example, its dependence on electronic transfer of funds) be its undoing? How long
will it take to restore the status quo ante? Will the state be able to kill so many
members of the tribe that it no longer exists? Human judgment will have to answer
these questions and guide the development of policies to cope with whatever contingencies result from whatever actions the nation or the tribe takes.

The Demand for Coherence in Reconstructing a State

The necessity for some agreed-upon measure of coherence in a modern nation
can be seen in the efforts to reconstruct Iraq. A coherent electrical system, water
supply, sewage system, and functioning governance seem to be necessities that

the rest of the world finds obligatory to restore in that nation. There does not seem to be any dispute over the specific nature of these systems; it even seems possible for representatives of a variety of governments to agree on the general nature of the government to be established. And there seems to be general agreement that all these systems need to be coherent, that all the pieces need to fit. In addition, there seems to be general agreement that achieving coherence will be an enormously difficult task because of Saddam's destruction of Iraq's civil society, and the Americans' and insurgent Iraqis' destruction of Iraq's physical structures.

The campaign for the political coherence of the reconstituted state of Iraq is another matter; it is a battle that is being fought by the various factions in Iraq and the U.S. troops on the ground. Brute force will be used to decide this battle. And the same is true for moral coherence, which is closely linked to political coherence in Iraq.

Moral Incoherence within a State

A hundred and fifty years ago Abraham Lincoln saw the critical role of coherence within a nation when he declared,

> A house divided against itself cannot stand; I believe this government
> cannot endure permanently half slave and half free. . . . I do not ex-
> pect the house to fall—but I do expect it will cease to be divided. It
> will become all one thing, or all the other.

Such all-or-none thinking is characteristic of the search for coherence. And indeed, it soon developed that one of the bloodiest wars of all time would be required to eliminate that incoherent state of affairs, and the nation did (mostly) become "all one thing."

But the demand for moral coherence has changed; it has run up against new trends in morality in our own time. One source of tension between tribes and the state is a conflict in the moral values. Elements within tribes voiced their anger at what they believed to be Western moral freedom that was so extreme it was an insult to their religion. Western states, however, exulted in their moral freedom and criticized the treatment of women within the tribes. This conflict in values and the consequent tension between nation and tribe meant that lives would be lost and societies disrupted. Differences in religion were once more poised to bring death and destruction.

Alan Wolfe makes these trends clear in his book *Moral Freedom,* in which he describes the current breakaway from the coherent Victorian code that had once prevailed:

Moral freedom has become so ubiquitous in America that we sometimes forget how path-breaking it is. We simply no longer live in a
world in which women are encouraged to stay home and raise their
children, government's word is to be trusted, teachers can discipline as
well as instruct, the police enforce laws against what is considered im-
moral conduct, and religious leaders are quick to offer—and their
parishioners are quick to accept—unanimous prescriptions for proper
Christian conduct. Now women will want for themselves a greater say in
how they ought to live, employees will look for jobs that give them some
say in the work they do, churchgoers will ask questions and not just receive answers, young people will manage their own sexuality, and political leaders will take moral instruction from the voters rather than
the other way around.[17]

Indeed, it is precisely that moral freedom enjoyed by the Western world that so
astonishes and so offends the Muslim tribes. That irritation or anger or outrage,
together with religious conviction, led to the shocking death and destruction in
New York City in 2001, and the outrage continues.

The success of the tribes' violent reaction against the state raises the question of whether the state, with its high degree of integration relative to the tribe,
is in fact the enduring social organization. It may not be. Indeed, the postmod-
ern state's very success in organizing itself may be its greatest source of vulnerability. The interruption of the tightly systematically organized structure of states
that provide a rich, integrated source of assets can bring down an entire system,
much as demolishing the World Trade Center buildings did. The coherence of
the elements of the modern state provides its greatest weakness, and also its
greatest strength.

The reverse is true for tribes, or clans. With a "big-man" organization (as
Diamond puts it) instead of an organized bureaucracy, a lack of formal integration frustrates the modern use of force against it precisely because it has a primitive organization and lacks integrated assets. Just as a slime mold can rapidly
reorganize after disorganization—there is so little to its original organization—
a tribe or a clan can also rapidly recombine its elements to its customary and
preferred low level of organization. In short, once the modern state achieves
its tightly organized bureaucracy, with its skills in written communication vastly
enhanced by electronics, and its concomitant demand for competent cognitive
coherence—without which it cannot function, questions begin to arise as to
whether it can maintain the adaptive flexibility that is necessary for its endurance.
In contrast, the casual, flexible, adaptive organization of the tribe may turn
out to make it the most enduring form of social organization, even though, or

perhaps because, it lacks the attributes of modernity. Does the reader—presumably immersed in modernity, with its blessings and its curses—think that is too high a price to pay for survival?

Implications for Tolerating Errors of Human Judgment

Differences in social organization have implications for human judgment. In a tightly organized society, a minor mistaken judgment can result in a catastrophe: the airline pilot who misjudges his location and turns right instead of left may disrupt an entire traffic pattern and put a hundred airplanes at risk; a train engineer who misreads a signal may create a head-on collision; the error of the corrupt accountant or CEO who mistakenly judges that he or she can "beat the system" can destroy the pensions of tens of thousands of employees. Any failure of judgment in a tightly organized system has the potential to bring down the system and threaten the well-being or lives of thousands. In short, in tightly organized and highly rationalized systems, both cognitive and social, errors of judgment will be infrequent, but when they occur they will be disastrous.

It is the weaknesses—the unplanned redundancies that create the backups, the uncertainties that induce checking of the information, the less-than-perfect validities that encourage seeking new data—that give loosely organized systems strength. Of course, that "strength" has its own price—a less-than-efficient organization. But loosely organized systems will produce fewer large errors of judgment, and fewer consequences of those errors will be seriously damaging.

It would be useful for organizations to make a judgment about the tradeoff between the efficiencies of tight organization and the consequences of error—human or otherwise—and the safety of loose organization and its consequences of error. This is occasionally done in engineering and studies of organizational behavior, but the types of human judgment—and their attendant errors—involved in each are seldom considered.

Conflict Resolution in Tribe versus State

Diamond includes in his table a notation about the different forms of conflict resolution in the four stages of society.[18] In bands and tribes, it is informal; in chiefdoms, it is centralized; but in states, it requires laws and judges. A large centralized society, such as the modern United States, which tries but has yet to achieve a coherent set of values, is thus likely to suffer outbreaks of violence periodically, despite its numerous judges and laws. Once a society develops a state and a bureaucracy and commits itself to the goal of coherence competence, it implicitly commits itself to the goal of encouraging, if not demanding, coherent behavior from its citizens. Next it creates laws to control the behavior of its members to fit the social ideal. Thus, a demand for coherence in those laws and their administration will follow. The persistence of this topic can be seen in a July 28, 2001, working paper titled "Predictably Incoherent Judgments."[19] As the title suggests, the concept of coherence was a key concept in this paper. The beginning is worth citing; it indicates that the authors understand the concept in the same terms as this author:

> Coherence in the law is a widely shared ideal. Almost everyone hopes
> for a legal system in which the similarly situated are treated similarly.
> But there are many obstacles to the achievement of coherence in the
> law. This Article is concerned with one particular test of coherence, and
> with two limitations that help cause many failures of that test in actual
> legal systems. We believe that these failures are also failures of justice
> and that they suggest a pervasive problem in existing legal systems.[20]

Because the authors are speaking in a legal context, the examples are in that context, but they are easy for the layperson to understand. They further write: "Our test of coherence is straightforward. We ask: When two or more judgments have been made separately, and each seems to make sense on its own, do they still make sense when considered together?"

That is a rather narrow conception of coherence, or so it appears to a non-lawyer, but the authors note that it "can be readily applied to decisions by juries and by judges." Then the authors broaden the concept: "More generally, we ask whether judgments made in isolation fit together in an orderly way when considered as part of the larger whole."[21] What this definition gains in scope, it loses in precision. Nor does it directly specify coherence in cognitive activity (it is unclear whether "makes sense" should be read as "meets a test of logical coherence" or, simply, and more loosely, "is common sense"). Nevertheless, we can now see that Sunstein and his colleagues are beginning to see judgments in terms of their coherence, which is something new.

This new turn of affairs—the appearance of the state, its bureaucracy, its demand for coherence competence in judgments of human affairs—provides the basis for the kind of twentieth-century ideological "philo-tyranny" described by another University of Chicago professor, Mark Lilla.[22] Indeed, it is the nature of this newly appeared bureaucracy—primarily the tightness of its grip and its rigid demand for cognitive coherence—that differentiates states from bands and tribes. And it is the degree of the bureaucracy's commitment to an ideology that determines the tightness of the grip of coherence, and thus marks the introduction of what Lilla calls *philo-tyranny*. It is philo-tyranny because (1) it is the philosophers (or intellectuals) of the society—those with the education and skills—who have the coherence competence required to set the policies and administer them within the bureaucracy; (2) it is tyranny that denies freedom of thought, freedom of expression, and freedom to suggest or advocate an alternative form of government; and (3) it is not the tyranny of a book, a person, or an idol—as has so often been the case in history—but precisely a tyranny of analytical coherence per se; the tyranny of an idea over reality. And the source of that idea is the society's intellectual, the slave of rationality. (Richard Posner, whom I discussed earlier, has a great deal to say about the "public intellectual" that will capture the reader's interest.)

Old as Lilla's theory of such a tyranny may be—it is reminiscent of Plato's theory of philosopher–kings—its application to the latter part of the twentieth century, and to the most respected academic members of this century, may disturb the modern intellectual (and perhaps the reader). And when Lilla reminds us of the behavior of many of the intellectuals who "were pilgrims . . . [to] Moscow, Berlin, Hanoi, and Havana" and describes them as "political voyeurs who made carefully choreographed tours of the tyrants' domains with return tickets in hand, admiring the collective farms, the tractor factories, the sugarcane groves, the schools, but somehow never visiting the prisons," he brings the false worship of rationality closer to home.[23] Such tyranny has a long philosophical history, but there were a few centuries of resistance to it. Oliver Wendell Holmes recognized it when he turned away from certitude and said he "detested the man who knew what he knew."

Resistance to philo-tyranny in the eighteenth century in the United States took the form of a written constitution that specified the separation of powers. Because this separation of administrative powers matches the separation of cognitive function, cognitive coherence—rationality—is prevented from exercising the tyranny that was so evident in those governments—e.g., the USSR, Maoist China—that lacked such separation. It is this separation of cognitive function, paralleled by administrative rule, that resists—and thus results in the cacophony of voices—the confusion of purposes, the uncertainty of maneuver, which have always typified the governance of the United States and other democracies and, one might add, human behavior itself.

Thus, the U.S. Constitution, with its separation of powers, produces political looseness and flexibility of organization that has insured its survival and may well continue to ensure its survival, this time against tribal aggression that is so suited to attacking rigid systems. But the fact of a written constitution—and its derivatives apparent in state constitutions, county laws, and city statutes—has provided the country with a mass of behavioral rules and regulations that often stymie the very purposes of law. One who has seen this is William Pizzi who, in his "Trials without Truth," provides example after example of how our highly analytical maze of laws prevents justice—and wisdom—from being served. And our tightly organized social and economic system favors a search for the coherence, namely, systematic, analytical interrelationships among its functional elements (its water supplies, power supplies, etc.). It is those systematic, rational relationships that have been built to eliminate human judgment that simultaneously provide the great strength and the great vulnerability of this system of social and economic organization. This distinction can also be seen in our cognitive activity, as I will demonstrate in the following chapters.

How Technology Drives the Need for Coherence Competence

There are numerous electronic worlds in the twenty-first century aside from the world of air traffic control that demand coherence competence from the person who wants to participate in that world. The airline pilot must develop the competence to conform to the coherent world of air traffic control. (It is essential for that world to be coherent in order for the traffic to be managed without collisions.) The pilot does not enter that world with the specific competence he or she needs; training is needed. But nearly all have the natural ability—innate coherence competence—to *be* trained to achieve the specific cognitive competence to perform in this completely coherent world.[24]

There are many other examples: traders who work in the various markets that control the world's economy; the scholars who use the Internet instead of a card catalog. All these electronic systems demand coherence competence; one mistake eliminates coherence, and trouble results. Do these coherent electronic worlds have the capacity to select for fitness? That is, do they actually select individuals for survival, as the natural world does (or did)? No one knows. But surely a coherent argument will soon be forthcoming. Were he writing today, would Wallace be retracting or redrafting his remarks about the selective function of coherence competence? Would Darwin now admit to the legitimacy of a broader conception of selection than *natural* selection that would include selection for coherence competence in addition to correspondence competence?

The Disparagement of Coherence

Before we leave the topic of coherence, the reader should know that not every student of judgment and decision making believes, as I do, that coherence (together with correspondence) is an important aspect of this process.

Gigerenzer and Todd, for example, disparage the significance of coherence in these remarks:

> We see rationality as defined by decisions and actions that lead to success in the external world, rather than by *internal coherence* of knowledge and inferences. Theories of mind that focus on internal coherence have led, in artificial intelligence, economics, and elsewhere . . . to models that assume that an individual must create elaborate representations of knowledge and solve impressive equations when making up [his or her] mind. The challenge ahead is not to construct models of omniscient minds, but rather of adaptive minds that can act quickly and reliably in their environments [italics mine].[25]

They add, "We have focused on adaptive goals in terms of correspondence criteria (e.g., accuracy, speed, and frugality) as opposed to coherence criteria (consistency, transitivity, additivity of probabilities) traditionally used to define rationality. Is there any role left for coherence criteria?"[26]

The answer is yes, there certainly is—and that is the matter of justification. Gigerenzer and Todd stack the cards against coherence by spelling out the argument for coherence in terms of correspondence criteria alone and then conclude that coherence of one's thought is unnecessary for these criteria. But there are some judgments—and usually very important ones—that demand justification before action is taken. However, the justification for correspondence judgments (accuracy, speed, and frugality) can only be determined *after* the judgment is made. You won't know whether the judgment was accurate, rapid, and "frugal" until later. Social-policy judgments (whether to build a road or a dam here or there, whether to apportion the city's budget differently, whether to privatize a health system) have to be made—and justified—before action is taken. Since no empirical criterion for the correctness of such judgments will be available, the justification will have to be made on the coherence of the argument for it, and on the argument's content. There may be possibilities for arguing by analogy, and so on, but the general principle holds that in the absence of an empirical criterion, coherence will be the criterion by which the judgment is justified.

I will have more to say about coherence below. I conclude this section by saying that it is unclear to me why these otherwise thoughtful and innovative psychologists should take this overly strong stand against the value and use of coherent cognition. The final two paragraphs of their book, however, illustrate the source of this stand. In these paragraphs, they offer an anecdote about some psychologists and economists arguing about the nature of reasoning (see their p. 365). One of the economists says flatly, "Either reasoning is rational, or it's psychological." Gigerenzer and Todd explicate this by saying, "To him, this inviolable dichotomy implied an intellectual division of labor: Rational judgment is defined by the laws of logic and probability, and thus should be the domain of rigorous economists and mathematicians; what we know about the human mind is irrelevant for defining sound reasoning. Only when things go wrong should psychologists be called in to explain why people can be irrational."[27]

But Gigerenzer and colleagues reject this argument; they think that this intellectual division of labor "is a huge mistake," and go on to say,

> This misleading idea has cursed the cognitive sciences since the antipsychologism of nineteenth-century philosophy, and it continues to obscure a realistic view of cognition to this day. A bit of trust in the abilities of the mind and the rich structure of the environment may help us to see how thought processes that forgo the baggage of the laws of logic and probability can solve real-world adaptive problems quickly and well.
>
> Models of reasoning need not forsake rationality for psychological plausibility, nor accuracy for simplicity. The mind can have it both ways.[28]

This eloquent statement, and the assertion that "the mind can have it both ways," becomes peculiar, however, in view of Gigerenzer and Todd's enthusiasm for ruling coherence out of a general theory of judgment and decision making. That effort (illustrated throughout their book and other in publications since) contradicts their argument because it suggests that the mind can't have it both ways but only the way that the correspondence strategy offers. As will be apparent from this book, it is my view that both experience and the ample research record show that Gigerenzer and Todd are right when they declare that "the mind can have it both ways." But they should be consistent with that declaration by admitting coherence and correspondence into their "adaptive toolbox"; they should grant the mind those two ways to cope with uncertainty (as they already have), and now study both of them.

Regrettably, the researchers who pursue the topic of coherence are as one-sided as Gigerenzer and Todd. But their approach is simpler. Kahneman, Thaler, and Sunstein don't argue the case for coherence and against correspondence; they simply ignore the work of the correspondence researchers and act as if coherence judgments are the only ones humans ever make. They don't trouble to defend this position (as Gigerenzer and Todd defend theirs). Although Sunstein takes little notice of Gigerenzer's concept of "ecological rationality," in his book *Risk and Reason,* he can be found grasping another concept—*richer rationality,* a concept introduced by Paul Slovic.[29] In his discussion of richer rationality,

Sunstein is persuasive in making the case that standard rationality needs to be "enriched." Both sides of this argument will be explored further in chapter 15.

It will be apparent to the reader that the disarray in this field will only be dissipated when researchers on both sides of this divide give up their one-sidedness, a one-sidedness that has plagued us since Wallace withdrew support from Darwin. This book is an attempt to encourage that reconciliation.

6

Kennedy and Khrushchev

Seeking—and Failing—to Learn about the Other

It is not only difficult to learn from history but also difficult to learn from, or about, another person, for the same basic reasons: irreducible uncertainty, entangled indicators, and entangled causality—and it doesn't matter whether the other persons are heads of state or the next-door neighbors. We will see from the evidence below that, even in the most crucial and important of human affairs, the most skilled politicians fail to reduce uncertainty, and that fallible indicators and causes remain entangled despite strenuous, if misguided, efforts to disentangle them.

The interchange between President John Kennedy and Chairman Nikita Khrushchev over a two-week period provides a striking example of these circumstances. Neither could find a coherent strategy in the other's communications, in one of the best-documented cases on record. The fact that heads of state and terrorists have tremendous destructive power means that the intractability of learning about another's intentions puts the world at serious risk.

What do we know about the Kennedy–Khrushchev situation? A definite fact: after 13 days of intense deliberation, interchange, and serious efforts to learn about one another's intentions, neither man succeeded. Neither could predict the other's judgments or behavior, a fact they both acknowledged and that, once it was grasped, mightily disturbed them. And what have we learned since? A similar situation would be no better today. And that is why we should examine this case closely. But unless we increase our understanding of the circumstances surrounding this incident, it seems clear it will repeat itself, because discerning another's intentions is essentially impossible for both participants and experts alike.

In October 1962, when President Kennedy learned that the Soviet Union had secretly placed nuclear missiles—weapons of mass destruction, as we would say today—in Cuba, weapons capable of reaching the United States, he immediately secretly convened a committee of several members of his cabinet and other trusted advisors—men he considered to have good judgment, if not wisdom—to strive to learn Khrushchev's intentions and to discuss the question of how the United States should respond. The committee met daily for 13 days of intense discussion and debate. Unbeknownst to the participants, the president had arranged for the round-table discussions to be audiotaped and thus recorded for history; the tapes were kept under lock and key for 35 years and were not made public in a form accessible to scholars until they were transcribed and edited by two historians, Ernest May and Philip Zelikow, and published in 1997 by Harvard University Press.[1] The book jacket does not exaggerate when it says that the transcripts capture "for posterity the deliberations that might have ended the world as we know it."

This 700-page book provides an extraordinary opportunity to see what Kennedy and his committee said to one another over these 13 days. In my view, it is a treasure, for the transcripts describe in detail the attempt of one person (John F. Kennedy) to learn—with considerable assistance—about the intentions of another (Nikita Khrushchev) under the most critical circumstances. We have no detailed record of Khrushchev's attempts to learn about Kennedy, as far as I know, although tapes were probably made. But we do know about the Americans. One learns exactly what President Kennedy says to Secretary of Defense Robert McNamara (and others) about Khrushchev's possible motives for his wildly aggressive maneuver, and what McNamara says in reply, and also the specific interchanges between the various members of the committee. It is rare indeed to have painstakingly detailed documentation of specific communications during such a historic episode. (But see Michael Beschloss's *The Conquerors,* in which he publishes documentation of discussions among world leaders—Roosevelt, Churchill, Stalin, and others—during World War II as they contemplated Germany's fate after its defeat and unconditional surrender.)[2]

The tapes are particularly valuable because they allow us to make inferences about the cognitive activity of the committee members and to ask ourselves whether that cognitive activity meets the standards of wisdom that Kennedy expected from these men under these circumstances in which every utterance would be examined critically by everyone present. Will we see the wisdom Kennedy expected, or at least hoped for? Will we find demonstrations of how to learn about the intentions of another party? The answer to these questions will leap off the pages.

We should also note what the historians who brought all this material together have to say about these documents. Although I have nothing but the greatest praise for their foresight in recognizing the importance of this material, and nothing but admiration for the stamina they exhibited in getting this job done, I admit to being perplexed by their own appraisal of their work. The historians May and Zelikow state,

> We come away from this study convinced that major policymaking episodes repay the closest possible examination. Only such examination can reconstruct key judgments within the little worlds in which they are made. Only by penetrating these worlds can we truly understand and evaluate that extraordinary human faculty that we label "judgment." And only by doing that can we learn to do better.[3]

And the editors must be congratulated in the their prescience when they state,

> If a government or a leader consistently relies on false intelligence reports, makes little effort to assess other governments, does not analyze policy alternatives, and has little open debate among senior officials who are overawed by an insecure and impulsive risk taker, we should not expect very good results unless the other relevant actors are weak, equally incompetent, or extraordinarily unlucky.[4]

Although May and Zelikow were ostensibly referring to Khrushchev, modern readers will find these words equally applicable to twenty-first-century leaders.

Although I of course heartily agree with their emphasis on the role of judgment in this crisis, I equally heartily disagree with the last sentence of the book, which states, "By coming fully to grips with the particulars of past moments of choice, we may become better able to handle our own [choices]." My view would be that it is precisely by focusing on the particulars "of past moments of choice" that we become *less* able rather than *better* able to handle our own choices.[5] The reader should look for any evidence that one leader learned about the other, and how he might have done it.

Kennedy's and Khrushchev's efforts are to be understood as exactly like the efforts any two persons make to learn about one another. The theory of human judgment outlined above was developed with that goal of generality in mind. Despite my differences with the historians, I certainly agree with James T. Patterson when, in his massive history of the United States from 1945 to 1974, he concludes his analysis of Kennedy's and Khrushchev's behavior in the Cuban missile crisis with the words "they were lucky as well as wise."[6] My own interpretation: they were much luckier than they were wise.

Why Place Missiles in Cuba?

President Kennedy and the committee members were eager to learn why Nikita Khrushchev had reached the judgment that nuclear weapons should be secretly placed in Cuba in October 1962. The committee members were puzzled and uncertain as to what Khrushchev was thinking, and indeed, at one point, Secretary of State Dean Rusk explicitly wondered whether Khrushchev was making rational decisions, a polite way of wondering whether Khrushchev had lost his mind. Although there was considerable tension about the situation in Berlin in 1962, Cuba was definitely secondary to Berlin in importance. So Kennedy was stunned when he was shown photographic evidence that proved that there were such weapons in Cuba and that there were preparations to create the conditions for launching them. Clearly, he had misunderstood Khrushchev and his priorities. He would have to learn more about him—quickly. Did he ever learn?

To answer the question of why Khrushchev's entirely unexpected maneuver was undertaken, Kennedy and his advisors would need to know what was in Khrushchev's mind. Did Khrushchev actually have a coherent judgment policy, a coherent plan in mind? As matters stood, the president and the committee were baffled; they couldn't imagine what such a plan could be or what his intentions were, and they could never decide what it was that Khrushchev wanted. What did he hope to achieve by this terribly threatening act? What was he prepared to do next? What response did he expect from the United States? What multiple fallible indicators of Kennedy's motives and plans was Khrushchev depending on?

Kennedy had met and talked to Khrushchev in Vienna in 1961, but that meeting accomplished nothing and was generally considered a disaster; the press reported that Kennedy had been humiliated. On his way home, Kennedy had described his meeting to the British prime minister McMillan; McMillan later reported, "The President was completely overwhelmed by the ruthlessness and barbarity of the Russian Chairman. It reminded me in a way of Lord Halifax or Neville Chamberlain trying to hold a conversation with Herr Hitler."[7] From that description, we gain an idea of Kennedy's view of Khrushchev before the events of October 1962.

Despite the vast intelligence-gathering resources of the United States and the expertise in the universities and think tanks, the tapes on the first day of the secret committee meeting show that Kennedy was reduced to this sort of puzzling: "What is the advantage [to them]? Must be some major reason for the Russians to set this up. Must be that they are not satisfied with their ICBMs. What'd be the reason that they would . . ."[8] In short, he is unable to find a coherent explanation for the "why" of Russian action. Moreover, he gets no help from his advisors, other than a comment from one of the generals to the effect that the Russians would have a launching base to "supplement their rather defective ICBM system." Later, a still-puzzled Kennedy would ask for help from a recent ambassador to the USSR but get only a vague and unhelpful answer. Indeed, during the entire 13 days, no one ever produced a clear and informative answer to Kennedy's question of "why"; no one among this group of experts had learned enough about Khrushchev's judgment policies—his goals, his preferred means, his intentions—to be able to provide anything more than a minimal explanation of his action, and thus it (and subsequent actions) remained—and still remains—a puzzle. In short, neither Kennedy nor his group of expert advisors could find coherence in the behavior of Nikita Khrushchev in the most startling and terrifying action undertaken by a head of state in the twentieth century.

There were concomitant events that illustrate the confusion and uncertainty that flows from poorly understanding another leader's intentions. During this period, China attacked and invaded India. Kennedy took time to discuss (and record the discussion) with B. K. Nehru, India's ambassador to the United States. May and Zelikow report:

> During their conversation Kennedy mused about the Soviet enigma.
> "Does anybody know the mystery of the Communist system?" he
> asked, half rhetorically. Why would China attack India? "What is it
> they are getting out of this? They take you on. Why don't they take us
> on in Viet Nam or something? Why did they take you on?"[9]

Ambassador Nehru said he did not know.

A lack of knowledge about Khrushchev's purposes made it difficult for the Americans to plan a response. Without knowing one's adversary's goals, let alone his or her judgment strategy, planning an effective response means operating under great uncertainty. The military facts and implications were obvious, however, and the response of the military people on the committee was as expected: they felt it necessary to remove the weapons either by a major air strike or an invasion or both. And their uncertainty about Khrushchev's purposes and plans made their plan seem urgent. Not knowing his aims meant not knowing what he would do next—and when he would do it. So the military advisors did what was expected of them: they asked for seven days to prepare; troops, planes, ships, and support were to be massed and ready before the 13 days were over.

But new steps were now taken in the Cuban crisis. The United States announced a quarantine; Soviet ships were to be stopped and searched. Most important, however, was the fact that contact had been established between the two leaders; on Friday, October 26, the first message arrived from Khrushchev addressed to "Dear Mr. President" in response to Kennedy's earlier letter to him. It was a long, rambling letter in four sections (six book pages), with sentences such as "War is our enemy and a calamity for all of the peoples."[10] What would or could the Americans learn from the platitudes in this long letter? What were they supposed to learn?

The Americans began to suspect that Khrushchev was, however vaguely, suggesting "a bargain that would exchange a non-invasion pledge for the Soviet withdrawal of their missile forces from Cuba."[11] Ask yourself why a leader of a huge country with nuclear missiles at his command would take six pages to make a suggestion that his readers would have to interpret?

But things got worse. The next day, Kennedy and his advisors found that the media had reported that a wholly different letter had been sent to Kennedy, and at the committee meeting called to discuss the letter, this conversation occurred:

> President Kennedy [apparently reading from news ticker copy handed to him by Sorenson]: Premier Khrushchev told President Kennedy yesterday he would withdraw offensive weapons from Cuba if the United States withdrew rockets from Turkey.
>
> Bundy: No, he didn't.
>
> Sorenson: That's how it is read by both of the associations that put it out so far. Reuters said the same thing.
>
> Unidentified: He didn't really say that, did he?
>
> President Kennedy: That may not be. . . . He may be putting out another letter. What is our explanation? But anyway, they've got this clear about how . . . Let's just go on, then. Are you finished there, Mr. Secretary? Pierre? That wasn't in the letter we received, was it?
>
> Salinger: No. I read it pretty carefully. It did not read that way to me.
>
> President Kennedy: Is he supposed to be putting out a letter he's written to me or putting out a statement?
>
> Salinger: Putting out a letter he wrote to you.
>
> President Kennedy: Well, let's just sit tight on it . . .
>
> [But the situation is still unclear to others.]
>
> Bundy: Is it a different statement?

Rusk then asked for the text of Khrushchev's statement to be brought to the committee, and Kennedy read the new statement from Khrushchev.

I report these words to indicate the confusion among the Americans. The recorded remarks that followed are too long to be included here, but they show considerable disagreement about what the Khrushchev message meant and what the U.S. response should be. The important point for us is that if Khrushchev had been sitting in on this meeting, he would have been as puzzled by the Americans as the Americans were by him. Matters were as confused as in any school board meeting or faculty meeting. In short, interpersonal learning in these critical circumstances was becoming impossible, even with these direct exchanges on a matter of enormous significance. If Khrushchev was looking for a coherent response from the American side, he needed to give them something coherent to respond to, but that was still far from happening. Nevertheless, around 10 A.M. on Saturday, the day after he received Khrushchev's long letter, Kennedy was acknowledging that the others would see the chairman's letter as "reasonable."

President Kennedy: As I say, you're going to find a lot of people think this is a rather reasonable position.[12]

But by 4 P.M. that same day, McNamara was saying:

McNamara: Let me go back a second. When I read that [Khrushchev's] message of last night this morning, I thought, my God! I'd never sell, I would never base a transaction on that contract. Hell, that's no offer. There is not a damn thing in it that's an offer. You read that message carefully. He didn't propose to take the missiles out. Not once is there a single word in it that proposes to take the missiles out. It's 12 pages of fluff.

McCone: Well, his message this morning offered a trade—his published message.

McNamara: Well, no, I'm speaking of the last night message. The last night message was 12 pages of fluff. That's no contract. You couldn't sign that and say we know what we signed.

And before we got the damn thing read, the whole deal had changed—completely changed. All of which leads me to conclude that the probabilities are that nothing is going to be signed quickly.

Now my question is, assuming that nothing is signed quickly, what do we do? Well, I don't think attack is the only answer. I think we ought to be prepared for attack, all-out attack. And I think we ought to know how far we can postpone that. But I don't think that is the only answer, and I think we ought to think of some other answers here.[13]

Let me pause and remind the reader that this is the same Robert McNamara who, later on, as a member of President Lyndon Johnson's cabinet, took us deeper and deeper into the Vietnam morass only to say later in his book about that disaster, "We were wrong, terribly wrong."[14] Nor will his role as the keen rationalist be forgotten soon. In a 2003 film documentary titled *The Fog of War*, which includes a focus on McNamara's hard-headed approach to war in the spirit of decision analysis, one voice says, "Rationality will not save us." But perhaps Khrushchev had intended no more than to throw the Americans into utter confusion; if so, he succeeded. However, if inciting confusion was not his explicit goal, it was an unintended consequence. So, we must ask, what did he intend to accomplish with that long letter?

In my view, he intended to teach the Americans what the situation really was, not merely what the situation was as he saw it, but what it actually was. That is why he delivered what is undeniably a lecture. We have seen what Kennedy thought of Khrushchev ("a son of a bitch"[15]). But what did Khrushchev think of Kennedy? The lecture in the long letter makes that clear: Kennedy in Khrushchev's eyes is a callow youth; a largely ignorant, rich, capitalist American, with an enlarged sense of his own importance, who, like all Americans, needs to be enlightened about the circumstances in which he finds himself. So Khrushchev did his best to help Kennedy understand what he obviously does not understand. The lecture in the letter makes that clear, for the letter focuses on improving Kennedy's understanding of the situation. That, Khrushchev thinks, will be the best way out of this impasse. In short, since Kennedy doesn't understand the circumstances, Khrushchev will teach him, and hope Kennedy learns. But Kennedy didn't. As is usually the case when people are being taught, or at least lectured, by people they don't like, what was learned (in this case, by Kennedy) was something other than what the "teacher" wanted the "student" to learn.

In short, these tapes illustrate, in unprecedented detail, poor interpersonal learning at the highest level of international relations in the modern world in a time of one of the most serious crises the world had ever faced. Do we find bounded rationality? Nothing but. (See chapter 15, p. 219, for a definition and discussion of bounded rationality.)

Perhaps Khrushchev did have a coherent plan in mind at the time he placed the nuclear missiles in Cuba. Giving him the benefit of the doubt, I'll say he could have. He would have had to convince the members of the Politburo that it was a good idea: there would have been no alternative to presenting a coherent plan, and, being good Communists, his colleagues would have been experts at critically examining coherence. His lecture to Kennedy doesn't describe that plan, however; rather, it simply explains the context in which it is to be executed. Therefore, even if Khrushchev did have a coherent plan for the Cuban situation, the Americans never learned what it was. In short, they never learned why he did what he did. Given the nature of the weapons that were to be used, and the consequences of their use—"the end of the world as we know it"—that failure of interpersonal learning is one of the most significant in history. So the historians have that story to tell. But who will prevent a recurrence with different actors?

Thus, the most momentous international events are found to be completely beyond the grasp of two of the most powerful officials in the world. Neither Kennedy nor his advisors could find in Khrushchev's communications a coherent view of the Cuban situation to which they could respond. And it was not only Mr. Khrushchev's mind that was a puzzle. Kennedy had not yet gotten over his view, gained in the Vienna meeting, of Khrushchev's character. In his conversation with Nehru, he "commented on the lower standard of behavior accorded to people like Khrushchev. 'If you're a son of a bitch [like Khrushchev], then every time he even looks at all agreeable, everybody falls down with pleasure.'"[16] Khrushchev's intentions, both military and personal, remained a mystery. And it was that mystery that made it impossible for Kennedy and his advisors to form a coherent response. Astonishingly, Khrushchev finally brought this impasse to an end by enlisting a reporter to communicate his conditions for the missiles' withdrawal to President Kennedy's brother. If readers are astonished that, at such a crucial moment in history, two men with the future of the world in their hands were completely puzzled by one another's actions and unable to communicate their views to one another, they should reflect on the possibility of this circumstance repeating itself today.

In short, the Kennedy–Khrushchev encounter teaches us how important it is for us to learn to enhance the process by which one person learns from, or about, another, particularly in regard to their intentions. And it may well be critically important for the immediate future, for as John Keegan, the military historian, puts it, "The challenge to the West's intelligence services is to find a way into the fundamentalist mind and to overcome it from within."[17] Without a serious, well-funded research program devoted to this topic, however, there seems little likelihood of developing the necessary knowledge and skill to find a way into the fundamentalist (or any other) mind. Without that knowledge and skill, we risk the reoccurrence of the grievous mistakes made by Cheney and Powell.

7

How the Drive for Coherence
Brings Down Utopias

In chapter 5, I linked the appearance of centralized bureaucracy to the appearance of writing and to the emergence of our ancestors' grasp of the value of—and, indeed, often the necessity for—the use of the coherence strategy in making judgments when no empirical criterion is available. That link between government and coherence indicates that coherence competence goes beyond narrative and mathematics and takes us into social arrangements and politics, and thus to *coherence societies*. Strong coherence societies are (or were) commonly known as *totalitarian societies* because totalitarian describes a society in which every aspect must fit together in what is intended to be a coherent whole. The "must" in that sentence is what destroys the potential utopian society; it is what has turned every utopia into a dystopia (a social disaster), for it prohibits personal freedom. That is, merely suggesting that the idea of controlling the society is a mistake, or should be modified, is a punishable offense. And when the "must" stems from a society that demands coherence based on a specific form of *religion,* disaster is almost inevitable, as is evident from the current situation in many Islamic countries. But coherence is present in other ways in other religions as well. For example, at the start of his career, 26-year-old Martin Luther King, Jr., in one of his first addresses to his constituents, made this appeal for coherence: "If we are wrong, the Supreme Court is wrong; if we are wrong, the Constitution is wrong; if we are wrong, God almighty is wrong."

The question central to utopias is whether the coherence that every utopia seeks and demands must necessarily destroy utopia itself. That question has been highlighted by the notorious failures of Communism in the USSR, China, North Korea, and Cuba. (Although fascist countries are enthusiastically totalitarian, they appear to abandon coherent thought in favor of romantic thought at the beginning. Their entire arrangement is arbitrary and based on the mandates of one man, for example, Hitler; it is the kind of society famously implicated in Kafka's *The Trial* and Orwell's *1984*.) The first signs of trouble appear when demands for uniformity of behavior appear, and by the time demands for uniformity of information appear, the utopia has already clearly become a dystopia. In the next phase—punishing persons who express ideas that do not fit—it is clear that the demand for coherence has rejected the possibility of accurate correspondence judgments, a second source of the failure of coherence societies. Thus, it is the coherence demanded by any utopia that necessarily brings the end of utopia.[1]

A significant feature of a coherent system of any kind, psychological, social, or physical, is its fragility and ready susceptibility to being upset, for only one piece of the system need fail for it all to fail, an attribute the dictator seems to understand well. As Václav Havel, the famous Czech dissident opposing his Communist government, put it,

> As long as it seals off hermetically the entire society . . . [the regime's version of itself] appears to be made of stone. But the moment someone breaks through in one place . . . everything suddenly appears in another light.[2]

Those who control a coherence society are intent on silencing any person or event apt to illuminate the situation. Because those in control cannot tolerate a break in the coherence of the story, they are willing to practice terror to prevent that crack from appearing.

Coherence is thus a feature of humankind's cognitive activity that is both a curse and a blessing: a curse because it demands total adherence to an idea and tolerates no deviation, and a blessing because that very adherence to an idea enables us to gain control of our thoughts and surroundings, as our scientific activity has shown. It is coherent cognitive activity that drives totalitarian dictators to their murderous actions, but it was coherent cognitive activity that enabled Galileo, Newton, and Einstein to give us a new view of how the physical world works. This contrast between good and evil presents a dilemma; this two-sided aspect of coherent thought creates our demand for the wisdom that rationality—also a matter of form, not content—denies us.

Nobody has made the danger of coherent thought clearer than Isaiah Berlin did when he described the attractiveness of a "final solution":

> The possibility of a final solution—even if we forget the terrible sense that these words acquired in Hitler's day—turns out to be an illusion; and a very dangerous one. For if one really believes that such a solution is possible, then surely no cost would be too high to obtain it: to make mankind just and happy and creative and harmonious for ever—what could be too high a price to pay for that? To make such an omelette, there is surely no limit to the number of eggs that should be broken—that was the faith of Lenin, of Trotsky, of Mao, for all I know of Pol Pot. Since I know the only true path to the ultimate solution of the problems of society, I know which way to drive the human caravan; and since you are ignorant of what I know, you cannot be allowed to have liberty of choice even with the narrowest limits, if the goal is to be reached.[3]

The abstractions of this dilemma can be made concrete by considering how information on the Internet should be organized. Should it be packaged in an obviously coherent form, thus taking advantage of the blessings of coherence? That is what Bill Gates would like to see. Or should we forego that blessing, as Cass Sunstein urges, to avoid the potential curse that coherence carries?

Coherence or Incoherence on the Internet?

Totalitarian societies seem to believe that eliminating new, dissenting information is essential. That is why totalitarian governments try to control the Internet, and why human rights organizations try to overcome barriers to Internet access. Cass Sunstein believes that the Internet makes it too easy, at least for some, to maintain coherence.[4]

He addressed this matter in a book titled *Republic.com*.[5] There he worried that, as a result of this growing power to control the organization of information, that information will become organized and presented so that persons with a given set of beliefs can filter out any and all information other than that that fits and reinforces their beliefs. He suggested that such filtering behavior will lead to a balkanized society, dividing people into groups that listen only to people who sound like themselves and see only that which conforms to what they already believe. No challenges to those beliefs will be able to penetrate the closed cognitive systems.

Sunstein sees all the ramifications of the filtering phenomenon—there are many—and in his book explains them all in eloquent detail. The results are not pleasant to contemplate. That is largely because the Internet provides the filtering mechanisms that make it easy for the user not only to seek out those sites that offer him or her confirmation of his or her beliefs but to filter out those sites that confront the user and challenge those beliefs. One could shut oneself up in a world of one's own construction, a world containing only agreeable ideas and events and occupied only by like believers. Just what a coherence society wants.

But not everyone sees what Sunstein sees. He provides a quotation from Bill Gates that shows Gates's pride in the Internet's filtering capacity:

> Customized information is a natural extension. . . . For your own daily dose of news, you might subscribe to several review services and let a software agent or a human one pick and choose from them to compile your completely "customized" newspaper. These subscription services, whether human or electronic, will gather information that conforms to a particular philosophy and set of interests.[6]

How can two brilliant people see things so differently? Where one sees a blessing, the other sees a curse. Sunstein agrees with Gates that sources other than the Internet do not offer filtering mechanisms as readily as the Internet does. But Sunstein believes that being unable to avoid differing and challenging points of view, as we ordinarily cannot in newspapers and magazines, is a benefit. Encountering these differing points of view stimulates to us think, he argues, and opens us to the possibility of the truth of a different belief. Loss of such opportunities leads to the homogeneity of belief and the consequence of division and polarization among believers that he depicts with skill and compelling examples.[7]

Sunstein's analyses are nuanced and sophisticated and describe a wide range of consequences of the balkanization he anticipates. And he brings his ideas to bear on Howard Dean's 2004 campaign for the presidency. Todd Purdum of *The New York Times* quoted Sunstein:

> If you get like-minded people in constant touch with each other, then they get more energized and more committed, and more outraged and more extreme. The intensity of Dean's support came less from his own personal efforts than from the fact that Dean supporters were in pretty constant touch with each other, whereas geography would normally isolate them and spread them out.[8]

And the scholar Jacques Barzun would support him, for he quotes Judge Stewart Dalzellas as saying, "Just as the strength of the Internet is chaos, so the strength of our liberty depends upon the chaos and cacophony of the unfettered speech the First Amendment protects."[9] Thus Barzun wants us to believe that the "chaos and cacophony of the unfettered speech" produced by the information revolution improves our judgment—by opening our minds instead of closing them. So, in his view, the leaders of the Chinese government are right to fear an unfiltered Internet; it may weaken their regime. Nonleaders in China, and non-Chinese, however, are right to fear the Internet that filters out their message; it may lead to misunderstandings and unnecessary disputes, if not worse.

The disagreement between Gates and Sunstein offers an example of the double-edged character of coherence that makes "filtering" on the Internet a curse from Sunstein's view but a blessing according to Gates. And it is precisely that double-edged character of curse and blessing that has been the bane of all attempts at developing a coherence (or coherent) society.

Two Types of Coherence Societies

Mark Lilla offers a third view about what I have called "coherence societies." He points out that the societies that gave rise to the term "totalitarian" (the USSR, Nazi Germany, and fascist Italy) no longer exist. But other coherence societies such as North Korea, China, and Cuba do exist, and do insist on allegiance to an ideology. That insistence distinguishes them from what Lilla calls "tyrannies," states ruled by dictators such as Saddam Hussein or Muammar Gadhafi, who demand personal allegiance rather than commitment to a set of coherent ideas. (Some demand both.) Lilla points out that whereas ideological coherence societies have almost disappeared, the tyrannical ones have multiplied. Moreover, the democracies seem uncertain about how to cope with tyrannical societies but may fear them so much they are prepared to declare war on them, as the United States did with Iraq.

A "holy book" is evidently key to an ideologically bound coherence society. The Communist countries had Karl Marx's writings, and China had Mao's "little red book" to supplement that. Fascism had Hitler's *Mein Kampf*. The Koran is the holy book of Islam and forms the basis for the Islamic "coherence society" that now dominates much of the world. Although not every Islamic society demands total allegiance to every aspect of Islam, by the twenty-first century, enough Islamic clergy had stressed the need for religious states that many people around the world became nervous about the possibility of a new form of a "coherence society," this one Islamic. The war between Iraq and the United States will increase that nervousness.

Democracies, on the other hand, seem to have no need for a "holy book." Although in the United States the Bible serves that function for Christians, and still may be found beside the telephone book in many hotel rooms, it has no direct political function. And much the same can be said for its place in the United Kingdom and Western Europe. Nor do nations new to democracy seem to need for a "holy book" of democracy. The absence of that need suggests that a strongly coherent view of democracy is also absent, which indeed seems to be the situation. (The nearest thing that U.S. democracy has to a holy book is *The Federalist Papers*, which is far from a coherent set of ideas, and which few Americans have read.[10])

Personal Tyrannies

Tyrannies, however, do demand coherence, although in a different form from that demanded by nations whose governments are based on ideology, because, although they are largely indifferent to ideology, they fiercely demand personal loyalty and conformity. Whether this demand is more difficult to meet than the demand for ideological conformity is unknown, but the absence of a clear set of rules suggests that the tyrant's demand is apt to be more whimsical and vague, and thus less predictable, and may therefore be more difficult to live with.

In his description of oppression in modern China, Perry Link treats the conflict between coherence and liberty directly. He suggests that vagueness of the restrictions (a) frightens more people, (b) pressures an individual to curtail a wider range of activity, and (c) maximizes what can be learned through forced confessions. For example, "When Li Shaomin was arrested, he asked his captors the reason, and they answered, 'You yourself know the reason' ";[11] thus, Shaomin might well offer up a misdeed about which his captors were ignorant. Also, such vagueness "allows arbitrary targeting"; if the restrictions on inferences to be drawn from what someone has written are vague, then the authorities have more latitude in labeling an act illegal.[12] In short, the distinction between the ideologically based coherence society, with its "holy book," and the tyrannically based coherence society is not merely an academic one, particularly if you live in one or the other.

Cognitive Coherence—Unrestrained by Common Sense— May Compel Despicable Behavior

The drive for coherence that is exhibited by those in control of a "coherence society"—a society driven by an ideology—stems from an intellectual or theoretical belief. That is, true believers will have a deep-seated, and (more or less) intellectually defensible, belief in a general theory of society. But many who are not true believers participate in a social system because of folklore, tradition, religion, or beliefs held by most members in the community, rather than because of an informed intellectual commitment. These nonintellectual beliefs are coherent only on a superficial level (they cannot stand up to analytical examination), but they are sufficiently similar to the coherent system to sustain participation in it. Such belief systems are seldom challenged by information from outside the community and are reinforced by local peer communications. And when the beliefs are religious beliefs, challenges to them often result in a strong and violent assault on the challenger.

When the meaning of rationality is exhausted by reasoning that does no more than meet the test of logic—and that is all that rationality entails—then there is potential for disaster; rationality fails us when it does not call our attention to, alert us to, or otherwise inform us about the lack of wisdom or the immorality in a potentially tragic belief system that otherwise meets the test of rationality. A current example of how the drive for rationality exhausted by logic leads to murderous behavior is that of Timothy McVeigh. When he was executed in a federal prison for killing 168 innocent persons, his cold, impersonal demeanor seemed a puzzle. But it shouldn't have been, for he had told us many times that he was driven to that act by the logical force of the argument that it was the only way to focus the attention of a federal government on the "crimes" (he believed) it is committing. And when you see McVeigh's impassive face, it appears to be the face of "cold reason," the face of a person who demands the clear, coherent thinking that found using bombs to kill innocent people logical and necessary. Although McVeigh could not be judged psychotic by any clinical standard—his reasoning process is without flaw—his premise was worthless. But no one was able to penetrate that closed system. No one suggested that McVeigh was insane; his actions were the product of a rationality that demanded only logical correctness. He was a perfect example of Sunstein's man whose rationality was "potentially dangerous for both democracy and peace."[13]

More than one modern (and ancient) philosopher has pointed to the dangers posed by the "rationalist" exemplified by McVeigh. Mark Lilla names the persons he believes would qualify as the tyrants of the twentieth century: "Lenin and Stalin, Hitler and Mussolini, Mao and Ho, Castro and Trujillo, Amin and Bokassa, Saddam and Khomeini, Ceausescu and Miloševic—one's pen runs dry."[14] All these exhibited the same drive for coherence; all were prepared to act ruthlessly to maintain—and convert others to—the coherence of their thought.

There are those whose need to maintain coherence coincides with their religious faith; they have been with us forever, enthusiastically torturing and killing nonbelievers. All this killing seemed to have ended, or at least diminished, with the beginning of the twenty-first century; religious faith, we thought, had put all, or almost all, of that kind of murderous activity behind it. Saturday and Sunday services, and faith, were doing what they do so well: ministering to the needy and the faithful. Until September 11, 2001. At that point, it became clear that the certitude of religious faith had once more driven a man—Osama bin Laden—and some of his adherents to large-scale murder, though that was hardly a new occurrence on the planet.

Oliver Wendell Holmes made the prescient assertion that it was certitude that leads to violence. "When you know that you know, persecution comes easy" was his plain statement.[15] It was certain radical Islamic groups' certitude provided by coherence that led to the beginning of the religious war against the United States in the twenty-first century. The radicals determined that it was their duty to deliver to the United States the worst treatment they could, even though this would mean terrible death for thousands of innocent people, including children. All this illustrates the folly of certainty, but the final paragraph of Edmund Morgan's great biography of Benjamin Franklin emphasizes the wisdom of uncertainty:

> [He was] a man with a wisdom about himself that comes only to the great of heart. Franklin knew how to value himself and what he did without mistaking himself for something more than one man among many. . . . He did it with a recognition of their human strengths and weaknesses as well as is own, in a spirit that another wise man in another century [Judge Learned Hand] has called "the spirit which is not too sure it is right."[16]

As the Oliver Wendell Holmes and Benjamin Franklins of this world have tried to show us, it is the person who is convinced by mere rationality that he or she is right who is devoid of wisdom.

The Drive toward Common Sense

There is no a priori reason that one argument—evil or benign—must always be more or less logical, more or less rational than another. There is no reason, for example, that the logic of the racist's argument must be more or less logically fallacious than the nonracist's in any specific case. If the racist's argument is found to meet the test of logic, then it can be rejected only because its content is offensive. It is just that interaction between content and process that drives us to reject opposing arguments and makes us want to use our "common sense," because common sense does not demand full logic.[17]

It is also that interaction between content (admired or repulsive) and process (logical or illogical) that creates the need for wisdom, which, after all, is merely the layperson's concept of common sense. A glance in any dictionary will show that the tie between wisdom and common sense is expressed in many ways (at least in English). Indeed, Webster's unabridged third edition devotes no fewer than six inches of a column to its definition of "wisdom," indicating not only that it has a relationship to common sense but also that it is a word with many implications. The reverse is also true; "common sense" will frequently be defined in terms of wisdom.

But here common sense is given a theoretical definition in terms of the cognitive continuum (chapter 16), not simply other words. That is, I provide a cognitive denotation, not merely a connotation, of its meaning. And that denotation is expressed in terms of the cognitive continuum. In short, common sense is here related to the *tactical* aspects of judgment and can thus be differentiated from wisdom, which is related to the *strategic and tactical* aspects of judgment. For wisdom also refers us to the question of whether the appropriate strategy and tactics were employed in making a judgment. And that distinction brings us directly to the cognitive aspects of utopias.

The Cognitive Aspects of Utopias

Utopias generally emerge from arguments, and the argument is usually that a particular social arrangement is not only the best, but the best possible, arrangement. The argument is usually based on logic of the "if p, then q" variety; that is, that if certain conditions are met (p), then certain conditions (q) will follow. The content of the argument is far more complicated, however, and generally involves the presentation of historical evidence, economic and political theses, and sociological facts that define p and q. All this makes any proposal for a utopia a massive cognitive undertaking. But even such complex arguments, no matter how coherent or corresponding to the facts they may be (although none, of course, can be perfect), are often overthrown by a simple appeal to "common sense," what one might call the "poor man's wisdom."

There have been many treatises on utopias, but *Visions of Utopia* (by Edward Rothstein, Herbert Muschamp, and Martin Marty), which returns again and again to the defining matter of order, makes exactly the right argument. The cognitive demand for order can be seen in the efforts to argue the case for why the utopia in question cannot fail. And thus it should be no surprise that threats to order are precisely what the leaders of coherence societies cannot tolerate. Inconsistencies with doctrine—right or left—are anathema and must be denied.

Traditionally, it has been the similarities and differences between various utopias' content that have drawn critics' and analysts' attention. And that is as it should be. But the fact that the form of cognition—coherence—that all utopias entail makes its own demands, too, has gone largely unnoticed, because the central role of cognition has gone unnoticed. Yet it is cognition that produces a utopia and that explains why a utopia is what it is and why. But the demand for coherence means that free thought that introduces incoherence in the argument for utopia cannot be tolerated, and thus that essential ingredient (free thought) of utopia is driven out, and the society eventually collapses. Freedom of thought and the demands of a coherence society contradict one another, and it is that contradiction that guarantees all utopias' failure.[18]

PART III

Tactics of Human Judgment

Gerd Gigerenzer. A thoughtful and penetrating researcher, one of the very few who saw the potential of Brunswik's contributions. (Reprinted with permission of Gerd Gigerenzer.)

8

Continua

Researchers centered their work on intuition from the beginning. It is the first thing anyone thinks about when they think about judgment; it is at the core of the mystery of the process of judgment. And its opposite—analytical thought—has been paired with it from the beginning as well. Isaiah Berlin referred to them as "rivals," and that certainly seems appropriate, for these two cognitive processes have been competing for our attention—and praise—since we have been pondering how we make our judgments. The topic goes back to antiquity, and our recent efforts are approximately two centuries old. In lectures given in 1907, William James referred to these cognitive "rivals" in terms of people who seem to be wedded to one or the other; he called the intuitive people "tender-minded" and the analytical types "tough-minded," which seems like a good idea, except that there is no sure evidence that these are really types.[1] Those lectures, and those representations, are fairly well known; hardly known at all are remarks by Thomas Jefferson roughly 100 years earlier, in which he not only separated these two cognitive processes in terms of people but by region as well.

The historian Garry Wills tells us that Jefferson labeled Southerners "fiery, voluptuary, indolent, unsteady, independent, zealous for their own liberties, but trampling on those of others (i.e., slaves) generous, candid, without attachment or pretensions to any religion but that of the heart."[2] All that is a fairly good representation of intuitive cognition. Northerners, on the other hand, are "cool, sober, laborious, persevering, independent, jealous of their own liberties, and just to those of others, interested, chicaning, superstitious and hypocritical in their religion." And that will serve as a representation of analytical thought. The reader will recall that Jefferson was a Southerner but widely traveled and well educated, so his conclusions are not due to naïvete.[3]

In short, intuition and analysis have had their place in the study of human thought for as long as we have been thinking about it. I have separated them from the cognitive strategies (correspondence; coherence) described in part II because they are very different concepts with very different consequences. Intuition and analysis are tactics that can and do serve both of these strategies well. But the conceptual separation of strategies and tactics is new, and they are generally confused in the literature. A very brief distinction follows.

A cognitive strategy refers to an overall plan related to a cognitive goal. The tactics of human judgment—both intuition and analysis, discussed in part III, and common sense, which we will examine in part IV—all operate within the two strategies described above in part II. Thus, a person can pursue the correspondence strategy—aiming for empirical accuracy—by means of intuition, or by analytical thought, or by using common sense. And one can also pursue the coherence strategy by use of intuition, analysis, or common sense. (All these terms are defined below.) It is important to distinguish between these tactics when we employ them in making our judgments, because they involve different cognitive processes and, as we now know, they even involve different parts of the brain. And, of course, it is important to be able to ascertain which tactics other people are using when they tell us what their judgment is. The following chapters provide the information that will allow the reader to distinguish among these tactics. But first, we need to place these tactics in the context of a "task continuum," a "cognitive continuum," and a "depth–surface continuum."

The Task Continuum

Consistent with the premise of ecological psychology, our theoretical concern begins with the environment, that is, the judgment task. Therefore, essential to the pursuit of ecological psychology is a theory of the task environment. What are the properties of the tasks with which judgment must contend?

The theory put forward here holds that judgment tasks lie on a continuum, with intuition-inducing tasks at one pole, analysis-inducing tasks at the other, and common sense–inducing tasks in between the two poles. That premise requires that we define the properties of each of these three types of judgment tasks independently of the judge's cognitive activity (otherwise the argument would be circular). Although much more work needs to be done with respect to a theory of a task environment, we can make some progress by noting that all tasks can be differentiated with reference to the *number* of indicators they offer, the *ecological validity*—or degree of fallibility—of the indicators, the *reliability* of the indicators (to what extent the information they offer can be trusted), and the extent to which each indicator is related to other indicators (the *redundancy* of the indicators), and others.

Because this is not a technical book, I will not list all the features that allow us to develop a theoretical description of judgment tasks and to differentiate them from one another.[4] It is these features (and others) that enable us to locate various tasks on the task continuum and thus differentiate among them in a systematic and orderly fashion.

If we make the simple hypothesis that the properties of the task will induce similar properties in the judge's cognitive activity, we can predict the judge's cognitive activity. The proof (or disproof) of our predictions will be informative. For example, when the task properties are those predicted to induce intuition, we can examine the cognitive properties of the subject's behavior and determine if the subject did indeed use intuition. Of course, that simple prediction is not apt to hold over many variations in these task properties, nor is it apt to hold over all variations in the content of the tasks. Nevertheless, it is a starting point; and, in fact, in the study cited above, this hypothesis held up quite well. And we can learn from the failed predictions how to modify the theory accordingly. The important point is that each study should list the properties of the task in the study, locate it on the task continuum, and present a prediction of the nature of the judgment (described in similar terms) that the task induces. Few studies of judgment meet that criterion, however, because few researchers recognize the importance of the task in determining the cognitive processes of the judge. But failure to meet that criterion leaves the results unanchored in the ecology, and that leads to the false generalizations that have plagued psychology.

The Cognitive Continuum

Central to the idea of the use of cognitive tactics is the concept of a cognitive continuum between intuition and analysis. It cannot be overemphasized that intuition and analysis should not be thought of as a dichotomy but as the endpoints of a cognitive continuum. That change—from a dichotomy to a continuum—is hard to achieve, inasmuch as the idea of a dichotomous relation between intuition and analysis has been a part of our intellectual history from the beginning. But it is time to move beyond that tradition. Once we acknowledge that various conditions select various forms of cognition—just as various environmental conditions have selected variations within and between species—we need to acknowledge that our cognitive activity should not be restricted to only two forms of cognition. Too many psychologists continue to hold onto the age-old theory that intuition and analysis constitute a dichotomy, without considering its validity. Even today, prominent theorists such as Nobel Prize winner Daniel Kahneman implicitly employ that theory when they describe cognitive activity in terms of System 1 and System 2, which simply represent the terms intuition and analysis.

The concept of a cognitive continuum is certainly an abstraction; no one has ever seen such a continuum and, of course, no one ever will. Yet this continuum can and does play a large role in our judgment processes, and that, in turn, can play a large role in the way we live our lives. I will have more to say about the cognitive continuum below in the discussion of common sense. At this point, I want only to remind the reader about the variation in cognitive activities that range from intuition to analysis.

The Competence of Various Tactics on the Cognitive Continuum

Although the struggle over the competence of intuitive versus rational analytical cognition remains a contemporary one, Egon Brunswik anticipated it in 1956 when he showed, by means of a simple experiment, how the question should be answered.[5] He induced the intuitive tactic in one group of subjects by asking them to estimate the height of a bar by visual perception, that is, simply to look at it and say how tall it was. That is an intuitive process: the subject is unaware of the process (no one can say how they know what the height of a bar is). Using intuition, the group's average answer was very close to being correct. But Brunswik also analyzed the distribution of errors in the estimates. He found it to be the usual normal (bell-shaped) curve. He then induced the analytical tactic in a second group of subjects by giving them the trigonometric information necessary for calculating the height of the bar. The subjects therefore had to rely on analysis to use trigonometry to calculate their answers. In this group—called the "reasoning" group—about half the answers were exactly correct, but the remaining answers were far from correct; thus, the distribution of errors was far from the normal (bell-shaped) curve.[6]

Brunswik gave particular attention to the "reasoning" method: the entire pattern of reasoning solutions

> resembles the switching of trains at a multiple junction [a few years later he could have likened it to a flowchart or decision-analysis

diagram] with each of the possible courses being well organized and of machine-like precision yet leading to drastically different destinations only one of which is acceptable in light of the cognitive goal.

He added, "This pattern is illustrative of the dangers in explicit logical operations."[7] This latter observation is critical, for it points to the fact that although reasoning (or rationality), as represented by logic, has its positive features and usually provides the exactly correct answer, it also has its dangers, in that it sometimes produces wildly wrong answers. This risk of employing rationality is seldom acknowledged and almost never considered when contrasting intuition and analysis. And he noted exactly what the dangers are: doing exactly the right thing in the wrong way, which can produce an extreme error, a result that has been observed only too often. He offers an explanation for this outcome:

> The relative ease of switching off at any one of a series of choice points in a basically linear, one-dimensional, all-or-none series of relays is at least in part the result of the precise formulation, yet *relatively* small number of basic cues, involved in most typical reasoning tasks.[8]

He then contrasts this risky procedure with *intuitive perception*, writing: "On the other hand, as we have seen, intuitive perception must simultaneously integrate many different avenues of approach, or cues." It is this use of many approaches (multiple fallible indicators) that protects the organism from the dangers reasoning poses. But one pays a price for intuition's protection against gross error; he notes, "The various rivalries and compromises that characterize these dynamics of check and balance in perception must be seen as chiefly responsible for the above noted relative infrequency of precision." It is this "organic multiplicity of factors entering the process [that] constitutes an effective safeguard against drastic error."[9]

These introductory remarks about cognitive tactics should prepare the reader to examine them in the examples provided below. But first we have another continuum to consider.

The Surface–Depth Continuum

The *surface–depth continuum* refers to the continuum between (surface) data that are close to the person making the judgments and (depth) data about objects and events that are remote in time or place from that person.[10]

Studies of the psychology of judgment and decision making began their work at the surface end of the continuum by investigating judgments about the distance between pinpricks on the skin, the loudness of sounds, and aspects of similar stimuli, giving rise to a discipline known as "psychophysics." Such studies included what I mean by data that are close to the person making the judgments—data on the skin, for example. As research went on, there was a gradual extension, a gradual reaching out, from presentations of data on the skin to "remote" presentations of data on paper, or information on a computer screen, and—most significant—to very remote data about objects such as persons, either in photographs, videos, or in person. The latter step, in the interest of gaining greater relevance to everyday experience, was an enormous one for psychology in those days, for it meant risking the loss of what small claim to scientific status psychology had achieved. Judging people's characteristics was far, far more complex than was judging the distance between two pinpricks on the skin, and thus far more susceptible to the dreaded criticisms of "softness" (as opposed to "hard science") and subjectivity. Taking this step entailed the pursuit of greater meaningfulness, but at the risk of the loss of scientific respectability. Nevertheless, they took the risk was taken, and by the 1970s the study of judgment and decision making had reached a reasonable level of complexity, without sacrificing scientific respectability. And indeed, that is how the study of "social perception" or "person perception" began.[11]

These steps resulted in psychologists' presenting information to their subjects in more-remote locations—in time or space, or psychologically (about which more below)—further from the subject, and thus more closely approximating, or representing, the conditions under which persons (and other organisms) normally make judgments. It was this movement along the surface–depth continuum, from surface to remote conditions, that increased the interest in judgment and decision-making research that we see today. Researchers could now address problems in the domain of everyday experience: how persons judge one another, for example—indeed, how persons judge *any* remote object. Even judgments of such remote ephemeral objects as values could be assessed in the same framework as could judgments of concrete remote objects, for complexity had been reduced to remoteness.

An Example of Surface and Depth Characteristics

You have just been introduced to a new person whom you know little or nothing about. You must interact with this person and you must be polite; you can't blurt out, "Who or what are you and what is your excuse for living?" You must try to find the answers to these questions by making use of multiple fallible indicators *at the surface*—that's all you normally have—to infer the depth characteristics of who and what the person is."

What does it mean to say "at the surface"? It means that you must look at those characteristics of the person that you *can* see, that our culture at this time deems important for this purpose—dress, makeup, mannerisms, language, physical characteristics, and other features—and use them to infer the important *psychologically* remote characteristics (for example, trustworthiness, intelligence, friendliness) that you *can't* see. Remember that all these surface characteristics are fallible indicators; not only can they be faked, but even if genuine, they will bear only an uncertain relationship to the remote depth variable in which you are interested. Are you interested in that person's intelligence? A high forehead is a very fallible indicator; level of vocabulary is better but not very good; peer evaluations are long on face validity but short on reliability. As you see, it will be hard—perhaps impossible—to completely eliminate uncertainty.

To take this a bit further, let me offer a general proposition. Persons who focus their judgments on objects, events, and ideas that are more remote, further away from the surface pole and closer to the depth pole, yet remain somewhere near the middle of the surface–depth continuum, are wiser than those who move to either pole. I will have more to say about this in chapter 20.

To sum up: there are three continua on which any judgment will fall: the task continuum, the cognitive continuum, and the surface–depth continuum. One must keep these in mind when trying to understand performance in any judgment situation.

9

The Cognitive Continuum
at the Supreme Court

Those requesting your judgment may have no interest in your reasoning, even if you are offering a coherence-based judgment. They may even prefer an intuition-based judgment without an explanation. They may ask no more of you than to hear you say, "I want you to do this because it is the right thing to do." Moral judgments are frequently of this character, mainly because thoughtful moral judgments are complicated; once one gets beyond simplistic clichés, they are hard to defend while trying to maintain a consistent point of view. Political ideologies are often expressed in intuition-based form that will claim coherence, if for no other reason than it is so hard to find empirical examples of the success of the ideology with which it corresponds. If you have noticed that it is these two areas of discussion—moral judgments and political judgments—that draw the greatest number of bitter disputes, you are right; it is no accident that coherence-based judgments that rely on intuition frequently induce severe conflict.

But there is a place to settle these disputes when they rise to the level of urgency, and in the United States that place is the Supreme Court. Surprisingly, even there we can find contention about the role of intuition and analysis in making coherent judgments. Of course, the justices do not call upon cognitive psychologists for help with such judgments; perhaps that is what encourages them to act as if they were cognitive psychologists. Below I will show how three different justices hold three different points of view, which places them at three different points on the cognitive continuum. That knowledge will enable the reader to predict how each justice will reach his or her conclusions. First, however, I want to show how the court itself has moved along the cognitive continuum over time.

Prior to 1984, federal sentencing of a convicted person was largely left to the judge's discretion. There was no clear system of rules that determined what sentence to mete out for a given crime. Widely different punishment for similar crimes became almost scandalous. Many offenders served no time at all, while others, who committed the same crime, were sentenced to 20 years. As Supreme Court Justice Stephen Breyer, then a member of the commission established to create the analytically based "sentencing guidelines," put it,

> People were fed up with a system in which a judge would order a twelve-year sentence, but the Parole Commission would make the offender serve only four years. If a judge, believing that an offender sentenced to twelve years would serve only four years and wanting him to serve twelve, gave him thirty-six years, he might find the Parole Commission requiring the offender to serve thirty of the thirty-six years.[1]

Breyer saw this as a struggle between intuitive, case-by-case (discretionary) judgments and the analytical demand for sentencing equality from case to case. He argued that he was seeking a compromise between these antithetical judgments (polar positions on the cognitive continuum) and urged the adoption of the sentencing guidelines that Congress had passed without opposition.

Although the guidelines were adopted and used for roughly 20 years, opposition to them was strong; many judges disliked them intensely because they felt that the guidelines robbed them of their dignity as judges and reduced them to little more than clerks who simply "looked up" the sentence for the crime.

As a result of this disputatious atmosphere, in 2005, in a 5–4 decision, the Supreme Court allowed a judge to move his or her cognitive activity from the analytical pole ("look it up in the book") along the cognitive continuum toward the intuitive pole, by authorizing the greater use of (intuitive) "discretion." The guidelines were not thrown away but were to be treated as "advisory." Furthermore, sentences could be appealed for their "reasonableness."

This movement of social-policy judgments on the cognitive continuum from the intuitive pole to the analytical pole and then to the center of the continuum illustrates how there is oscillation between the poles of the cognitive continuum as various constituencies demand the kind of cognition that favors their interests. Thus judges' cognitive activity was first ordered to move from intuition to analysis. But the change in the Supreme Court's view in 2005 directed the judges' cognitive activity to be moved to the center of the continuum by ordering "reasonableness" (that is, by demanding some unspecified combination of intuition and analysis). It is easy to see that all the ambiguities associated with the center—reasonableness and common sense—will soon appear. Some critics will demand more analytical rigor, some will argue for more discretion (and already have), and the oscillation will go on.

Oscillation on the cognitive continuum is likely to be a rewarding, if difficult, topic of study.[2] It may well be that the most fruitful approach will be to document its occurrence in individual cases. In what follows, I show how three different justices show their preferences along the cognitive continuum.

Brennan

William Brennan, the deceased justice of the Supreme Court who is a hero to the liberal community, in 1987 sturdily and emphatically diminished the importance of analytical cognition at the Court. In an important lecture to the Cardozo Law School, he made it plain that intuition had a strong place in the application of justice at the Supreme Court. In what must be one of the strangest statements ever made by a Supreme Court justice, he indicated that there must be a place for "the insights of passion" in the dispensation of justice when he said, "Attention to experience may signal that the greatest threat to due process principles is formal reason severed from the insights of passion."[3] What makes this pronouncement so strange—reaching perhaps to absurdity—is that most of us think that the purpose of courts of law is precisely to explicate due process principles so that formal reason *would* be "severed from the insights of passion." Indeed, one might have thought that this separation was absolutely fundamental to the rule of law and that any justice who didn't make that separation would not keep his or her seat for very long.

All this becomes even stranger when we discover what Brennan means by "passion." He said that he chose that word deliberately, and then explained, "By 'passion' I mean the range of emotional or *intuitive* [italics added] responses to a given set of facts or arguments, responses which often speed into our consciousness far ahead of the lumbering syllogisms of reason."[4] Curiously, Brennan is exactly correct in his description of the process of intuition; judgments based on intuitive process do "speed into our consciousness far ahead of the lumbering syllogisms of reason." Despite his correct, albeit limited, description of intuition, throughout his lecture he failed to acknowledge that although intuition has the advantage of quickness, those "lumbering syllogisms" have the advantage of defensibility by virtue of their retraceability, which rapid intuitive judgments do not, precisely because of their lack of retraceability. That is the price we pay for the "speed" with which they enter our consciousness in contrast with the "lumbering" entry of analytical cognitive activity. But if there is one thing Supreme Court justices must be able to do, it is defend their judgments by explicit appeals to their logical and judicial base; otherwise, their implicit intuitions will be left to stand against the implicit intuitions of their peers and of the untrained and unlettered. One would suppose that the ability to provide careful, analytically derived, transparent, reasoned arguments was the whole purpose of a legal education.

Curiously, Justice Brennan never seemed to recognize the incongruence of his remarks with the requirements of his "job," as Holmes would have put it. I have seen no criticisms, from either Supreme Court justices or any commentators on the Court, of Brennan's praise of the use of intuitive tactics.

Scalia

Now we have a sitting Supreme Court justice, Antonin Scalia, whose cognitive activity is at the opposite end of the cognitive—and political—continuum from that of Brennan and so holds exactly the opposite view of how judgments should be reached. In his recent book, *A Matter of Interpretation: Federal Courts and the Law,* Justice Scalia takes up the matter of how laws should be understood and interpreted.[5] Not only is he uninterested in the emotions and intuitions that interested Justice Brennan, but Scalia goes further and tells us what justices *should* be interested in—and it is *not* emotions and intuitions. His view is that it is neither the law's legislative history nor guesses as to the lawmakers' intentions nor what the law ought to be in the eyes of the judge; rather, it is the *words in the statute* that should guide the judge's interpretation and application of it.

He calls this approach *textualism*, which he distinguishes from *strict constructionism*. (Strict constructionism refers to the process of trying to imagine exactly what the framers of the Constitution had in mind when they wrote what they wrote.) Scalia wants us to ignore all that and simply pay close attention to the exact wording of the statute as it was written. And he believes that textualism will result in judges doing what they are supposed to do, that is, interpreting the law, not making the law, which, he believes, is the regrettable consequence of the other approaches to interpretation. In short, Scalia wants to see the justices stick closely to the text, which means that he rejects the intuitive approach of which Brennan spoke so approvingly.

Unsurprisingly, then, Scalia accepts, indeed praises, the use of explicit analytical tactics. He makes that clear in his vigorous response to charges that his textualism is "formalistic." He welcomes that charge because it enables him to elaborate on the foundation of his views about how judges and lawyers should think: "Of all the criticisms leveled against textualism, the most mindless is that it is 'formalistic.' The answer to that is, *of course it's formalistic!*" (italics in original).[6] That rebuttal offers Scalia an opportunity not only to explain his fundamental views of the law but to emphasize his adherence to analytical tactics: "The rule of law is *about* form" (italics in original).[7]

Thus, Scalia's cognitive activity appears at the opposite end of the cognitive continuum from Brennan's. That can easily be seen in Scalia's preference for form, because form is precisely what analysis demands and what intuition foregoes. The strong demand for retraceability of analytical tactics means that the form of organizing information must be examined to determine whether the correct form was used and whether it was used correctly. Scalia then gives an example: "A murderer has been caught with blood on his hands, bending over the body of his victim; a neighbor with a video camera has filmed the crime, and the murderer has confessed in writing and on videotape. We nonetheless insist that before the state can punish this miscreant, it must conduct a full-dress criminal trial that results in a verdict of guilty. Is that not formalism? Long live formalism. It is what makes a government a government of laws not men."[8] There will be no intuitive inductive leaps, no matter how narrow the leap, in Justice Scalia's court. And (almost) everyone is for a government of laws, not men (or women). There is no room for the "insights of passion" in Justice Scalia's plea for a long life for formalism.

On June 20, 2002, six of the justices delivered themselves into Justice Scalia's hands. He could hardly have asked for an opinion that would provide more grist for his mill than the one handed down in *Atkins v. Virginia*, in which the majority of the Court used as a major part of their argument the idea of a "national consensus" that the mentally retarded should not be subject to the death penalty. Scalia's scorn for this reasoning is best seen in his own words:

Today's decision is the pinnacle of our Eighth Amendment death-is-different jurisprudence. Not only does it, like all of that jurisprudence, find no support in the text or history of the Eighth Amendment; it does not even have support in current social attitudes regarding the conditions that render an otherwise just death penalty inappropriate. Seldom has an opinion of the Court rested so obviously upon nothing but the personal views of its members. . . . Beyond the empty talk of a "national consensus," the Court gives us a brief glimpse of what really underlies today's decision: pretension to a power confined neither by the moral sentiments originally enshrined in the Eighth Amendment (its original meaning) nor even by the current moral sentiments of the American people.[9]

What aggravated Justice Scalia was the reliance on poll data and the action taken by 47% of the state legislatures. This flew in the face of his textualism and reliance on analytical, coherent cognition.

Before leaving Justice Scalia, it should be noted that journalists have not been oblivious to his demands for formalism, and at least some have noted what they believe are inconsistencies in his application of his principles. I mention this because it is precisely consistency that formalism demands, and when it is absent, the argument upon which it is based fails. So, one can expect that when one bases one's judgment on its coherence (as Scalia does), opponents will be quick to seize upon inconsistencies. Adam Cohen provides us with a nice example in his *New York Times* column when he claims that Scalia

> likes to boast [that he follows his] philosophy wherever it leads, even
> if it leads to results he disagrees with. But it is uncanny how often it
> leads him just where he already wanted to go. In his view, the 14th
> Amendment prohibits Michigan from using affirmative action in col-
> lege admissions, but lets Texas make gay sex a crime. . . . He is dismis-
> sive when inmates invoke the Eighth Amendment ban on cruel and
> unusual punishment to challenge prison conditions. But he is support-
> ive when wealthy people try to expand the "takings clause" to block
> the government from regulating their property.[10]

The correspondence strategy will be susceptible to criticisms of fact, but as may be seen from Cohen's example, the coherence strategy upon which Scalia relies is susceptible to criticisms of inconsistency; in either case, the critic will charge hidden motives as the source of error.

Scalia's enthusiasm for the use of "formalism" (he means analytical thought) is not confined to him or other Supreme Court justices. Indeed, it has become widespread throughout the legal profession—so much so that two lawyers, Jean Stefancic and Richard Delgado, have decided it is a threat to the integrity of the profession and have written a book about the role of formalistic thinking and what they believe is its pervasive, and deleterious, effects.[11] They even give it a role in the massive annual departure of lawyers from the profession (40,000 per year, according to Benjamin Sells).[12] No doubt, the use of analytical thought is growing within the legal profession, as it is everywhere, and possibly that will have regrettable consequences; our question will be, What is to take its place? As we have seen, other equally famous Supreme Court justices— William Brennan, for example—will be pleased to offer "the insights of passion." But Scalia will reply, "Should we not prefer a government of laws, not men?"

Is there no middle ground? The theory that there is a cognitive continuum suggests that there must be. We can find that middle ground in the life and work of the most famous justice of them all, Oliver Wendell Holmes.

Holmes

Where would Holmes have stood in this argument between the worth of intuition and analysis in the cognitive activity of Supreme Court justices? Earlier we saw that Holmes, perhaps the most distinguished justice in the history of the Supreme Court, diminished the importance of analytical, coherent reasoning at the Court (see below), and thus, by implication, emphasized the importance of intuition. Indeed, he was explicit about this in his celebrated book *The Common Law,* where he famously wrote, "The life of the law has not been logic; it has been experience." He followed that surprising announcement with these words:

> The felt necessities of the time, the prevalent moral and political theories, intuitions of public policy, avowed or unconscious, even the prejudices which judges share with their fellow men, have had a good deal more to do than the syllogism in determining the rules by which men shall be governed.

And to make his thoughts perfectly plain, he concluded, "The law cannot be dealt with as if it contained only the axioms and corollaries of a book of mathematics."[13]

So, Holmes stood squarely in the middle; he was strongly opposed to the certitude demonstrated by Brennan's strong belief in intuitive tactics and equally opposed to the certitude afforded by Scalia's strong commitment to analytical tactics, so he wouldn't be joining either of them. He would follow his philosophy of work at the Court, namely "jobbism." He used that strange word to indicate that he would do what he thought his job required. He might even follow his own description of his job—"decide first, then deduce." He would decide just how far formal analysis would need to be followed before becoming absurd, or morally repulsive, and how far "the felt necessities of the time, the prevalent moral and political theories, [his] intuitions of public policy" (see above) would take him in either direction and then express himself in his own terms.

You can see from these words from our most scholarly Supreme Court justices that all three had firm convictions about intuition, analysis, and common sense, and how these cognitive tactics should be employed in the pursuit of justice. Brennan supported the use of intuition, Scalia despises its use and demands the analytical processes of formalism, whereas Holmes was prepared to do what he believed his job required him to do in any specific case. Therefore, it is apparent that cognitive scientists and legal scholars have something in common; both endeavors consider these cognitive activities to be essential substantive aspects of their discipline.

You will also see from those words that the justices held preferences for which cognitive tactics are most appropriate for judicial judgment and were eager to express those preferences, although of course, none could justify them (though they tried). But that is to be expected, inasmuch as none of these jurists had any acquaintance with the scientific literature on these topics. Should they have had such acquaintance? Well, perhaps not Holmes, but Brennan and Scalia were and are modern, learned men; they should have been acquainted with the major features of what they were talking about. Had that been the case, the discourse might have moved forward from Holmes's day to Scalia's. Justice Breyer, for example, is apparently aware of research in judgment and decision making.[14]

There is no doubt, however, that the discourse should move forward. For example, Justice Scalia's entire thesis depends on his confident assumption that "textualism" will indeed evoke agreement on the meaning of a specific text. For if it doesn't, textualism will be abandoned.

Yet Lawrence Tribe, a distinguished professor of constitutional law at Harvard University, in his chapter entitled "Comment" on Justice Scalia's thesis, expresses no such confidence. Indeed, he concludes his 30-page "Comment," which includes 75 footnotes, with an expression of complete pessimism on that point. For he finds that he and Justice Scalia have no formula for deciding which parts of the Constitution are susceptible to his approach, and that "may trouble some, and may inspire others, but [it] seems to me, in either event, our inescapable fate."[15] In other words, he holds exactly the opposite assumption from that of Justice Scalia; he believes that it is our "inescapable fate" that we will live with disagreement over how to interpret the Constitution.

Is this impasse a result of amateurish interpretations of major concepts in cognitive science, specifically intuition? Would it help if better-informed and more explicit versions of these concepts were put forward—and used? Would it help if, instead of arguing over the hypothetical ability of Justice Scalia's textualism to evoke agreement, we first sought agreement over which cognitive tactics— and strategies—could be justifiably employed to interpret which sections of the Constitution? Indeed, that is the issue that seems to divide Holmes, Brennan, and Scalia. They make it clear that these terms, central to cognitive science, are also central to legal scholarship. Therefore, to answer my questions above, I believe it would help both disciplines if they clarified the meaning and function of these terms as they apply to the judicial "job." But it is doubtful that they will succeed if they pursue this task in terms of seeking rationality; they will find themselves mired in disagreements over just what that term signifies.

The reader will note that I have carefully selected my justices and their remarks so that my theory of a cognitive continuum will be nicely represented, with Justice Brennan at the intuitive pole, Justice Scalia at the analytical pole, and Justice Holmes vacillating somewhere in the center. I have done this to illustrate the applicability of the theory, not as proof.[16]

The Future of Torture

The reader might be forgiven if he she is wondering whether all this talk about the three justices and the cognitive continuum might not be too abstract and removed from today's events. In order to reassure you that such is not the case, I will relate the above remarks to one of the most pressing issues of today: did the United States in 2003 become a nation that accepts torture of its prisoners? For if it did, many new questions will arise about the call for human rights that numerous U.S. presidents have issued, and the frequent claim that the United States is the bulwark against those nations that destroy human rights (Saddam Hussein's Iraq, for example). Is the United States, in fact, a nation that preaches one thing and practices another, as so many claim?

What makes the matter of torture more relevant is the likelihood that that the abuses alleged to have occurred in the Abu Ghraib prison in 2004 will occur more frequently in the future. That sounds like a prediction, and it is. It is a prediction that follows rather readily from another, namely, that the future will bring us more preemptive wars. Preemption will occur more frequently because of the nature of modern weaponry; it has such strong capability to make a rapid strike that no nation can count on advance notice from its adversary. It would be "irrational" to do so. Condoleezza Rice, the former national security advisor and now secretary of state, made this "irrationality" plain when she indicated that the United States should not wait for the evidence that Saddam Hussein possessed nuclear weapons to appear in the form of a "mushroom cloud." In a memorandum to the deputy counsel for the president, John Yoo wrote, "The Framing generation well understood that declarations of war were obsolete."[17]

The fact that preemption depends entirely on information (intelligence) about what the purported enemy is planning to do has lacked emphasis; it is crucial to understand that preemption is based on intelligence; it is intelligence that excuses preemption. And if the heads of state, or the generals, find it necessary to acquire information, there will be strong pressure on those in a position to get it to do so at any cost.

The systematic use of torture to extract military information is a recent development (although long known to police departments, for these also thrive on information). Historically, torture was more likely to be used as punishment, as for example in the case of John McCain, who was harshly tortured by the North Vietnamese for failing to cooperate with them. And the effectiveness of torture as punishment is undoubted. Torturing for information, however, has a bad reputation in terms of its effectiveness. Too often, it is claimed, the prisoner will give the interrogator *any* information, false or contrived, to escape the pain and suffering.

Nevertheless, despite its poor reputation, the urgency of getting information about the enemy's intentions as soon as possible leads directly to the possibility of torture. In his introduction to *The Torture Papers*, Anthony Lewis makes this situation clear with a simple anecdote. He tells of his meeting in Israel with Jacob Timmerman, a newsman tortured in Argentina. Timmerman asks Lewis whether he "would agree to torture a prisoner if he knew of a terrorist outrage that would shortly take place." Lewis replied, "After trying to avoid the question, I finally said, 'Yes, I would.'" But Timmerman said, "No! You cannot start down that path."[18]

This is precisely the situation that the U.S. troops in Iraq and Guantánamo faced. The Americans believed that their prisoners had knowledge of a terrible threat to the lives of many people. Should they resort to torture to extract that knowledge, whether or not they could be sure that the prisoner did in fact have the desired knowledge? How were the many lives of those at risk to be balanced against the principle of due process? Is this not a challenge to students of judgment and decision making?

Lewis, long known for his strong and outspoken stand on civil liberties and the rule of law, acknowledged that he *would* resort to torture. So it should not be surprising to find that others less committed to the rule of law would do the same, and indeed, have done so. For example, in her essay titled "From Fear to Torture," Karen Greenberg quotes an October 2002 memo from the commander of the U.S. Southern Command, James T. Hill, that shows the dilemma the military command faced: "Despite our best efforts, some detainees have tenaciously resisted our current interrogation methods.[19] Our respective staffs, the Office of the Secretary of Defense and Joint Task Force 170 have been trying to identify counter-resistant techniques that we can lawfully employ."[20] That quote sums the problem up: What can we *lawfully* do to make these guys talk, and thus give us a chance to save American and Iraqi lives?

That plea for advice about lawful methods brings us back to judgment and decision making over the use of torture, and the wisdom of the Supreme Court. How will the members of this Court, the last resort of rationality and rule of law, *think* about this problem that pits the lives of people—possibly large numbers of people—against due process, one of the most important human principles we have achieved? This problem, the very one Timmerman confronted Lewis with, will soon be at the doorstep of the Court. Can we imagine what cognitive processes will be brought to bear on the issue by different judges? For that is how this problem will be treated; justices will have to exercise their judgment under uncertainty. By making use of the three continua described above, and the prior positions of the three justices described above, we should be able to predict how they will vote on this matter. I now turn to that topic.

Brennan on Torture

The key statement in Brennan's speech before the Cardozo Center was, "Attention to experience may signal that the greatest threat to due process principles is formal reason severed from the insights of passion."[21] Brennan's, and many others', lack of confidence in "formal reason" or "rationality" alone leaves us uncertain about his stance; where would he stand on the torture at Abu Ghraib? Or to put it more simply, how would he have answered the question Timmerman put to Lewis?

It seems to this author that if Brennan is to maintain a coherent view, he must agree with Lewis, stand against the formal reason of the Constitution, and declare that his "passionate insight" is that torture is appropriate in these circumstances because the lives of hundreds, thousands, or tens of thousands are at stake. He might even resort to quoting whoever it was who said, "The Constitution is not a suicide pact."

Scalia on Torture

It will be somewhat easier to find Scalia's position, on the assumption that he maintains a coherent view. For he makes clear that his textualism is formalistic. He welcomes formal reasoning with enthusiasm and he asserts, "The rule of law is about form." So it appears that Scalia will have no truck with the insights of passion; he wants us to pay attention to the words in the Constitution and apply them; due process is threatened not by formal reasoning but by departure from it. And since the Constitution is clear in its demand for due process, there will be no torture. Or will there?

The latter question arises because there is another formidable actor in this drama who is not on the Supreme Court but who may persuade Justice Scalia that he can "have his cake and eat it too"; that is, another actor may lead Scalia to other writings that will allow him to depart from the Constitution while appearing not to. The other actor, John Yoo, is formidable because he is a brilliant lawyer with considerable credentials (a professor of law at Boalt Hall School of Law at the University of California, Berkeley, and a former deputy assistant attorney general, Office of Legal Counsel, in the Department of Justice), who has already found the words Scalia needs, should he wish to condone torture as a way to get life-saving information. And indeed, Yoo's words have already influenced powerful members of the Bush administration to take a more benign look at the process of torture as an information-collecting technique. What did Yoo say to move Scalia in that direction? What would he *have* to say to influence Scalia to accept the practice of torture as *lawful* while maintaining his commitment to the analytical pole of the cognitive continuum?

We know from Scalia's remarks (above) what Scalia would demand: no use of multiple fallible indicators to arouse passion, and clear cold sentences with readily understandable words logically ordered to lead to an inevitable conclusion. That's what he means by formalistic. Did Yoo manage that? He certainly tried, for he had a great deal to say on the matter.[22] Although I lack legal training, I discern that he certainly made a case that would meet Scalia's demands for formality (no "insights of passion" here).

I cannot relay here all that Yoo had to say in his several drafts; his language is precise and detailed. But his task was determined by the situational demand for intelligence to be obtained as rapidly as possible. It was the president, through his counsel, Alberto Gonzales, and others, that made the task clear.[23] The upshot of the numerous memoranda and reports that ensued can be seen in Greenberg's conclusions:

> Ultimately, what the reader is left with after reading these documents is
> a clear sense of the systematic decision to alter the use of the methods
> of coercion and torture that lay outside of accepted and legal norms, a
> process that began early in 2002 and that was well defined . . . before
> the invasion of Iraq.[24]

That sort of material should be enough for Scalia; it is sufficiently formal, detailed, and analytical to require a reply in kind if the argument is to be refuted. But in fact it was refuted in kind, as *The Torture Papers* makes clear. Scalia will have plenty of formal analyses to ponder analytically. Since we are unable to read Justice Scalia's mind, and he has not yet made it up, so far as we know, I cannot predict how he will vote, unless he votes in terms of his politics, which have become clear over the years. If so, I assume he will vote to support the administration's (and Yoo's) argument. In either case, there is little doubt about form; we shall see a carefully reasoned, analytical argument, a very risky procedure.

Holmes on Torture

Oliver Wendell Holmes's judgment on this matter should be easy for us to predict. Holmes believed not only that the law *is* removed from the formalisms that Scalia wants (see the paragraph above on "felt necessities of the time") but that it *ought* to be so removed ("the law cannot be dealt with as if [it were] a book of mathematics"). So, Holmes removed the law from the strict rules of a coherence strategy and placed it clearly in a strategy of correspondence with the "prevalent moral and political theories" and "even the prejudices which judges share with their fellow men." Taking him at his word, then, we would expect him to have stood with the Bush administration and supported the use of torture to extract information, thereby adopting a romantic view of policymaking.

I acknowledge that it is hard to imagine this somber, dignified, well-educated Bostonian signing off on the constitutionality of torture. But, remember; he made it clear that he had had enough of abstractions; he was mindful of his bloodied uniform hanging in his closet, and when he saw "a clear and present danger" (his words) to his country and its citizens, he would want to act on it; he thought that was his "job."

Convergence

My conclusion, then, is that, given the way each of these illustrious justices speak about how they exercise their judgment, all three would, in their own way, support the practice of torture by the United States in the twenty-first century.

Would it be *wise* for them to do so? Within the framework of this book on wisdom, the answer must be yes, although only Holmes would appear to be flexible (to take advantage of the range of cognition of which humans are capable). If the reader will recall that analytical cognition rarely makes errors, but when it does, those errors are likely be very large, Brennan brings us the intuitions we need to counter the rare, but severe, mistakes of Scalia's analytical work. And thus we are—possibly—presented with wisdom; but it takes the combined efforts of all three justices. Can we arrange for such wisdom in the cognitive activity of one person? Perhaps that was true of Holmes. And perhaps that accounts for his reputation.

10

Intuition

Seeking Empirical Accuracy the Easy Way

Intuition has always been a mysterious process because it is an unconscious process of integrating information. Because it is unconscious, that is, because you are unaware of how you do it, and therefore can't explain it, the process remains mysterious. That is a critical feature of intuition. To many people its mystery suggests it's a very powerful form of cognition, but to many others it means that intuition deserves no credence at all. They are likely to say, "If you don't know how you reached your judgment, why should we trust it?" In either case, it is no longer mysterious to students of judgment and decision making; it was one of the first topics to be studied, and progress has been made, so we are no longer seventeenth- or eighteenth-century philosophers in the Age of Enlightenment arguing about the unknown properties of a mysterious process. Nevertheless, the fact that intuition is a process we all recognize, yet that remains mysterious to many, is a matter of profound significance that affects the most serious and important judgments of laypersons and our leaders in war and peace.

There is no dispute about the fact that in any judgment situation the easy tactic is to be intuitive; that is, go with your instincts, rely on your gut, or do what your heart tells you. It is quick, often instantaneous—almost all "snap" judgments are intuitive, and because you can't explain what it is that you did, it will always seem easy. For example, when you make a judgment about the distance or movement of an object when you are driving down the highway, or when you shoot a basket, or recognize friendship in another person, you do it rapidly and *thoughtlessly*: you don't reflect on how you ought to do it, or whether you are meeting all the criteria for a sound judgment. Such snap judgments may be defended in minor matters. Yet even very powerful people acknowledge that they make very important decisions in this fashion. When the heirs to the Hewlett-Packard company were trying to decide whether to merge with the company that made Compaq computers—it is difficult to imagine their facing a larger decision—one of the heirs explained how his decision would be made: "I guess a decision comes down to your gut feeling about things."[1]

Football players (and fans) know that during games, place kickers kick the ball intuitively, that is, without thinking about "mechanics": how their leg should move or where their feet or hands should be (though certainly between games they and their coaches use practice to make good mechanics second nature, and they put plenty of thought into it then). It is strongly believed that if they are made to think—and thus to lose their intuitive competence—they will lose their accuracy. So, it is a well-known trick for the opposing team to call a time-out just before a field goal attempt in order to "make him think about it." They hope that during the time-out the place kicker will think about the details of kicking and will thus lose his intuitive, that is, thoughtlessness, skill, and thereby his accuracy, too.

Perhaps the best example from football comes from an article in *The New York Times* titled "Thinking Quarterback May Think Too Much." This headline referred to a coach's irritation at his quarterback's performance; the coach had lamented: "At times he is too analytical." He thought the quarterback was thinking too much about where to throw the ball and should, instead, "just throw it."[2] (Of course, when the throw is intercepted, the coach will say, "He ought to think more about what he is doing.")

The place kicker's intuitive judgments are quick and easy, they come naturally, and the kicker doesn't have to defend them; in fact, they can't be defended, because no one can retrace the process. When you are asked why you made this judgment and not that one, or asked to retrace and defend your judgment, if you are honest, you will simply say, "I used my intuition," or instincts, or gut, or such. Your listener will understand (most of the time) that this is your way of saying, "I don't know how I reached that conclusion; I just did," just as you did when you said, "My, isn't that a beautiful [or ugly] photograph or painting." Imagine trying to explain why Van Gogh's paintings are beautiful. It easy to see why intuition was the favorite cognitive tactic of the Romantic philosophers who are supposed to have held that "God is a poet, not a mathematician."

It is essential to understand that although intuition involves cognitive activity—your brain is doing something—for our theoretical purposes it is *not* thinking. Thus, when authors index "intuitive thought," as do Ian Buruma and Avishai Margalit, they are indexing an oxymoron; if a person is thinking, he or she is not engaging in intuitive cognition.[3]

Professionals Like to Claim to Be Intuitive

Intuition is commonly used by economists to predict the markets, and by doctors to predict their patients' health. Indeed, it is a common feature of the way most professionals (and nonprofessionals)—indeed, all of us—make judgments about other people. When we refer to a "judgment," we are assuming the use of intuition. For judgment is what we have always employed when we lack the analytical tools—like mathematics—to help us. Indeed, this process is part of our evolutionary heritage from the days when there were no mathematical tools.

Because the central aspect of intuition is a rapid cognitive activity that cannot be retraced (at least by the nonprofessional person), easy, nonretraceable intuitions appear everywhere, often where you least expect them. For example, they can appear in the judgments of those who are in control of the U.S. economy. Bob Woodward, the well-known journalist, reports that Nicholas Brady, secretary of the treasury during the first Bush presidency and former head of the huge brokerage firm Dillon, Read, made much of his use of intuition. According to Woodward, Brady liked to justify his judgments by saying, "I feel it in my bones." And Woodward says, "When he tried to articulate it, the words could sound like hash [to Alan Greenspan]."[4] This is typical when a person is trying to explain what he can't explain but rather feels.

Brady's "hash" was apparently unconvincing to Greenspan, but what is remarkable is that he convinced many; after all, he did become secretary of the treasury. (In chapter 14, I will describe the very different approach of another financial expert, Robert Rubin, who also became secretary of the treasury.) I mention this to show that it is not only followers of spiritual gurus from India, or Romantic philosophers from Europe, who put their faith in mysterious judgments that cannot be retraced or defended by logical arguments; easy, nonretraceable intuitive judgments often command respect—and are used to justify action—at all levels of societies, everywhere, and in all professional disciplines. As I have shown elsewhere, all the great figures in science, engineering, law, philosophy, economics, and medicine have expressed their belief in the efficacy of intuitive judgments and thus have added to their credibility, albeit almost certainly undeservedly so.[5] Scientists, however, have learned several things about intuition that you should know.

What Do We Know about Intuition?

Earlier I said that intuition was an "unconscious process of integrating information," but I did not say what kind of information. Intuition uses information that comes in the form of multiple fallible indicators (discussed in detail in chapter 3). When intuition is used to make a judgment within the strategy of seeking empirical accuracy—correspondence with the facts—then it is information from multiple fallible indicators that is "put together" or integrated into a judgment. Thus, intuition is a process that is compatible with an environment that presents information in the form of fallible cues; cues that are valid on certain occasions but not others, and thus are often in error, and therefore fallible. Clouds are fallible indicators of rain (sometimes they indicate rain and sometimes they don't); the expression on someone's face is a similar fallible indicator, for sometimes it reflects another person's feelings and sometimes it doesn't. Similarly, the tone of someone's voice is a fallible indicator of mood. None of these cues to the mood of another can be trusted all the time. There are some untrustworthy indicators, some more untrustworthy than others, in all professional fields and in everyday life, and we—professionals and nonprofessionals alike—all use them without knowing how we do it, an empirical fact demonstrated many times by judgment researchers.[6]

Second, it is the process for integrating this usually subtle but always less than fully trustworthy, information from fallible cues that has always been the central focus of the mystery. Sometimes we can identify the indicators we use—economic indicators are all over the newspapers—and sometimes we can't. But we never can describe the process for putting them together in a judgment or a prediction; you will never see a description of *that* process in the newspapers. But the mystery is now (almost) gone among students of judgment and decision making. According to them (at least most of them) the process is an astonishingly simple one: the process we humans (and other animals) use is little more than adding up (or averaging) the information from the indicators. That is, if I see three different indicators of a person's intelligence, I just add them up, or average them. For example, if I hear an unusually brilliant observation from someone, and my neighbor tells me that he hears that kind of thing from that person very often, and then I find that she holds a very high position at a university, I add (or average) all that up and reach the judgment that the person involved is very intelligent. And whereas it is usually believed that persons (especially experts) put together the information from a very large number of indicators, in fact, it is seldom more than three or four. Some investigators have found that, in some cases—they will argue that it is in many cases—only one indicator is used, and surprisingly, it is highly effective to do so![7]

Professionals (doctors, stockbrokers) who make intuitive judgments will always quarrel with this conclusion; it annoys them because they say it oversimplifies what they do. But empirical tests always prove that the professionals are wrong about this; these conclusions hold up. As a result, it is simple to build a quantitative model of intuitive judgments within the correspondence strategy. This is called an *additive model* when there are three or four indicators, or "take the best" when only one is used.[8]

Third, you should know that because intuition-based judgments are very rapid, they are largely unaffected by time constraints because intuition itself requires so little time. Thus, time deprivation is not a threat to the intuition tactic, even when several indicators are used. The opposite is true of judgments based on analysis. And that is something to remember when you hear about someone making a judgment "under stress." Remember that because intuitive judgments require very little time, stress or no stress. So time deprivation itself is not a threat to intuitive judgments inasmuch as intuitive judgments are always made in very brief periods of time.

Intuition in Medicine

The field of medicine provides us with some of our best examples of the use of intuition. Perhaps the most striking examples occur when more analytical cognitive tactics fail. Possibly, intuition is acceptable in medicine because of the long tradition in which medicine has been depicted as an "art" in addition to a science. But modern physicians have also made great efforts to achieve a coherent, fully defensible, scientifically based description of the patient's disease. The "art" of medicine lies in applying knowledge that is not yet fully coherent, of which there is a great deal. And in view of the plethora of information available to modern physicians, they are bound to feel a sense of defeat when they cannot apply all this knowledge. So, when the diagnosis is not obvious, the physician is uncertain about what to do for the patient, or there are conflicting opinions, then— surprising as it may seem—a physician is apt to resort to "feelings" to provide that explanation. Doctors may also explain to the patient (or themselves) that medicine is as much art as science. Although some modern physicians will have a sense of failure when doing this, others seem to revel in it. One who apparently enjoys it is Dr. Jerome Groopman, who writes books about it.[9] Dr. Groopman has set himself the task of convincing patients (and other doctors) that they should trust their instincts to do what is best for their patients. Contrary to many other modern physicians with a strong background in science (which he has), he apparently believes that intuition (specifically, trusting one's instincts) has a justifiable place among the physicians' cognitive resources.

Dr. Groopman is no ordinary doctor. He holds an endowed chair at the Harvard School of Medicine, is the chief of experimental medicine at Beth Israel Deaconess Medical Center, and is a leading researcher in cancer and AIDS. He also writes articles for *The New Yorker* and contributes articles to national newspapers and magazines. The question for us is, should we listen to him when he asks us to trust doctors' instincts? He tells us that he teaches his students, "Doctoring was a balance between the sixth sense of intuition and the tedious reiteration of diagnostic lists."[10]

One wonders what this prestigious doctor tells his students about just where that "sixth sense" is located—in the bones? gut? heart?—and just how it works. He explains to patients, "Armed with knowledge, steadied by family and friends, and calling on intuition, we can gain clarity and insight, and are prepared to make the best possible decisions."[11] Apparently, he wants his patients to call on their own intuition for insight.

But for all this man of science's persistent reliance on and advocacy of intuition, he never explains just what intuition is and how it works, or even how it differs from analysis, common sense, mysticism, or mere guesswork. It remains a process buried in mystery. That he continues the mystery is a grave departure from science and, perhaps, a grave (no pun intended) disservice to his patients. For Dr. Groopman should know (or be told) that there is a science of cognition in general, and judgment and decision making in particular, and has been for some time. (Dr. Alvin Feinstein, formerly a colleague of his at Harvard, could have brought him up to date some time ago with his 1967 book *Clinical Judgment*.) And because he is an authoritative doctor, people depend on him not only for medical advice but also for help in the matter of reaching very serious decisions. But it is clear that what he calls his intuition is a process impossible for him to describe, and thus impossible for him to defend, and so should be impossible for him to use or advocate.

Atul Gawande, another Harvard physician, much younger than Dr. Groopman, and becoming famous while still in his residency, also writes for *The New Yorker* but differs from Dr. Groopman in that he reads at least some of the literature on judgment and decision making and, as a result, knows what has been learned about the use of intuition in medicine. Dr. Gawande knows that ignoring what has been learned is very expensive; patients will suffer more incorrect diagnoses when doctors rely on their intuition instead of an algorithm, say, or "tedious reiteration of lists," as Dr. Groopman put it. And, in fact, recent autopsies have revealed misdiagnoses in a startling 40% of cases, although we don't know how many of these errors were based on some doctor's intuition and how many on analytical work.

Another well-known physician, Dr. Sherwin Nuland, also takes the opposite view from Dr. Groopman; he supports systematic analytical cognition. For example, when writing about the tragedy of a patient who died at Mount Sinai Hospital after surgery, apparently because of lack of supervised care, he had this to say:

> Flying by the seat of doctors' pants is no way to get to a destination safely. Every step in the process of patient care must be analyzed by itself and in tandem with all others, with a view to decreasing dependence on individual moment-to-moment decision-making by individual personnel. Insofar as is possible, operational errors must be corrected and a method established of subjecting the system to ongoing critical review.[12]

Dr. Nuland has seen too much intuition in hospital systems and thinks it is responsible for the enormous death rate from medical mistakes. He wants the entire system to be shifted to one based on analytical tactics. Here is the age-old rivalry between intuition and analysis being acted out in the twenty-first century regarding the most serious of matters—life and death.

But we must be careful in matters of this sort. Although we shouldn't be intimidated by men of Dr. Groopman's status, we must be mindful of the fact that there is still much to be learned about intuition and analysis. Each has its own assets and liabilities (as we shall see in the next chapter). At this point, however, we can say that Dr. Groopman cannot justify his appeal to intuition by appealing to reason, for reason demands explication and retraceability, and Dr. Groopman cannot retrace the cognitive processes that led to his intuitive judgment; if he could, it wouldn't be intuition. Nor can he justify his intuitive judgment by appealing to empirical accuracy, because he doesn't keep score; he doesn't offer us a list of intuitive diagnoses or prognoses that he has made, nor does he provide a comparison of hits and misses when he was "trusting his instincts" and when he was relying solely on his scientific knowledge. In the absence of logical, medical, or empirical justification, it is hard to see how the use of intuition in relation to a patient's future can be defended. And because these are medical judgments about a patient's health, and life, they do need justification. Why is there no scientific approach to the evaluation of those intuitive guesses?

In a long article in *The Washington Post,* Sandra Boodman described the need to reduce error in medicine, a need made apparent in 1999 when the Institute of Medicine reported that 98,000 hospitalized Americans die every year from preventable errors.[13] It is impossible to say how many of these preventable errors are due to misdiagnoses or other doctor-related errors (the report indicated the largest number were medication errors); without a scorecard, no one can say. Boodman reports that Michael Millenson, a scholar of medical practice, says the problem of medical error was first presented in 1955. She quotes him as saying,

> You won't believe the number of times I've heard a doctor say, with a straight face, "I don't make mistakes." There's an old saying in aviation: The pilot is the first one at the scene of an accident. Well, in medicine, if someone makes a mistake, who gets hurt? It's not the doctor. Who pays? It's not the hospital. Nobody's doing this on purpose, but they're not losing money on it, either.

But there is a (barely) perceptible trend toward "keeping score," a greatly disliked procedure in medicine. It received some publicity in 2002 in connection with mammography, when some record-keeping work by an HMO radiologist led to keeping track of the test's effectiveness (the scores were shockingly poor) and thus provided feedback not only for radiologists (and their employers) but for patients. Will that example lead Dr. Groopman and others to track their intuitive judgments? History suggests that getting them to do will be a long and very slow process. It would not be unreasonable, however, in light of the large amount of research on intuition, to assume that a large proportion of these errors are due to the use of intuitive guesses about patients' illnesses. (Research by members of the Society for Medical Decision Making should aid in error reduction.)

It is also clear that the fatigue endured by the 100,000 interns and residents who work 80 to 120 hours per week, often unsupervised, threatens good judgment. (This may change; recent studies are providing clear evidence of sleep deprivation–induced errors.)[14] Curiously, airline pilots' restrictions on the number of hours they can continuously fly apparently never excited the curiosity of the medical profession.

Why Intuition Lives a Long Life

Roughly a decade ago, the National Cancer Institute introduced the idea that, in situations in which there is irreducible uncertainty about procedures, the decision should be left to the patient. It appears that the fact that the patient "will be the first at the scene of the pain" outweighs the fact of expertise. The oddness of turning a difficult decision over to the least informed person concerned was not lost on editorial writers, but the idea caught on and has persisted. Indeed, it has taken on a certain authenticity and has even been given a name, "autonomy," which means that patients should make informed decisions for themselves. Exactly why a person who can hardly be called "informed," who has little or no knowledge of the disease, little or no experience with such decisions, is sick and perhaps lying in strange and threatening surroundings, and is distressed at the imminent possibility of pain and death, is considered in the best position to exercise his or her judgment and make such decisions has not been explained, so far as I know. Atul Gawande describes this situation well: "The conundrum remains: if both doctors and patients are fallible, who should decide? We want a rule. And so we decide that patients should be the ultimate arbiters." But Dr. Gawande doesn't like this rule; he says,

> "But such a hard-and-fast rule seems ill-suited both to a caring relationship between doctor and patient and to the reality of medical care, where a hundred decisions have to be made quickly. . . . The doctor should not make all those decisions and neither should the patient. Something must be worked out between them." Gawande then suggests that "the real task isn't to banish paternalism; the real task is to preserve kindness."[15]

But the patient isn't consulting the doctor for a dose of "kindness"; that can be found elsewhere. The "real task" for the doctor is to improve his or her ability to do what no one else can do: bring scientific medical knowledge to bear on the patient's illness as best possible. Evidence-based medicine (EBM) is now getting its share of publicity as a means for doing that, and it may serve to educate the public (and many doctors) about the choice they have to make between "intuitionists," such as Dr. Groopman, and the hard-eyed EBM doctors.

The seriousness of doctors' misplaced confidence in their intuitions is documented by Shannon Brownlee, who reports that it is the lack of reliable information that

> hampers the efficiency of the health-care market and prevents doctors and hospitals from learning what constitutes high-quality care. It has been more than a decade since the manifesto of "evidence-based medicine" was published in the Journal of the American Medical Association, yet much medical care is still based more on intuition than on science.[16]

Perhaps doctors who studied with Dr. Groopman want it that way. But the reports of health and medical practice in the United States indicate they are wrong. Brownlee states,

> Doctors don't know, for example, whether regular mammograms for women in their forties save lives, and they ignore evidence that Celebrex, a widely prescribed and much ballyhooed prescription painkiller, is no more effective than ibuprofen, which costs one tenth as much.[17]

(Since then Celebrex and Vioxx have been shown to be risky.)

> In one well-known example a clinical trial ended in 2002 showed hormone-replacement medication, which generated $1.2 billion in sales in 2000 and which women have been taking for more than thirty years, does not lower the risk of heart attack, as previously believed; in fact, it appears to raise it.[18]

Brownlee cites other examples of procedures that intuition encourages doctors to prescribe, and that do more harm than good.

Intuitive Learning

We begin to make empirically accurate judgments intuitively at an early age because making empirically accurate judgments is part of our genetic endowment, and our environment demands it. No one has to teach us to judge the larger object to be larger, irrespective of its distance from us. Indeed, no one would know how to teach us to do that.

That may be true for empirical judgments directed toward correspondence competence. But what about coherent judgments? It's the reverse; we have to be taught almost everything. We certainly do have to be taught to do arithmetic, algebra, and the rest of the mathematics we learn. If we are to learn about probability, we have to be taught, and it isn't easy, as any student of statistics will tell you. Nor is it an accident that our understanding of statistical logic came rather late in our history. It was similarly with respect to logic; if we are to learn, for example, about "truth functional inferences," we must be taught. Learning to make logically correct, analytically justified, coherent judgments takes work (as you probably already know). And it is always accompanied by a high degree of awareness of what is being learned.

Now the question is whether coherent competence can be learned intuitively. Can you intuitively learn to solve problems demanding a high degree of coherence competence without awareness?

The best-known example of this is the putative phenomenon of insight. I say "putative" because some doubt remains about insight; do people actually learn to solve a problem without awareness of how they did it? Usually "insight" also implies a rapid solution, no trial and error, and a means unknown to the problem solver; thus it also implies a solution reached by intuition.

But these conditions imply that learning, which is supposed to occur over time, isn't the process at work here, because insight occurs all at once. You have probably heard it described as the "aha!" phenomenon; the person, or animal, just "saw" the solution, without trial and error. Does this happen? Almost certainly it does but not very often, and usually the circumstances are such that one can't be sure exactly what the process was, even in experiments designed to investigate the question.

There are examples of autodidactic geniuses who produce the "aha!" response, but I don't know of any scientific work that explains how this happens or that even provides a good description of it. The fringe cultures have urged positive answers upon their disciples for ages (it's an easy way to "truth"), but dependable examples are hard to find. So my answer to the question of whether coherence competence can be achieved intuitively is a tentative "maybe." (There is a literature on learning without awareness, but the process is described best under "multiple probability cue learning," which is directed toward correspondence, not coherence.)[19]

Intuition and Social Policy: Why Administrators Seldom (If Ever) Learn

The question of learning is of critical importance in the matter of making social policy, and learning from history. We hear everywhere the pained cry about our political leaders: "Why can't they learn"? Or more specifically, "Why can't they learn from their mistakes?" And, of course, it is a complaint that covers more than politicians. All administrators, including generals and admirals, are berated for their failure to learn. Why is it that these policymakers are seldom seen to have the ability to learn?

The answer is that policymakers can, of course, learn as well as anyone else, given the same opportunity; the reason it seems that they can't learn is because they don't have the opportunity. So the charge is correct: they seldom do learn—as administrators—because they seldom can, and that is because the information they get is not conducive to learning. In addition, the feedback they get about the consequences of their judgments is generally absent or flawed. Their apparent failure to learn is not due to the special failings of administrators or bureaucrats; it is due to a learning situation that makes learning next to impossible for anyone (historians included, about whom I will have much more to say in chapter 17).

It is the same situation anyone faces when trying to learn from uncontrolled situations. That the situation is uncontrolled is precisely the cause of the difficulty, because it means that irreducible uncertainty from an indicator to what is indicated prevents incontestable inferences and/or deductions. Removing these barriers means removing these forms of uncertainty by creating controlled situations (experiments), and that is exactly what scientists do in order to make justifiable conclusions possible and allow knowledge to accumulate. But exerting that control retroactively is exactly what administrators and historians cannot do, because the situation is over and done with; it can't be manipulated. And if it is a prediction the administrator must make, feedback may be years in coming, or it may never come. Undoubtedly, the past may allow learning *that* something did or did not occur ("Washington slept here") but will not allow learning about *why* it occurred (Why was Washington there? Why did the Bush administration make a preemptive attack on Iraq?). In short, it is not because we (administrators, policymakers, or historians) somehow lack the competence to draw correct conclusions from past events that we fail to "learn lessons," it is because the situation of irreducible uncertainty and entangled causality won't permit us to rule out plausible alternative hypotheses about puta-tive cause and effect, or hypotheses regarding the relation of indicators and what is indicated. All this can be summed up as irreducible ambiguity in feedback, to which we can add long delays in feedback, usually amounting to years—often decades—and sometimes centuries.

The discipline of mathematical statistics was created as a branch of mathe-matics because of that irreducible uncertainty; its purpose is to reduce it *concep-tually,* to allow us to make transparent, justifiable conclusions in spite of it. And that discipline has been successful; it has become the methodological foundation of the substantive disciplines of medicine, pharmacology, meteorology, psychol-ogy, and the social sciences. But it does not yet underlie the study of history. In chapter 17, I will provide detailed examples of how esteemed historians attempt to learn from history and, in my view, fail.

The assumed failure of politicians to learn may not fit easily into my argu-ment, however. Perhaps politicians are not in office to learn lessons in the first place; maybe they simply want to stay in office. Unfortunately, that may well be true, but politicians must also face the consequences of mistaken policies, even if the information that led to the mistakes is flawed. Moreover, their constituents be-lieve in the myth that they *can* learn and therefore often demand that they *must* learn. They can't, however, although neither politicians nor constituents know this.

But if politicians and administrators have difficulty learning, what about the rest of us?

An Astonishing Farce of Misperception

In modern literature, an author will use his or her skills to draw distinctions between the correct and incorrect use of fallible indicators in the judgment of others upon meeting them, and the plot will generally describe how these distinctions play out. The widely known author of numerous prize-winning novels, Philip Roth, makes note of precisely this aspect of social life in *American Pastoral* by suggesting that people are usually wrong in their inferences about others, thus,

> You get them wrong before you meet them, while you're anticipating
> meeting them; you get them wrong while you're with them; and then
> you go home to tell somebody else about the meeting and you get them
> all wrong again. Since the same generally goes for them with you, the
> whole thing is really a dazzling illusion empty of all perception, an as-
> tonishing farce of misperception. And yet what are we going to do
> about this terribly significant business of other people, which gets bled
> of the significance we think it has and takes on instead a significance
> that is ludicrous, so ill-equipped are we all to envision one another's in-
> terior workings and invisible aims? Is everyone to go off and lock the
> door and sit secluded like the lonely writers do in a soundproof cell?

After this rather powerful description of the practice of social misjudgment in which we all participate, Roth comes to an astonishing conclusion:

> The fact remains that getting people right is not what living is all
> about anyway. It is getting them wrong that is living, getting them
> wrong and wrong and wrong and then on careful consideration, get-
> ting them wrong again. That's how we know we're alive: we're wrong.
> Maybe the best thing would be to forget being right or wrong about
> people and just go along for the ride. But if you can do that—well,
> *lucky you* (italics in original).[20]

The interesting thing about Roth's remarks is how different they are from those a psychologist would make, for psychologists think that "getting people right" is what we should strive (hard!) to do. Roth disagrees entirely with that goal. It may well be that Roth is serious about this, that making errors in perceiving people is "living." And maybe it is. It's also expensive and dangerous (as is living). But making errors about people can cost you your job, and your marriage, and your friends. It may even cost you your life—as every police officer knows—if your mistake involves a misjudgment at night on a dark street.

The surface–depth distinction and the surface–depth continuum provide a good idea of why accurate people perception is so difficult and why an author like Roth would conclude that we are continually getting others wrong. The fallible surface indicators from the other person of the depth variable (honesty, integrity, etc.) and the often error-ridden perception of these indicators explain misjudgments; indeed, the more we peer into the mechanisms for the transmission of information, the more improbable it seems that anyone ever makes accurate judgments of another's "inner person." Yet we find confidence in reading people everywhere, even in the office of the president of the United States. George W. Bush boldly informed us that he could trust Vladimir Putin because he, Bush, could "see" Putin's "soul" by peering into his eyes.[21]

U.S. Involvement in Iraq: What "Lessons" Will Be Learned?

No one will dispute the fact that the road to the date of Iraq's election was hard for all concerned, filled with unexpected casualties and chaos in the streets and in government. Not only did what many consider to be a "quagmire" take many lives, both American and Iraqi, but the war also cost the United States its credibility, when its stated reasons for invading Iraq were found to be dubious at best. Saddam Hussein's weapons of mass destruction were never found. Moreover, the pride and honor of the United States were badly stained, perhaps indelibly, when widespread torture in its military prisons in Iraq was discovered. All these unanticipated events led people to ask questions that could be fully anticipated: Why did all of this happen? What is to be learned from this?

It is the last question that psychologists must answer, as must politicians and military historians—but the psychologists don't, or at least they don't answer clearly. Indeed, the whole question of human learning, once a leading domain of psychology whose princes searched for the "laws of learning," seems to have been abandoned. Today the elusive "laws of learning" and the learning psychologists are never mentioned when our school system, our political leaders, and our editorial writers try to improve matters. Instead, there is a general wailing by all those interested: "Why don't they ever learn?"

This phenomenon, failing to learn, takes a highly disturbing form in Iraq, where chaos has erupted. And it is not only the politicians; even military professionals express grave doubts about our capacity for learning. Those doubts are revealed in remarks in *The Atlantic Monthly* made by Bruce Hoffman, the acting director of the RAND Corporation's Center for Middle East Public Policy and a senior fellow at the U.S. Military Academy's Combating Terrorism Center. His position as an expert on both Middle East policy and the military combat of terrorism gives him a special authority and lends particular importance to his remarks.

Hoffman began his article by quoting Secretary of Defense Donald Rumsfeld: "We know we're killing a lot, capturing a lot, collecting arms. . . . We just don't know yet whether that's the same as winning."[22] Hoffman thought that remark "encapsulates the confusion and frustration that plagued U.S. counterinsurgency efforts around the world for more than half a century—most notably in Vietnam, El Salvador, and now Iraq."[23]

That is a long learning period, and, as Hoffman implies, we should have learned something about how to carry out counterinsurgency efforts effectively. But if we haven't learned, Hoffman, surprisingly, notes that the *insurgents* have. He states, "Guerrilla groups and terrorist organizations, on the other hand, learn very well. They study their own mistakes and the successful operation of their enemies, and they adapt nimbly."[24] He believes that our inability to learn is not due to a general human failure to learn from experience; he thinks guerillas and insurgents don't suffer that inability. Whether that distinction is true or not (I find it to be part of the myth of learning by policymakers), these remarks bear directly on the issue of learning from past experience. *They* learn, but *we* don't. I don't think that is true. Hoffman has only anecdotal evidence. I don't think either party learns, because the learning situation won't permit it. So that brings us to the central issue: Let us suppose all these military people, the formal military of the United States (or the West generally) and also the insurgent and terrorist groups, do *want* to learn from their histories; the psychological question is: can they do it? In short, is the military in any better position to learn from the past than policymakers and academic historians? What would that "better position" be?

One answer to that question comes immediately to mind: the military has better information for learning about their domain than politicians and professors do. That answer raises a new question, however: better information for learning what? After all, there are different things to learn. First and foremost, we need to distinguish between learning *that* and learning *why*. Learning *that* is mainly about learning the facts, as in learning that the Allies won World War II, or that the Allied invasion of France was successful. Learning *why*, however, is far more complicated, because learning "why" entails the search for an explanation. Once we have made this distinction, we can see that the military really doesn't have an advantage over politicians or historians; they may have access to more facts—a debatable point—but they surely face the same difficulties as anyone else when it comes to learning about "why" under irreducible uncertainty.

The "Fog of War"

The barriers to anyone's trying to learn under uncertainty all stem from the irreducible uncertainty of the information in the environment.[25] In the special cases of politicians and military planners, delayed ambiguous feedback is a formidable barrier. It is these two features of warfare that led Clausewitz to create the famous phrase the "fog of war." It is not only irreducible uncertainty in the facts one observes, it is also the irreducible factual ambiguity of their causes, and the uncertainty and ambiguity associated with the delayed feedback from actions taken in a chaotic environment—all of which combine to make it impossible to learn what led to what with any useful degree of certainty. For an excellent example of the "fog of war" in contemporary terms, see the first chapter of *The 9/11 Commission Report* describing the confusion in the military and aviation centers upon hearing of the attacks.[26]

Does the Practice of Science Drive Out Intuition?

Since science is a practice that relies entirely on the analytical treatment of agreed-upon facts, one would expect scientists—particularly physical scientists—to be indifferent to claims about the power of intuition. Curiously, however, physical scientists seem much more proud of their intuitive abilities than of their analytical abilities. Indeed, the more sophisticated the scientist, the more likely we are to find praise for intuition. For example, here is Freeman Dyson, a renowned physicist, explaining in the magazine *Nature,* how "it was Fermi's intuition, and not any discrepancy between theory and experiment, that saved me and my students from getting stuck in a blind alley."[27] Dyson, of course, assumes that everybody knows just what he means by "intuition" in that passage, but do they? Perhaps not, but Dyson knows what he means, for when Dyson was queried about this by a colleague of mine, he was gracious enough to reply,

> Of course, I mean by physical intuition the same kind of ability that chess grandmasters have to grasp in a moment the essence of a complicated situation. This is an ability that requires both an inborn talent and a long-continued intensive training. It has not much to do with analysis. It comes from experience rather than from analysis. Yours sincerely, Freeman Dyson.[28]

Crisp as that reply is, it is not the reply that most cognitive psychologists, or other students of intuition, would give. Be that as it may, we can see from that exchange how central the concept of intuition is and how easily its meaning is taken for granted, even among those who should know better.

Dyson was also enamored of the intuitive powers of the great physicist Richard Feynman and provides us with graphic descriptions of Feynman at work. For example:

The reason Dick's physics was so hard for ordinary people to grasp was that he did not use equations. The usual way theoretical physics was done since the time of Newton was to begin by writing down some equations and then to work hard calculating solutions of the equations. This was the way Hans and Oppy and Julian Schwinger did physics. Dick just wrote down the solutions out of his head without ever writing down the equations. He had a physical picture of the way things happen, and the picture gave him the solutions directly, with a minimum of calculation. It was no wonder that people who had spent their lives solving equations were baffled by him.[29]

All these implications for the special use of mysterious powers, however, can be reduced to paying attention to Hans Reichenbach's admonition in 1938 to distinguish, as he put it, between the "context of discovery," which freely makes use of intuitive cognition, and the "context of verification," which demands analytical cognition.[30] With that distinction in mind, we need no further confusing remarks about mysteries, other than to say that while discovery remains largely mysterious, that is a problem for psychologists, not methodologists, to solve. Nevertheless, we can be grateful to astute observers such as Freeman Dyson for pointing out to us the critical role of intuition in the "context of discovery."

We can also be grateful to Dyson for his description of Feynman's use of diagrams rather than equations, for we can now see how Brunswik used comparable tactics in his efforts to move psychologists from the theme of physicalism to the theme of ecology (as described in chapter 15). The "lens model" diagram of judgment, based on Brunswik's principle of probabilistic functionalism, serves much the same purpose for psychology as Feynman's diagrams did for physics. These diagrams literally provided a new way of looking at things. This cognitive similarity among Feynman, Darwin, and Brunswik in their use of diagrams— essentially the use of pictures—to introduce a comprehensive, revolutionary idea demonstrates the power of *visual coherence* to provide conceptual coherence, which is what a comprehensive, revolutionary idea presents. That is probably why those early humans chose to paint animals in the caves in what is now France; painting them made them whole in a way words could not, as Gestalt psychologists would like to remind us, and as artists do remind us today.

Analysis

Seeking Empirical Accuracy the Hard Way

The slow, hard, highly defensible way to reach a judgment—whether in the correspondence or coherence strategy—is to be analytical. Analysis is hard because it demands that you know how to reason and that you know how to be explicit about your reasoning so that you can defend that reasoning, in terms of both logic and substantive knowledge. In short, you have to think, slowly and carefully: this is *not* intuition; it is its opposite.

It helps if you know how to do it. And you will know how to do it only if you have been taught how to do it. That's why they have university courses that teach you how to do it. (Note that there are no courses in "intuition.") No mystery is allowed in the analytical process; indeed, that is the purpose of analysis, to drive out the mystery that Dr. Groopman not only accepts but praises. In contrast to Dr. Groopman, Alan Greenspan offers a good example of the use of analysis within the correspondence strategy when he explains why he believes an interest rate change is or is not appropriate. He mentions each of the indicators he has taken into consideration, often describes how much weight he is giving to each, and adds them up. Thus, he does explicitly what Dr. Groopman does implicitly, and that makes his judgment process available for review and criticism, although, of course, his predictions may be in error. Nevertheless, we know how he reached his judgment, and that means that there is a possibility of improvement, always absent from the opaque process Dr. Groopman uses.

Analysis is slow (in contrast with the rapidity of intuition) because it involves step-by-step reasoning, demands careful review, and assumes your reasoning will be checked—if not by you, by someone—because, unlike intuition, analytical cognition must be retraceable, and usually is retraced by someone who wants to be certain about the answer. And because you have been analytical, you will be able to provide a specific answer to a request for defense of a judgment (e.g., "first I considered this, then that, etc., and I did that because . . ."). That ability to retrace your judgment will serve you well, provided your reasoning process can stand up to criticism; it will be embarrassing if it doesn't.

If you are a weather forecaster, those depending on you want accuracy; that is what you are paid for. But accuracy is all they are interested in. If you forecast "rain," they are interested only in whether it does in fact rain; your reasoning for why it will rain will be of little interest to anyone except other forecasters. And because you are a professional, you have to be accountable. That is, you have to be able to retrace your cognitive activity for your peers, and in order to do that, you have to know what you are doing when you do it. You should at least be able to give a clear account of the steps you took, the information you used, and why you used that information and not some other information. In general, modern professional forecasters of any variety—meteorologists, economists, physicians—are expected to be analytical, and thus accountable and subject to criticism. Despite Dr. Groopman's urging, fewer and fewer professionals, including politicians, get away with relying on their intuition.

Analytical cognitive processes are the bedrock of science and the tools of scientists. Not only do they make it possible for scientists to pursue the logical consequences of their theories and hypotheses, and thus, perhaps, discover new possibilities, they make it possible to convey the entirety of their thinking. The whole purpose of such analytical processes is to leave no ambiguities.

Analytical judgments are often made in the political realm, both national and international. Usually one selects certain indicators and argues that the indicators show that a section of the country or a nation will take a certain path unless they observe the author's advice. Here is an example from a well-known columnist at *The New York Times,* Thomas L. Friedman, who writes on international affairs. In his November 20, 2001, column, he contrasted Pakistan and Bangladesh, both of which are Muslim countries. Pakistan, however, at the time of his column was strongly committed to Osama bin Laden and strongly anti-American, while Bangladesh was not. Friedman made use of fallible indicators to explain:

> Over the last ten years . . . Bangladesh has had three democratic trans-
> fers of power, in two of which . . . Muslim women were elected prime

ministers. Result: All the economic and social indicators in Bangladesh have been pointing upward lately, and Bangladeshis are not preoccupied with hating America. Meanwhile in Pakistan, trapped in the circle of bin Ladenism—military dictatorship, poverty, and antimodernist Islamic schools, all reinforcing each other—the social indicators are all pointing down and hostility toward America is rife.[1]

Notice how Friedman bases his case on the use of fallible indicators; there is no coherent theory of international relations that will allow him to make this comparison: he simply notes the indicators (possibly selectively) and draws the obvious conclusion that it is democracy that makes the difference. Thus he finds, "It's democracy, stupid!"[2]

The main characteristics of analytical judgment are that it is a slow process, (which gives rise to the expression of "analysis paralysis") that is highly controllable and retraceable, and the person using it must be keenly aware of the steps being taken. All these attributes make analysis one of our most valuable cognitive activities.

The Risks of Rational Analytical Thought

The person using analysis is not, however, always aware that its fragility makes it a dangerous, if effective, process. That is, analytical judgments (especially those based on mathematics) are generally exactly right, if done exactly right, but when they are done wrong, they are usually terribly wrong, as I point out in chapter 20. It was Secretary of Defense Robert McNamara, known for his strong advocacy of analytical judgments, who in his memoirs made the risk of error very clear when he declared that, as a result of his analytical work regarding Vietnam, 58,000 American youths were dead, thousands more were wounded, and countless Vietnamese were dead or wounded. He stated that "we were wrong, we were terribly wrong." The nation seemed to agree with that evaluation.

Analytically based judgments are usually right, but when they are done hastily, or are misapplied by novices, they are frequently wrong. And when there are errors, they often lead to catastrophes, some of which are extreme indeed. The American bombing of the Chinese embassy in Yugoslavia is perhaps the best example of an analytical error that was so bad it defies belief. Here is an action—sending a huge bomb capable of great destruction—that one would have expected leaders to undertake only after careful consideration. In fact, in all likelihood the decision to take this action did involve the greatest care and (analytical) thought. But the bomb was sent in error because the map used to ascertain the coordinates of the intended target was out of date. That is typical of analytical error: a perfectly correct system is used perfectly incorrectly. Yet as the information base becomes more digitized, that is, develops more of an "on or off " character (this map or that one), a greater number of analytically based extreme errors (doing exactly the right thing in exactly the wrong manner) are more likely to occur.

There is still a school of thought within the judgment and decision-making field that accepts as legitimate only judgments that are based on analytical tactics; they scorn judgments based on intuitive tactics. (I am not a member.) Members of this school of thought, however, seldom if ever consider the different types of errors generated by each tactic (infrequent but large in the case of analytical tactics, frequent but rarely large in the case of intuition-based tactics). Further, this school seldom considers vulnerability to disruption: analytically based tactics are more vulnerable to disruption, whereas intuition-based tactics are less vulnerable. I am of the view expressed so well by the historian Jacques Barzun: "Wisdom lies not in choosing between [intuition and analysis] but in knowing their place and limits."[3]

Terrorism and the Vulnerability of Analytical, Coherent Systems

The age of terrorism has given new meaning to the fragility and vulnerability of coherent, analytical systems. But we have been oblivious to the fact that such systems are vulnerable to disruption by enemies. The electrical power grid of the United States is one of the great achievements of coherent thought, as is the air traffic control system, the system for distributing natural gas, and, indeed, almost every system invented by human beings since World War II. That period seemed to mark a time when systems took hold of our imagination, and, we can now see that *system* really refers to a "coherent, analytical system." Once systematization became not only the goal but the standard for distributing required natural resources such as gas, electricity, water, and the like, *system* meant that the system should be analytically perfect. What we failed to realize—because we were not then under threat—is that coherent analytical systems are fragile, and that fragility means that the system is readily vulnerable to attack precisely because of its coherence; rupture the coherence, and the system—generally the complete system—comes down. Furthermore, anyone familiar with any coherent, analytical system and its content can position himself or herself to rupture the system; learning about one specific system merely requires learning about the details.

That is why adolescents can break into important systems that control gas, water, or electrical systems, and even military and financial systems. For example, in 1998, a 12-year-old hacker, exploring on a lark, broke into the computer system that runs Arizona's Roosevelt Dam. He did not know or care, but federal authorities said he had complete command of the system controlling the dam's massive floodgates. *The Washington Post*'s Barton Gellman made this disturbing observation:

> Unsettling signs of al Qaeda's aims and skills in cyberspace have led some government experts to conclude that terrorists are at the threshold of using the Internet as a direct instrument of bloodshed. The new threat bears little resemblance to familiar financial disruptions by hackers responsible for viruses and worms. It comes instead at the meeting points between computers and the physical structures they control.[4]

So the even-handed, empirical evaluation of, and restraint on, reasoning goes back to the middle of the twentieth century, to Brunswik's empirical demonstration of the properties of both intuitive perception and reasoning, and also the assets and liabilities of each, together with an explanation of the source of these assets and liabilities. It is probably true that this small demonstration marks the first scientific treatment of this age-old process of checks and balances. Nor was Brunswik's emphasis on the "drastic" errors of reasoning a mere academic exercise; it can easily seen in a wide variety of contexts—the marketplace, for example.

Drastic Errors in the Marketplace

One of the most intriguing and visible attempts to combine the analytical tactic and coherence strategy with the correspondence strategy—to treat them as partners—can be seen in the efforts of the brainy principals of one money-management fund (Long-Term Capital Management) to make themselves super-rich. They were going to achieve this much sought-after goal by applying the principles of (coherent) probability theory to the (apparently incoherent) behavior of the financial markets in a new and different way. And at first it certainly looked as if they might bring it off. There was every reason to believe in the cognitive competence of the fund's management; it included two Ph.D. economists who had won the Nobel Prize for work on exactly this kind of problem. Could there be better grounds for belief? And the first few years of the effort saw spectacular success. The predictions of their mathematical model were backed by hundreds of millions of dollars. (Because the events they were betting on involved only tiny discrepancies between buying prices and selling prices, to make it worthwhile the bets would have had to be huge ones, and they were.)

Success came immediately. The gross value of one dollar invested in the fund in 1994 grew to more than four dollars (i.e., the value of the fund had quadrupled). Unhappily for the investors, by 1998 it had crashed to a value of less than 50 cents. The original investment was now worth only half its original value. That is a spectacular loss, surely the result of a "drastic error." This crash was spectacular, not only because it involved the loss of several billions of dollars of investors' money, but also because the crash was on the brink of escalating into a national disaster prevented only by the extraordinary combined resources of the many Wall Street banks that rescued the fund. How could smart guys like this make such a catastrophic mistake in judgment? It couldn't have been ignorance, and it wasn't Enron-like accounting or other evil doing: so, what was it?

Roger Lowenstein tells the story of this fascinating series of events in *When Genius Failed: The Rise and Fall of Long-Term Capital Management.*[5] That story is of particular interest to us because of the reason this fund failed: it was not because of a failure of competent cognitive activity. The managers did not suffer a sudden loss of "genius": they were just as smart the day after the fund's failure as they had been day before; their test scores would have been the same. Nor were they careless—they did not make any mistakes in mathematics, data management, or the like. They were doing what they routinely did, and the system was doing what it routinely did. And no one believes that they tried to use phony accounting. The fund failed not because of the managers' ignorance or stupidity but because of their complete, but incorrect, commitment to the infallibility of their coherent judgment system. Failure was thought to be so improbable that it could be ignored. (Possibly, they forgot Sir Ronald Fisher's remark that "the improbable is inevitable.")

But the improbable is exactly what happened to the Nobel Prize winners. They treated the bond market much as the owners of the casino treat their gaming tables, and sure enough, the market behaved as they expected—for a while. And those associated with the endeavor became very rich indeed, for a while. But then in 1998 the improbable occurred: the Russian economy collapsed. The Russians defaulted on their loans, an unthinkable event—at least to the managers of the Long-Term Capital Management; it was not included in their theory of the behavior of the bond market. The managers' belief in the infallibility of their system was to prove expensive for a lot of people.

Rigid Adherence to a Coherent Belief System

This episode also teaches us something about coherence and information. For surely the managers had as much information as anyone about the shaky state of the Russian economy; they simply refused to believe that it would default on its bonds. Why? Because, Lowenstein tells us, they were convinced that "nuclear powers do not default." And that illustrates another very important danger of committing to the goal of coherence; when fully committed, as these managers were, one tends to ignore information that does not fit one's coherent view. The information is rejected because you "know" it is somehow false or irrelevant. It must be so; otherwise, the coherence of your judgment disappears because of the information that does not fit. Rejecting information that others who are not so committed to a particular belief accept as genuine and relevant permits us to apply the term *fanatic* (a fanatic being doctrinaire or dogmatic) to those who reject it. That is, a fanatic is a person so convinced of the truth of his or her view that he or she literally cannot imagine its falsity. Persons so strongly in the grip of coherence are often accused of being stupid, but they are not. Indeed, as we see from this example, even persons brilliant enough to win the Nobel Prize can become victims of beliefs or judgments strongly grounded in coherence that turn out to be wrong.

Do all heavy traders on Wall Street depend so much on coherence? No, they do not. In fact, George Soros, who has been called one of the greatest currency speculators and is one of the richest players in the financial markets, thought that the Long-Term traders were foolish to place so much faith in the unbending coherence of statistical logic. When Long-Term traders came to him for help as their fund was spinning out of control, Lowenstein reports that Soros said, "The idea that you have a bell curve is false. You have outlying phenomena that you can't anticipate on the basis of past experience."[6] So he kept his money and didn't help out.

Was it irrational of the Long-Term traders to ignore the possibility of a Russian default? No, they could have given you a perfectly coherent explanation of why they were prepared to ignore this possibility. It simply would have been empirically wrong, although their argument would have been totally coherent. For it is possible to have entirely coherent theories that turn out to be empirically wrong. One might say that the managers of Long-Term Capital were ignoring the *dangers* of explicit logical operations, and thus lacked wisdom.

George Soros Requires Both

In reviewing a book by George Soros, Robert Skidelsky, a well-known economist and author, comes to grips with the relation between coherence and correspondence when he states,

> Some philosophers, faced with the difficulty of making true statements about the world, have concluded that truth is a matter of logical coherence rather than correspondence with the facts. Soros rejects

this solution. He adopts what might be called a loose version of the correspondence theory of truth; reality does in the end impose some limit on what can be truthfully believed, but there is plenty of play for . . . the gestation and persistence of false beliefs.[7]

What this comes down to is that Soros—who made his money (lots of it) in the financial markets—argues that it is not enough to depend on the coherence strategy alone; one must test the theory or model against the specific empirical facts of interest. However, the uncertainty or ambiguity between theory and fact is usually sufficient to allow empirically false theories and models to live a long life. Although that can hardly be doubted, it will serve the reader well if she or he keeps in mind this fundamental difference in these two strategies, observes how they are being employed, and takes seriously the ambiguity that allows satisfactorily coherent but empirically false information to live a protected life. (I will come back to this in chapter 20 in my discussion of wisdom.)

Although Soros's knowledge about the application of the normal probability distribution was certainly useful information for him, it did not prevent his fund from losing almost as much money as the Long-Term Capital Management Fund; his fund lost $2 billion! His enormous profits prior to the fall indicate that giving up the normal curve as a model for the behavior of the market (while the Nobelists were depending on it) was a financial benefit—he became one of the richest men in the world. But life in the financial world is never simple. Relinquishing that model created another problem: predicting the occurrence of those outlying phenomena, those unanticipated events (Enron, WorldCom, etc.) that shock the market. That is, he had to go beyond acknowledging the existence of unanticipated events and actually anticipate them. He failed at this, and that is what cost his fund $2 billion. The problem was—as it always is—finding the model to use in place of the normal probability curve that would incorporate such events as the fall of the ruble. Is there such a model? Perhaps not. Turn to common sense, that "in-between" process? Soros would simply depend on his—or his expert's—judgments of the relevance of information about day-to-day events, and buy or sell accordingly. If so, that "commonsense" strategy failed as badly as did the strategy of ignoring those outlying phenomena.[8]

Does Learning Occur?

So, what did the principals of Long-Term Capital do next? What did they learn from this experience? They had received obvious, unambiguous feedback that told them that their belief system was wrong. That system may have been coherent, but it did not correspond with the facts of the market. There was no doubt about that. So, did they say, "George Soros is right: we should not put our trust in mathematical models based on the normal probability distribution; such models are subject to the vicissitudes of 'outlying phenomena' that are perhaps not present in the model"? No, they did not. Before long, they had a new model at work in the market.

So what did the investors learn? Not to trust genius? Not to trust mathematical models? No, they did not. Roger Lowenstein probably has given this matter more thought than anyone, and he knew what should be learned by everyone; he believes that all concerned should heed Merrill Lynch, which cautions that mathematical models "may provide a greater sense of security than warranted; therefore, reliance on these should be limited." That satisfied Lowenstein; he said, "If Wall St. is to learn just one lesson from the Long-Term debacle, it should be that."[9]

But how could a sophisticated person like Lowenstein be satisfied with such a mealy-mouthed recommendation? Does he really believe that one can learn from such a tentative, weasel-word admonition? What does *may* mean: maybe you can trust such models, but maybe you can't? Why does he think we are looking for a "sense of security" rather than a return on investment? And "warranted"? Who is to decide how much of a sense of security is "warranted"? Why didn't he demand that Merrill Lynch give us some quantitative information, such as the probability of the failure of a mathematical model (in terms of its relative frequency)? That would clarify what is "warranted." Merrill Lynch didn't do that because it couldn't.

Instead we get a useless platitude that, surprisingly, Lowenstein swallowed. Of course, no one learns from useless platitudes. So, in November 1999, after losing $4.5 billion, the principals of Long-Term were back in business. They used the same fuzzy, have-it-both-ways language that Merrill Lynch did, and according to Lowenstein, "raised 250 million [dollars], much of it from former investors in Long-Term Capital"![10] (Discussions about the probabilistic nature of financial forecasting continue; on October 1, 2005, *The New York Times* carried a column by Joseph Nocera that was sharply critical of Nassim Nicholas Taleb's best-selling book *Fooled by Randomness: The Hidden Role of Chance in Life and the Markets*.[11] Taleb takes up the place of randomness and our failure to incorporate it in our judgments and uses the Long-Term Capital disaster as an example. Nocera says this book was translated into "more than a dozen languages, and has sold around 100,000 copies.")

A cautionary note regarding errors of judgment: although it is true that analytical cognitive processes are apt to produce infrequent but drastic errors, and intuitive cognitive processes are apt to produce more frequent but small errors, we need to take into account—as always—the nature of the context in which the judgment is made. For intuitive judgments can also lead to drastic error. A graphic example can be seen in the case of a crash of the Staten Island ferry in New York Harbor. After the collision, it was revealed that the ferry pilots had no instruments—no analytical methods—for measuring its speed; instead, they had to rely on their intuitive judgment of its speed.

That tragic incident and the pilots' cognitive activity bring to mind an incident of roughly 150 years ago, when Mark Twain was a trainee riverboat pilot on the Mississippi. In the days before riverboats commonly used navigational aids—infallible indicators that replaced the fallible indicators Twain had to learn to use—Twain was told by his instructor that he would have to learn to use his intuition for a number of important tasks. When Twain queried the instructor as to how he could learn to do this, he was told, "by and by you will just naturally know." Twain's instructor apparently meant "trial and error." Twain did learn to pilot the riverboat more or less safely using his intuitive cognitive skills, but errors on the river could be extremely costly. Ultimately, the cost was too high, and navigational aids were installed. In today's engineered waterways, filled with traffic and navigational aids, pilots have equipment that provides infallible information such as buoy markers and speedometers, which they would learn to use analytically.

But the pilot of the ferry *John F. Kennedy* that "coasted into the side of the dock" in New York in the twenty-first century was not so different from Mark Twain's pilot instructor in the nineteenth. When he was asked to explain his actions at the helm, "[he] could not, saying that 'past practice' was his only guide," for he had "no speed indicator whatever."[12] In short, he was relying on his intuitive skills to estimate the speed of the ferry, just as his predecessors in the nineteenth century had relied on theirs. Unhappily, on this occasion, his intuitive skills did not serve him (or his passengers) well. Nevertheless, the captain said, "I'm 20 years with the system; I work like that . . . I don't want to change anything."

The latter comment is often heard after an intuition-induced accident; intuition seems to define us, and changing that seems tantamount to changing us.

12

Intuition

Seeking Rationality the Easy Way

There has always been tension between two major theories of cognitive activity. One theory, described in chapter 3, proposes that cognition works by aggregating information in a linear way, that is, by seeking surface indicators of depth information and simply adding or averaging their values. This process is known as the "linear model," and there is little doubt that *Homo sapiens* and many other animals, birds, and insects do just that. There are three important research questions about this process: Under what conditions does it occur? What are the consequences? What parts of the brain are involved in that activity? We already know the answer to the first question: This sort of activity happens in a very wide variety of circumstances. Progress is being made with regard to the second and third questions.[1]

However confident we may have become with respect to the ubiquitous character of the "linear model," psychologists have also known for nearly a century that cognition works in other ways as well. The most prominent science-based alternative was provided by the Gestalt psychologists as far back as the early part of the twentieth century. They discovered that when we perceive physical objects, we unconsciously seek coherence—and find it, whether it's there or not! Because they were German, they called such coherent intuitive perceptions *Gestalts*. Anyone who has ever opened an introductory psychology textbook has without doubt found a lot of it devoted to Gestalt psychology. The big discovery was that it was one's intention to perceive a gestalt that often led to perceptual illusions. The Gestalt psychologists became masters at creating figures that induced visual illusions that are rather fascinating. The textbooks present numerous perceptual illusions—involving symmetrical objects such as circles, parallelograms, cubes, and so on—that were the favorites of the Berlin psychologists (almost all of whom were driven out or killed by Hitler).

The important point for us is that the illusions, which attracted so much attention, are errors (for example, seeing incomplete figures as complete), and these errors are caused by our urge to see a figure (a circle, a square) as coherent (complete or perfect) even if it is in fact incoherent (incomplete or imperfect). An illusion of this sort is a positive error; it is an error toward coherence and away from the actual deviations from coherence present in the object shown. The Gestalt psychologists showed beyond doubt that the urge to create such coherence from incoherence "just comes naturally"; that is, it occurs without effort, and we are unaware of how, and often unaware of when, it occurs. Thus, seeing these illusions (errors) toward coherence—seeing coherence when it isn't there—is a cognitive activity generally beyond our control, and such illusions are hard to avoid, even when we know better. Indeed, if we didn't read that chapter about Gestalt psychology in the introductory textbook, we wouldn't be aware of most of these illusions. That suggests that the urge to see coherence, even when it isn't there, is "built in" to our nervous system—just as the linear model is—and prompts the neuroscientists to seek the neural correlates of that activity. And because the illusory effect is so strong and so hard to eliminate, it can be argued that the urge to seek coherence is a product of evolution; it is a part of our biological history.[2]

The Gestalt psychologists tried to extend their ideas beyond visual perception; they argued that those erroneous intuitive judgments of coherence were not limited to visual perception but are part of a general tendency to seek coherence; it is part of the "whole of experience." For example, it frequently occurs in memory, a phenomenon often described as "selective remembering" (and thus parallel to selective perception) to provide a coherent picture of the past. And it is essentially what we mean by "social stereotyping" (assigning features to a person that we think "ought to be there" in order to preserve coherence). These are important social phenomena, examples of which can be found in your newspaper almost every day.

Indeed, famous students of judgment and decision making would later refer to "cognitive illusions" to describe errors of judgment such as "confirmation bias," which is discussed below. Gestalt psychology never worked out a coherent general theory of its own that gained acceptance, however; as a result, it remains fragmented and limited to curiosities, such as those represented by perceptual illusions. Nevertheless, serious students of conceptual coherence, for example, Paul Thagard, still rely on Gestalt psychology for a point of departure.[3]

A Coherent View of Uncertainty

Mathematical theories are of course coherent; they have been proven to be so by virtue of the hard analytical labor that went into producing them. The essential strength of mathematics lies in coherence. And the theory of probabilistic relations has been worked out over the past 200 years or so into set of widely known theorems and rules. But since we apply probabilistic judgments frequently, it is not surprising that some cognitive psychologists (particularly those with a good knowledge of mathematical statistics) wonder if we humans actually follow those analytically established rules—intuitively—when we make probability judgments. For example, they wondered if, when a person says, "I think there is a high probability of rain," or when the doctor says, "I believe that the probability she has pneumonia is very high," or when a president declares, "There is a high probability that the enemy possesses weapons of mass destruction," the person was making the same calculations a statistician does when he or she declares that there is a certain probability that an event will occur. It would be quite wonderful if we could indeed, without any training in, or knowledge of, mathematical statistics intuitively match the product of the analytical work that led to the laws of probability. Can we? Put that way, it seems doubtful, yet nearly everyone assumes that we can make this match when they express a probability in relation to a problem that requires such calculations. But, of course, untrained people won't know which problems do require mathematical treatment—coherence—and which don't; we learn that from this book, and it is the next topic.

Coherence in Probability Judgments

In the 1970s, two psychologists, Amos Tversky and Daniel Kahneman, set out to discover just how good—that is, how coherent—are the processes that lead to our intuitive probability judgments.[4] They used a simple method in all their studies; it involved setting up a problem requiring a simple calculation (e.g., what is the joint probability of x and y?) using everyday materials, then they gave the same problem to untrained individuals and checked to see if their answers were the same as the one derived by calculation; they were not. This result held true over a wide variety of problems, content, and persons. Few, if any, persons ever got the right (calculated) answer to any problem by intuitive means; sometimes the answers were wildly wrong, and sometimes quite close to the accurate one. Since the calculated answer provides the criterion for accuracy, they concluded that our intuitive search for coherence is not as competent as our intuitive search for correspondence. Inaccuracy, it was claimed, was due to the subjects' implicit, incoherent calculations of probabilities.

This was no small claim, and it is this claim, or "discovery," that led to Kahneman's receiving the Nobel Prize in economics. But since it is this conclusion that Gigerenzer and his colleagues strongly contest, we need to review our procedure for ascertaining intuitive competence in the search for coherence.

First, note that justification for asserting that the calculated answer is the correct one, and that the subjective answer is wrong, rests on the coherence of a mathematical argument. (No contradictory statements will be permitted.) If our intuitive judgments don't match the calculated ones, then they fail the coherence test, and we can conclude that we are observing a less-than-competent intuitive process.

Since we are dealing with intuitive cognition, however, and intuitive cognition by definition is nonretraceable, we can't ask that a person be accurate or competent in retracing or describing their cognitive activity. But it is important to recognize—and researchers have not always recognized—that we do have different criteria for evaluating the competence of intuitive coherence-seeking judgments and the competence of intuitive correspondence-seeking judgments; the criterion for the accuracy of intuitive coherence-seeking judgments is the analytically derived judgment (that provided by mathematical proof). Note that we can't compare the intuitive cognitive process with the analytical process (the mathematics) to discover if it is the same as the analytical one because no one, not even the subject, knows what the intuitive cognitive process is. And matching answers won't tell us whether the processes are the same. That is, if the answers given by the subject match the calculated answer, we still could not conclude that the subject used the same process as the calculation did.

This is an important point, and worth an example. Imagine trying to figure out what is in a watch makes it work. Suppose that someone suggests it works because it has an hourglass inside to tell time. By offering the hourglass as a hypothetical model of the process, and then comparing the elapsed time indicated by the watch and that given by the hourglass, we can see whether the elapsed times match. Suppose they do, as they normally will; would it be proper to decide that what makes the watch work is a little hourglass inside the watch? It is easy to say no to that explanation because of the incongruity of the materials; we know there is no hourglass inside the watch case. But it is a common error to conclude that if a hypothetical model provides the same outcome, or answer, as does the mechanism one is trying to model, one has hit on the correct hypothetical model for the process.

This error is committed even by engineers making critical decisions about the validity of models for important environmental decisions. For example, the U.S. Department of Energy explained in a report that "a common method of verification is the comparison of a [computer] code's results with the results obtained analytically."[5] That is an exact parallel to comparing the time given by a watch and an hourglass and thus verifying the hourglass as a correct model of the mechanics of a watch.

Researchers in cognitive psychology are aware of this distinction and have taken the position that only the competence—not the process—of intuitive coherence-seeking cognition can be evaluated by comparing the answers provided by intuition and those provided by calculation. That means that if the intuitive answer does not match the mathematical one, it is wrong; thus the psychologists' finding that, since their subjects' answers did not match the mathematical answers, this meant that people's intuitive (coherence) judgments were wrong. I have no quarrel with that conclusion. (It is essentially Karl Popper's method of falsification.[6])

Should we accept the conclusion that our intuitive probability judgments that seek coherence are incompetent?

First, we need to ask how we are to know when a coherence judgment is required of us and when we should seek coherence. A coherence judgment is required when there is no empirical criterion for evaluating the accuracy of a subject's judgment. Absent an empirical criterion, we ask the subject to justify his or her judgment. ("Explain your answer!") That is a very practical and important requirement, and one will have to provide such justification many times a day in most offices—people would ask for justification even more often if not for their politeness. But it is a critical issue in important cases. When the judgment was made to drop the atomic bomb on Hiroshima, there was no empirical criterion whereby the correctness of that judgment could be determined; those who argued for or against that history-making act had to appeal to an argument for dropping or not dropping that weapon. The critical feature of that argument was its coherence. Not unexpectedly, the correctness of that decision is still being debated a half century later.

A similar situation developed when the justification of the judgment to invade Iraq was left to Secretary of State Colin Powell in his address to the UN Security Council on February 5, 2003. But Powell's speech was a muddle of both coherence seeking and correspondence seeking; the fact that it was a muddle became apparent when he made his emotional appeal for acquiescence. And, of course, it later became apparent, and widely acknowledged, that the data he offered were badly flawed. As Powell himself said on NBC's *Meet the Press*, "Some of the sources were weak, some of the sources didn't hold up. They failed. And some parts of the intelligence community knew that some of these sources probably shouldn't have been listened to."[7]

Historians may someday use this speech as an example of exceedingly poor form combined with exceedingly flawed substance in relation to one of the most important questions of the day. Students of judgment and decision making may use this episode to demonstrate the need for professional and scientific participation in the defense of critical judgments.

A further possibility is that we are incompetent in achieving intuitive coherence in our cognitive processes in probabilistic judgments even if we are given dependable information. It now seems clear to many that people cannot intuitively reproduce such coherent equations as those in the probability calculus that is used to calculate the answers to the problems the researchers put to their naive subjects. Yet it now seems somewhat naive of the researchers (and certainly of the economists) to imagine that people would have such intuitive competence. After all, it was only about 200 years ago that mathematicians worked out these equations. Does this difference between what our intuition tells us and what the equations tell us make a difference to anyone but the researchers? Yes, indeed: people are still naively offering intuitive probabilistic judgments in situations in which it is possible to calculate the probabilities. It is a part of the attraction of sports that careful records are kept that allow statistical analysis. As might be expected, people are often insulted to be told they are wrong, and further insulted when they are told they can't make such judgments competently, especially when they think have been doing so for a long time; it is taken as a slur on their capacities for wisdom. But we must remember that these errors are made with respect to coherence and say nothing about empirical correctness. (Curiously, people are not offended if they are told that their intuitive empirical estimates—of the height of a tree, for example—are wrong. Yet such estimates are usually reasonably accurate! No one says a tree that is 2 feet tall is 50 feet tall, or vice versa, even under ambiguous visual conditions.)

In short, when extending these research results to circumstances other than straightforward calculation problems that one might find in a textbook, we should be very aware of the context of the information given, and also very aware of the task—that is, achieving coherence or empirical correctness. There will be many occasions when we should consider the possibility of the application of these findings, and a consultant will help. But we should remember that it is essential that we first separate coherence problems from correspondence problems (a step academics have often failed to take).

This separation can often be made simply by looking at the person's function or role in the organization in which they work. For example, the troops in the field or the workers in a factory generally make correspondence judgments; these will be focused on empirical objects and events rather than plans. Officers or supervisors, however, generally make judgments based on plans or policies, and these generally demand coherence in cognitive activity. Officers and supervisors can usually explain their judgments, whereas troops or workers generally answer in terms of the empirical success of their efforts. Thus, we ask for different types of cognitive competence from each type of function; the troops and the factory workers must be correspondence competent, and the officers and managers must be coherence competent. Consequently, researchers should supply different types of information for each type of function in the organization. This will be accomplished only when researchers become more adept at making this distinction.

Political Judgments: How Intuitive Efforts Can Lead to Romanticism

Earlier, I addressed the question of the use of intuitive cognition in pursuit of coherence and noted how the absence of an empirical criterion creates the need for a coherent justification of a judgment. If we cannot appeal to an empirical criterion (the presence or absence of rain when rain is forecasted), then we are driven to seek a rational justification, that is, driven to appeal to a coherent model. But what happens when we have no coherent model to which we can appeal? That question brings us to the matter of political judgments, because most political judgments rest on what is hoped to be coherence.

Does the lack of empirical justification and/or coherence justification leave us speechless? Far from it; although political judgments (usually) lack both types of justification, we seem to have plenty to say about political matters, and usually utter our judgments with great confidence. In order to bring this topic within our general approach to judgment and decision making, I refer again to the topics of romanticism and rationalism (see p. xxii), for it is these grand concepts that hold our ideas together. And lest the reader think I am veering off into a morass of philosophical concepts, I turn next to showing how these two ideas are very useful and practical ones for understanding the current political world.

Romanticism as a Cognitive Theory of Political Judgments

I am not a philosopher, so I begin with the observations of the famous philosopher Isaiah Berlin, who wrote in 1959,

> The disintegrating influence of romanticism, both in the comparatively innocuous form of the chaotic rebellion of the free artist of the nineteenth century and in the sinister and destructive form of totalitarianism, seems, in western Europe at least, to have spent itself."[8]

Let's look carefully at this sentence; it carries a lot of explanatory material not only for developments in the twentieth century, but also for the first war of the twenty-first century, and has a strong connection to our study of cognitive psychology.[9]

First, we should ask what features of romanticism we are talking about. I restrict myself to romanticism's cognitive features, its choice of mode of cognition that: (1) enthusiastically accepts intuition and eschews analysis, (2) embraces poetical interpretation and ignores computation, (3) enlists the aid of the immediacy of the visual while rejecting the time-consuming denotations of science and mathematics, (4) confidently seeks the relationships between abstract ideas, and (5) scorns demands for concreteness and explicit methodologies. Romanticism often relies on the mystical and encourages a dependency on it by utilizing symbols such as flags, songs, and the staging of patriotic and religious events. (It was no accident that astrology played a role in the Reagan administration.) In short, romanticism rejects the rational. Thus, romanticism is a concept with which students of human cognition, particularly judgment and decision making, should be familiar, for romanticism is the philosophers' term for what is here called the intuitive search for coherence in the world around us. Thus, it is not surprising that it finds its place in international relations, a domain in which empirical criteria for our judgments are either ambiguous or altogether lacking, and in which agreement on a functional coherent model has (since the demise of Marxism) been conspicuously absent. When heads of state reject the role of reason and make strong appeals to our emotions by focusing on such concepts as "freedom," "liberty," "strength," "our shores," "our heritage," and the like in their speeches, while ignoring the complexities on the ground, they are following the path of romanticism.[10]

Adolf Hitler carried profane romanticism to its bitter and hideous end in the 1930s and 1940s, and Isaiah Berlin had Hitler's fascism in mind when he referred to the "sinister and destructive form of totalitarianism." (I describe the profane form of rationalism in chapter 13.) For it was Hitler's passionate tirades, his parades and many flags, the many songs sung so loudly, the emphasis on blood and on the Aryan mysticism of the *volk,* and the proud encouragement of so much ruthless brutality, that embodied so well the profane form of romanticism. All this is shown in the famous documentary by Leni Riefenstahl, who filmed the Nazi Party rally in 1934, which Louis Menand described so effectively in an article in *The New Yorker.*[11] Menand observed that such demonstrations—and their documentation—do not "speak truth to power" but try "to speak power to truth."[12]

Romanticism's appeal to the emotions carries particular importance for political leaders, for the strong appeal to intuition leaves no room for an appeal to reason; there is no reason in the presentation—one can cheer or curse a flag, but one cannot argue with a flag.

In 1959, however, Berlin believed that this form of romanticism had "spent itself." And in a hopeful note that brings his remarks close to cognitive psychology, he says, "The forces that make for stability and reason are beginning to reassert themselves."[13] With that remark, he suggested we were seeing a shift from the intuitive search for coherence in our world to a more rational cognitive tactic in that search. But are we? It is easy to find disturbing indications of a return to romanticism in George W. Bush's approach to international relations. In his book that describes an interview with President Bush, Bob Woodward quotes the president as saying, "I just think [my judgment is] instinctive. I'm not a textbook player. I'm a gut player."[14] Bush also told Woodward, "I can only go by my instincts."[15] And Condoleezza Rice said her job was to "translate President Bush's instincts into policy."[16]

The recurrent references to relying on one's instincts are certainly reminiscent of the romantics of the early twentieth century. Remarks of this sort, and the good-versus-evil approach Bush takes in his speeches, in addition to the declarations that "you're either with us or against us," are part of a romantic view of the world; they do not reflect the rational view of the complexity of the world introduced by the Enlightenment. The romantic view relies heavily on the intuitive search for a coherent view that considers which problems are important, what makes problems important, and how problems should be solved. It is a view that the rationalists of the last two centuries would have rejected, perhaps scorned, as overly simplistic and impossible to justify other than by an appeal to intuitions and the emotions they arouse.

It may well have been Bush's intuitive search for coherence that encouraged the CIA to offer its flawed intelligence to the president and his advisors. Current searches for explanations of what can only be called a massive failure of information seeking and reporting have focused on personnel ("we need better people") or reorganization of the agency ("the system is broken"). Both miss the point. The failure of the CIA resulted from a lack of understanding of the main operation of the agency, namely, human judgment under uncertainty. Making judgments about physical, behavioral, or cognitive events under great uncertainty is the fundamental job of the agency. That it is good at making these judgments is the reason the agency exists. Of course, other agencies also employ people to make judgments about objects and events under uncertainty (isn't that what the secretary of the treasury does every day?). The difference lies in the greater uncertainty of the data the analyst at the CIA examines compared with the data the analyst at the treasury department examines: virtually every piece of information the CIA examines is subject to deliberate distortion, faulty reporting, or intrinsic uncertainty, and there is no simple mechanism for distinguishing among these. In a large number of cases (all? most? nobody knows how many) the final judgments that wind up in the president's daily brief include irreducible uncertainty.

This is exactly the kind of judgment situation that a "gut player" welcomes (witness the appeal of horse races). Anyone who demands that the "gut player" analytically justify his or her judgments will be disappointed; indeed, those who make such demands will soon learn that requests for justification are not welcome, particularly in a "you are with us or against us" environment. The staff will quickly learn that analytical work in the face of irreducible uncertainty is of no interest to the "gut player." (See, for example, Richard Clarke's memoirs recalling his service as an intelligence advisor to the president.[17]) If it comes down to a question of your "gut" versus the "gut" of the commander-in-chief, there is little doubt which "gut" will make the final judgment.[18]

But micromanagement is the last thing a romanticist is interested in. President Bush's appearance on the flight deck of the *Abraham Lincoln* is exactly what a romanticist appreciates; it was the modern equivalent of flags and songs. What a romanticist wants is an appeal to the "gut," which encourages the use of powerful symbols. Jimmy Carter, on the other hand, eliminated as much fanfare from his office as possible and minimized the rest (no more "Hail to the Chief"; he carried his own suit bag to the helicopter, and he spoke to the nation while wearing a cardigan sweater); slogans were rare.

Changing the Focus to the White House

The reader should note that I have shifted the focus of the discussion from a change at the CIA to a change at the White House, to which the director of the CIA reports. That is, I shifted to a consideration of the recipient of the information, whereas the usual approach is to consider the provider of the information. I do that because it is the cognitive activity of the recipient that is critical. If the recipient is a romanticist—that is, a person using the intuitive tactic to achieve a coherent policy—that person will demand information that best suits that cognitive activity. If, however, the recipient is using analytical tactics to achieve a coherent policy, that person will demand information that best suits that form of cognitive activity. And because the person using the information is in control of the situation, he or she will soon get what is wanted, or there will be a new director of the agency. In short, any attempt to improve communication in a hierarchical situation should begin with the needs and requirements of the user.

13

Analysis
Seeking Rationality the Hard Way

When those requesting your judgment want to know why your judgment is what it is, they will be demanding justification for your judgment. If you are using the correspondence strategy, where judgments are tested against an empirical criterion, you can reply, "Look at my record; it shows that I am right 85% of the time. That is better than any other judgment system you can find." Thus, because you had empirical criteria for your judgments, you had the luxury of being able to measure the accuracy of your judgment directly. That is a comforting situation for all concerned, unless your judgments are so bad that you are ashamed of them—though even in that event, at least you found out how good (or bad) your judgments were. But if you are working within the coherence strategy, and your challengers will not accept your use of the rapid intuitive tactic, life will be far more complicated; your defense of coherence will have to appeal to some rational system. That is, you will have to depend on the explicit coherence of your justification to persuade your challenger. Unfortunately, coherence is difficult to represent by a number, or anything other than a verbal explanation. Someone may say, "Put it in writing!" That means your justification will take time and will (almost always) be resting on the use of language, not numbers, a notoriously ineffective method for this task. Time-honored though they may be, verbal attempts to persuade others of the coherence of your thought do not have a good track record.

If you are fortunate enough to be able to place your judgment problem in a numerical, mathematical framework (and there are several available for this purpose), your justification of your judgment will be transparent, and that will be good—provided that your challengers agree on the appropriateness of your choice of mathematical framework.[1] And your challengers will have to be indifferent to the time that it takes you to reach your judgment, for these procedures often take considerable time and resources.

Unhappily, flaws in reasoning are common; the frequent 5–4 decisions at the Supreme Court suggest that almost half the members of the Court thought that those in the majority were wrong in their reasoning. That leaves us with a strange situation; no one believes that analytical judgments, such as those reached in mathematics or science, should be decided by voting. (There are no votes on the correctness of the proof of a theorem.) A vote is an acknowledgment that the problem remains subject to various interpretations, and, therefore, the true answer is uncertain—buried somewhere. So we know that, in principle, even the most esteemed judgments that claim to be the product of rationality are often found to be wrong, or at least heavily in doubt. Unhappily, we have no "third way"; if our best efforts at rationality lead to competent dispute, we are at the mercy of that dispute. That is why the Supreme Court is composed of an odd number of members; it allows disagreements to be settled by votes, and ties can be broken without resolving the dispute.

This state of affairs should not be surprising. As I pointed out earlier, we have been dealing with coherent systems of thought for only a few thousand years, in contrast with our millions of years using the correspondence strategy. We are relatively new at explicating and resolving differences between coherent systems of thought. No one knows exactly how recently we began trying to be coherent, but the latest estimate suggests that making bone tools (which requires some sort of coherent image of what a specific tool should look like before it is made) dates back to roughly 70,000 years ago. However, for millions of years, our forebears made empirical judgments based on multiple fallible indicators, a process that requires no logical effort. It is hard for human beings to analyze information without committing a logical error because logic is so fragile; one slight mistake and the entire argument fails (the Chinese embassy gets bombed by mistake). Nevertheless, analytical work represents the best cognitive behavior we can muster; when it is appropriate to the problem, it will serve us very well. And we have developed very good methods for finding error and checking judgments, especially when those judgments are susceptible to mathematical examination. But all analytical judgments are vulnerable to the error of using the wrong model perfectly, and this error is often not discovered until it has been made, and (usually) awful consequences have followed. Supreme Court justices may not refer to specific breakdowns in their peers' logic, but law professors who have the competence (and energy) to do so do not hesitate.

Reason: An Aid or Hindrance to Justice?

Earlier, I mentioned that the famed justice Oliver Wendell Holmes, Jr., was well known for his skepticism regarding the place of logic and reason in the administration of the law. Consider his famous sentence in 1881: "The life of the law has not been logic: it has been experience."[2] Holmes was also well known for his sharp negative comments about the place of reason in the administration of the law. Louis Menand, in his splendid history of Holmes's era, *The Metaphysical Club: A Story of Ideas in America,* provides this startling example: "When he was on the Supreme Court, Holmes used to invite his fellow justices, in conference, to name any legal principle they liked, and he would use it to decide the case under consideration *either way* [italics mine]."[3]

Now this is a strange invitation from a Supreme Court justice. Could—or would—a current justice, say, Ruth Bader Ginsberg or Antonin Scalia, try this gambit? It is, in fact, an arrogant expression of Holmes's skepticism regarding logic in the work of the Court. And it is a part of his attitude toward general principles. Menand reports on a letter Holmes wrote to a colleague in 1899 that reads, "But all of the use of life is in specific solutions—which cannot be reached through generalities any more than a picture can be painted by knowing some rules of method. They are reached by insight, tact and specific knowledge." Menand interprets the latter statement thusly: "Even people who think their thinking is guided by general principles, in other words, even people who think thought is deductive, actually think the way everyone else does—by the seat of their pants. First they decide, then they deduce."[4]

But Menand gives the word *experience* too large a task; it is better to rely on Holmes's own explanation of what he meant. He clarifies his meaning in the very next sentence:

> The felt necessities of the time, the prevalent moral and political theories, intuitions of public policy, avowed or unconscious, even the prejudices which judges share with their fellow-men, have had a good deal more to do than the syllogism in determining the rules by which men should be governed. The law embodies the story of a nation's development through many centuries, and it cannot be dealt with as if it contained only the axioms and corollaries of a book of mathematics.[5]

What was Holmes seeking if he did not accept "axioms and corollaries"? Whereas he said that the proper judgments are "reached by insight, tact and specific knowledge," what he should have said is that they are reached by wisdom, because that is what his remarks imply and because that is what he was seeking. At this point, we see the necessity for the use of the concept of wisdom, for rationality continues to fail us.

Not only is the rejection of rigorous, narrow logic becoming more and more apparent, it is now being confirmed by scientific findings. It is no longer a question of whether ordinary humans can intuitively achieve rational judgments of the wholly logical kind, as the rational-expectations economists imagine; it is now more a question of how rationality itself should be defined (irrespective of how it is achieved) and how it should be used. As a result of all this, we are beginning to look at the economists' most distinguishing attribute in a new and uncertain way. The rational expectations view is faltering, but its replacement is not yet a mature theoretical system. Only a clear separation of cognitive strategies from tactics will bring us closer to that replacement.

In our own history, Benjamin Franklin conveyed his impression of his famous contemporary John Adams in a manner that demonstrated an ability to discriminate wisdom from folly. Franklin's biographer, Edmund Morgan, writes,

> Franklin closed his letter [about Adams] with the fairest and most quoted assessment anyone ever made of the character of John Adams: "I am persuaded . . . that he [Adams] means well for his Country, is always an honest Man, often a Wise One, but sometimes and in some things, absolutely out of his senses."[6]

To which I would add: driven, no doubt, by his faith in rational, analytical cognition.

Statistical Solutions

There is an increasing interest in the pursuit of rationality by means of simple statistical reasoning. It has been brought to the public's attention not only by meteorologists but by sports analysts, who gain publicity by their statistical analyses. Because meticulous records are kept of the performance of teams and individuals over long periods of time, it is easy to calculate the relative frequency of various activities (home runs, for example) and then state with confidence the probability that the activity in question will occur. Indeed, any set of records can be examined in the same way, and now that records are electronically stored, such statistical calculations will soon replace all the wisdom of the old pro, whose long experience formerly made him the sport's wise man. I label this the "hard way" to achieve rationality, even though it involves only some simple knowledge of statistics, because most people are averse to learning statistics and will consider it hard to do.

Moving on from simple relative-frequency statistics to more complex procedures will bring an encounter with fairly difficult ideas. Although it was invented in the seventeenth century, one such procedure, called Bayes's theorem, is now becoming widely used. This theorem invites the participant to express his or her probabilities of the likelihood of events at the outset and then incorporates this information with new information about the task. It is this mathematical integration of data that provides the coherence people seek. Unhappily, Bayes's theorem is not the kind of procedure that amateurs can readily use, and thus gaining coherence through analytical procedures remains difficult, and few nonprofessionals can manage it.

Profane Rationalism

In chapter 12, I discussed profane romanticism, rationality's opposite; indicated its abuse by Adolf Hitler in the twentieth century; and suggested that there were signs of the reappearance of romanticism in the twenty-first century. So, it would be natural to ask: Were there signs of profane rationalism in the twentieth century that match Hitler's profane romanticism? And are there indications of profane rationalism in the twenty-first century? The answer to the first question is yes: Stalin's sadistic abuse of the Marxist theory of scientific socialism offers an example of profane rationalism in the twentieth century. However else one might describe the Communist period in the Soviet Union, it represents scientific, rational socialism gone wildly awry; the gulag and millions of murders testify to that.

But Stalin and his people were also great flag wavers who sang songs, held great rallies, and refused to acknowledge mistakes. Does that not mean that Stalin and his cohorts were romanticists just as much as Hitler was? Yes, they held romantic views of their party, of the Soviet Union, and of their struggle toward their goal of overthrowing—and killing—the capitalist devils, all repeated by the Chinese in the days of Mao. But they did not hold romantic views of the nature of social dynamics: far from it. They knew—or thought they knew—exactly how society worked, and it had nothing to do with the glorification of their forebears, who, in fact, were their oppressors. The same is true for the Chinese under Mao.

More to the point for students of judgment and decision making in the twenty-first century is the question of whether there are signs of such abuse of rationalism today. The answer to that is: probably.

The first possible example of profane rationalism would be the maximizing principle (discussed on p. 179). Carried out by nation-states, maximizing is a clear derivative of rationalism, and the false-positive errors and injustice that it produces are equally clear, even though it may claim justification on the basis of the "lesser evil" principle.[7] Because of its indifference to the false positives it creates, however, and because it does not pretend to be based on proof of guilt, maximizing often creates injustice. (Franz Kafka's 1937 novel *The Trial* achieved lasting fame because of its convincing depiction of the consequences of maximizing.)[8]

Profane romanticism doesn't demand thought because it is based on unconscious cognitive processes. But profane rationalism does take thought, because one must think to achieve coherence. And that thinking often leads to the *utility maximization* advocated by decision analysts acting as consultants. Utility maximization can result in absurdities such as handcuffing "little old ladies" arrested for minor traffic violations, or the legal absurdities that stem from fine-print interpretations of the law. The same utility maximization also results in mandatory sentencing, which is easily justified on rational grounds yet has been enthusiastically opposed by judges and civil libertarians, largely on moral grounds.[9]

For an extreme case, consider the argument of those who justify the bombing of Hiroshima on the grounds that it saved a million Japanese lives in addition to a million American lives. That assertion involves very simple and difficult-to-dispute rationality, yet many people consider it profane rationalism—rational, but horrifying in its immorality.

To summarize, rationalism becomes profane when it offends the common morality. When rationalism encounters a problem that induces people to bring their intuitive judgment of common morality to bear, the result is an encounter between two cognitive tactics that have nothing in common. The result is the predictable never-ending dispute. The same holds for a romantic view that encounters a rationalist tactic. The argument that follows is highly unlikely to be resolved peaceably.

Part I began with a quotation from the famous economist Amartya Sen in which he rejected the conventional notion of rationality. It turns out that he is far from alone in his rejection; his reservations are supported by many empirical studies conducted by what are often called "behavioral" economists and psychologists. And indeed, the researchers who undertake these studies that challenge the conventional views are being rewarded with prestigious prizes. The question now is what standard of rationality will (or should) replace the conventional one. Answering that question will require both a theoretical effort and an empirical one. In chapter 15, we will examine research efforts that hope to provide the answer.

14

Robert Rubin

Embedded in an Uncertain World

Robert Rubin is a highly respected former secretary of the treasury, director of the White House National Economic Council, and, at the time of writing, a director of Citigroup, one of the nation's largest financial institutions. He was also an advisor to President Bill Clinton during one of the nation's most prosperous periods. So, when he writes about "probabilistic thinking," we should see what he has to say, for he certainly had plenty of experience battling uncertainty under the most pressing circumstances.[1] But when we do see what he has to say, we find that he literally does not know what he is talking about. (Given his status in the financial and political world, however, my conclusion is hardly likely to send him into a depression.)

Yet, it is quite frequently said that if we really want to learn about judgment and decision making, we should sit at the feet of extraordinarily successful men such as Mr. Rubin. He allows us to do just that, for he wants to share with us his broad and significant experience as a decision maker. Most important is his intention to "explain [his] method of decision making." His fundamental view, he tells us, is that "all decisions are about probabilities."[2] In short, he accepts uncertainty as the central feature of the tasks he has faced in his professional life. He also tells us how he dealt with that uncertainty because he believes (correctly) that we need to know, and, he points out, "While a great many people accept the concept of probabilistic decision making and even think of themselves as practitioners, very few have internalized the mindset," as, we are led to assume, he has.[3]

He makes his method very clear: "For me, probabilistic thinking has long been a conscious process. I imagine the mind as a virtual legal pad, with the factors involved in a decision gathered, weighed and totaled up."[4] Clear as this description may be, it is surprising to find Rubin explaining it to us. Not only is it widely used, he can hardly claim to have originated this technique, because, as is widely known, Benjamin Franklin was advocating it more than 200 years ago. Franklin's biographer, Walter Isaacson, quoted this forefather as saying, " 'My way is to divide a sheet of paper by a line into two columns, writing over the one Pro and the other Con.' " Isaacson noted, "Then he would list all the arguments on each side and weigh how important each was." He further quotes Franklin: "Where I find two, one on each side that seem equal, I strike them both out; if I find a reason pro equal to some two reasons con, I strike out the three.' " Isaacson observed, "By this bookkeeper's calculus, it became clear to him 'where the balance lies.' "[5]

The readers of this book will recognize this "bookkeeper's calculus" immediately as a straightforward analytical tactic (since, as Rubin notes, it is completely conscious) that uses multiple fallible indicators. Rubin is somewhat unusual in that he specifies his method of organizing the data from the indicators; that is, he says he weighs them, and then they are "totaled up." Most people who describe their judgment process may go as far as explaining that they write down the factors they consider, and weigh them, but few go so far as to admit they simply add them up and see which side of the argument gets the highest score.

But Rubin is clearly mistaken when he refers to his technique as a "conscious" process; it is shot through with subjective judgments. Not only are his "weights" subjectively derived, but he announces,

> To describe probabilistic thinking this way does not, however, mean that it can be reduced to a mathematical formula, with the best decision jumping off a legal pad. Sound decisions are based on identifying relevant variables and attaching probabilities to each of them.[6]

That's certainly part of an analytical process, as noted above, but Rubin overlooks its subjectivity. Selecting the relevant variables? Assigning the probabilities? How do you do that? Rubin doesn't tell us because he can't—the process is buried in his subconscious. Nor does he say exactly what a sound decision is— that is, whether it is a coherent one, or one that corresponds with a criterion. He concludes, "The ultimate decision then reflects all of this input, but also instinct, experience, and 'feel.' "[7]

So who knows what went into that "sound" decision? Worse is still to come: the final sentence includes the undefined term *instinct* (it is somewhat disconcerting to see a man of Rubin's stature inappropriately using this term in this context), and *experience* (what experience?), and *feel* (so obviously ambiguous that Rubin puts it in quotes, as if to acknowledge that). So, the analytical activity is pushed far from the analytical pole of the cognitive continuum to some point near the intuitive pole. And that movement means that Mr. Rubin winds up advocating "common sense" but dignifies it by calling it "probabilistic thinking." That is not very impressive—or instructive.

Of course, Rubin has proved that he is a very smart man and surely has made many millions of dollars, perhaps hundreds of millions of dollars, (possibly) using this technique, and he successfully employed it in his years in government and high finance. So it's hard to criticize him without seeming to be picky, or even foolish. But if Mr. Rubin were to describe this method to an undergraduate class in judgment and decision making that had already had a few weeks of instruction, he would be harshly criticized by the students (especially if they were my students).

What criticisms would the undergraduates make? They would probably begin with Mr. Rubin's remark that this "has long been a conscious process" and point out that he doesn't recognize that at least half of it isn't. He even identifies the parts that aren't but blissfully incorporates these in his procedure. Most important, he doesn't tell us how he incorporates them, and that's because he doesn't know, and can't know, because they are used unconsciously. Second, they would note that he doesn't recognize that this is the same unconscious process most of us use most of the time. Sometimes we begin at the intuitive end of the continuum—instead of the analytical end where Mr. Rubin prefers to begin—in which case we blend, in his words, "instinct, experience, and 'feel'" and then proceed to be analytical, but the resulting process is the same. In either case, we employ a blend of intuition and analysis that we defend as common sense; therefore, contrary to his notion of "probabilistic thinking" as something he does in contrast to what others do, he is using a process we all use, but he's unjustifiably calling it something else. The entire paragraph is unworthy of a secretary of the treasury who purports to tell us how useful his so-called method of "probabilistic decision making" is.

Yet all this is quite interesting, indeed fascinating, mainly because it seems that Rubin, despite his convictions about the centrality of uncertainty in his professional life, has yet to discover that there is an academic discipline that purports to study this process; that there are roughly 50,000 academic papers on the topic; that there are a Judgment and Decision Making Society and a Medical Decision Making Society, each with thousands of members; that there are several professional journals; that all major universities (including Harvard, his alma mater) offer a variety of courses in this subject; that, in short, what he seems to believe is a new practice that he needs to explain to us is actually part of a fairly well-known academic subject. If Rubin does know all this, it is quite astonishing that a person of his many accomplishments would not make his readers aware of this, rather than presenting his experiences as if they were unique. Worse still, he doesn't seem to recognize that his practices are far from what he preaches.

Preaching versus Practice

I searched through all of Rubin's examples of his judgment and decision making in the hope that I would find examples of his use of the "virtual legal pad," but—remarkably, in view of his emphasis on the practical value of his "probabilistic method of thinking"—I could not find any case in which he explicitly used the method he described on page xi of his book until I reached page 373. There he says that because he had "received many calls to go on television and discuss the economic implications" of the events of 9/11, he "kept working through the question of how to think and talk about the consequences of September 11, making notes on a legal pad as usual."[8] I find it significant that Rubin's first explicit reference to his "virtual legal pad" occurs in connection with planning how to talk to a television audience, because that is exactly how all economists (in my experience) explain matters to a television audience: they refer to multiple fallible indicators, explain the direction they are "indicating," and implicitly add them up and present their conclusion. This is true even of Alan Greenspan, who is, in my opinion, the greatest economic communicator of them all. This phenomenon suggests to me that economists assume that presenting a coherent story that involves interdependent indicators to a television audience is too confusing for the audience. Or perhaps they don't have a coherent story to tell.

But when you see how Rubin actually goes about his "probabilistic decision making," you see immediately why he does not practice what he preaches. Here is an example of the kind of problem Rubin typically faces. In this case, Rubin and his staff are trying to form an economic plan for the Clinton administration. He first explains how things work:

> Interest-rate effects are only one part of the argument for fiscal soundness . . . but they were our focus at that moment. Bond holders were demanding a higher return, based both on the longer-term fiscal outlook and on the risk that the politics of reestablishing fiscal discipline would

be too difficult and that, instead, our political system would attempt to shrink the real value of the debt through inflation. We thought that lowering the deficit and bringing down long-term interest rates should have an expansionary effect that would more than offset the contractionary Keynesian effect and that, conversely, the expansionary effects of the continued large deficits would be more than offset by the adverse impact on interest rates.[9]

Contrary to what we have been led to expect, the "virtual yellow pad" is nowhere to be seen. (Nor would Ben Franklin see two columns labeled *pro* and *con*.) Instead, what we see is the coherence strategy hard at work. The interdependence of variables is prominent, as he points out the connection between lowering the deficit and bringing down long-term interest rates, and the expansion that would effect, etc.). It is the same logic as "the planes cannot leave Dallas for San Francisco because the planes in San Francisco cannot leave for the Midwest because of the weather there." And that kind of logic demands coherence, which is exactly at the heart of every example (except the one to be given to a television audience) that Rubin gives us.

I use this example from Rubin's book because it is likely that many social-policy problems are like this one: they present very complex interrelationships about which most people know little—and about which very little may actually be known—and which are very hard to keep track of. We can handle the air traffic control problem easily because it involves visible objects in visible space. But trying to maintain a coherent understanding of the abstractions Rubin presents is very difficult, even if you are an economist. Rubin occasionally shows that he is aware of such difficulties. For example, he cites his encounter with the finance minister of Brazil:

> I remember Pedro Malan, the finance minister of Brazil, telling me in October of 1998 how difficult it was to explain to his people that their currency was under attack and interest rates were higher in part because the Russian Duma had failed to raise taxes.[10]

That problem is a very neat counterpart of the air traffic problem: you can't do something here because of what is happening there.

Why is it that an intelligent, sophisticated man such as Robert Rubin does not practice what he preaches? The answer can only be lack of awareness: he is not aware of the distinction between correspondence strategies of judgment and coherence strategies of judgment. So he slips from one to the other unaware of what he is doing. And that is the point of asking the reader to read this chapter: people can be successful for many reasons besides brilliant decision making. They can also sincerely believe that they know exactly how they made all those brilliant decisions when, in fact, they don't. The nature of judgment and decision making, as the reader surely knows by now, is such that only those people who use analytical procedures analytically know how they did it. Indeed, that is the great advantage of all those flow charts the decision analyst presents. But that is a far cry from what Rubin tells us he does, or wants to do.

In short, Mr. Rubin may be far more successful politically and financially than any of us can hope to be, but it isn't because he knows anything about "probabilistic decision making." If the reader wants to learn about that, she or he would be better advised to turn to the academic sources described in earlier chapters.

PART IV

Themes Guiding Research

Kathleen Mosier. A bold researcher, the first to introduce the ideas of correspondence and coherence into the field of aviation psychology. (Reprinted with permission of Kathleen Mosier.)

15

Current Research Themes

It has often been said that the last thing fish will discover will be water. This metaphor applies with force to the themes that guide the researchers in the field of judgment and decision making, and perhaps researchers everywhere. There are few researchers who are prepared to seek out and understand the differences between the thematic character of their work and that of their peers and explain them to their students. These differences, and the blindness thereto, became apparent during the latter part of the twentieth century, a time when the problem of understanding and evaluating intuitive, and even analytical, rationality became prominent.[1]

This chapter will identify and describe the "unifying ideas" that are being pursued in this field at the beginning of the twenty-first century. They are somewhat surprising, or certainly would be to a mid–twentieth-century psychologist. None would have predicted the emergence of judgment and decision making as a sub-field of psychology that would involve researchers from economics, business, statistics, medicine, sociology, and other related fields, nor would anyone have predicted the sharp rise in uncertainty in modern life. The themes themselves would hardly have been guessed; no one anticipated the slow disappearance of physics as the major theme that inspired academic psychologists for over a century or the steady increase in the adoption of ecology as a new theme.

The coherence and correspondence strategies that are used in human judgment, and the three major tactics that are basic to human judgment, were described in parts II and III. This chapter describes the thematic identities of the several research programs in the twentieth century. I group these programs within the judgment strategy they have chosen to study, for it turns out that the researchers separate themselves persistently and rather sharply in terms of these strategies. Seldom, if ever, do researchers working within these strategies cross the strategic boundaries that separate them, a situation that has changed little since 1973 when it was first described by Paul Slovic and Sarah Lichtenstein.[2] The situation is different with regard to the tactics of judgment; all the researchers widely, if unsystematically, recognize two tactics, intuition and analysis, but rarely mention common sense.

Correspondence Researchers

Egon Brunswik's Ecological Theme

Few undergraduates in psychology in the twentieth century had heard of Egon Brunswik (1903–1955) although, or perhaps because, he was the first experimental psychologist to formally challenge psychology's traditional methodological orthodoxy and its close dependence on physics. And that is the principal reason for Brunswik's absence from psychology professors' lectures and their textbooks. His theme for psychological research differed too much from the conventional "stimulus—organism—response" (S-O-R) theme in psychology; as a result, it was generally ignored, and when not ignored, scorned. It was a challenge conventional psychologists did not wish to confront, for Brunswik made it clear that he believed, and wanted to show, that psychology was on the wrong track, that is, had developed the wrong overall theme and the wrong research methodology.[3]

Brunswik announced his theme of environmental texture as far back as 1935 in a joint article—written in Vienna—with a leading psychologist of the time, Edward Tolman, then chairman of the psychology department at the University of California at Berkeley. The theme was made plain in the title of their article: "The Organism and the Causal Texture of the Environment."[4] The softness implied by the word "texture" meant that "causal texture" lacked all the elements of the powerful and hard measures of physical science.

From the 1930s forward, the S-O-R theme ruled, but by the 1960s the scientific and intellectual community—and the psychologists who had been in the grip of the physical-science theme—became enthralled with the advent of the computer; now Brunswik and Tolman's theme involving "texture" wouldn't stand a chance, and it didn't get one. The computer became a strong contender for the "model of the mind." Yet, if Brunswik and Tolman wanted to differentiate themselves from that theme, the choice of the word "texture" as a thematic representation of the environment was a stroke of genius. Nothing could better delineate their approach from that of physics or the digital logic of the computer. Imagine trying to apply the term "texture" to Newtonian mechanics or a computer program. Nothing would make it clearer that the ecological theme was different. Opponents simply thought it was hopelessly wrong—indeed, that it meant an abandonment of scientific psychology—while admirers thought that its time had come.

Unexpectedly, however, by the latter decades of the twentieth century, the scientific and intellectual community had become more interested in "ecology," and laypersons became more environmentally sensitive; concomitantly, the theme of the computer as a "model of the mind" lost much of its charm. The theme of environmental texture, the idea of *Homo sapiens* trying to cope with an environment consisting of interrelated, or "entangled"—and thus "textured"—objects and events, contrasts sharply with the theme psychologists took from physical science that led them to focus on, and hope for, the exact mathematical laws of behavior. Concomitantly, the search for the "laws of learning," the prime topic of the 1940s and 1950s, was abandoned. The two concepts of "texture" and ecology, however, offer a more biological conception of what psychology must cope with. It might be said that "the times have caught up with" Brunswik.

Curiously, the "textural" theme dates back to Darwin. The final paragraph of his classic *Origin of Species* contains his famous reference to the "entangled bank":

> It is interesting to contemplate an entangled bank, clothed with many plants of many kinds, with birds singing on the bushes, with various insects flitting about, and with worms crawling through the damp earth, and to reflect that these elaborately constructed forms, so different from each other, and dependent on each other in so complex a manner, have been produced by laws acting around us. There is a grandeur in this view of life, with its several powers, having been originally breathed into a few forms or into one; and that whilst this planet has gone cycling on according to the fixed law of gravity, from so simple a beginning endless forms most beautiful and most wonderful have been, and are being, evolved.[5]

With this final paragraph, Darwin wanted us to see that, despite the physicists' success in constructing the laws of physical events, living organisms have evolved (and are evolving) and survive in "entangled" interrelationships among other living and evolving organisms, all coping with the fallible indicators that are others' behaviors. Brunswik and Tolman saw the importance of Darwin's view for psychology, and, in particular, wanted us to see that the psychology of perception and cognition must cope with an "entangled" form of objects and life events. That conclusion led to their theme emphasizing the "texture" of the uncertain information drawn from the objects and events with which we (and other organisms) must cope, both in terms of thought and action.

It is that textural quality of the "entangled bank" that leads us to say that we live in systems of interrelated interdependent (not independent) variables, which is another way of indicating that psychologists should focus on ecosystems. Moreover, because "entangled banks" consist of systems of interrelated variables that change, we have to come to grips with the fact that we do not live in a static ecology. Our social ecology is a rapidly changing one; people move in and out of it; the people themselves change over time; their relations to one another change over time, and one learns new things about each person in the ecology. Even Herbert Simon's passion for the chess analogy now seems weak, for we now see that the pieces have minds of their own.

All this leads to an irreducible uncertainty in the information that this ecology provides us. In short, we make judgments in a textured, dynamic, irreducibly uncertain ecology, and a theory of judgment tasks will have to take account of those features. One task of this book is to explain Brunswik's general theory of how organisms survive in such circumstances, and to show its applications to the ecology in which we now live. In his argument, he looked carefully at psychology's research methods and concluded that they were wrong-headed and deficient. It is to that issue that we now turn.

Asymmetrical Experiments

Brunswik began by pointing to an inconsistency in the logic used by experimental psychologists. He asked why the logic that is applied to generalizing from the conditions under which the results are obtained is not applied to generalizing to the conditions to which they are intended to be applied. That is, if psychologists demand that the logic, and methods and procedures, of sampling statistics must be applied to the *subjects* in the experiment, why should not such logic, methods, and procedures be applied to the *conditions* of the experiment? Otherwise a double standard of inference is used, with one standard for subjects that demands specifying the number of subjects, their method of selection and so on, and a second standard for conditions that ignores the first standard.

It's hard to see why that appeal for consistency in generalizing should have been ignored, but it was. Psychologists, steeped in the theme of classical physics, generally regarded this demand as impossible or irrelevant, and thus unworthy of their consideration.

But, in 1944, Brunswik showed that this demand was relevant and could be met. His method was straightforward. He followed one subject as she walked around Berkeley in the course of her day, stopped her every so often, asked her what object she was looking at, and asked her to judge the size of that object. He then measured the size of the object and compared her judgment of its size with the actual size of the object. Surprisingly, her nearly 200 judgments were found to correlate almost perfectly with the objective sizes of the objects. Brunswik had discovered that at least one person possessed empirical accuracy under conditions that maintained the essential conditions of the "entangled bank" in which the subject lived; he had applied the same logic to the sampling of conditions as to the subject. By representatively sampling the environment of a modern human, he broke the double standard. At one stroke, he had learned something new and important and demonstrated the practicality of a new approach to psychological research that was both consistent and effective. Of course, to demonstrate that this result was not unique to the one subject he studied, he would have to study another. (He didn't have to do this because his results were soon replicated by a psychologist at another university.)

Psychologists then (and even now) steadfastly ignored this study and its results and implications for the simple reason that they were not obtained under the usual conditions—rule of one variable—advocated by countless textbooks. But, as I have indicated above, these are the wrong conditions if one has any interest at all in generalizing the results of the study to the natural—or any—world of many entangled variables. Ignoring Brunswik's views—and ignoring this study—was a serious mistake for psychology for at least two reasons: First, the empirical result of the study is itself of considerable importance because it demonstrates the high degree of accuracy of our judgments under natural or highly informative conditions. Prior to that study we did not know we possessed that competence, and we would never have learned that we do, if Brunswik had stuck to the (wrong-headed) rule-of-one-variable method.

Second, the result (and the method) had strong practical and academic implications. For example, the conventional psychologists who set up the Army Air Corps' procedures for selecting pilots during World War II did stick to the "rule of one variable" method and did not find what everyone knew—that people do have good depth perception and make accurate judgments of size. Their method of testing for size constancy required them to use a procedure that asked subjects to look down a tunnel that eliminated all the cues of the natural environments pilots fly in, and then to match two rods with respect to their size. The tunnel was used to make certain there was only one variable. Traditional method triumphed over logic and good science.

Thus, at a time when the nation was encouraging young men to become pilots in the Army Air Corps, a task situation that was utterly unrepresentative of the flyer's task environment, utterly irrelevant to flying and landing an airplane, and unjustified other than by an appeal to "scientific method," was used to select and reject applicants. (James J. Gibson, the other "ecological" psychologist, famous for his work on perception, later criticized this procedure for the same reason.) This gross misrepresentation of the situation and futile expenditure of research efforts were never acknowledged, and Brunswik's study was seldom presented in undergraduate textbooks. Indeed, in all likelihood, the instructor had never heard of it, or would have dismissed it as "unscientific" because it didn't follow the rule of varying one variable and hold all others constant.

Such miscarriages occur in all sciences, and there are many instances in the history of science where important findings were overlooked. Brunswik repeatedly tried (and failed) to interest his scientific friends (and enemies) in his experiments and methodological innovations, and his work is still largely unknown. And here I must mention a coincidence: while writing the above paragraph, I received an e-mail from a renowned professor in one of the most prestigious U.S. universities, who was inquiring about Brunswik. The e-mail said, "I vaguely remember a paper (I think by Brunswik) when a researcher studied vision not by creating stimuli in the lab, but by following people around in their day-to-day life and assessing how they inferred distance based on the kind of cues in their natural environment." This e-mail appeared 60 years after Brunswik's article was published, a fact that should stimulate the modern student to think critically about the progress of methodological improvements. Brunswik's introduction of "representative design," the only serious alternative to the dogma of the rule of one variable, remained in the shadows from 1944 until 2001. As a result, the mistaken methodological theme that has guided psychology since its beginning continued to stifle research that attempts to discover how we make judgments and decisions in our normal environment.

Nevertheless, there are breakthroughs. A recent example should be briefly mentioned here because it is a paragon of ecological research in the Brunswikian tradition and advances that tradition.[6] In this example, the researchers thought that one's environment might well reflect the personality of the person who lives in it. Furthermore, they thought that "individuals select and craft physical environments that reflect and reinforce who they are."[7] In order to pursue this hypothesis they chose two environments: a person's office and his or her bedroom. After examining these rooms, researchers found systematic relationships between descriptions of the rooms and specific personality measures. The researchers then found that it was possible for persons who did not know the rooms' occupants to discern with a significant degree of accuracy the occupants' personalities. In short, the personality system matched the environmental texture. Although the number of categories is very small (N = 2) for each person studied, the content of the categories is very large and highly representative of the occupant's ecology. I do not offer this example as a methodological model, but I do find it useful as an example of the possibility of productive research that follows from an ecological point of view.

Herbert Simon's Theme of "Bounded Rationality"

Although Brunswik and Simon achieved visibility at about the same time (in the 1940s) and wrote seminal articles at about the same time (Brunswik in 1955, Simon in 1956) and were actually on the Berkeley campus of the University of California at the same time, they never met. Simon went on to fame, but Brunswik went on to near obscurity, rescued only by a fluke of history.[8] The difference in these two careers—one rising to become a Nobel laureate, the other being largely ignored—lies precisely in the nature of the themes they chose to replace the conventional theme in the field of psychology. Simon's replacement theme involved hitching his ideas to the game of chess and the choice of the computer as a general model. When he introduced this theme, it was clear that he was "in tune with the times." At that time, the scientific and technological communities were enthralled with the computer as a model of how we humans think, solve problems, and make decisions. Simon provided the analytical framework for our beliefs that there was a close connection between the computer's "processing of information" and our cognitive processes. The pursuit of this metaphor was vigorous and widespread, and it made "stimulus–response" psychology seem quaint, even obsolete. Brunswik's theme of environmental "texture," on the other hand, was "out of tune" with the times, so much so that it was almost never described to students.

Simon began his work as a student of cognitive competence by studying how administrative decisions are made, and he won the Nobel Prize in 1978 for what was ostensibly his work in economics. But it was really his work in cognitive psychology—essentially, decision making—that got the attention of the Nobel committee. It was the game of chess that gripped Simon's imagination and guided his theory about problem solving, judgment, and decision making throughout his life, and thus provided the thematic identity of his work. (He was no mere observer of chess players; he participated in the game and became a chess master.) And when the computer arrived, it became part of the thematic identity of his work. Simon leaped on that new invention in the 1960s and modeled his theories on it; he applied such concepts as "memory," "buffer," "program" (he wrote several), and the like to human cognition throughout his work.

Simon linked the concept of coherence to the cognitive processes involved in chess, and it was this link that formed the core of his theory. For it was the lack of coherence he found in human thought that led to his major innovation, the idea of "satisficing." That is a simple but powerful idea that one can easily imagine arising from the chess environment. You will see the players think for a few minutes, such thoughts generally being "if I move here, she'll move there, but if I move there . . ." until the imagination becomes overwhelmed. And when they are satisfied with their contemplated move (or exhausted by thinking about it), they stop thinking and make the move, thus exhibiting Simon's "satisficing" behavior, a term now firmly established in the field of judgment and decision making.

Simon's more important idea of "bounded rationality" follows from the idea of "satisficing" because it implies that the chess player does not pursue each and every alternative move and all its consequences, as full rationality demands. (Only the early "Big Blue" computer chess program that competed with Kasparov did [almost] that.) That is because cognitive activity is restricted by time, energy, capacity, resources, imagination, and similar limits, and is thus "bounded." Simon's genius lay in his brilliant extensions of this idea from chess to other features of our lives that require our judgment and problem-solving efforts. Thus, Simon received the Nobel Prize, richly deserved, all because of his fascination with the game of chess, his appreciation of the power of the computer analogy, and the strength of his imagination in seeing how these could be made to apply to significant human cognitive processes such as thinking.

And, indeed, it is precisely the cognitive process of imagination that is at the core of the "bounded" rationality of which Simon speaks. That is, it is the ability (or inability) to imagine future consequences that provides the "bounds" that defy rationality. As the president of the United States was attempting to persuade the world of the necessity of war against Iraq, one of the most compelling opposing arguments was that certain difficulties would follow initiating such a war. As James Fallows pointed out, "If we can judge from past wars, the effects we can't imagine when the fighting begins will prove to be the ones that matter most."[9] In short, failures of imagination are likely to occur and may well be fatal. Indeed, *The 9/11 Commission Report* announced that it was a "failure of imagination" of the U.S. leadership that made the terrorist attack on the United States possible. ("Failures of imagination" simply result from one's having a strong coherent view of matters; if your view is tightly coherent, it won't allow any other view to gain any credence. It is that phenomenon that led Holmes and Berlin to disparage certitude.)

I want to briefly describe the nature of the game of chess so that the reader will see how the theme of the chess match had both a liberating and restrictive effect on Simon's theorizing. Chess is a structured game with rigid rules; it has a small board with boundaries, a specific and limited number of locations for pieces, and a specific and limited number of pieces, each of which has specific, limited properties. I could mention other features, but the reader will see that chess and the chessboard form a very peculiar representation of the environment from the point of view of a participant in the twenty-first century. Yet, Simon thought this was exactly the right place to study human cognition; he once suggested that chess should be thought of as the *e. coli* of psychology (*E. coli,* a bacterium found in the intestines of mammals, had, at the time Simon was writing, become molecular biologists' "standard" experimental organism). He also thought that the computer analogy was an excellent one; he became sufficiently enamored of the computer's power that he predicted that a computer would soon defeat a human at chess. He was right, although his prediction was too optimistic by about 20 years.

Genius that Herbert Simon might have been, I disagree entirely with his choosing chess as the overall model for research in judgment and decision making. I acknowledge that chess might well provide a model for a few, rather peculiar judgment tasks, and that the study of chess players has provided some useful hypotheses about analytical cognition. But the game is so limited in its structure, and the demands it makes on the person are so restrictive, that it is misleading, in my view, to recommend it as an overall model. He didn't see that the very special circumstances of the chess game made it inappropriate for representing anything but similar special circumstances, those that strongly induce analytical cognition. More important, perhaps, is that he didn't link the driving feature of chess, the search for coherence under extraordinary circumstances, to cognitive activity. That would have been a daunting task, but a man of Simon's extraordinary abilities might have made progress. (His autobiography, *Models of My Life,* is a fine source for understanding his approach to psychology.[10])

Gerd Gigerenzer's Theme

Simon's principal idea, "bounded rationality," has been taken up by Gerd Gigerenzer and his colleagues and comprises the core of their work. Gigerenzer wants to show the generality of this idea. First, he wants to show that coherence is of little importance and that correspondence is everything. And he applies Simon's bounded rationality to that aspect of human judgment, but with a different name; he calls it "ecological rationality." In fact, it more closely resembles Brunswik's theme than Simon's.

Gigerenzer is one of the few psychologists who recognized the significance of Brunswik's theme. Moreover, he has elaborated on it, combined it with "bounded rationality," and confronted conventional psychologists with both. In the preface to their book, Gigerenzer and Todd directly challenge the conventional notion of rationality by asking, "How can one be rational in a world where vision is limited, time is pressing, and decision-making experts are often unavailable?" That is a page right out of Simon's book, so to speak. And they make the nature of their theme plain by stating, "In this book we argue that rationality can be found in the use of fast and frugal heuristics, inference mechanisms that can be simple and smart. The laws of logic and probability play little if any role in the performance of these components of the mind's adaptive toolbox—these heuristics are successful to the degree they are ecologically rational, that is, adapted to the structure of the information in the environment in which they are used to make decisions."[11]

So, Gigerenzer and his colleagues introduced yet another conception of rationality. Moreover, they stated plainly their objections (that follow from Simon's work) to the broad, unqualified acceptance of the common notion of rationality. And Gigerenzer's beliefs about the nature of the cognitive process that should replace it are also based on Simon's; he emphasizes "fast and frugal heuristics, inference mechanisms that can be simple and smart [meaning empirically accurate, not logical]."

This was a highly significant step in the withering of the standard conception of rationality, both in its role as a descriptor and as a prescriptor of rational behavior. That is, Gigerenzer and Todd challenge (as did Simon) the standard "rational expectations" theory, the bedrock theory of economics, in both senses; they deny that rational expectations theory accurately describes the way humans make judgments, decisions, and choices, and they deny that rational expectations theory *prescribes* how people should make judgments, decisions, and choices, thereby depriving anyone of using that theory as a way of justifying their judgment, decision, or choice. That denial, based on empirical tests, immediately raises a most serious question: If that theory will not justify our judgments, what will? Are we now left with no way to justify one decision-making method as "better," that is, more logical, than another? Wouldn't that mean chaos?

Duncan Watts is one who sees this situation for the disaster it could be. He writes,

> Perhaps the most successful attempt at a general theory of decision making to emerge from the social sciences is known as *rational expectations theory*. . . . Developed by economists and mathematicians in order to inject some scientific rigor into debates over human behavior, rationality has become the de facto benchmark against which all other

explanations must be compared. Unfortunately . . . rationality makes a number of assumptions about human dispositions and cognitive capabilities that are . . . outrageous. [italics in original][12]

(These are the assumptions laid out by Gigerenzer and Todd above.) And, Watts adds, "More unfortunately still, no one appears to have come up with anything better"—anything better, that is, than what has been shown to be descriptively and prescriptively useless.[13]

Nobody but Gigerenzer. But Watts doesn't know this. He does know that "in the 1950s Herbert Simon and others proposed a far more reasonable-seeming version of rationality, called bounded rationality, that relaxes some of the more unlikely assumptions of [rational expectations theory]."[14] As Watts saw it, however, bounded rationality does not provide the answer we so badly need. The problem with bounded rationality, he asserted, is that "once one starts to violate the assumption of perfectly rational behavior, there is no way of knowing when to stop."[15]

Gigerenzer did find a way, however, and that was through Brunswik's emphasis on the need to include the ecology as a reference point for behavior. He insisted on the ecological, rather than the purely logical aspects of rationality, that is, the "structure of information in the environment." It is that insistence that makes it plain that his theme is derived from Brunswik's theme emphasizing the uncertain aspects of the environment, or ecology. In short, Gigerenzer becomes a committed student of the correspondence strategy in human judgment.

Thus, it is Gigerenzer's acceptance of Simon's view of cognitive processes (bounded) that brings Gigerenzer close to Simon, and it is Gigerenzer's acceptance of Brunswik's concept of the role of the (uncertainty-ridden) environment that brings him close to Brunswik. It is that combination of ideas that answers Watt's complaint that without reference to rational expectations, "there is no way of knowing when to stop." Gigerenzer tells us that the ecology—not some theory of what rationality implies—tells us "when to stop," that is, tells us when we are right or wrong, and thus affords us a criterion for rationality. And that is Gigerenzer's theme.

Stanislas Dehaene's Theme

There has always been an uneasy relationship between psychology and what medicine has called neurology but what is now called neuroscience, and sometimes neuropsychology. By "uneasy relationship" I mean that neither field had much interest in the other, but thought that they should, somehow. Neurologists were mainly interested in the pathology of the anatomy of the nervous system rather than the relationship between the brain and behavior. The neurologists' conception of the nervous system seemed to many psychologists to resemble something like an old-fashioned telephone switchboard. On the other hand, one prominent psychologist (Donald Hebb) famously suggested that most psychologists seemed to think the brain had all the complexity of a "bowl of mush." What this came down to was that each discipline found the other to be largely irrelevant to its purposes.

This changed considerably when brain imaging appeared in the 1980s; both groups developed a strong interest in this new technology because of its ability to present detailed pictures of cognitive activity in various regions of the brain. That was exciting! (One prominent form is called "functional Magnetic Resonance Imaging" [fMRI] to distinguish it from imaging of a static condition.) Representatives of both disciplines could be seen standing around the MRI scanner explaining to one another what was happening. That was new, and the telephone switchboard was gone. Out of all this there appeared, together with molecular biology and genetics, a new, vigorous, and exciting discipline: neuroscience. Thus, we are now developing knowledge about brain structure and function that is related directly to human judgment. Such knowledge creates an opportunity for neuroscientists and students of judgment to compare notes and to develop a theme for guiding research.

Before the development of fMRI, our knowledge about neuroscience was largely about brain anatomy and the localization of specific functions such as speech, motor activities, and vision. Such knowledge, while of considerable importance, was not tied to the more general psychological aspects of a cognitive variety, such as intuition, common sense, and analysis. Therefore, it was difficult to link modern studies of judgment and neuroscience. But fMRI does make it possible to relate specific cognitive functions to specific brain function. Stanislas Dehaene, who is both a mathematician and a neuropsychologist, took advantage of that development in his pursuit of the origin of mathematics. Thus it is not surprising that Dehaene's theme links evolution to mathematics and cognition.

Earlier, I suggested that our ancestors' cognitive activity relied on the correspondence strategy and intuitive tactics in the search for food, shelter, and mates. The use of the coherence strategy and the tactic of analytical cognition seems to have appeared only relatively recently, when there were social and environmental demands for them. But in those earlier remarks, I did not address the question of the evolution of quantitative cognitive operations, such as counting and measuring. Yet, understanding the evolution of these fundamental operations is necessary for our study of human judgment. Fortunately, Dehaene's strong interest in how the mind creates mathematics takes us a long way toward understanding this topic. In his book *The Number Sense: How the Mind Creates Mathematics,* he provides us with the information we need to understand why intuition is easy for us (it happens quickly and effortlessly), and why analysis is hard (it is slow and often requires repetition).[16]

The Approximate Man

Dehaene's clinical examination of a patient marked the beginning of the development of his theme. A severe blow to the head had destroyed much of the left side of the patient's brain, specifically the left temporal, parietal (side) and occipital (rear of the head) lobes. Dehaene was particularly interested in this patient because our ability to calculate is located in these general areas. He wanted to learn how badly his patient's ability to do simple calculations was impaired as a result of his injury. So, Dehaene began by asking him, "What is 2 plus 2?" The patient replied, "3." That answer is surprising because it suggests that although the patient had lost his ability to calculate precisely correct answers to simple arithmetic problems, he had not lost his ability to find an approximately correct and reasonable answer. That was completely unexpected. Ordinarily, a patient with an extensive injury to the left side of the brain would either be able to calculate or not; for the patient to provide an approximation was a new experience for Dehaene. Moreover, he learned that approximation was a persistent response by this patient, so he named his patient "Mr. N, the Approximate Man."

And just as Dehaene was intrigued by the "approximate man," this author was also excited to learn of this "approximate man." For the discovery of this form of behavior in a man with this specific brain injury to the left side of his brain suggests that although his analytical capacity (precise calculation) had been lost, his intuitive capacity for approximations had not been. Apparently, intuitive judgments could still be produced by the intact right side of his brain. Mr. N never gave wild or absurd answers but always gave appropriate approximations. Dehaene writes, "In experiment after experiment, a striking regularity emerges: Though Mr. N has lost his exact calculation abilities, he still approximate," that is, make quantitative approximations.[17] (As I will show below, Mr. N's injury put him in the same cognitive situation as our ancestors. His inability to make exact calculations resulted from his brain's loss of function, however, whereas our ancestors' inability to calculate resulted from an intact brain's lack of knowledge.)

Dehaene's pursuit of the problem of brain function led him to conclude, "The brain is not a logical machine, but an analog device."[18] That conclusion carries meaning for the theme of this book; it suggests that rationality, defined as hard analytical cognition, is not a natural function of the human brain. One has to be taught to use it.

The next section in Dehaene's book is titled "When intuition outruns axioms" and further elucidates the theme of his work.

Field Studies: The Piraha

His careful clinical studies of brain-injured patients led Dehaene to conclude that "the brain is not a logical machine, but an analog device," and this conclusion has received support from equally careful field studies by Paul Gordon of a primitive tribe, the Piraha, in Brazil.[19] The Piraha are a tribe with an "innumerate" language; also, they do not draw. Gordon set out to address the question of "whether language can determine thought." From studying these people whose language had no counting system, he found that "numerical cognition is clearly affected by the lack of a counting system in the language. Performance with quantities greater than 3 was remarkably poor." And Gordon also ascertained from further statistical analysis of their performance that "it is suggestive of an analog estimation process."[20]

It is these rather startling discoveries of the apparent primordial nature of analog, or intuitive, cognitive mechanisms that lead me to link Dehaene (and Gordon) with Simon, Brunswik, and Gigerenzer. And there are further findings from brain research that investigates lesions on the right side of the brain that support Dehaene's conclusions about the patient with lesions on the left side.

For example, Marian Gomez-Beldarrain and colleagues studied patients with right frontal lesions and found that they were "unable to assess and use advice to make predictive judgments."[21] That is, Gomez-Beldarrain and her colleagues' findings of a diminished capacity to accept advice because of brain lesions parallels Dehaene's study of the "approximate man."

The study of the brain is now affected by a theme that has developed from research on judgment and decision making, just as research on judgment and decision making is also being affected by brain research. Brain research is moving from the early work that focused on the anatomical location of different psychological functions to exploration of various theoretical issues, as illustrated by the above studies.

Coherence Researchers

The Sunstein/Kahneman/Tversky/Thaler Theme

Among the psychologists—and economists and lawyers—who pursue the theme of coherence competence, the work of Cass Sunstein should be considered first because he is one of the most thoughtful and prolific students of judgment and decision making. Although a prominent professor of law, and author of numerous books in that field, he examines judgment and decision making particularly as it relates to the field of economics. He is interested in the fact that the classical economists continue to favor the competence of *Homo sapiens* intuitive rationality; modern economics is based on the idea that human economic behavior follows from "rational expectations." Economics has boldly claimed that rational-choice theory provides a coherent theoretical base and that its accurate predictions of behavior have allowed it to achieve both coherence and correspondence validity. (It is these economists that Amartya Sen and other economists criticize for their narrow definitions of rationality.) Sunstein is particularly critical of what he sees as the disparity between the predictions made by classical economic theory and the way people actually behave. Thus, it is the "behavioral economists" and Sunstein's "new legal realists" who have sharply challenged the classical economists.

In *Behavioral Law and Economics,* Sunstein and his colleagues address this topic directly: "It would be highly desirable to come up with a model of behavior that is both simple and right. But conventional economics is not in this position, for its predictions are often wrong."[22] Thus, the psychologists, and now "behavioral lawyers" and "behavioral economists," who are opponents of rational-choice theory, deny the classical economists' claims of empirical justification. But the main reason they reject the rational-choice theory is that in so many experiments that they have carried out themselves, the actual behavior of individual persons is not what the classical economists' narrow definition of rationality predicts.

It is important to note, however, that the behavior these researchers are interested in is the *coherence* of the elements of the subjects' judgment process. They do not examine the empirical accuracy of their subjects' judgments as Gigerenzer and his colleagues do; they ask their subjects about the value of various objects under different conditions and examine whether their judgments obey the laws of the probability calculus, a far different task. Curiously, those who pursue this theme consider those who pursue the correspondence theme to be wasting their time, and those pursuing the coherence theme believe those pursuing the coherence theme to be wasting theirs.

Additionally, those who share Sunstein's belief completely disagree with classical economists about fundamental issues; the former are persuaded that intuitive rationality is a myth, yet the economists take intuitive rationality as the foundation of economic behavior. Proponents of all sides of this disagreement have been blessed by Nobel Prizes (Gary Becker for the classical economists, Herbert Simon and Daniel Kahneman and Vernon Smith for the behavioral economists).

Bounded Rationality with a Twist: Sunstein's "Incomplete Theorization"

In his book *Designing Democracy,* Sunstein introduced the concept of "incomplete theorization."[23] "Incomplete theorization" is a direct intellectual outcome of his earlier writings on bounded rationality, a fact of considerable importance, although Sunstein doesn't make this connection. (Surprisingly, bounded rationality is not even in the index of his book.) When addressing the "trouble"—he means the never-ending disputes—that deliberation generates in democracies, he urges "incomplete theorization" as a remedy.[24] That is, he praises the value of turning to *incomplete* abstractions when people cannot agree on particulars and takes note of the putative conflict-reducing advantages of "incomplete theorization."

> The use of low-level principles or rules allows judges on multimember bodies and also citizens generally to find commonality and thus a common way of life without producing unnecessary antagonism. . . . Both rules and low-level principles make it unnecessary to reach areas in which disagreement is fundamental. . . . Perhaps even more important, incompletely theorized agreements allow people to show each other a high degree of mutual respect, or civility, or reciprocity.[25]

This soft approach to "deliberative trouble," with its explicit tolerance of incompleteness and (unfounded) claims for better interpersonal relations is something of a surprise, coming as it does from a (tough-minded) law professor rather than a (soft) psychologist.

Sunstein's enthusiasm for "incomplete theorization" seems perfectly compatible with his preference for bounded rationality. Indeed, bounded rationality provides the cognitive basis for the applicability of "incomplete theorization." To see how central this idea is to Sunstein, consider the following statement:

> In constitutional law, incompletely theorized agreements are especially valuable when a society seeks moral evolution and progress over time. Consider the area of equality, where many democracies

have seen considerable change in the past and will inevitably see much more in the future. A completely theorized judgment would be unable to accommodate changes in facts or values. If a culture really did attain a theoretical end-state, it would become too rigid and calcified; we would know what we thought about everything.[26]

(This jibes with what I discussed in chapter 7.) So, Sunstein agrees with Simon (and Gigerenzer) that unbounded (standard) rationality is impractical, unobtainable, and undesirable.

All this seems to constitute a restatement of Sunstein's antipathy toward full rationality. But it also seems a rejection of full commitment to the coherence strategy as "too rigid and calcified." And it appears that this stance is compatible with Sunstein's experiments (with Thaler and Kahneman) in which he observes the participants' failure to achieve full rationality, an assumption at the basis of classical economics. In this book, he is even prepared to urge the abandonment of this standard in the legislature! (Many would argue that his goal has already been achieved, to our great embarrassment.) Yet it seems fair to ask: how will this plea for "theoretical incompleteness" stand up against the arguments of his colleagues in the legal profession whose competence lies precisely in their ability to destroy their opponents' "theoretically incomplete"—that is, incoherent—arguments? How will those law professors who seek coherence in their students' papers react to a student's plea for the value of "theoretical incompleteness"?

In short, Sunstein's appeal for the general use of "theoretically incomplete" assertions follows nicely from his reliance on the theory of bounded rationality (which he shares with Gigerenzer) and the experiments he conducts with Thaler and Kahneman, but he leaves open the question of the conflict-reducing potential of full rationality. Indeed, he leaves open the possibility of quarreling— "deliberative trouble"—that arises in different forms, some of which are not susceptible to "theory" at all.

Failure of Intuitive Rationality under Uncertainty: Proved?

The answer to that is: not quite. And this disagreement is broader than a dispute between psychologists and classical economists. When Kahneman and Tversky's work is brought together with the work of Sunstein and his colleagues, it is fair to say that it demonstrates, although does not prove, the existence of a general failure on the part of human beings to achieve—by intuitive means—coherent, rational judgments under uncertainty. Although the limits of this demonstration have yet to be made clear, that qualified assessment of human judgment is of the utmost importance, because intuitive rationality is often used to achieve coherent judgments in judgment and decision making; specifying the limits of the failure of intuitive rationality will therefore be critical.

All this wrangling is important because, if the broad claim for the incompetence of intuitive rationality is true, it casts serious doubt on the intellectual capability of our species, or at least that is what many have concluded. Lola Lopes and Greg Oden captured the significance of these generalizations, and the paradox to which they led, as far back as 1991 when they reported on the reaction of print media to them:[27]

> On the one hand, there is a large body of research that documents striking failures of naïve humans when confronting relatively simple tasks in probability theory, decision making, and elementary logic. On the other hand, there is the continuing belief of psychologists and computer scientists that by understanding human problem-solving performance we will be better able to build machines that are truly intelligent. One can only wonder at the puzzlement of lay readers who come across articles like one published recently in *Newsweek* that spent several columns describing people's failures at decision making in scathing terms ("sap," "sucker," "woefully muddled") only to conclude that researchers hope to "model human decision makers'" rules of thumb so that they can be reduced to computer software and so speed the progress of artificial intelligence, the aim of which is "not to replace humans but to give them an important tool."[28]

(The paradox of hoping to model cognitive processes that have already been shown to be flawed remains unresolved.)[29]

Thus, we see the importance of the choice of theme, for Sunstein and his colleagues chose to begin with the premise that intuitive rationality was defective—a hypothesis introduced by Simon and explored extensively and empirically by Kahneman and Tversky (and Vernon Smith). Following that theme meant that the researcher would proceed by accepting conventional rationality (and the statistical technique known as Bayes's theorem) as a standard, and then using the experimental results of Kahneman, Tversky, and others to show that humans fail to achieve that standard. Sunstein and his colleagues believe that by using similar experiments they have discredited the basic premise of classical economics and thus are able to dismiss its claims to legitimate explanations and predictions of economic phenomena. That is indeed a large conclusion.

But much more needs to be done to determine the limits of these conclusions, and many researchers are now asking for better demonstrations of the empirical generalization of these conclusions—in other words, better evidence that these same results will be found outside the laboratory. As Robin Hogarth put it when he addressed a conference on risk,

> Researchers who study people's decision making processes seek results that are generalizable. However, conclusions are often based on contrived experimental 'incidents' with little understanding as to how these samples of behavior relate to the population of situations that people encounter in their naturally occurring environments (i.e., the so-called real world).

He went on to describe a different method:

> Specifically, use was made of the ESM (Experience Sampling Method) to sample decisions taken by undergraduates and business executives. Each day participants received several ESM messages (on their mobile telephones) at random moments at which point they completed brief questionnaires about their most recent decision making activities. Issues considered here include types of decisions and feedback (expected and received), and confidence in both decisions and the validity of feedback. Results show important differences between the populations of decisions experienced by the two groups of participants and also raise some fascinating theoretical issues. For example, most participants were quite confident of the outcomes of the decisions that they took and, yet, did not receive or did not expect to receive any feedback as to the outcomes they would experience.[30]

(Note the resemblance of Hogarth's argument to the argument underlying Brunswik's study of the person making perceptual judgments outside the laboratory.)

So despite Nobel Prizes and many experiments, we are left with dubious conclusions about an important topic. The classical economists and those who cling to the traditional narrow definitions of rationality will continue to base their work on these definitions. The "behavioral" economists, lawyers, and the psychologists will continue to gnaw away at the descriptive power of the traditional beliefs about rationality, and the philosophers and judgment researchers like Simon and Gigerenzer will continue to hack away at the prescriptive value of traditional rational-expectations theory. But it is unknown when the conventional beliefs will be replaced. (I will offer a replacement below.) First we need to understand the gap between the idea of coherence and correspondence researchers.

Confusion about Heuristics Separates Coherence and Correspondence Researchers

The reader may be puzzled by what seems to be a determined effort on the part of those who pursue the different themes of coherence and correspondence to deny the significance of the other theme. Gigerenzer and his colleagues, for example, reject the idea of a world ruled by a physicalistic theme, and choose instead the theme of an ecological world, much like Darwin's "entangled bank," emphasizing the organism's adaptation to its environment. That is, these researchers see the world as a mass of probabilistically interrelated objects and events to which individuals successfully adapt (which brings them close to the evolutionary psychologists Cosmides and Tooby, and other anthropologists). Thus Gigerenzer and his colleagues celebrate their discovery of simple heuristics (such as "take the best cue and ignore the rest") that, because they are claimed to be "fast and frugal," allow us to achieve competent intuitive judgments that correspond to—are more or less closely empirically related to—the uncertain ecological facts. (Cognitive coherence is not expected, or even desired, and Gigerenzer gives it little credence.)

So, whereas Sunstein, Kahneman, Tversky, Thaler, and colleagues find that intuitive cognitive heuristics are ever-present in our economic choices, Gigerenzer and his colleagues declare that the choices of Sunstein his colleagues fail the test of coherence and thus lead us into "irrational" judgments. As a result, they conclude these failures of rationality make "rational (coherent) expectations" theory obsolete. They do not offer a different criterion of rationality; they simply find a litany of "biases" that prevent people from achieving rationality. They claim that their research has shown that humans fail to achieve the standard criterion of rationality in judgments under uncertainty, a view that has angered some, but earned Kahneman a Nobel Prize.

Although both Gigerenzer and Sunstein give the concept of "heuristics" a major role in describing and explaining judgments and decisions, "heuristics" are given very different roles in these very different themes. Following the lead of Kahneman and Tversky, Sunstein and his colleagues find that heuristics, although sometimes helpful, lead us to "biases," that is, errors in judgment. Thus, "heuristics" occupy a negative role in this theme and are therefore to be avoided in favor of rational (internal, coherent) probability calculations. But Gigerenzer has the opposite view; heuristics, he claims, will "make us smart" because they help us achieve correspondence competence, that is, help us make empirically accurate judgments. And, he believes, that's all that counts; coherence competence has no value whatever. So these two themes assign opposite values to the use of heuristics in the judgment process.

Who Is Right?

Although Gigerenzer and colleagues acknowledge the work of Kahneman and Tversky (mainly to criticize it) and also the work by Sunstein and his colleagues, the latter are utterly indifferent to Gigerenzer's work, which is somewhat puzzling. We can hardly attribute that to ignorance of the others' work (although Thaler's writings clearly suggest that possibility). But it is often the case that the choice of different themes leads to indifference to others' work. It may well be that Sunstein believes that the theme on which Gigerenzer's work is based is so implausible as not to deserve recognition. Gigerenzer, however, makes explicit his scorn for Sunstein's main claim that our intuitive competence is flawed; Gigerenzer and Todd specifically indicate that they believe that the coherence strategy simply has no relevance to human judgment.

Despite all this disagreement, these two groups of researchers share a common reliance on Simon's concept of "bounded rationality." Neither group seems to find their common interest in bounded rationality to be noteworthy. Gigerenzer adopted bounded rationality to explain the cognitive activity of his subjects and why their performance was superior to that of Kahneman and Tversky's subjects. Gigerenzer insists that bounded rationality provides the answer because it explains that there is no need to fully explore every branch in the decision tree, or problem space (as standard rationality requires), and that to do so wastes the scarce resources of time and cognitive efforts. That is why it is critical that Gigerenzer show that the subjects in his experiments perform better than those in Kahneman and Tversky's experiments. Gigerenzer will claim that his experiments make the "biases" (errors) that are the main attraction of Kahneman and Tversky's work "go away," all the while claiming that these biases make no difference anyway because they are merely biases away from internal compliance with probability laws and therefore inconsequential. Gigerenzer and colleagues not only critically analyze Kahneman and Tversky's experiments with the aim of refuting their validity but conduct experiments based on the ecological theme and show results that, they assert, support it.

Although Sunstein takes little notice of Gigerenzer's concept of "ecological rationality," in his book *Risk and Reason: Safety, Law and the Environment,* he can be found grasping another concept: *richer rationality,* one introduced by Paul Slovic.[31] In his discussion of richer rationality, Sunstein persuasively makes the case that standard rationality needs to be "enriched," thus again indicating dissatisfaction with standard rationality.

The "Real World"

Gigerenzer and Todd spoil their discussion of ecological rationality by using the journalistic term "real world" in place of a meaningful theoretical term describing the ecology, or the environment. For example, they write,

> Real organisms spend most of their time dealing with the external disorder of their environment, trying to make the decisions that will allow them to survive and reproduce. . . . These real-world requirements lead to a new conception of what proper reasoning is: ecological rationality.[32]

This criticism of their use of journalistic phrases such as "real organisms" and "real world" may seem pedantic, but it is precisely by the use of these meaningless terms that the authors avoid being specific about exactly which environmental circumstances they are talking about, how the circumstances differ from one another, and the consequences for cognitive activity. That specification is at the core of ecological rationality. Thus, they are not only ignoring their own demands for task specificity, they are ignoring the demands made by the concept of a task continuum.

If Gigerenzer and Todd want to substitute ecological rationality for standard rationality—a substitution I endorse—they should be specific about exactly how they intend to describe the various ecologies they have in mind. How are the ecologies that demand intuitive cognition to be described and differentiated from those that demand analytical cognition? If no differentiation is necessary, what is the importance of all the talk about the "structure of the environment"? The meaningless term—"real world," not to mention "real organisms"—allows these authors to escape the burden of developing a theory of the significant parameters by which various "structures of the environment" are to be described. That means that an ecological theory is missing. In short, ecological psychologists must, just like biological ecologists, talk about the parameters that describe and differentiate ecologies.

For example, one of the critical parameters of any judgment-task ecology is feedback; some ecologies provide immediate and unambiguous feedback, some provide delayed and ambiguous feedback, and most important, many provide no feedback whatever. Each of these ecologies is just as "real" as any other. But Gigerenzer and Todd address none of them. Indeed, the tasks that offer no feedback are precisely the ones that demand "maintaining internal order of beliefs and inferences." In short, such tasks (or ecologies) demand coherence as their justification, just the process that Gigerenzer and Todd dismiss as unimportant. Yet these are the judgment tasks with which policymakers are regularly confronted.

(Should we allocate the money to the welfare department or the highway department?) And these, of course, are precisely the tasks that Sunstein focuses on (while neglecting the correspondence tasks that Gigerenzer focuses on!). It is plain that by restricting their theme to a "real world" that is made up only of correspondence tasks, Gigerenzer restricted the range of applicability of the heuristics, just as Kahneman and Tversky, and now Sunstein, restrict theirs to tasks involving coherence.

Most impressive, however, is the work by Martignon and Lasky (who are among Gigerenzer's colleagues) described in Gigerenzer and Todd's book.[33] They show in great detail exactly how difficult, time-consuming, and resource-consuming it would be to perform an unboundedly rational procedure—do all the mathematics—in a wide variety of tasks, which is exactly the point emphasized by Simon and by Gigerenzer and Todd. And they leave the reader with no doubt whatever as to how unrealistic it is to propose Bayes's theorem as the operational (behavioral) expression of rationality in anything but a very simple task. Thus, its prescriptive irrelevance is evidence for the unlikelihood of its descriptive validity. And that also makes clear why it is mainly statisticians, who thoroughly understand the complexity of Bayes's theorem and have access to the necessary computing facilities to handle it, who use this procedure regularly to good advantage.

The unlikely relevance of Bayes's theorem to judgment research is closely related to a second reason that Gigerenzer rejects Kahneman and Tversky's conclusions regarding *Homo sapiens'* use of flawed intuitive rationality involving the use of probabilistic information. He argues—and demonstrates—that performance in the intuitive use of probabilistic information improves if the information is given in "natural frequencies" (e.g., one person out of ten) rather than probabilities (e.g., the probability of this event is .10).[34] This empirical finding is crucial to Gigerenzer's concept of "ecological rationality," for it demonstrates what he means by that term; such numbers as "one person out of ten" are a part of our common ecology, but probabilities such as "p=.10" are not. The first is easy to understand because of the concreteness of its referent (it is easy to visualize one person standing among nine others), but the second is not because the referent for the statement "the probability of this event is .10" is abstract. It subsumes not only knowledge of a numerical system (as does the first) but something more, specifically a ratio of a numerator and a denominator that includes a reference class. Everyone is familiar with the first, and we are notoriously ignorant regarding the second. So, it should be no surprise that we are intuitively incompetent in using uncertain information when it is presented in terms of probabilities instead of "natural frequencies."

There is also a post hoc explanation of this differential competence. *Homo sapiens* didn't begin to use probabilities in the abstract sense in which they are used in mathematics until the seventeenth century. But we can guess that they were conveying uncertainty to one another via the use of "natural frequencies," perhaps some 5,000 years earlier when they began to write.

Gigerenzer gives a nice example of the incomprehensibility of forecasts expressed in probability terms by citing U.S. National Weather Service attempts to convey weather information in terms of probabilities: "There is a 30% chance of rain tomorrow. Most Americans thought they knew what that meant. However, studies showed that some people understood this statement to mean that it will rain in 30% of the area, others that it will rain 30% of the time tomorrow, and others that it will rain on 30% of the days like tomorrow."[35] But if the reader has any doubt about the difficulty of probabilistic reasoning, she or he need only ask for an opinion from any teacher of statistics, or consult the research on "debiasing," which generally concludes that debiasing is impossible.[36]

Thus, Gigerenzer's theme of ecological rationality is a bold approach to human judgment that derives from biology (ecology is a sub-discipline of biology). It is bold because it challenges age-old ideas about rationality and because the promotion of the concept of "ecology" marks a twenty-first-century change from the worship of physics to an interest in biology. That change will have a profound effect on the choice of methods in psychology, for it will change the focus from traditional systematic design (from physics) to representative design, about which more below. Although Gigerenzer's efforts are certainly bold, they are not new, because this is precisely the approach Brunswik took in the 1930s.[37] Thus, Gigerenzer's theme can be said to be a derivative of Brunswik's.

Looking for a New Anchor

The disarray in contemporary research in judgment and decision making makes the situation regarding rationality regrettable, for the tattered concept of rationality—or reason—is now beside the point. Even affect is becoming legitimized; "if it feels good, do it" has lost its pre-modern stigma; emotion is getting its due. The problem is, no one knows what its "due" is. In short, we have lost the anchor that rationality once provided us. Simon's bounded rationality is only justified by correspondence, by empirical correctness; it doesn't help us achieve or justify the coherence we claim. In fact, it gives up on rationality at the beginning—scorns it, as a matter of fact—by declaring it impossible to achieve, and foolish to consider.

Oliver Wendell Holmes saw all this, but his insight lay fallow in lawyers' tomes for almost a century. Worse, when scholars like Simon reached the same conclusions, Holmes's original thoughts were ignored, not only by Simon but by all concerned (including the "behavioral lawyers"). More important than the failure to appreciate Holmes is the current general failure to recognize the limitations of the concept of "rationality" that Holmes was emphasizing. Even Holmes's sneer at the application of "the axioms and corollaries of a book of mathematics," which he considered useless guides to serious judgments, has not been addressed by those who take rationality as the super-criterion by which all judgments are evaluated—and this includes many researchers in the field of judgment and decision making.

This section addressed the question of "who is right" about how rationality should be defined. The answer is that neither the work by the coherence group (represented by Sunstein) nor the correspondence group (represented by Gigerenzer) provides a satisfactory answer, because each is incomplete. The coherence group fails because it addresses only questions of coherence competence; the correspondence group fails because it considers only questions of correspondence competence to be relevant. The correspondence group, however, deserves credit for addressing the problem of rationality directly and enthusiastically, and falls short only by failing to develop a theory about the parameters of the ecologies toward which judgments are directed.

One of the reasons this divide has occurred is that each group holds to what it believes is a coherent point of view, and to shift to the other view would amount to what Thomas Kuhn, in his groundbreaking approach to the history of science, called a "paradigm shift." As Kuhn noted, paradigm shifts are "all or none." I share that view because, as I have noted, when we shift from one strategy to another, we *alternate* between them. Intuitive tactics, on the other hand, allow compromise between tactics because we *oscillate* along the cognitive continuum.

But the process of judgment is difficult to study because it is the one cognitive process that includes, and is the product of, many others. Memory, perception, learning, motivation, inductive inference, deductive logic—all these have a role in almost every judgment made; all these play some part in organizing the information upon which judgment is based. Given that sort of complexity, it is no wonder that judgment is one of the last fundamental processes to be studied by psychologists. And it is that complexity that has called upon the wide diversity of disciplines for contributions.

The diversity of the subject matter of judgment and decision research is matched by the diversity of the professional backgrounds of those who contribute to it: psychologists, neuroscientists, mathematicians, statisticians, political scientists, physicians, management scientists, systems analysts, engineers, and others participate in the research and teaching. Diverse as the backgrounds of the contributors to judgment and decision research may be, the questions that held them together are few and straightforward—how accurate is human judgment? How rational—that is to say, how justifiable—is human judgment? How valuable is intuition? It was through the pursuit of these questions that new ideas about judgment and its justification and value were developed and, most important, tested.

Although the disciplines may be diverse, and the ideas they pursue may be different, research methods are not. The traditional research methods introduced and employed by experimental psychologists dominate the field. In chapter 16, I indicate why I believe these traditional methods have restricted the development of the field, and why research methods need to be changed if we are to successfully take the next step beyond rationality, which is understanding the nature of wisdom. When describing the theme of my research, I argue that our methods must become compatible with the new biological theme of psychology, rather than continuing to mindlessly follow the twentieth century's physicalistic theme.

16

The Author's Theme

The author's theme urges that we recognize the role of coherence and correspondence in the study of human judgment. Once understood in this manner, it becomes clear that understanding the important field of human judgment cannot go forward, cannot eliminate the current disarray, without our acknowledging the role of coherence and correspondence. The fact that these two strategies have been studied largely, if not entirely, independently is a minor handicap to the pursuit of our topic; the independent pursuit of each without the acknowledgment of the importance of the other gave a certain intensity to the pursuit of each strategy that might not otherwise have been there. But, given the development of research on each strategy, it is now time to bring the investigators together.

The author's theme with regard to rationality can be seen in part III, in which the tactics of human judgment and the concepts of a task continuum, a cognitive continuum, and a surface–depth continuum are described. Because these concepts are useful tools for showing change in cognition over time, they will lead us to develop a more dynamic approach to the study of judgment and decision making. Certain properties of coherence and correspondence, and the various tactics of intuition, common sense, and analysis, should be briefly noted.

First, the two *strategies* cannot reach a compromise; there is no middle ground between coherence and correspondence. In making a judgment, one is doing one or the other; it is impossible to do a little of both in one judgment. The opposite is true for the *tactics* of judgment, and it is the role of the task continuum and the cognitive continuum to make the role of compromise between the polar activities of intuition and analysis clear. That distinction leads to another: in seeking wisdom in making judgments, one will alternate in all-or-none fashion between strategies but will oscillate between tactics. This distinction has seldom been given its due in theory or research.

I should call the reader's attention to the long history of these concepts. I will not attempt a description of their role in the history of thought, other than to say they have appeared in numerous guises. In the early twentieth century, when physical science was at its peak and prominent scientists (Heisenberg, Gödel, Einstein, Mach) were philosophers as well, these concepts generally appeared as opponents in the form of empiricism (correspondence) and rationalism (coherence). The struggle for the right to claim truth was serious, unimpeachably dignified and rigorous, sustained and unending—but perhaps it has ended; some claim it has.[1]

Vicarious Functioning and Vicarious Mediation

The author's theme builds directly on Brunswik's ideas about the nature of *Homo sapiens* and is indebted in many ways to the contributions of Gigerenzer, Simon, Darwin, and the many other ecologically minded scientists mentioned in this book, although I trust I have made clear certain differences I have with these scholars. And while acknowledging the contributions of the other themes mentioned here, the main theoretical and methodological theme is unequivocally the one initiated by Brunswik.

Brunswik's conception of the nature of the human organism had much in common with his conception of almost all organisms, and that was the preeminence of the achievement of the organism's stable relationship with its ecology, despite its irreducible uncertainty. The manner of the achievement of that stability is shared by humans and other species; it rests on the use of the cognitive strategy of correspondence and the tactics of what Brunswik was pleased to call *vicarious functioning*, by which he meant the use of a variety of intersubstitutable, fallible (observable) indicators to achieve a reasonably accurate inference about the (not observable) matter of interest.

The concept of vicarious functioning did not drop miraculously from the theorist's dreams. Vicarious functioning was deduced as a necessary feature of the achievement of stable relationships, necessary because of the nature of the ecologies of the world. Brunswik called vicarious mediation that feature of nature that makes vicarious functioning mandatory for survival. Thus *vicarious mediation* refers to the ecology's tactic of conveying uncertain information through a variety of fallible indicators. The term *vicarious* carries the same meaning here as it does in connection with vicarious functioning, namely intersubstitutability; that is, one form of mediation of information can substitute for another. For example, that person I just met (an object in my environment) can convey his intention to be friendly by a warm handclasp; but if I am carrying something, he can give me a warm smile, or a pat on the back. Most important: vicarious mediation in nature is what selected those organisms that were able to develop the skill of vicarious functioning to match it. That skill is the robust flexibility, the shiftiness in our cognitive activity, represented not only by vicarious functioning but also by movement on the cognitive continuum to match the movement of tasks on the task continuum.

That description of *Homo sapiens*' cognitive activity was appropriate for them while they were living in the natural world of millennia past, but it needs to be modified—only in degree, not substance—for life in today's world. In today's world, cognitive tasks have moved considerably—especially since the introduction of the personal computer—toward the analytical pole of the task continuum and thus have commanded cognitive activity to move in that direction. The positive consequences have been enormous for millions of people—those who could manage to adapt through training and education; for those who could not, the negative consequences have been enormous. Robust flexibility is still the most valuable cognitive asset, but the center of that activity has moved sharply to the analytical pole.

Robust flexibility has been known to us as "common sense" for as long as we have been talking about how we think. It would be hard to overemphasize the implicit role of common sense in the history of *Homo sapiens* during its "civilized" period, say from 5000 BCE to the present. Its persistent, if implicit, centrality is outdone only by the superficiality of its treatment by intellectuals during that period. And the last half of the twentieth century is no different, for both history and science have turned a blind eye to this cognitive activity as consistently as our forerunners did. This chapter is intended to change that.

Common sense probably earned its name because it is the way we make our judgments most of the time, and therefore we use that term to refer to a "common"—that is, frequent—tactic. It is also "common" in the sense that it belongs to the common people; it does not require schooling: no one goes to school, particularly a university, to acquire common sense, whatever it is. Indeed, there is a folk belief that a college education deprives you of whatever common sense you might have acquired, a folk belief that, although much exaggerated, does contain a kernel of truth. And then there is the widely accepted belief—also with a kernel of truth—that bureaucracies are completely devoid of common sense. So it is a concept with a great variety of folk meanings, and, as result, it is shunned by researchers in the field of judgment and decision making and by most psychologists. But it will not be shunned here, because once it is given meaning in the context of the present (Brunswikian-type) theory, it becomes a useful, even necessary, concept.

The loose use of the term *common sense* continues. Here is today's striking example of a demand for common sense in the midst of a world crisis: Thomas Friedman wrote a column in *The New York Times* in which he addressed the impasse over the question of how aggressive the UN should be toward Iraq. Friedman said that Iraq could be dealt with "if we, the Russians, the Chinese, and the French 'pursue them with a little more common sense.' "[2] How easily a columnist can appeal to his readers with the concept of common sense! But we can be sure that neither he nor his readers could explain just what that entails, especially in this context.

Would cognitive psychologists do any better? No. Cognitive psychologists are of course aware of common sense, but they ignore it because it is a layperson's term and therefore they believe it has no scientific merit. By defining it in the terms of the above paragraphs as *robust flexibility*, I give it a scientific base that derives from its place on the cognitive continuum, together with intuition and analysis.

The Author's Theme: Robust Flexibility on the Cognitive Continuum

Robust flexibility is the overall theme-derived descriptor for the effective cognitive activity of human judgment. *Flexibility* refers to the ease of oscillation of cognition on the cognitive continuum from one pole to the other. For example, one often makes a judgment in which some analytical reasoning occurs but is not satisfactory as justification for a defensible judgment. When this occurs, we turn to some fallible indicators, make the best intuitive use we can of them, and then we reach a judgment, thus moving toward the intuitive pole of the continuum. Or it might work the other way: our intuitions suggest two or three plausible judgments, but they are unsatisfactory because they leave us with too much irreducible uncertainty (as our friends and enemies will be happy to point out to us). At this point we turn toward the analytical pole of the continuum and reason as carefully as we can about our intuitive judgments, trying to create a more defensible judgment. But then after some analytical work, we realize that although our analysis may be an improvement, we are still uncertain about our judgment.

Feeling the need for more support for a judgment, we turn back to intuition, and once again make use of multiple fallible indicators. Cognition, in short, can be dynamic![3] Our dynamic efforts will seem like "common sense" to anyone to whom we explain our judgment. It may even seem like wisdom. And, indeed, that is how I shall define wisdom in chapter 20.

I use the term "robust" to reflect the long-established fact that this cognitive process produces good empirical accuracy in a wide variety of circumstances; that is, it has ecological generality. There is no specific point of compromise on the cognitive continuum between intuition and analysis that permanently defines robust flexibility for all circumstances: on one occasion it will lie closer to the intuitive pole of the continuum and analytical reasoning will contribute little; on another occasion, it will be the reverse. That ambiguity is what makes common sense so hard to define precisely, and why no good definition is likely to be found outside a theory of judgment.

No one knows how just how often during the day we employ our intuition, or our analytical abilities, or our (quasi-rational) common sense. Much depends on one's occupation and/or profession. Those involved in the performing or visual arts are likely to employ their intuitive capacities frequently; judging the value of artistic creations is highly intuitive, that is, based on the appraisal of multiple fallible indicators. Examining what artists (broadly defined) do and the fact that there is often considerable disagreement among them in their judgments suggests that that is the case. But a conversation with professional artists will leave you with the opposite impression; they will impress upon you the important role of analytical cognition in their work.

Scientists are more likely to engage in analytical cognitive activity inasmuch as they must have logical and empirical bases for their judgments and are more readily held accountable for their departures and lapses than others. Scientific thought strives to be fully analytical, within both the correspondence strategy and the coherence strategy, but of course we have also seen the role that scientists claim for intuition in their work. Engineers, and others in mathematically oriented professions, and also lawyers, are likely to engage in hard analytical cognition. Computer programmers engage in purely analytical work. (I once had a professor who made a point of severely scolding any student who said or wrote "I feel . . ." He would shout, "Scientists think! They do not feel!" A few shouts of that kind soon erased any further use of that expression, in or out of his presence. While this professor's behavior may seem quaint, it was his way of teaching us that every scientific problem should be cast in analytical terms, and thus every cognitive effort should match the problem, that is, analytically.)

Most people are not at the extremes; they are not artists, scientists, engineers, or musicians; most people visit the ends of the continuum rarely, and then only under duress; most vacillate near the middle. It is surprising, unanticipated change in outside circumstances (commonly called *stress*) that leads to cognitive change and often drives people to the ends of the continuum.

The concept of the cognitive task continuum is the basis for my assertions about different occupations and the kinds of cognitive activity they will induce in their participants. My argument is that occupations vary widely in the relative amounts of intuition and analysis they require, and they do so *within* any occupation as well. Thus, tasks will vary in the amount of intuitive and analytical cognition they induce and also in the degree of oscillation they induce. And when they are not engaged in their professional work, the artist, scientist, lawyer, engineer, carpenter, plumber, electrician, computer programmer—in short, virtually everyone—employs robust flexibility (common sense) in their everyday judgments; that is, we all engage in as much analytical work as required, and in as much intuition as will suffice, because intuition is by far the easiest. Not every task has to be performed perfectly or with full justification, as Gigerenzer has emphasized.

It is easy to be deceived by our assumptions of what professional occupations demand and what practitioners like to claim. For example, although we are inclined to assume that the courts themselves exhibit, and from lawyers demand, impeccable logic, recall the statement of Supreme Court Justice Oliver Wendell Holmes: "It is the merit of the common law that it decides the case first and determines the principle afterwards," a rather shocking admission of the minimal role of legal principles in favor of common sense, and where it would be least expected.[4]

The Flexibility of Cognition and Action

It should now be clear what has long stood in our way in the effort to define and understand common sense. That commonly used expression cannot be understood until we understand intuition and analysis. And that is what has defeated most efforts, for most researchers, even Nobel Prize winners, still rely on the incorrect conventional assumption that a dichotomy divides intuition and analysis. Once the dichotomy is dispensed with, and a continuum is acknowledged, the recognition of movement on the continuum easily follows; from that proceeds the recognition of oscillation. It is that flexibility (movement on the cognitive continuum), combined with the robustness that ensues, that made *Homo sapiens* the superior animal in the natural world and now allows its exceptional achievement—though not without problems—in the world of its own making.

No one has yet drawn formal distinctions between Simon's bounded rationality, Brunswik's quasi-rationality, and everyone's common sense and my robust flexibility. Perhaps that is because there are strong common elements in these concepts. They all find a narrow ecological slot for standard rationality (if a clear definition of that term can be developed). Perhaps it would be best if all four of these terms were used interchangeably.

Artificial Intelligence and Robust Flexibility

Where does the concept of artificial intelligence fit in this framework? Artificial intelligence (AI) is one of the most important developments in the history of cognitive science, and it has been enormously successful in attracting researchers. It has had success in the application of computer-based solutions to minor analytical problems. It has not been so successful in fulfilling its other promise(s), such as becoming a general substitute for, or description of, natural intelligence. Its main failure is its inability to replicate the common sense of young children; it can't grasp simple concepts such as "why lions don't live in fish tanks."

There are other problems with AI, but the failure to cope with what the AI people call common sense is an outstanding one. That problem is an easy one for judgment researchers when cast in the framework of a compromise between intuition and analysis described above. There will be many occasions in everyday life when it will be obvious when such compromises are at work, and it will be easy to replicate those conditions in the laboratory. In fact, it has been done many times when studying judgments under uncertainty, without naming the process "common sense."[5]

Why has AI failed to solve this problem? It is because AI researchers have never developed a theory of cognition but rather assume only that cognition is a replica of a computer program. Just what the program should be remains a mystery. That failure also describes why AI has been so successful in diagnosing standard failure problems in fixed, repetitive, logic-based circumstances. The fixed nature of the diagnostic task makes it clear what the program should be.

The Growing Demand for Common Sense in Government

When you are not sure what you want, or what you mean, it is common, even if you are an expert, to make demand that *others* use common sense. In her June 5, 2005, op-ed column in *The New York Times,* Diane Ravitch, a respected expert on education, tells us that the National Assessment Governing Board should review the test makers' deletions of potentially offensive words by applying their "common sense." No criterion is mentioned, of course, because no criterion for common sense has ever been established. (Odd that an expert on education doesn't know that.)

In the mid-1990s, however, Phillip K. Howard made a determined attempt to show how government was failing because of its abysmal reliance on bureaucratic rules and lack of common sense. His book was titled *The Death of Common Sense,* and it immediately became a best-seller.[6] It caught the attention of most of the major figures in government, including then president Bill Clinton, then presidential candidate Bob Dole, and others, who not only promoted his book, but also bought many copies to give others. With his anecdotes and examples, and a certain appealing prose, Howard had clearly touched a population sensitive to his thesis, "common sense is best"!

Never mind that his work lacked a definition of common sense, analytical criticism, and a workable remedy for the problems he described in such a compelling manner. He had said what people—particularly those interested in failures of government—wanted to hear, in a way they understood. Many people, it turned out, were dissatisfied with what they had come to believe was an over-application of nitpicking bureaucratic rules. In terms used here, they believed that the role of analytical cognition had been exaggerated: in government, cognition had moved too far to the analytical pole of the cognitive continuum. That meant that common sense was lacking. Howard had put into understandable words what many had been thinking for some time.

A second interesting feature of Howard's book was that his remedy was to urge the greater use of human judgment, which, of course, brings his thesis close to the ideas in this book. But he offered no indication of why or how judgment, however conceived, would make things any better. After all, common-sense judgments have had their failures (which Howard knows as well as anyone else does), and these have done much to promote the use of analytical rules. Yet Howard doesn't show us any evidence that would lead us to believe that the greater application of human judgment would be better than the application of those silly rules he enjoys telling us about. It is enough for him to provide anecdotes about ridiculous behavior by bureaucrats applying ridiculous rules. And that was enough for all those politicians who bought his books in such prodigious numbers.

About seven years later, Howard tried again, with a new book, *The Lost Art of Drawing the Line: How Fairness Went Too Far.*[7] The message was the same, the style was the same, and the remedy was the same: scrap those rules and apply human judgment (apparently, he doesn't consult textbooks on human judgment that reiterate the failures of human judgment). This time, however, Howard's work drew a critical review from Cass Sunstein, who came down hard on Howard's lack of serious evidence for his thesis.[8] This review is important for us because it offers a detailed analysis of the weakness of the "just use your good judgment" point of view.[9]

Sunstein acknowledged the importance of Howard's first book: it influenced the Clinton administration's "reinventing government" initiative, which attempted to focus attention on results and performance and allow people to find their own way to make workplaces safer or the air cleaner. Howard also appeared to affect the thinking of prominent Republicans; Senator Dole took a great deal of interest in Howard's diagnosis of the problem. It is highly likely that the Bush administration's efforts at regulatory reform have been influenced, at least indirectly, by Howard's claims. Sunstein also noted, "*The Death of Common Sense* was in many ways a fine book. Howard is an unusually vivid writer."[10]

The success of Howard's book of anecdotes and persuasive remarks is instructive, for his thesis flies in the face of the past 50 years' research on human judgment. His success suggests that knowledge does not influence policymakers' reflections about their judgments, but clever examples do. Sunstein's critique explains Howard's success this way: "Howard radiates decency, and his heart is in the right place, and about some things he is surely correct."[11] But Sunstein knows enough about human judgment research to know what the book lacks, and he says what it is:

> The problem with his [Howard's] book is that it is not so much an argument as a mood. He compares authorities from heaven with laws from hell, without making a sufficient effort to explore, at the level of theory or practice, the factors that will lead to the right mix of rules and discretion in the actual human world.[12]

Sunstein could hardly have been clearer in his call for the analysis of judgment in terms of a cognitive continuum; he agrees with Howard's "mood," although he criticizes him for leaving matters there. But are these critics of rationality going to be satisfied with common sense if it ever does appear in officials' judgments? Aren't they, like Justice Holmes, really seeking wisdom?

The Modern Enlightenment

Should deductive logic always be the accepted standard of rational cognition? Although philosophers have pursued this question since the Counter-Enlightenment (roughly the eighteenth century), few psychologists have shown interest in it.

It is the thesis of this book that it will be common sense (robust flexibility) that replaces rationality as the desirable cognitive tactical response to problems involving uncertainty that stem from fallible indicators, entangled causality, and other elements of our task environment that induce our judgment. To say that the wisdom of common sense will replace analytical cognition as the more desirable form of cognitive tactics is to say that cognition at the analytical pole of the cognitive continuum will no longer be seen as the ultimate criterion of rationality. Analysis will thus be replaced by some broad region on the cognitive continuum between the analytical pole and the intuitive pole of the cognitive continuum, the specific location depending on the nature of the task, that is, the location of the task on the task continuum. And the match, or congruence, between the point on the cognitive continuum and the task continuum will provide us with a definition of wisdom.

Here, I must remind the reader of Gigerenzer's plea for ecological rationality (see p. 99) that was based on Brunswik's ecological psychology and can be traced to the latter's "quasi-rationality."[13] Gigerenzer and Todd assert that "heuristics are successful to the degree they are ecologically rational, that is, adapted to the structure of the information in the environment in which they are used to make decisions."[14] Thus, Gigerenzer and Todd imply that the "structure of information in the environment" varies and that successful cognition must be "adapted" to that environment.

Although I share the general sentiment Gigerenzer and Todd expressed in their definition of ecological rationality, it must be noted that their definition is tautological, for the meaning of *successful* is apparently exhausted by "adaptation"; cognition that is not adapted to the environment cannot be "successful cognition," and "successful" cognition could hardly be anything but "adapted" to the structure of the environment. Thus, Gigerenzer and Todd's definition of ecological rationality suffers from a definition of successful cognition that is not independent of "adaptation." Nevertheless, Vernon Smith, who shared the Nobel Prize with Daniel Kahneman, found Gigerenzer and Todd's concept of ecological rationality appealing. But Smith was taken by a slightly *different* definition written by Gigerenzer and Todd: "A heuristic is ecologically rational to the degree that it is adapted to the structure of the environment."[15] (The tautological character of this conception is not as clear in this definition as in the earlier one, although it cannot be ruled out as long as the term *adapted* remains ambiguous. I can agree with this definition if the term *adapted* is replaced by the weaker term *related*.)

The concept of ecological rationality obviously appealed to Smith (though it apparently does not appeal to Kahneman). Smith encountered the expression *ecological rationality* after he had written his prize lecture, and employed it in his title because it fits with his interest in developing the idea of two kinds of rationality, which he identifies as *constructivist* and *ecological*.

That position is analogous to the one I asserted above, namely, that instead of positing analytical cognition (rationality) as the one and only justifiable and defensible form of cognition, one should observe that it is the match between the form of cognition and the nature of the task ("the structure of the information in the environment") that defines not *rationality* but *wisdom*.

A prime example of the fact that quasi-rational cognition already has a strong foothold in our search for wisdom in justice is the current use of plea bargaining in U.S. courts. Plea bargaining appeals to a search for wisdom in the commonsense application of formal, written law that is a complete surrender neither to intuition nor to an unbending application of written law that ignores situational particularities.

A Theory of Common Sense

Once *common sense* is given meaning in the context of the present (Brunswikian-type) theory, it becomes a useful concept. Thus, common sense is not here defined arbitrarily, nor is it assigned a meaning chosen from the folk tradition. Rather, its definition here follows from the postulate of a cognitive continuum and task continuum.[16] Common sense is defined as the match, or congruence, between the location of cognition on the cognitive continuum and the locations of the task on the task continuum. Without knowledge of the location of the task, the area surrounding the midpoint of the cognitive continuum (that is, any area in which both intuition and analysis are employed) is defined as common sense. The specific point on the continuum occupied by any specific judgment is determined by how much intuition and how much analysis is employed. A judgment that is primarily analytical (one based largely on calculation, or a set of verbal rules, as, for example, the legal codes) will occupy a point near the analytical pole. A judgment that is primarily intuitive (one based largely on unconscious processes, as, for example, a literary or personal judgment) will occupy a point near the intuitive pole.

Thus, commonsense judgments are located at various points on the continuum. Different locations simply mean that the person making the judgment is using different relative amounts of intuition and analysis. Using the tactic of employing common sense generally means being as analytical as time and knowledge permit, so as to be able to defend one's judgment as much as circumstances will permit. But if you still cannot provide a fully defensible answer, you are permitted, even expected, to rely on your intuition, to "go with your instincts" as much as is necessary. That latter part of your judgment is partly based on intu-ition and will thus be beyond your reach; it will be inexplicable. And that, of course, is what makes that part of your judgment process mysterious and hard to describe, and why you say "I feel" instead of "I think." You recognize when you have reached that point when, in response to the query "Why do you say that?" you reply, "I don't know, I just feel that . . ."

The Common Use of Common Sense

Is there any naturalistic evidence for the kind of cognition I have described as "common sense"? Yes. It is to be found almost everywhere. It is prevalent in the regions where folk wisdom prevails and where it is simply not good manners or good sense to push a judgment too far, either toward analysis or intuition. The analytical part of your judgment is undertaken to provide some clear deductions from your premises, to eliminate obvious contradictions or absurdities, and to show that you have some knowledge of the subject. But in ordinary circum-stances, no one is pretending that the process is perfectly logical; the term *com-mon sense* is used to avoid having to meet that standard. The intuitive part of your judgment is generally based on folklore that people are reluctant to chal-lenge. It sometimes begins with "Any damn fool knows . . ." As a result, com-monsense judgments are generally accepted because they seldom fly directly in the face of empirical fact and they are sufficiently ambiguous to be difficult to contradict. And for those of you who hold common sense in high regard because of its supposed balance, you must give some consideration to the adage that claims "the common sense of today is the science of yesterday."

In addition to finding this cognitive compromise between analysis and intu-ition in anecdote and personal experience, we find it has occurred in numerous experiments on learning in uncertain situations, although the term *cognitive com-promise* is seldom employed.[17] The demand for common sense, and its ubiqui-tous use as an explanatory concept, is also found in the work of scholars, partic-ularly historians.

Movement on the Cognitive Continuum

The concept of a cognitive continuum is a fruitful one that can advance our grasp of the subject. For example, we can see that cognition can move over time on the cognitive continuum from one polar position to the other. Thus, when we move from a rapid, off-the-cuff, intuitive judgment to a (literally) thoughtful, slow, retraceable consideration of the information in the task, we move from one pole of the continuum to the other. And, of course, in any judgment task, cognition may move from one pole of the continuum to a point somewhere between these poles and back to the original pole. This type of movement back and forth along the continuum is called *oscillation* (in contrast to *alternation* between strategies). That difference in terms is intended to describe the fact that as cognition oscillates, change occurs in terms of the different relative amounts of intuition and analysis in tactics, whereas change in strategies between coherence and correspondence is a matter of all or none, not degree.

Oscillation on the continuum can be observed as a person tries to "make up his or her mind." It often follows this path: intuition seems unsatisfactory because it cannot defend its conclusions, so one turns to analysis, which then seems unsatisfactory because there isn't time to consider all features of the task and because one doesn't quite know how the information should be organized, and therefore one returns to an intuitive attempt. Or the person making the judgment may work out a fairly satisfactory analytical judgment and then seek to bolster it by an appeal to his or her intuition (does it feel like the right answer?) or vice versa. That is, one does not oscillate forever but stops somewhere on the continuum. The result is a quasi-rational judgment; that is, one that is almost but not quite a rational judgment, a compromise between intuition and analysis. It is my contention that most judgments we make are quasi-rational in form; the layperson's term (and now mine) for this is *common sense*. In short, the tactics most of us use most of the time are neither fully intuitive nor fully analytical: they are a compromise that contains some of each; how much of each depends on the nature of the task and on the knowledge the person making the judgment brings to the task. And over time, the person will move his or her cognitive activity across the cognitive continuum.

Design engineers know that oscillation is what they must try to prevent in the design of an information system, such as a display panel for a power station, an airplane, or even the dashboard of a car. They want to design the system so that even though the eyes of the operator may range over all the gauges and dials, his or her mind—that is, cognitive activity—will remain focused on the analytical pole of the continuum. Artists have the opposite goal; they strive for a presentation that induces cognitive activity to oscillate, and that will be stimulating and enriching to the observer. And that, of course, is what artists want to happen to their audience and what engineers don't want to happen to the operators who are reading the instruments the engineers have created.

If movement on the cognitive continuum can cause joy and intuitive understanding when one is observing an artistic production, it can cause havoc in an engineered situation, not to mention serious problems in interpersonal understanding. Such oscillation makes your judgments hard to anticipate. Just when you think you finally understand how your colleague makes his or her judgments, he or she has decided that you don't and has moved to a different tactic. And that often continues, as close attention to any conversation will demonstrate.

Oscillation on the Cognitive Continuum

Sometimes oscillation is self-generated, produced by a person in response to his or her satisfaction with his or her cognitive activity. And sometimes oscillation occurs because of changes in task conditions. That is, what began as a task that induced analytical cognition changes to a task that now induces intuition; but intuition may then produce an insight into the possible use of analytical tools, and the person moves back to analysis. The postulate of a cognitive continuum makes it possible to describe and understand that kind of cognitive activity. Without it, the study of such dynamic activity would not be possible. One striking example of the division of labor between these two strategies occurs in the cockpit of the modern jet airplane that carries a pilot and a copilot. It is a customary practice in such airplanes during the approach to the runway to have one pilot look out the window at the field ahead and to have the other pilot focus on the instruments. Thus, one pilot is using a correspondence strategy and the other is using a coherence strategy.

Unfortunately, however, most research in judgment and decision making has taken place in what might be called static tasks; that is, tasks that do not change their properties over time. Probably 95% of all the research in research in judgment and decision making is based on static tasks, tasks whose properties do not change during the time the subject is making his or her judgments, although we learned long ago that people can track changes that occur over time in the relative importance of indicators in a learning task.[18] And although that experiment of long ago demonstrated people's ability to track changes in, indicators we have no experiments (to my knowledge) that examine how difficult it is for people to shift from one point on the cognitive continuum to another, to shift from intuition to analysis or vice versa: to oscillate between the poles of the continuum. Cognitive shifting may be sharply affected by aging.

The Task Continuum, Cognitive Continuum, and Judgments under Stress

The concepts of a task continuum and cognitive continuum have not been widely investigated, but their utility has been explored in my book *Judgments under Stress*.[19] Because it is extremely difficult to create convincing stressful conditions in the laboratory that are sufficiently representative of stressful conditions outside the laboratory, very little research of any use—either theoretical or practical—has been done.[20] One source of material exists, however, that has seldom been explored, and that is the description of episodes of extraordinary circumstances, particularly in the military and in aviation, where careful and extensive documentation is frequently available. Although using such material can often be frustrating because it is fragmented or unreliable, it can compensate for its shortcomings by describing conditions that cannot easily be recreated in an experiment. *Judgments under Stress* makes use of such documented episodes rather than developing laboratory experiments.

The concept of a task continuum is invaluable when examining conditions post hoc because it allows the discovery and description of differences among the tasks being investigated, irrespective of whether they are in aviation, medicine, or another field. The formal analysis (number of indicators, reliability of indicators, interrelationships among indicators, etc) that leads to such descriptions makes the differentiation of tasks possible. Indeed, it is precisely in this regard that the journalistic term *real world* proves useless, for it provides no means for discriminating among tasks but instead seduces the reader into thinking that a tie to an ecology has been established, when in fact it has not. The use of the task and cognitive continuum was demonstrated in a laboratory experiment; its generality can be seen in *Judgments under Stress,* where it is applied in several domains: flying a plane, engaging in naval warfare, launching a space shuttle, fighting a forest fire and so on.[21]

How Movement on the Cognitive Continuum Saved an Airplane

In order to illustrate the utility of the concept of a cognitive continuum anchored at the poles by intuition and analysis, I take an excerpt from my book *Judgments under Stress* to show how this concept offers a (post hoc) description of the cognitive activity of a flight crew at a time of potential disaster.

> At the start of our analysis, the flight system is operating normally
> [that is, analytically], and the operators of the system are operating

normally [also analytically]. An unanticipated event then occurs for which there is no prearranged response anticipating this event. There is no emergency plan for this event. The operators' cognitive efforts are thus twice deprived; on the one hand, they are deprived of normal technological support from task coherence because of the technological breakdown of the system; on the other hand, they are deprived of cognitive coherence because sufficient knowledge to cope with the event is not available, either through training or expert assistance; help cannot be obtained from experts because no resource has anticipated this event. As a result, the operators do not know what to do, a fact that is made plain by Captain Haynes's communications with the control tower. The airplane is now out of control.

Deprived of both task coherence and cognitive coherence, the operators must move their cognitive activity to make it congruent with the new conditions. If ever there were circumstances that required people to think differently, these were surely those circumstances. And due to the lack of anticipation, these circumstances are now almost entirely intuition inducing. That is, the operators must resort to dependence on multiple fallible indicators to tell them what the aircraft is doing; the operators have proved that it is impossible to bring analysis to bear on their circumstances. The disruption of normal conditions have resulted in task conditions becoming intuition inducing, and thus driving the operators to use multiple fallible indicators. Task-cognition interaction has changed. Does that mean that degradation of performance is inevitable? No, for intuitive cognition is now congruent with intuition-inducing task conditions. It will be the robust properties of intuition that will make survival possible. For it is precisely in these conditions, in which only multiple fallible indicators are available, in which intuition is robust.

This explanation is consistent with the excellent performance of the crew of UAL 232. They gave up their analytical efforts to restore the coherence of the technological system and turned to orienting the aircraft to correspond with the empirical demands of flight. They turned to the perceptual-motor task of achieving the appropriate orientation by visual means, and thus managed to get the airplane to an airport.[22]

Skeptics—and we should all be skeptical of anecdotal reports—will be unimpressed. It is my contention, however, that there is a wealth of material to be gained from documented episodes that affords excellent opportunities for learning. The event described also shows the disadvantage of resorting to journalistic terms such as *real world* to describe task conditions. Had I merely used *real world* to indicate the circumstances in which these events occurred, the reader would have been deprived of the essential information necessary to understand what had occurred.

I offer these examples in order to show that the general approach described here is not without its practical applications, that the theme I have adopted, and which I urge upon the reader, can be applied to a wide range of problems.

PART V

Looking Backward

Michael Doherty. A meticulous experimenter who documented the empirical wisdom of Brunswik's theory. (Reprinted with the permission of Michael Doherty.)

17

Trying to Learn from History with Bernard Lewis and Jared Diamond

The status of history as an intellectual discipline has long been debated. Can we really learn anything other than the content of the story? Is it nothing but story-telling? These perennial questions and similar ones have slowly but surely taken center stage as democracy has replaced aristocracy as the source of public authority, thus allowing the judgment and decision-making process to come under wide critical review. History, broadly defined as past experience, has become more and more relevant to the process of forming social policy. And that, in turn, has led to a demand from the public that its policymakers *learn* from history, and especially from their mistakes. But if there is one universal complaint against legislators, and other policymakers—including the military—it is that they *fail* to learn: "Why can't these people learn?" is a common complaint from their constituents.

No one, however, looks at the conditions under which the legislators and others are expected to learn. It is my contention that if those conditions were to be examined, it would become obvious that it is impossible for legislators, or any policymakers, to learn from history.

And they don't. So it is common for editorial writers, public intellectuals, and columnists to complain about "lessons not learned" (by others). It is also common to read, "One of the most important lessons learned from [some event] was that *we should never* or *we should always* [something]." But it is a rare case indeed when we can learn from the circumstances of history, with its multiple causations; unreliable, uncertain, or potentially deceitful data; interrelated and confounded data; and poor and/or delayed feedback.

There is, of course, no dispute about the fact that we can learn *that* something did or did not occur. But learning *that* is not the question of interest. The question all policymakers—and the rest of us—are interested in is answering *why* something did or did not occur; that is the only way of avoiding disaster or achieving success. Jared Diamond's important book *Collapse: How Societies Choose to Fail or Succeed* deals directly with the problem of learning *why,* as the book jacket explains: "Why do some societies, but not others, blunder into self-destruction?" (I will examine his efforts below.)

Here we need to mention the many barriers to learning *why.* First, it is hard to know which variables, factors, or indicators are important across cases. Second, multiple causation among entangled (correlated) variables makes it difficult to ascertain which variable was the causative agent. Third, the long delay and poor quality of feedback from the effects of an action (or inaction) enables many new variables to enter (and old ones to exit) the equation. And there is the irreducible uncertainty in the system of interrelationships among variables, factors, or indicators that is so daunting to investigators. These are the essential conditions that make learning outside the controlled conditions of the laboratory so difficult and that lead to situations where explanations are contested for hundreds of years.

"Can we learn from history?" is not a question to be reserved for "egghead" academicians or policy "wonks." It has taken on a new seriousness as more people become more educated and citizens increasingly demand that their leaders learn. Historians, like other social scientists, are participating ever more closely in the policymaking process, although word of their participation is slow to surface. One of the historians discussed below is a close advisor to the highest-ranking members of the Bush administration on the topic of problems arising from the U.S. invasion of Iraq. The centuries-old question of how to learn from history is now acknowledged as obviously relevant to matters of great concern, a view that was absent in the past.

The importance of learning from experience has even become obvious to the troops in the field in Iraq, who complain that the army hadn't learned what the troops needed to know to handle the chaos of street warfare in Iraq; because the army didn't know, the troops weren't taught. An article in *The New Yorker* describes how some soldiers discovered that other soldiers wanted to know what they had learned from their experience.[1] They found they could share their knowledge with other soldiers via the Internet, and they did. Their sites were soon very busy indeed.

But one officer was astute enough to see the difference between learning *that* and learning *why*. The author reports that Captain Jason Miseli said, "What they [the soldiers sharing their knowledge] actually did was . . . of limited value . . . It's the *why*" (italics mine). Nevertheless, so eager were the troops to learn what they should have been taught, even if it was of limited value, that "ten thousand, or more than a third of all captains in the Army . . . went to the site sixty-seven thousand times and looked at more than a million pages."[2]

It is the historians, naturally enough, who responsibly take on the task of learning from history so that we may be guided more successfully in the future. And it was the esteemed Middle East scholar Bernard Lewis who recently assumed one of the most difficult of these tasks. His book *What Went Wrong?* asks what went wrong in the Middle East and tries to answer it.[3] "What went wrong" is clearly a question directed at learning. And "what went wrong" is exactly the question that policymakers, and others, frequently ask. So it is interesting and useful to look at how a renowned scholar seeks to answer this question with respect to the nations of Islam at a time of great tension between these countries and the West; it is clearly a bold, ambitious, and worthy undertaking. It is my contention that it is precisely this kind of learning that is impossible to achieve.

Note that Lewis's question is different from that grand question of the past "Is history a science?" That is the type of question left to scholars such as Isaiah Berlin, who addressed it in his widely reprinted article "The Concept of Scientific History."[4] It is now more a matter of, "Can you tell us how things work? Or, at least, how they worked in the past? Or, even better, why they worked the way they did in this particular case?" It is this latter type of question that Lewis addresses when he asks "what went wrong" with Islam between 600 and 1600 AD.

Trying to Learn from History with Bernard Lewis

Lewis begins by reminding us that Islamic nations were the dominant powers in the world for roughly a thousand years, militarily, economically, technologically, and intellectually. Moreover, they controlled vast amounts of territory. All that came to an end by 1600, however, and for the past three or four centuries they have lagged far behind Western society. Indeed, Islamic nations have been recognized economically only because of riches they earned through no efforts of their own, but simply because they happen to sit on vast amounts of oil. Lewis states that in contrast with Western Europe, "the world of Islam had become poor, weak, and ignorant."[5] That widely held opinion has given new visibility to the question of what went wrong, the question Lewis asks in the title of his book.[6]

But the question I want to raise is a different one: It is not "What went wrong?"; rather, it is "Can the Islamists (or anyone) learn what went wrong?" Specifically, can Bernard Lewis learn what went wrong? Perhaps more important, can we, the reader and this author, discover how Lewis *learned* what went wrong, if he in fact did? Perhaps the assumption that such things can be learned is false and unfounded. If so, Lewis took on an impossible task. I ask these questions because they follow from—they are the practical consequences of—asking whether or not policymakers can learn. That question is at the heart of democratic life, yet is seldom, if ever, examined. For while learning may or may not be the essential characteristic of a sustainable society, nearly everyone believes it is, with little or no scientific support. That is in contrast to totalitarian societies, where the correct answers are always known in advance. Lewis's book offers an excellent opportunity to see how an accomplished historian goes about answering this fundamental question.

"What went wrong?" is what policymakers, and their constituents, usually ask after it becomes apparent that a disaster has followed from the pursuit of a social policy. Recall the numerous times this question has been asked regarding the disastrous end of the Soviet Union, or with respect to the highly educated society of Germany's welcoming Adolf Hitler in the 1930s; it is the basis of Diamond's *Collapse*. Asking what went wrong and pointing to the collapse of other societies, and to the potential catastrophes awaiting us, raises questions of great import, for they imply that we may, or may not, have the wit and motivation to prevent these unpleasant events from happening to us. But the question of what went wrong, and books about collapse and catastrophe, implies that an answer will be forthcoming, and further implies that a method of inquiry exists to provide it. Is that the case?

The structure of the task such questions entail leads me to deny that such a method exists. It is my belief that the conditions of that inquiry (irreducible uncertainty, entangled causality, and delayed, ambiguous feedback) make it impossible to find an answer that will stand up to methodological criticism. And that means that completely defensible answers will not be obtained, and that means unending dispute and conflict. So it will be instructive to see how Lewis answers the question he poses.

Lewis's answer is clear, and he makes his method plain in his conclusion; he assembles facts and draws logical deductions and inductive inferences from them. Although he does not name his method, it is apparent that he is following the method advocated by the philosopher Karl Popper of falsifying, or rejecting, various hypotheses, to try to prove them correct. (Below I will show how Diamond uses the method of *proof* of a hypothesis rather than *disproof*.) Lewis follows the well-known logic of *modus ponens,* which is: if *p,* then *q.* That is, if a certain condition, *p,* exists, then *q,* a certain consequence, should follow. For example, in Lewis's pursuit of what went wrong, the first hypothesis he puts to the test is a conventional explanation: things went wrong because of (*p*) the Mongol invasion of Arab territory in the thirteenth century that (*q*) destroyed Muslim power and Islamic civilization. He then tests this proposition empirically, and describes what he calls "flaws in this argument," namely, "some of the greatest achievements of the Muslim peoples" came "after . . . the Mongol invasions."[7] He thus falsified this form of "if *p,* then *q,*" because the deduction doesn't hold, empirically. For although *p* (the invasion) happened, *q* (the collapse of the Muslim society) didn't happen. His falsification of this "if *p,* then *q*" rules out that explanation of what went wrong.

Then he turns to another hypothesis and refutes it by the same procedure, namely, assembling facts that show that the logical *q* (sociocultural disaster) did not empirically follow a certain specified condition *p.* He continues by testing the common conjectures for the failure of the Islamic societies against the empirical facts and falsifying each one in turn. That's important, because once he has falsified all the common conjectures, he can now turn to his own conjecture, which concerns the matter of freedom, and deduce the consequences of the absence of freedom. That is, his conjecture is that it is the absence of freedom that caused the downfall of the Muslim empire. His deduction is clear: "To a Western observer, schooled in the theory and practice of Western freedom, it is precisely the lack of freedom—freedom of the mind—that underlies so many of the troubles of the Muslim world."[8] Here we see that Lewis has shifted tactics from *modus ponens* (if *p,* then *q*) to *modulus tollens* (if *not p,* then *not q*). He will now attempt to refute the truth of that deduction with the facts. So he lists the conditions of freedom that he believes are necessary for cultural advancement and then examines Islam for their appearance. Specifically, his hypothesis is that without (*p*) ("freedom of the mind from constraint and indoctrination, to question and inquire and speak; freedom of the economy from corrupt and pervasive mismanagement; freedom of women from male oppression; freedom of citizens from tyranny") we should not observe *q,* that is, advancement by the Muslim world. And since his examination of the facts of the history of the Muslim nations will not allow him to refute that argument (which is no freedom [*not p*] no advancement [*not q*]), he accepts it, just as he accepted the conclusions from all his other refutations. Lewis therefore concluded that denial of freedom led to the downfall of the Islamist states because he could not refute this hypothesis, and that is his answer in *What Went Wrong?*

Why Bernard Lewis's Conclusion Should Not Be Accepted as Beyond Dispute

To examine Lewis's conclusions in the context of the theory of judgment in this book, we begin by placing his methods (*modus ponens, modulus tollens*) on the cognitive continuum. Since his methods entail pure logic, they belong at the purely analytic pole of the continuum, but the manner in which they are used does not. For although in a purely formal sense it appears that Lewis's work involves merely the simple case of "if p, then q"—and what could be simpler?—it is not altogether clear exactly what p or q entails. To see what each entails will require inferential logic; that is where the trouble always begins with rationality, on the inductive part.

Defining p and q

A closer look at the definition of p (the conditions that prevailed) shows us that p is not clearly defined: "freedom of the mind from constraint and indoctrination, to question and inquire and speak; freedom of the economy from corrupt and pervasive mismanagement; freedom of women from male oppression; freedom of citizens from tyranny"—all this sounds concrete when these terms are piled up as they are, but, in fact, they are rather vague terms. These elements are not defined for the reader; rather, readers will be required to infer what they mean, and thus we cannot place this argument at the analytic pole of the continuum; it belongs closer to the center, closer to common sense. So the argument is not logically impeccable after all, because once definitions are attempted, there will be dispute over inferential judgments about just how much freedom, or tyranny, there is at any one specific point in time and place. There will be instances of repression, and counter-instances, and someone will have to weigh their relative importance.

Ambiguities in Feedback

Similar problems arise with q, the consequences—in this case the fall of Islam. Remember that Lewis indicated that the 1,000 years of the practice and policies of Islam (from 600 to 1600 AD) had left it "poor, weak, and ignorant" in contrast with Christendom, a description sure to evoke dispute.[9] But the consequences of any actions almost always are a product of subjective judgment, and are thus ambiguous and the source of dispute. No doubt, defenders of Islam would dispute the application of the term *poor* to Islam; they would likely point to the Muslim religion as a source of spiritual riches denied to the "infidels" (who "know the price of everything but the value of nothing"). Nor would they agree that the Muslims are weak, but rather would say they possess strengths of which the infidels can know little, and in fact it is the infidels who are ignorant, because they know only what is unimportant. It may well be that Lewis will win the argument; my point is that this is no longer purely an argument involving deductive logic: it has come down to the relative strength of inferences regarding the facts; the strength of correspondence has begun to compete with the strength of coherence.

Subjective Inferences Create Uncertainty

By raising these points, I intend to introduce doubt about Lewis's claim to have learned what went wrong; and by introducing the matter of "irreducible uncertainty" regarding both conditions (p's) and outcomes (q's), I wish to drive the point home. The uncertainty is irreducible because questions will arise concerning exactly how much freedom or tyranny there was in specific places at specific times. Because people's subjective judgments will be required for answers, we will have to settle for approximations. Meticulous historian that he is, Lewis himself can be counted on to provide us with examples of ambiguity, that is, examples of progress where it is not expected, and lack of it where it is expected. And he does. For example:

> Westerners tend naturally to assume that the emancipation of women
> is part of liberalization, and that women will consequently fare better
> in liberal than autocratic regimes. Such an assumption would be false,
> and often the reverse is true. Among Arab countries, the legal emanci-
> pation of women went farthest in Iraq and in the former South Yemen,
> both notoriously repressive regimes. It has lagged behind in Egypt,
> one of the more tolerant and open societies.[10]

Thus Lewis teaches us that freedom and emancipation are not simple ideas; they can be, have been, and will be decomposed in many ways by many different people. But those many ways share one significant characteristic; they are "soft." That is, the measurement of p is person-dependent, highly dependent on human judgment; it is no longer purely rational, it is quasi-rational, or boundedly rational. And the same is true for q, the consequences of p, the definition of *wrong* in "what went wrong." All of which brings us right back to applying Simon's concept of bounded rationality, from which Lewis could not escape because he is trapped in the vicissitudes of an uncontrolled, uncertain environment.

Lewis's Bounded Rationality

A second reason that Lewis's judgment cannot be placed at the analytical pole is that, as Simon would predict, Lewis's rationality is "bounded," that is, he "satisfices." For although Lewis does an impressive job of exploring the conventional hypotheses for the downturn in Islam (exploring numerous conventional p's), he does not, because he cannot, explore *all* of them—which is exactly Simon's point. When Simon said, "Since my world picture approximates reality only crudely, I cannot aspire to optimize anything . . . Searching for the best can only dissipate scarce cognitive resources; the best is the enemy of the good," it is as if he were standing in Lewis's shoes, and perhaps those of every historian.[11] For Lewis's "world picture" will "approximate reality only crudely" (he would not deny that), and "searching for the best" (that is, examining every hypothesis imaginable) would "only dissipate scarce cognitive resources" (and Lewis would surely agree with that). Further, Simon's phrase "the best is the enemy of the good" helps us see that if Lewis had actually tried to explore all the hypotheses imaginable, he never would have finished his book and we would have been deprived of the "good," namely, an excellent historical description of the downfall of the Islamic empire. Therefore, the pursuit of wisdom has its benefits over the pursuit of full, unbounded rationality.[12] It seldom occurs that we see such a thorough, scholarly effort as that undertaken by Lewis to systematically consider a series of hypotheses to account for a complex social phenomenon. That is why I chose his study for an example of an attempt to learn. If it is indeed impossible for Lewis to learn with certainty after such an effort, it will be even more difficult in the ordinary circumstances of policymaking. For in the case of social policy—in contrast with historical analysis—each explanatory hypothesis will attract a constituency of its own that will demand exploration of its self-serving hypothesis, and will charge bias by the policymakers should they refuse, or if they find no support for the hypothesis. But Lewis's study of what went wrong in the history of Islam amounts to an honest, thoroughgoing, highly competent scholarly attempt to learn what went wrong, and bounded rationality was the method used to integrate information.

Bounded Rationality and Cognitive Conflict

Once we acknowledge that irreducible uncertainty will induce both correspondence and coherence, conflict and dispute will almost always follow, as it has in this case. Aside from Said's attacks, there has also been the work of noted historian William Dalrymple, who has recently noted, "Lewis's ideas have largely formed the intellectual foundations for the neo-conservative view of the Muslim world. Lewis has addressed the White House, and [Vice President] Dick Cheney and [consultant to the Bush Defense Department] Richard Perle have been named as disciples." Dalrymple also notes,

> Lewis has had such a profound influence that, according to the *Wall Street Journal*, "The Lewis doctrine, in effect, has become U.S. policy." If that policy has now been shown to be fundamentally flawed and based on a set of wholly erroneous assumptions, it follows that for all his scholarship, Lewis's understanding of the subtleties of the contemporary Islamic world is, in some respects at least, dangerously defective.[13]

Thus, we see the power of what I believe to be the myth that historians and policymakers are able to learn why specific events occur. For if it is true that the Lewis doctrine has become U.S. policy, then it is clear that judgments and decisions made in high places (in good faith) based on such "learning" can and do strongly influence significant events in the history of the world. And, indeed, why shouldn't they? What better source for informed judgments than the conclusions drawn by a noted scholar on the basis of published research? Myth-based conclusions are unsustainable, however.

We must not ignore the language employed by Dalrymple to criticize Lewis's attempt to learn what went wrong" His language reflects a form of bounded rationality that does not nearly reach the rationality—also bounded—by Lewis and will easily be criticized by him. If that happens, Dalrymple will probably reply. And so the dispute will go on, and the resultant confusion will insure that we will be further than ever from learning what went wrong. Each side will refer to "politics." Neither policymakers nor historians will be well served by this exchange. Until we make it our practice to bring scientific findings (and we need more of them) to bear on the question of learning from history, we shall all suffer from repeating it.

Jared Diamond's Attempt

Bernard Lewis is not the only historian who is making an explicit attempt to learn what went wrong. Jared Diamond, who achieved fame with his *Guns, Germs, and Steel: The Fates of Human Societies*, is a professor of geography who writes—and thinks—in sweeping historical terms and has now applied his talents to a new topic: *Collapse: How Societies Choose to Fail or Succeed*. It also addresses Lewis's question of what went wrong but in much grander terms; he wants to learn (as the book jacket puts it) *why* "some societies, but not others, blunder into self-destruction" and asks, "How can our world best avoid destroying itself?" His scope is extraordinary, for he examines not only such esoteric places as Easter Island, Pitcairn Island, and Iceland, but also Montana; his book is a masterpiece of geographical history aimed at learning why things went wrong for some societies and why things went right for others. So his book addresses directly the issue I have raised: is it possible to learn "why" from history? Clearly, Diamond is making the case for a positive answer and, in doing so, is adding a warning: "We had better."

Using almost a full page of *The New York Times* on New Year's Day, 2005, Diamond offered his thoughts and conclusions about what we should learn from history.[14] He begins his article by asking his readers to reflect on the future of the United States because it is "seemingly at the height of its power." He asks, "Where will we stand 10 years from now, or even next year?" and points out, "History warns us . . . [that] . . . once-powerful societies collapse . . . quickly and unexpectedly." He then offers five causes of such collapse "that have been especially important," but cautions us to think of these as a "checklist of factors that should be examined, but whose relative importance varies from case to case." This approach offers an example of rationality that is as bounded as Lewis's, yet is different from Lewis's, for, in contrast to Lewis, Diamond cautiously sets out no hypotheses to be tested and makes no rigorous deductions or inferences but simply offers five causes that he believes "have been especially important." Despite the caution, however, he then goes on to provide historical examples of the operation of these causes and uses them to warn us of the consequences of failing to heed them. And he takes these examples very seriously; indeed, one is easily tempted to believe that these examples actually offer *proof* of their causal significance. But no proof has been offered. Are there counter-examples? Of course, and his critics have been quick to point them out. That is the difficulty with this method; in the case of bounded or quasi-rationality never-ending dispute always follows.

I mention Diamond's article because I think the prominent placement of the article is indicative of the growth of the public's interest in, and concern over, learning from history and using it to inform us of the future of the entire global society. More attempts such as those by Lewis and Diamond will be seen. This highly practical curiosity will bring us to face more directly and frankly the question of *how we learn*—or fail to learn—from our past, and will force us to consider what has helped us and what has hurt us, and why. The new challenge, therefore, is not to acquire new factual information (although, of course, that is almost always useful) but to decide what to do with it once we have it.

It is instructive to note that Diamond chose exactly the opposite method to that employed by Lewis. Whereas Lewis followed Karl Popper's method of *falsification* (attempting the *disproof* of hypotheses, rather than their proof), Diamond follows the more conventional (and often discredited because less rigorous) method of attempting ex post facto *proof* of a hypothesis, even using single examples for proof. He is aware of the fragility of his method, which he calls "comparative analysis," and shows that he has given its assets and liabilities considerable thought.[15] In the end, however, he makes clear the fact that he must resort to bounded rationality (without using that term) by stating, "Only from the weight of evidence provided by a comparative study of many societies with different outcomes can one hope to reach convincing conclusions."[16] As the reader now well knows, however, weighing the evidence when forming a judgment usually produces different weights from judge to judge (without awareness of such by the judges), and dispute commonly ensues.

Diamond devoted the final pages of his widely acclaimed *Guns, Germs, and Steel* to consideration of the possibility of history's becoming a science.[17] He helpfully contrasts the differences between the physical sciences (physics, chemistry) that can manipulate the conditions—experiments—of interest with those sciences (astronomy, geology) that cannot. But he fails to describe and explain the *methodological* differences; that is, he does not show us exactly what methods historians should adopt or create to achieve their goal. As a consequence, his own work suffers from criticisms such as those presented by Clifford Geertz in his review in the *New York Review of Books*.[18] Geertz is a well-known professor of anthropology at the Institute of Advanced Study at Princeton, so his comments should interest us. And they do (although he calls Diamond an "evolutionary psychologist," which he is not). Geertz takes note of Diamond's "sweeping, relentlessly environmentalist account of the reasons for the emergence of the modern West" in *Guns, Germs, and Steel,* and finds the same type of account in *Collapse*.[19] *Collapse* may be "relentlessly environmentalist," but it is more than that; it includes the story of how the industrial sector can be relentlessly destructive as well, although Diamond makes a point of being evenhanded, and very nearly manages to be. More seriously, Geertz reduces Diamond's empiricism to a mere formula: "Look at this, look at that; note the similarities, note the differences: find the thread, tell the story—a natural history of societal failure."[20] A formula it may be, but it is an extraordinarily successful one. *Guns* sold over a million copies and received a Pulitzer Prize.

Ultimately, however, Geertz disappoints, for he doesn't bring his knowledge and skill as a social scientist to bear on Diamond's methodological weaknesses. We are led to expect Geertz to do this as he winds up his piece (which includes a review of Richard Posner's *Catastrophe: Risk and Response*).[21] He notes, "What is

most striking about Diamond's and Posner's views of human behavior is how so-
ciologically thin and how lacking in psychological depth they are. Neither . . . has
very much to say about the social and cultural contexts in which their disasters
unfold."[22] From this, we expect Geertz to unload a barrage of criticisms of their
work, but nothing happens; he gives us a few examples of what he means, but no
general principles, no analytical work. And Geertz concludes with this thin sentence: "Monographic examples should take us further than either Diamond's
chronicles or Posner's scenarios toward whatever understanding and whatever
control of the disruptions and disintegrations of modern life are actually available
to us."[23] Perhaps they should, but where does that pious remark take us?

From my point of view, the significant omission in Diamond is the distinction between learning *that* something happened, and learning *why* something
happened. Clearly *Homo sapiens* can learn *that* something happened, such as that
whoever lived on Easter Island disappeared. But learning *why* they disappeared is
another matter. The conditions necessary for establishing causal connections are
simply not present; that is why scientists do experiments—to create the conditions for learning why. But historians cannot do experiments, and that is why
Diamond must resort to what he calls the "comparative method." But that won't
do for the task at hand, although it is helpful. It is disappointing that Diamond
does not address this topic directly in *Collapse*, because his chapters that show
what happened are extraordinary in their scholarship and clarity of exposition.
But his explanations of *why* are not as well justified as we would like, because he
does not directly address the methodological issues involving causal inferences
under uncertainty.

No doubt there will be more books like Diamond's, and if we are lucky,
they will profit from the criticisms of Diamond's work. For there is no topic
more important, and no topic less accessible to the people who need to know
about it, and that is all of us.

Form versus Content

There is an important difference between the historian and the scientist that
should be made apparent to the reader, for it occurs not only in this chapter but
in all the cases in this book where we look at famous men exercising their judgment under uncertainty, and that is the difference between form and content.
The historian is interested in the content of the interchange; he or she wants to
know who said what to whom and, if possible, learn the why, and what came of it
all. The cognitive scientist, or at least this cognitive scientist, is interested in the form
of the interchange. I want answers to such questions as "Will we find participants

using the coherence strategy, or the correspondence strategy? Will there be a re-sort to intuitive rationality? What were the consequences?" The distinction be-tween form and content is easy to understand; the historian is trained to analyze content and its sources, and every kind of cognitive scientist is trained to analyze the form of an expression of an idea, or even the form of persuasion.

The distinction between content and form is important for another reason. In the above chapters, I have often shown the compelling nature of coherence in judgment strategy, and the similarity in the formal aspects of those strategies even when employed by very different people, for example, Timothy McVeigh, Osama bin Laden, and other dangerous fanatics. And I explained the similarity between Isaiah Berlin and Oliver Wendell Holmes in their antipathy for certi-tude and the man who "knows what he knows." That antipathy seemed to pro-duce a paradox; was Holmes really offended by those who wanted to abolish slavery? Didn't the content of the belief held with absolute certainty make a dif-ference to Holmes? As I pointed out above, Holmes could and did point to the blood on his uniform when his antipathy to certitude about abolition was chal-lenged, but we have to ask: did he not make the distinction between men who wanted to enslave others and those who wanted to free men from slavery? Of course he did. We all make such distinctions between the content—usually the values—of a judgment or a belief, and the form of the cognitive activity that produces or holds it.

There is a sharp difference between content and form, which holds consid-erable significance for us. Briefly, we can choose (within the limits of our history) to be pro- or anti-slavery, but once we choose to justify that belief by using the coherence strategy, we must operate within the properties of that strategy; we must make the elements of that strategy "hang together," that is, work within the rules of standard logic or be criticized for that failure. Or if we choose to im-plement that belief with the correspondence strategy, we have to assemble the multiple fallible indicators that will support the judgment. No such rules govern our choice of content.

The Use of the Cognitive Continuum
in Learning from History

It will come as no surprise to anyone that the question of learning from the past remains problematical, although the myth that good history will allow us to learn remains strong, and we read every day about "lessons learned," or more frequently "lessons not learned." So the expectation is strong. The above examples from highly respected historians show that they don't present serious methodological defenses of their efforts, nor do they anticipate the consequences of the weakness of their methods, namely, extended dispute over their conclusions, dispute that is unlikely to produce more than invective or dismissal. In what follows, however, I want to show that the application of the concept of a cognitive continuum offers a possible solution to this longstanding problem.

Different Historians' Methods Occupy Different Places on the Cognitive Continuum

By placing Lewis's attempt to learn what went wrong in the context of Popper's method of falsification, that is, suggesting that Lewis proceeded by using *modus ponens* (if *p*, then *q*) to falsify the hypothesis that ([*p*] the Mongols' barbarity [*q*] destroyed the advanced Arabic culture), and his use of *modulus tollens* (if *not p*, then *not q*) to conclude that it was the absence of freedom [*not p*] that destroyed the advanced Arabic culture [*not q*], I thereby placed this aspect of Lewis's method at the analytical end of the cognitive continuum. He thus proceeded to disprove various hypotheses by means that were rigorous and analytical and thereby justify his conclusion about what went wrong.

Lewis's next step, however, did not rest on such rigorous, retraceable means. As I indicated above, when we examine the properties of "freedom of the economy from corrupt and pervasive mismanagement; freedom of women from male oppression; freedom of citizens from tyrannies," we find that these elements lack precise definition (as Lewis acknowledges); readers are thus required to infer what they mean, and therefore this argument will no longer occupy a place at the extreme right pole of the continuum. So the argument is not logically impeccable after all, because once definitions are attempted, more intuitive cognitive processes will be involved; there will be dispute over the inferential judgments about just how much freedom, or tyranny, there is at any one specific point in time and place, and these disputes will put the generalization in jeopardy.

It is important to note, however, that the change in cognitive activity that Lewis asks of his readers does not vitiate his argument; it simply recognizes the process that has to be used—inductive inference—to establish what Gigerenzer would call *ecological rationality* and justify his conclusion. Thus, the efforts of historians to learn from history cannot escape bounded rationality, and therefore the end to dispute is not in sight.

Diamond's approach moves us even further away from the analytical pole of the cognitive continuum in the direction of the intuitive pole. We get a direct suggestion of this shift when, after a page and a half of explanation of his method, he concludes, "Only from the weight of evidence provided by the comparative study of many societies with different outcomes can one hope to reach convincing conclusions."[24] From this statement, we know that Diamond is employing the inductive method; his dependence on outcome feedback ("different outcomes") from his comparison of many societies will in the end depend upon the differential weighting of many fallible indicators (the weight of evidence) that will be the basis of his judgment. To ascertain how far along the cognitive continuum in the direction of the intuitive pole his judgment will be pushed will be a difficult but not impossible problem. But it will be a worthy task, for such work will tell us a great deal about the cognitive activity of historians, and how to improve it, and how to reduce important disputes.[25]

Diamond's attempts to learn from history are, of course, impressive and may well mark the beginning of a new, more science-based form of history (and I hope they do). But the next efforts will have to include much more (and better) science, at least as far as psychology is concerned. Diamond's casual remarks about group decision making are not only naive but are based on sloppy work. (His remarks on page 439 of his book, about the Cuban missile-crisis deliberations, are utterly wrong and misleading and therefore a disservice, as would have been apparent to him had he read the transcript of the meetings; see my comments in chapter 6). Much as I admire Diamond's work (on occasion, I am awed by it), his methodological efforts leave much to be desired. Nonetheless, his stories are fascinating and his conclusions are interesting, stimulating, and, it is to be hoped, will encourage our greater use of science in attempts to learn from history.

To illustrate how badly we need the greater use of science, I close this section with a quotation from one of the great historians of our time, Gordon Wood, reviewing a history of the American Revolution that showed many parallels between "Great Britain's eighteenth-century war in North America and the United States' recent experiences in Viet Nam and Iraq." Wood concludes that the suggestion that "the history of Britain's quagmire has something to teach us today . . . would probably be wrong," and adds, "History has no lessons for the future except one: that nothing ever works out as the participants quite intended or expected. In other words, if history teaches anything, it teaches humility."[26]

That is a shocking conclusion from an accomplished historian. Did he need to invest his life in the study of history to learn humility? Isn't humility taught in a thousand different ways, on a thousand different days? We need more than humility; we need guidance from our history that will help us manage our future. That is Diamond's view, and mine. We need to learn from human experience, but not experience alone, how to cope with the serious challenges ahead. And the history of our past performance should help us do that. But it won't be the history we have had, nor will it be the historians we have had, who will help us do that. It will be historians such as Diamond, who conclude their books with chapters titled "The Future of Human History as a Science."

To sum up, the impressive work by Lewis and Diamond brings us to the threshold of a new grasp of our history, and a new hope for realistic perceptions of the future because their work offers examples of how we might go about learning from our history. If their work, and the work that is yet to come, does not overcome all obstacles to fully justified judgments based on learning from the past, it may well be that the brain of *Homo sapiens* does not possess the means for doing so. That may seem far-fetched, but we already have striking examples of our limitations from Mercator, Gödel, Einstein, and Heisenberg, discussed below in relation to our attempts to achieve wisdom (see chapter 20).

18

Toward Better Practices

Scientific knowledge of human judgment should become an integral part of the judgment process that is applied to the development of our social policies. When that happens, we will be able to move away from our present chaotic, conflict-inducing practices and perhaps even end our use of war as a means of settling our religious and ideological differences. Let me briefly remind the reader of the costs of the failed and erroneous judgments of some recent leaders. Although few among us have a direct memory of World War I, nearly all of us have read enough about it to be aware of what happened—the gross, senseless killing and maiming of millions of soldiers and sailors and innocent people for reasons few any longer know or care about—all as a result of the misguided—that is to say, stupid—judgments of the well-educated leaders of these societies, who seem to have had no better idea of their purposes than we have of ours. Although the World War II was a well-justified effort to restrain a society that had lost its senses, as shown by the poor judgment of its citizens and its leaders, the lives of 25 million people (some estimates say 40 million) was a terrible price to pay. And the absurdity of recent wars, for example, the war in Vietnam, has become all too apparent. Now humans find themselves in the midst of another war, the rationale for which has disappeared. There is little to be pleased with in the way people have managed their affairs involving neighbors throughout history. And with societies—of which our own is an outstanding example—affording their least thoughtful members the means of enormous destruction, we must do better soon; as we have been told so often, we now have the capability to wipe out all of humanity.

I address first the matter of wars because of the obvious evidence of the enormous death, destruction, and moral disgrace they impose on the human population. But wisdom in the form of good judgment is needed everywhere because of our increasing power to modify the world for good as much as for evil. Better judgment is badly needed in medical practice, education, social welfare, and law, and in coping with natural hazards, and, of course, in coping with poverty, all of which could save many lives and improve the human condition.

The purpose of this book is to take us a small step further on the path to the wisdom that will enable us do better. That step, as I see it, will require not an appeal to myths, or religion—both have a terrible history of turning us against one another—but to the science that will be as good as we can make it. And that is why this book attempts to bring some understanding of the current science of the psychology of judgment and decision making to the attention of the lay reader.

Different This Time?

The plea for the application of scientific knowledge to social problems has been made many times before—sadly, with little result. There are reasons for this that we should consider if we are to make progress toward the goal of moving from myth and superstition to wisdom.

First, science has its own goals, and the advancement of knowledge—not its application—is the prime goal. Therefore, studies are not designed with application in mind. There is nothing wrong with that. There are occasions, however, when the need for knowledge is so compelling as to demand an answer to the question of how our hard-won scientific knowledge can be put to use. That is the situation we are in now. One or two more "crises" that lead to the call for the use of nuclear weapons—of which there are tens of thousands available—and civilization, and possibly humankind, may disappear forever. Military power's threat to civilization is real and poses a challenge to science itself. In short, the need for scientific knowledge is now compelling enough to make the attempt to put it to work for us, not only to prevent catastrophic war but to improve the human condition.

Second, when it is said that "studies are designed for the advancement of knowledge," we can ask "What kind of knowledge?" When most of us demand "pure" science, we think of "objective," "value-neutral" science of the sort that

Einstein had in mind. Isaiah Berlin tells us, "His [Einstein's] conception of external nature was that of a scientifically analyzable, rational order or system; the goal of the sciences was objective knowledge of an independently existent reality."[1] That is the science we envision was practiced when the "law of the lever" was discovered by Greek scientists, when Galileo discovered the relationship between gravity and the rate of time of the fall of objects, and when Newton discovered the laws of mechanics; all these evoke a picture of a scientist utterly indifferent to, and protected from, the vicissitudes of the social and political world around him.

Even these pure cases weren't so pure, however; Galileo found that his astronomical discoveries were of considerable interest—indeed, frightening—to the religious authorities, and they made him recant: myth prevailed. And even now, evolutionary biologists are under attack from conservative elements who want to remove the study of evolution from our schools because they believe it challenges their religious beliefs and the teachings of the Bible (a removal even the Roman Catholic Church, old enemy of Galileo, opposes). But that vision of "pure science" that hangs over the practice of academic science today has hampered the growth of the applicability of scientific knowledge to social problems; it has seriously affected economics and psychology, particularly the psychology of judgment and decision making. That is the vision that John Kenneth Galbraith fought against—and perhaps defeated—in economics, and it is that vision—not yet defeated—that this book resists in psychology, for reasons that are very different but that lead to the same end. It is those reasons we consider next.

A Different Vision of Science and Society

Although this book does rely on the past half century's scientific work on human judgment, it does not follow mainstream research. As a result, much that is in this book is unorthodox and iconoclastic, meaning that it does not rely on the conventional approach to psychology. Mainstream research in the psychology of human judgment has produced much that is valuable and has added substantially to our knowledge base, but it is essentially without theoretical guidance, is methodologically backward, and thus wanders without a clear purpose, other perhaps than to show that our common assumptions about our cognitive activity, particularly uncertainty and probability, are wrong. Interesting as that clouded view may sometimes seem, it lacks theoretical guidance, ignores modern research methods, and therefore does not produce the cumulative science we need.

Psychology is not the only science to struggle with the problem of the usefulness of its work, however. Economics has also found that the work that pleases economists is seldom the work that pleases those who seek scientific knowledge about economic or social problems. John Kenneth Galbraith struggled to convince his colleagues that their practice of "blackboard economics" (a reference to economists' heavy use of mathematics) was serving *neither* academic economics *nor* society well.[2] Although the senior members of the profession battled Galbraith for decades and made his academic appointments problematical, he slowly made headway. Parker reports,

> In the early 1990s . . . the American Economic Association appointed a commission of twelve economists . . . to undertake a multiyear study of their profession . . . . It found that that nearly two thirds believed that they had for too long mistakenly "overemphasized mathematical and statistical tools at the expense of substance" and that the time had come to overhaul and revise economics' core suppositions."

In addition, Parker wrote, "Too many prospective employers found that economists weren't being trained for 'anything but other graduate programs.'"[3]

That report vindicated Galbraith, for that was exactly what he had been trying—against strong opposition—to tell the senior members of the graduate programs at the most prestigious schools for decades. Interestingly, modern economists have turned to the behavioral economists to remedy this situation. As noted in chapters 2 and 3, the behavioral economists followed the work initiated and developed by psychologists—researchers in the field of judgment and decision making, primarily Amos Tversky and Daniel Kahneman. It was their research that provided the basis for making economics useful (or so it seemed), and Parker's biography of Galbraith recognizes that.[4]

But the history of this turn in economics was more complicated than Parker shows, for Kahneman was not to emerge from this struggle for meaningfulness outside academic graduate schools unscathed, his Nobel Prize notwithstanding. Gigerenzer and his colleagues had for years criticized Tversky and Kahneman's work for its lack of relevance to what Gigerenzer chose to call the "real world."[5] The major conclusion drawn from Kahneman and Tversky's work was that untrained persons—and often trained persons—were incompetent in their judgment and in their use of probabilities. Gigerenzer's objection to this conclusion was that Kahneman and Tversky framed the problems they gave to their subjects in such a way as to be unfamiliar to them and thus induced the answer they wanted. That is, Gigerenzer has made much of the fact that many of the studies that Kahneman and Tversky used to show the inability of untutored persons to cope with uncertainty consistently presented information in terms of *probability,* a concept often misunderstood even by professionals. Gigerenzer argues—and attempts to demonstrate—that if the same information been presented in terms of relative frequencies, which Gigerenzer claims is the more "natural" way of expressing information, the subjects would have demonstrated more competence, and he has some evidence for this.[6] Thus, he cast some doubt on exactly how far Kahneman and the behavioral economists have moved the professional economists toward work that can be considered useful.

However, Brunswik anticipated all this. He wrote treatises and did experiments as far back as the 1930s and 1940s to demonstrate the problems caused by the artificiality of psychology research that made its conclusions useless outside graduate schools of psychology. As late as 1988, psychologists interested in application were complaining about the uselessness of the work in their own area of specialization. Here are Wickens and Flach, acknowledged experts in the field of aviation psychology, doing just what Brunswik had warned of:

> The science has produced an enormous catalog of information about a few rather esoteric laboratory tasks, yet has contributed very little to our understanding of how humans function outside the laboratory. . . . We have missed the big picture."[7]

Just as Galbraith warned against "blackboard economics," Brunswik warned against artificial "rule of one variable" experiments that every psychology student is taught is the only way to do research.

Although Brunswik and Galbraith did not know one another, both opposed the uncriticized dominance of the physical-science model because of its remoteness from life sciences. Brunswik's career thus paralleled Galbraith's in his analysis, conclusions, and aims; and he, too, was harshly criticized—essentially ostracized—by the senior members of his profession for his unorthodox views. Like Galbraith, Brunswik had also urged—and demonstrated—that the departure from the physical-science model of scientific work and the adoption of the biological model would allow us to solve the problem of how to harmoniously advance academic work and make more usable its results. Brunswik differed from Galbraith, however, in that he became discouraged and ended his own life in mid-career. Galbraith seemed to have become more invigorated by the opposition, and published extensively well into his nineties. By then he could claim, with considerable justification, to have taken economics a long way toward being a useful science.

I was fortunate enough to have been a student of Brunswik's and, as this book shows, I embraced his ideas wholeheartedly. The research in the field of judgment and decision making that is reported in this book is largely based on Brunswik's development of the biological, rather than physical-science, view of psychology, as a means of advancing academic work and thus the usefulness of psychology. That is to say, he described new ways of doing research, introduced new methods that allowed psychologists to avoid having to choose between being academic and "truly objective" and being "useful"; he showed how psychologists could achieve both goals. Of course, as the senior members of any profession will, the senior economists objected to Brunswik's work, mainly by turning their backs, and progress has been slow. But the fact that basic science and application goals can be achieved can be seen in the work reported here.[8]

Surprisingly, there seems to be an actual convergence of economics and psychology regarding the move from physics to biology as the model for both disciplines. That possibility can be seen in the remarks by the behavioral economist Vernon Smith (who was, with Kahneman, co-recipient of the Nobel Prize) that indicate his support for the field of *ecology* as a model for economics. That is a statement that could hardly have been imagined in the twentieth century.

19

Ineptitude and the Tools of War

Imagine yourself in the Oval Office with Franklin Roosevelt and his advisors in 1939—the year the Germans began World War II with the invasion of Poland—when a letter from Albert Einstein appears advising him of the possibility that "extremely powerful bombs of a new type may be . . . constructed."[1] Although it had taken two months to reach him, that news was welcome indeed to Roosevelt because explosive capability was all the warriors of 1939 could think of. They thought in terms of specific objects and populations in specific places that could be destroyed by blowing them up. Therefore, the bigger the explosion the better. So when Albert Einstein's letter advising him that the new physics of the twentieth century could be used to make bigger and better explosives, Roosevelt was glad to hear it. And that, as the world will never forget, was done with memorable success (and sorrow, in Japan).

Things are different today. As noted in chapter 8, instead of facing a modern, highly organized nation, we now face a tribe, or any rate a loose confederation of people, united by their religious devotion and hatred of those with different religious views. It is that hatred and the destructive actions that follow from it that have made members of this confederation—loosely known as al-Qaeda—enemies of the modern Western World. The nuclear weapons stored by the United States and others do not intimidate or deter these enemies, for they possess few important assets vulnerable to destruction by explosion and cannot even be located in terms of their geographical coordinates. They are everywhere and nowhere, which is also true of their weaponry; their most destructive maneuver was carried out on 9/11 with hardly any weapons at all.

But, in fact, they do have a weapon. The weapon they possess is just of a different kind. That weapon is information; members of al-Qaeda possess information about where, when, and how they will strike. It is our uncertainty, our lack of that information, about where, when, and how—not if—the attacks will occur that creates the fear of catastrophe. It is the uncertainty that looms over the nature of the future catastrophe—what kind of weapon will be used?—explosive? biomedical? biochemical?—and where will it placed?—in a subway? a nuclear plant? an airport? Will they use something of our making, such as an airplane filled with thousands of gallons of jet fuel? That uncertainty creates the fear that never goes away. And that is a new circumstance, very different from the fear of the air raids of World War II, the nature of which everyone understood.

That fear has been made evident, plausible, and pervasive by two events: first, the publication of *The 9/11 Commission Report*, which concludes,

> The lesson of 9/11 for civilians and first responders can be stated simply: in the new age of terror they—we—are the primary targets. The losses Americans suffered that day demonstrated both the gravity of the terrorist threat and the commensurate need to prepare ourselves to meet it.[2]

Second, nothing could make more clear the fact that the Western world is desperate to acquire information about al-Qaeda's intentions—yet baffled about how to do it—than the crude, bumbling, highly embarrassing efforts at the Abu Ghraib prison. Not only did these efforts embarrass the United States, they provided al-Qaeda with proof of their beliefs about the low character of the American infidels. Certainly, something better—morally and practically—than torture is needed to gain information, and one place to start is to find people who will think of something better than torture, a barbaric medieval tactic.

But so far, the agencies responsible for providing such intelligence have done little but earn a great deal of skepticism—and worse—since September 11, 2001. No other country—not even Great Britain—will trust information from U.S. agencies with good reason: they can point out how right they were not to trust Colin Powell's plea before the UN Security Council asking for their troops and money by presenting claims about the reality of Saddam's possession of weapons of mass destruction (discussed in chapter 4).

Preemptive War Is Different

All this takes us to the question of the wisdom of preemptive war. Since the enemy is indifferent to national borderlines, nations will no longer be reserving military action until troops make clear, unambiguous border-crossing assaults. The Gulf War in 1991, which saw Iraqi troops marching across the border with Kuwait, may well be the last of the "border-crossing" kind. (For example, the Chechen rebels do not march across the border into Russia; instead, they attack Russian theaters, schools, and airplanes within their borders.)

Preemptive war is to be expected. If preemptive war is indeed the war of the future, it must be recognized that such wars will be based on intelligence, not "acts of aggression," and that such intelligence will always involve uncertain inferences about intentions. Indeed, the entire justification for the invasion of Iraq now rests on the judgment of the intentions of Saddam Hussein.[3] Thus, human judgment will be involved to a greater degree than ever, inasmuch as judgment will be the basis for the preemptive war, just as it was in the American invasion of Iraq in 2003. Should the information upon which the judgment to invade be found to be flawed—as in the case of the American invasion—then the justification is flawed.

If it is indeed true that wars of the future will inevitably be based on judgments made under uncertainty, then it seems reasonable to conclude that we should know as much as possible about how such judgments are formed. When we needed to know as much as possible about making bigger and better explosive devices, we concentrated our energies on that goal and started the Manhattan Project, which successfully created the atomic bomb in 1945. Although the aftermath of that event includes horrible deaths, deception about radiation and fallout, and general dismay at the destruction of life and property, the new Manhattan Project (called something else, perhaps) would be conceived with a different goal, namely, that of improving our understanding of human judgment to the point where it can be used with justifiable confidence. By contrast, in 2003, human judgment proved to be untrustworthy, and its failures were explained in amateurish ways.

Are present judgments good enough to rely on for our defense? Do we know what went wrong with past judgments?

**Current Explanations of Human Failure
of Intelligence at the CIA**

Before explaining what the specific goals of the new Manhattan Project should be, we should look at the current explanations of human failure that have been applied to judgments regarding enemy activity as described in the *The 9/11*

Commission Report and the press. The 9/11 Commission charged with examining the efforts of the United States to anticipate and prevent the attacks on the World Trade Center made the structure of the arrangement of the intelligence agencies—the intelligence system—the main target of its criticism. The Commission's report emphasized the need for structural changes in the bureaucracy, as did the congressional committee that oversees intelligence. It is not surprising that this type of recommendation should be made; people do what they know how to do and what they have always done. Special committees, such as the 9/11 Commission and the congressional committee, have focused on rearranging committee structures for generations and will continue to do so in response to failures, for the foreseeable future. And, of course, sometimes that is the right solution. But when Richard Posner, a prominent author and a judge on the United States Court of Appeals (7th Circuit), reviewed the Commission's report, he did not think it was the right solution. He challenged the Commission's suggestion that it was "systematic failures in the nation's intelligence and security apparatus that can be corrected by changing the apparatus." Posner thought that the Commission's recommendation was a "leap that . . . is not sustained by the report's narrative."[4] He wrote, "The Commission's contention that 'the terrorists exploited deep institutional failures within our government' is overblown."[5] My choice of words would be different from Posner's; I would say "misdirected" rather than "overblown": Roosevelt did not merely create a different committee structure in response to Einstein's letter; rather, he initiated a research project to meet the problem. Further, as Posner notes, it is hardly likely that a mere rearrangement of committee structures will suffice to solve the problem of how to prevent the kind of catastrophe that occurred on 9/11. Numerous others agreed with Posner, among them Benjamin DeMott. DeMott made a more vigorous and focused criticism, claiming that the entire report was a "whitewash" of the president's failure to recognize and understand the numerous warnings he had, in fact, been receiving about al-Qaeda.[6] Thomas Powers, also a prominent journalist, presented the same argument, that it was not the structure of the system that was at fault but the president's failure to pay attention to the warnings he was receiving.[7] Richard Clarke, who was the national coordinator for security, infrastructure protection, and counterterrorism in the Clinton administration and continued in that position in the Bush administration until he was demoted by Condoleezza Rice, took the same view as DeMott and Powers, namely, that the problem was the president's failure to take the warnings seriously. He presents his argument in detail in his book *Against All Enemies.*[8]

I agree with Posner, DeMott, Powers, Clarke, and many others that the real cause of the failure was not the system but rather human judgment under uncertainty that produced the same weaknesses that research has demonstrated hundreds of times. It was human judgment under uncertainty that made the errors associated with the catastrophe of 9/11, and it is human judgment under uncertainty that will make the errors that fail to prevent the next catastrophe. All the research—and there are many hundreds of studies—make it clear that it is impossible to perfect human judgment in conditions of uncertainty. That does not mean that human judgment should not be used; generally, there is no alternative, and often it performs very well. But examination of the task structure will tell us when it will perform well, when it will perform poorly, and what precautions should be taken under various circumstances. And such knowledge is readily available from numerous academic sources.

Aside from administrative structure, two other explanations—both psychological—have occasionally been offered by a variety of sources. One is that the members of the intelligence agencies were victims of "groupthink." The concept of *groupthink*, introduced in 1982 by the noted psychologist Irving Janis, has not had a long and successful life.[9] Although it now appears in dictionaries, it is seldom employed in a serious way by contemporary psychologists.[10] Its most successful application was made by G. Moorhead, R. Ference, and C. P. Neck, who found much to support Janis's claims in their study of the tragic *Challenger* launch. But as I noted in 1996, "these authors seriously weaken their support of the 'groupthink' concept by stating that 'the groupthink symptoms result from the group characteristics, proposed by Janis, but only in the presence of the moderator variables of time and certain leadership styles.' "[11] This modest achievement is hardly the kind of material on which to try to build an explanation of national intelligence failures. Yet even serious investigators such as Jared Diamond have succumbed to the widespread use of this dubious concept.[12]

The second psychological explanation—often repeated—is that our intelligence agencies failed because they did not "connect the dots." This explanation barely rises above slogan status, but it will remind readers of the concept of *coherence*, and justly so. A reminder based on word association does not suffice for an explanation. In fact, the more common danger is not that one fails to seek coherence in the data or information available, but that one instead finds coherence ("connects the dots") when it doesn't exist, as so many mistaken conspiracy theories tell us. The confusion about "connecting the dots" that indicates the low value of slogans is reflected in remarks by the rejected head of the CIA in a September 8, 2004, speech: "In a post-9/11 environment, when our analysts were bitterly accused of not connecting dots, we were probably connecting too many," Mr. Tenet said. One wonders how the question of connecting the dots when you shouldn't, or not connecting them when you should, can be decided without understanding the search for coherence.

The connect-the-dots explanation, in fact, was given a much different meaning when some sections in some agencies (primarily the FBI) failed to inform others about the information those sections had that would have been informative when added to the information others had. That situation is common among all bureaucracies, but probably more important among intelligence agencies for the reason that people in these agencies are (justifiably) continually seeking coherence in the behavior of the enemy—that is, trying to discover what its strategies and tactics are, or what they are going to be. (Chapter 6 described the unsuccessful efforts of Nikita Khrushchev and John Kennedy to find coherence in each of their arguments in their exchange of letters.)

The great barrier to success in making correct inductive inferences about terrorists' behavior is not that we fail to see coherence or that we fail to exchange information—although of course that happens in badly managed agencies. Rather, it is the uncertainty in the dots that one is trying to connect; moreover, we cannot determine the nature of the connection, a matter seldom mentioned. By "uncertainty in the dots" I mean the fallibility of the source of the information. It is also difficult to recognize a dot when it appears. It is very convenient when a dot represents reliable (but possibly irrelevant) information such as that someone enrolled in flight school (with its association to airplane hijacking), but too often the information is no better than information from the source's cousin's erstwhile friend—and no one else; most dots would more accurately be represented by a freckle.

In short, dots will vary in their credibility, or fallibility, a matter that the connect-the-dots explanation does not address, and that variation makes it very difficult to judge. And there will be a variety of coherent stories created to address the question of how the dots should be connected. Since there will be many possible ways of connecting them, there will be a dispute as to which form of connection is the true one, a dispute that will also raise questions about the differential credibility of various dots. The present users of the dots explanation do not address that issue either.

A third way of avoiding the task of seriously trying to reduce our uncertainty is simply to rely on the judgments of "gut players" (as George W. Bush has described himself). Relying on one's gut—using your intuition—is a psychological explanation of a sort. But however valuable intuitive cognitive processes may be in situations appropriate for them, and however many anecdotes are told about the success of certain gut players (who are usually careful not to keep track of their failures), intuitions are not what should be relied upon for life-and-death matters, primarily because intuitive judgments irresponsibly rely on multiple fallible indicators that are combined into a judgment by unconscious mechanisms. The intuitive process cannot be retraced (that is why the layperson locates it in the gut). Therefore, intuition has no place in the process of important judgments, such as invasions of other countries (or medical judgments, as I explain in chapters 6 and 8).

Posner is certainly correct when he points out, "The problem isn't just that people find it extraordinarily difficult to take novel risks seriously; it is also that there is no way the government can survey the entire range of possible disasters and act to prevent each and everyone of them."[13] Precautions are usually taken only after a disaster or near-disaster occurs. You were not required to take off your shoes in the airport until a terrorist actually put explosives in his. It is matters of precisely this sort, problems we now cannot prevent, that the new Manhattan Project should address; it should try to find ways to solve these problems, to the extent they can be solved. These problems include matters that judgment and decision researchers have yet to consider, either for lack of imagination or lack of funds. Researchers should be allowed to turn their imaginations loose on these problems. But they should be joined by others—particularly, young others—who have not been exposed to the theories, methods, and procedures that members of the judgment and decision community use. In short, new and different themes should be encouraged.

The current remedies and psychological explanations for the failures of intelligence are so amateurish that they are hardly worth our notice. Moreover, we cannot rely on Congress to supply us with more than outdated terms from psychology (*groupthink*) or vague concepts (connect the dots). All these inadequate remedies remind one of the nineteenth-century physics that Einstein told Roosevelt should be replaced by twentieth-century physics in the effort to defeat the Nazis, as indeed it was. We are somewhat worse off than Roosevelt was because the twenty-first century's psychology of human judgment has yet to reach the level of nineteenth-century physics. For us to acquire the necessary knowledge of human judgment, we will need the new Manhattan Project. In what follows, I make some suggestions about how the general approach to the study of human judgment presented here could provide a useful beginning for that project—that is, for the development of the knowledge basic to a national intelligence system for the twenty-first century.

Application to Military Intelligence

The difficulties of acquiring reliable information in military situations has been obvious ever since, and perhaps before, Clausewitz introduced the phrase "the fog of war." And the nature of the task has remained as ambiguous as the fog itself. Therefore, I begin with some premises about the framework I offer.

Work should begin with the clear conceptual separation of judgments directed toward correspondence or coherence. Some military judgments will necessarily involve the correspondence strategy because they will be directed toward establishing facts, that is, they will be judgments directed toward the existence of certain objects, events, or persons at specific times or places. Other judgments will be directed toward establishing relationships between and among objects, events, and persons and will evaluate the coherence of such relationships. In the military, the former will likely be the duty of the frontline troops, whereas the latter will likely be the duty of the commanders. In the intelligence agencies, both will be engaged; each is discussed below.

Judgments Involving Correspondence Competence

When the 9/11 Commission addressed the topic "Institutionalizing Imagination: The Case of Aircraft Weapons," it referred to the problem of identifying *indicators*, a term with which the readers of this book will be familiar.[14] The report noted: "North American Aerospace Defense Command imagined the use of aircraft as weapons . . . and developed exercises to counter such a threat."[15] These exercises employed a method long used by (and perhaps invented by) judgment researchers working within Brunswik's ecological theme.[16] Following the researchers, the military developed scenarios of various possible episodes that included multiple fallible indicators. As the Commission authors put it, "The challenge was to flesh out and test these scenarios."[17]

But that was not the challenge. That error was produced by a lack of familiarity with the scientific work on the problem of judgment under uncertainty that uses such scenarios. In fact, the challenge is to be found in *measuring* the fallibility of each of the indicators and discovering the fallible *relationships* among the indicators, for this is the structure that creates uncertainty, and reducing or eliminating the uncertainty is at the root of the difficulty of military intelligence, or any other judgment under uncertainty. In adversarial situations, there will be little solid information about the degree of fallibility of various indicators (aided by the ever-present danger of deception) and little possibility of producing that information. (Similar circumstances arise in studying medical judgments. Although there is considerable knowledge about various symptoms [fallible indicators] associated with specific diseases, the degree of fallibility is seldom known; textbooks are content to use such phrases as "often associated with," "occasionally associated with," or "frequently associated with" a disease, but the true degree of association has seldom been measured, and is therefore unknown.) The military situation is far more difficult because the indicators in military situations seldom repeat themselves and because the enemy will be engaged in deception; thus, military information will always be suspect in a way that medical information is not. As a result, the fallibility of any of the indicators will generally be unknown and often unknowable.[18]

The researchers who employ such scenarios in order to study military judgments are careful to specify the degree of uncertainty offered by each indicator and thus are able to ascertain the effect of various degrees of uncertainty in a judgment task (and also to ascertain other features of the task such as the number of indicators, other statistical properties, their content, and so forth). Indeed, the military (and other agencies) has put millions of dollars into research based on these procedures, and still does. Did the intelligence agencies learn anything about military judgments from this research?

The intelligence agencies certainly should have learned from the research, for the Commission report states:

> [The] intelligence community . . . has devoted generations of effort to understanding the problem of forestalling a surprise attack. . . . Rigorous analytical methods were developed . . . and several leading practitioners discussed them with us. These methods . . . seem to have at least four elements in common:
> 1.   think about how surprise attacks might be launched;
> 2.   identify telltale indicators connected to the most dangerous possibilities;
> 3.   where feasible, collect intelligence on these indicators; and
> 4.   adopt defenses to deflect the most dangerous possibilities or at least trigger an earlier warning.[19]

The report then states, "With the important exception of analysis of al-Qaeda efforts in chemical, biological, radiological, and nuclear weapons, we did not find evidence that the methods to avoid surprise attack that had been so laboriously developed over the years were regularly applied."[20] The Commission then (boldly) turns to suggesting "possible ways to institutionalize investigation" and takes up an examination of the "four elements of analysis just mentioned." It then concludes, "The methods for detecting and then warning of surprise attack that the U.S. government had so painstakingly developed in the decades after Pearl Harbor did not fail; instead, they were not really tried."[21]

It is hardly surprising that these methods were "not really tried." Members of the Judgment and Decision Making Society, particularly Ward Edwards and

Cameron Peterson, attempted—as much as 40 years ago—to impress upon the CIA and other defense agencies the importance of quantifying probabilities in judgments, to no avail. And this matter is now resurfacing: in an article in *The Washington Post,* Michael Schrage wrote,

> "Unfortunately, the odds are excellent that this multibillion-dollar structural shuffle—capped last week by the appointment of veteran diplomat John Negroponte as the new national intelligence director—will do little to improve the quality of intelligence analysis for this country.
>
> Why? Because America's intelligence community doesn't like odds. Yet the simplest and most cost-effective innovation [that] that community could adopt would be to embrace them. It's time to require national security analysts to assign numerical probabilities to their professional estimates and assessments as both a matter of rigor and of record. Policymakers can't weigh the risks associated with their decisions if they can't see how confident analysts are in the evidence and conclusions used to justify those decisions. The notion of imposing intelligence accountability without intelligent counting—without numbers—is a fool's errand.[22]

There is little likelihood (my probability is .05) that any more will come of Schrage's article than came of the hard work by Edwards and his counterpart (Martin Tolcott) in the Office of Naval Research to get the administrators in the Defense Department to change their ways as a result of scientific research. Low-level officers and enlisted men and women may be persuaded to pay attention to research, but as the challenge to judgment increases, defeat is almost certain. That was true of the atomic bomb—and was one reason for instigating a project (the Manhattan Project) that evaded the military bureaucracy; it is also a reason for a new Manhattan Project.

As the Commission report suggests, the research certainly could have helped if it had been tried. Had a new Manhattan Project produced this knowledge, it surely would have been tried. But research on human judgment will always have a hard time getting off the shelf, for the reason La Rochefoucauld explained: "Everyone complains of his memory, and no one complains of his judgment" (see p. xvi). People who have had trust placed in their judgment do not welcome information that may cast doubt on it. It will take the weight of a new Manhattan Project to persuade many a CEO or general or admiral or president to develop sufficient humility to accept the idea that he or she could improve his or her judgment.

Judgments Involving Coherence Competence

Correspondence strategies will be applied mainly to the establishment of empirical fact: Did this suspected agent meet with that one? Where? Who else was there? The 9/11 Commission's report is replete with the judgments of American agents in relation to such facts, and these judgments will be established on the use of multiple fallible indicators. The appropriate skills and training should be enhanced by recognizing that making use of these techniques and computer skills involves applying the correspondence strategy.

In contrast, coherence strategies will be applied mainly in the effort to discover the coherence of the enemy's plans for attacks. For example, the 9/11 report describes efforts—generally ineffective—by American agents to discover coherent plans made by terrorists; the case of the 19 hijackers provides the notorious example. Although it is uncertain to what extent various groups of terrorists actually do have coherent plans, it would be foolhardy to assume that they have none, in view of the numerous successful terrorist attacks that have already occurred. (The 9/11 attack certainly required a coherent plan conceived over a long period of time.)

In short, establishing a fact is a different cognitive matter than is establishing the existence of a plot, and people not only should know when they are responsible for doing which, but also should be appropriately equipped for what they are asked to do, in terms of both theory and practice. One of the reasons for recognizing different cognitive functions in different tasks is that such recognition makes it possible for one to provide a check on the other. For example, the discovery of a plot by the group seeking coherence might find their judgment challenged by the correspondence group on the grounds that the facts were not trustworthy. The 9/11 report describes an event of this sort when some agency members stopped an attempt by other agency members to kill bin Laden at a compound in Afghanistan when they determined (on the basis of fallible indicators) that the attempt would create too much collateral damage, and that it was uncertain that bin Laden was still there.

A significant problem is created when there is an attempt to communicate the meaning of a coherent "picture" of what is going on. In chapter 6, I presented the poor state of communication between Chairman Khrushchev and President Kennedy and his group of high-level advisors at the time of the Cuban missile crisis. The transcript of the meetings of that committee makes obvious the failure of each side to present a coherent view of the situation to the other side. The 9/11 Commission's report also indicates that the president's daily brief did not make clear the terrorist threat to the United States, although it remains uncertain whether this was the president's fault or the fault of the briefing message. The title of chapter 8 of the report repeats what has become a well-known phrase used by the director of the Central Intelligence Committee: "The system was blinking red." It is hard to take that phrase as indicating anything but clear and present danger; thus, we must assume that "clear and present danger" is the message that the director was trying to convey to the president. Yet the report makes it clear that at no point do we see a government agency, or a president, acting as if there were blinking red lights in front of them.

It must be acknowledged that our understanding of the correspondence strategy is far greater than our understanding of the coherence strategy. We know far less than we need to know about discerning a coherent strategy on the part of the other, as chapter 6 on Kennedy and Khrushchev illustrates. In that case, two heads of state each failed to make the coherence of his thoughts obvious to the other, despite using direct communications. The research that we have tells us that despite the publicity about the 9/11 failure to connect the dots, it is far more likely that the error will be that the dots will be connected when they shouldn't be. That is, people are more likely to see coherence when it isn't there, than not to see it when it is, although I hasten to add that we need to know far more about this than we do. That, in itself, will be one of the tasks of the new Manhattan Project.

Let me remind the reader that the above remarks are not intended to be recommendations for a government agency but suggestions for topics the new Manhattan Project might consider. Nor is this a recommendation for physically or administratively separating personnel engaged in the establishment of fact at a particular moment from those working on the uncovering of a plot. There should, however, be some recognition of the different cognitive efforts involved.

If by some miracle a new Manhattan Project is created, how will we know if it's been successful? Success will not be as easy to recognize as in the case of the first Manhattan Project, whose success was marked by the explosion of a bomb. Nevertheless, it should not be impossible to ascertain progress in our understanding of judgment under uncertainty. We already know how to do the research to get the work under way. Judgment tasks that now produce disagreement and dispute should be resolved more readily, accuracy should be more readily achieved, and coherence should be more readily obtained. And the benefits should not be restricted to military intelligence but to judgments under uncertainty in a wide variety of circumstances, including medicine.

Let me give a concrete example of what the work of the new Manhattan Project might entail.

The New Manhattan Project at Work

In the week of October 3, 2004, the CIA released a report by Charles Duelfer, its chief weapons inspector, whose findings are generally significant. The outstanding finding was to confirm once again that, contrary to the numerous assertions by all the top members of the Bush administration, Saddam Hussein possessed no weapons of mass destruction, nor had he possessed any since 1991, the year the Gulf War ended, roughly 15 years ago. Regrettably, the Bush administration chose to ignore this aspect of the Duelfer report and chose instead to emphasize the report's conclusions regarding Saddam Hussein's intentions, which they interpreted as hostile and aggressive. While this sharp shift in emphasis was not unexpected in political circles (this is what politicians of all stripes do), students of judgment and decision making will find this shift to be important and worthy of study. The reason it is important is that a judgment about the presence (or absence) of independently real objects can be tested for its accuracy by independently ascertaining whether those objects exist by commonly accepted means (for example, direct observation by means of the five senses). When such efforts provide high inter-observer agreement, as would be the case with weapons of mass destruction, the data are then taken as demonstrable fact. Judgments about intentions, however, are a far different matter, and generally speaking, are a common source of dispute; they are not subject to direct empirical tests, as are judgments about weapons of mass destruction. The reason for that is that a person's intentions are located far back on the proximal–distal continuum and thus subject to all the difficulties of making judgments under high uncertainty of all the information relied upon. Because of the usually large uncertainties about their accuracy because of the remoteness on the proximal–distal continuum, judgments about intentions must meet stringent criticism. Therefore, when the Bush administration shifted its emphasis from the Duelfer report's denial of the existence of weapons of mass destruction—the basis for the invasion of Iraq—to inferences about the intentions of Saddam Hussein, the administration shifted from a judgment that could be directly tested for its empirical accuracy to a judgment that could not be so tested. Judgments about intentions can be tested only by considerable study, since direct observation of intentions is impossible and can ordinarily be performed only by analyzing multiple fallible indicators within the correspondence strategy or the coherence strategy.

We do not need to consider which is appropriate at this point. Rather, I call attention to the similarity of these two judgments to those of going to war because of conventional reasons—border crossing—and going to war preemptively. Conventional warfare is justified by direct observation of an offensive act (similar to observing weapons of mass destruction), whereas preemptive war is based on an inference of intention based on multiple fallible indicators (similar to the intentions discussed in the Duelfer report, and in the justification of the U.S. invasion of Iraq).

This is not complex, but the difference between these judgments is significant for public policy matters such declaring war, which is so costly in terms of life, property, and public debt. Straightforward as it may be, the difference between judgments of empirical fact and judgments of intent would not be immediately apparent to most politicians. It did not, however, escape the attention of one *New York Times* reporter, for shortly after the Duelfer report appeared, David Sanger wrote a long article devoted almost entirely to this shift in judgment from one depending on the existence of independently real objects (WMD) to one relying on an abstraction (an intention).[23] Sanger did not see this in the psychological terms I have used in the above description but as a shift in "defining one of the signature philosophies of his [Bush's] administration— his doctrine of preemptive military action."[24] Sanger also quoted Joseph Nye, a Harvard professor who is an expert in matters concerning the presidency, as saying, "He [Bush] is saying intent is enough." Sanger also quoted Nye as saying, "The Duelfer report pushed him into a box where capability is not the standard [forpreemption] but merely intention."

There are further differences between these judgments, which need not be discussed here. They could be and would be discussed in the new Manhattan Project, and their policy implications explored and made clear. At present, the only places in which such matters are discussed are universities or other academic forums, where policy implications are generally given little attention. Such was also the case at the time of the Manhattan Project. The virtue of the Manhattan Project was that it translated ideas into action, and that should be the virtue of the new Manhattan Project. It should translate its development of knowledge regarding human judgment and social policy into action.

Does Government Provide Honest Feedback on Policy Outcomes?

Many people lost confidence in government reports during the Vietnam war, and there has been an erosion of confidence in the government since the Iraq invasion. For example, two recent events have raised questions about whether the Bush administration intended to deceive the public about its plans for the invasion of Iraq. On June 8, 2005, Elisabeth Bumiller wrote in *The New York Times* that the British government received a report from its "senior policy advisors more than half a year before the war in Iraq began" that became known as the

Downing Street memo, which said, "American intelligence was being 'fixed' around the policy of removing Saddam Hussein in Iraq." This memo indicated that the British senior policy advisors were telling the prime minister and his government that the Bush administration was fixing intelligence to justify the invasion of Iraq. Bumiller noted that the memo "created anger among the administration's critics, who see it as evidence that the president was intent to go to war with Iraq earlier than the White House has said." When asked about this at a joint press conference with the president, Mr. Blair said, "No, the facts were not being fixed in any shape or form at all," and the president also denied that this was the case.[25] But in her article, Bumiller pointed out,

> [Their] statements contradicted assertions in the memorandum that
> was first disclosed by *The Sunday Times of London* on May 1 and
> which records the minutes of a meeting of Mr. Blair's senior policy
> advisors more than half a year before the war with Iraq began.[26]

The fact that the two leaders of the two nations that have been at the forefront of the war in Iraq must confront the minutes of a meeting that directly contradict their many public utterances about their intentions does little to diminish doubts about their veracity, and that leads to a loss of confidence. And this means that the feedback that is so critical for evaluating our correspondence judgments has become untrustworthy.

Adding to the doubts about the validity of feedback from the government is the following quotation from a senior advisor that is certainly one of the most astonishing and sophisticated of all the remarks made so far by any member of the Bush administration. In an article in *The New York Times Magazine* in 2004, Ron Suskind wrote,

> The aide [a senior advisor to President Bush] said that guys like me
> [i.e., reporters and commentators] were "in what we call the reality-
> based community," which he defined as people who "believe that solu-
> tions emerge from your judicious study of discernible reality." I nodded
> and murmured something about enlightenment principles and empiri-
> cism. He cut me off. "That's not the way the world really works any-
> more," he continued. "We're an empire now, and when we act, we create
> our own reality. And while you're studying that reality—judiciously, as
> you will—we'll act again, creating other new realities, which you can
> study too, and that's how things will sort out. We're history's actors . . .
> and you, all of you, will be left to just study what we do."[27]

In short, the new "empire" will create its own reality, and thus will create its own justifications for its actions, regardless of the truth of the matter. That means that it will create the feedback for the judgments we all make about the events that appear in the new empire. If this actually occurs, how will we ever be able to determine what is going on?

What Is Going On?

In the previous pages, I emphasized the problem of learning from the past, and I drew the distinction between learning *that* some event had occurred, and learning *why* it had occurred. I then explained the difficulties involved in learning *why*. But since I did not emphasize the difficulties in learning *that,* the reader may have assumed that these difficulties are minor. Not so. Uncertainty, unreliability of data, indeed, all the problems of making inferences from multiple fallible indicators remain, including the two instances just mentioned, all combining to make judgments about empirical reality seriously suspect.

In the beginning of this chapter, I said that members of al-Qaeda possess a weapon of a different kind. That weapon is information; members of al-Qaeda possess information about where, when, and how they will strike. Thus, it is the uncertainty about where, when, and how—not if—the attacks will occur that creates the fear of catastrophe. And it is that uncertainty that drives Westerners' search for information about al-Qaeda's intentions and practices; that uncertainty can be reduced only by relying heavily on judgments. Therefore, it is knowledge about the process of judgment under uncertainty that we need. I propose that the need is so urgent and the absence of an institution in which that need can be fulfilled so evident that a new Manhattan Project should be established.

Conclusion

Einstein's letter did not get to Roosevelt's desk very quickly, nor is there any record, so far as I know, of Roosevelt's immediate reaction to the letter. He did not see it until two months after it was written, when one of his assistants presented the letter to him on October 11, 1939, after the Germans had invaded Poland (65 years ago to the day that I am writing this). Roosevelt then appointed a Uranium Committee and it approved $6,000 to purchase uranium. But for two years, nothing more was done. The atomic-bomb project began on December 6, 1941, the day before the Japanese bombed Pearl Harbor. The Manhattan Project began in August 1942, three years after Einstein sent his letter.

I mention these details to indicate how difficult it is to direct the attention of government (even when it is headed by a Franklin Roosevelt) to new developments (even when they concern "extremely powerful bombs of a new type"). On the assumption that such circumstances (or worse) still prevail, together with the fact that I am not Albert Einstein, nor am I talking about a bigger "bang" and greater devastation, but the esoteric matter of judgments under uncertainty, the likelihood of establishing a second Manhattan Project seems minuscule. Nevertheless, it is my belief that a similar letter (or other conveyance) describing the military importance of judgment under uncertainty is likely to receive attention from someone, somewhere in the U.S. government. I say this because the 9/11 Commission's report makes it plain that protecting the country against acts of terrorism remains a critical function. It also makes plain that our ability to acquire information about when, where, and how the attacks will take place rests on the power and accuracy of human judgment under uncertainty.

I have provided examples but have not specified in any detail the specific future contributions that the members of the judgment and decision-making community might make to the problems addressed here. That is because I cannot say what they will be, any more than Einstein could be specific about what the research on uranium would bring. Nevertheless, on the basis of the productivity of the work in the field so far, I am sufficiently confident in the intellectual capacity of the people who work on this difficult topic to urge the development of a new Manhattan Project immediately, with the hope of reducing the ineptitude with which we are meeting the threat of death and destruction today.

20

The New Search for Wisdom

Because *wisdom* is such an abstract idea, and because it has such a long history, I will begin with some examples of what I am talking about. Abraham Lincoln provides me with an opportunity to show what it means to apply cognitive theory to the concept of wisdom.

Lincoln at Cooper Union, 1860

On February 17, 1860, Lincoln gave a speech at Cooper Union in New York City that turned out to be so important that several books have been written about it. Two were recently reviewed by James M. McPherson, a noted historian of the Civil War period. Although I am not citing that speech as evidence of Lincoln's wisdom, it was a smashing political success; it moved Lincoln from being dismissed as a gangling, awkward, backwoods bumpkin to being accorded the status of a serious contender for the nomination, eventually becoming president, and gaining an honored place in world history. The speech, an hour and a half in length, was recognized immediately as an extraordinary one and was printed in full in the five major New York newspapers. Only one brief portion of it will be reported here, but this fragment will suffice to show the usefulness of the concept of the cognitive continuum and how masterful Lincoln was in moving on the cognitive continuum from the rational-analytical pole to the romantic-intuitive pole of that continuum, and thus using the full cognitive power of a member of our species. His point of departure at the rational-analytical pole was the demonstration of an inconsistency, a logical contradiction in the position adopted by the "Southern people" when they opposed a ban on slavery and, as McPherson noted, "were threatening to take their states out of the Union if a Republican president was elected on a platform restricting slavery (to those states which already accepted it)."[1] Addressing his remarks to the people of the South, Lincoln said:

> But you will not abide the election of a Republican president! In that
> supposed event, you say, you will destroy the Union; and then, you
> say, the great crime of having destroyed it will be upon us! [Laughter].
> That is cool. [Great laughter]. A highwayman holds a pistol to my ear,
> and mutters through his teeth "Stand and deliver, or I shall kill you,
> and then you will be a murderer!" [Continued laughter].[2]

Having used the rational-analytical tactic to ridicule the contradiction in his opponents' logic, he moves in his concluding sentence to the intuitive-romantic pole of the continuum: "Let us have faith that right makes might, and in that faith, let us, to the end, dare to do our duty as we understand it."[3] It is the emphasis on faith and duty that places this at the romantic-intuitive pole of the cognitive continuum, and it was that move that "brought the audience to their feet with an ovation that went on and on."[4] (The best appeal a logical contradiction can make to our emotions is to evoke murmurs of assent, or ridicule and laughter; appeals to the intuitive-romantic predilections of an audience, however, can bring ovations.) Further evidence of the consequences of that move comes with McPherson's astute observation that "Lincoln's phrase 'right makes might' became a Republican slogan in the presidential campaign of 1860. It also became a rallying cry for the North in the terrible war that followed."[5] The appeal to intuition and the use of slogans (and flags) remain essential components of the romantic tradition, as the "gut player" George W. Bush showed us from the flight deck of the aircraft carrier *Abraham Lincoln*. The rational-analytical tradition remained a resource for Lincoln, however; his speeches and memoranda showed that. Lincoln, in short, was a man who could move his cognitive activity on the cognitive continuum to suit the demands of the task, and therein lay a good part of his wisdom.

Lincoln was, of course, not alone in this capacity. Oliver Wendell Holmes also demonstrated the ability to use the entire spectrum of the cognitive continuum, and also movement on it as the task's context demanded. He was admired for his ability to exercise rigorous logical thought and had a keen appreciation for the value of the intuitive mode of cognition as well. This book contains many examples of brilliant statements by Holmes vividly attesting to both.

Theory of Wisdom

The search for the definition of wisdom is an old and tangled one. Both the goal and the search are now perhaps more desirable than ever because of our unprecedented power to put our thoughts into action and thus create misery in addition to comfort, and evil in addition to good. In order to build a theory of wisdom, all manner of thinkers have sought its defining character, from the beginning of our intellectual endeavors in Asia, Arabia, Europe, and the United States. Traditionally, the search has consisted of thinking hard about what wisdom is and what it isn't, who has it and who doesn't, and how one might find it. But it wasn't until the latter half of the twentieth century, when empirical methods were first brought to bear on the matter of wisdom, that matters changed.[6] Thus, the twentieth-century recognition of human judgment as a topic to be investigated empirically and theoretically opened the door to a new approach to the study of wisdom. And finding that there are two distinct strategies of human judgment—correspondence and coherence—appears to be a further step. As indicated throughout this book, the correspondence strategy of judgment involves looking at a multiplicity of indicators, cues, information segments, and data sources that we can see, and reaching a conclusion about the state of affairs that we can't see. When one makes correct judgments of this sort we attribute wisdom to that person.

The coherence strategy, on the other hand, requires one to organize information in a logically defensible form, and that process has taken us into the development of logic and mathematics and has supported our development of science. Although we share with other species the competence to make the judgments that correspond with the features of the physical world, our use of coherent cognition, which distinguishes us from all other species, gives us the ability to create the coherent worlds that transform the cognitive activity demanded of us and evokes our potential for the coherent competence to cope with it.

Unfortunately, that very competence regarding coherence encourages us to defend the coherence of our religions and our social and economic theories to the point where we are prepared to maim and kill other people on a large scale, and also to disfigure our planet. Thus, we face a dilemma: should we encourage our coherence competence in the hope that it will enable us to develop the wisdom necessary to eliminate the death and destruction brought about by the defense of coherent thoughts, or should we discourage that cognitive activity because of its terrible history and encourage the pursuit of correspondence alone? Clearly, although the latter may have been possible centuries ago, it can no longer be attempted. That leaves us with the difficult and challenging problem of how to continue to create coherent views of the world and its problems without becoming slaves to that coherence—since surely that slavery would be unwise, however we defined slavery.

The Challenge

Our search for wisdom thus takes us beyond rationality and brings us to a challenge and a dilemma: how can we derive the advantages of our coherence competence without suffering from its disadvantages? Our intolerance for forms of coherent judgments of how the world should work that are in disagreement with our own has led, and leads to, murder and destruction as we try to drive out those competing views. But it is our coherence competence that has brought us our understanding of the physical universe, and all the advantages that go with that understanding. We need to learn how to make use of our extraordinary ability to achieve competent coherent judgments without demanding that others abandon coherent judgments that differ from our own. That is the challenge that evokes the search for wisdom and stimulates the demand that we continue the search after thousands of years of failure. In what follows, I suggest a solution.

A Guiding Metaphor: When Mapping the Mind, Seek Compromise and Acknowledge Limits

It is well known that because the world is round, and not flat, it is impossible accurately project the landmasses and oceans onto a flat map. That means that every flat paper map provides a distorted picture of the Earth: The features on the map do not accurately correspond to the physical features of Earth. The standard projection one sees is the Mercator projection, named for its originator, Gerard Mercator (1512–1594), who was a fine scholar, an artistic engraver, and perhaps the greatest mapmaker of all time. Recall that the Mercator projection makes the longitudinal (north–south) lines parallel to one another and perpendicular to the equator, despite the fact that, on the globe, longitudinal lines converge to points at both the North Pole and the South Pole. As a result, this projection misrepresents the physical size of landmasses and the distances between them. Because of this misrepresentation, landmasses and the distances between them at the polar regions are much exaggerated. (Greenland, for example, is made to look very large compared to more southern landmasses, but, in fact, it is small—about the size of Arizona.)

As a result of these well-known distortions, many alternative projections to the Mercator projection have been proposed and presented. But none has succeeded perfectly; none is perfectly accurate. Every map is a compromise; each has its own distortions. Navigators must choose which distortion will least affect their travel and thus pose the least danger. Although I know of no mathematical proof that a perfect projection is impossible, 500 years of trying to develop a perfectly accurate projection have not led to success; instead, they have led to the *acceptance of imperfection*—and some disasters—by the navigators of land, sea, and air. So, rather than continuing to reject imperfect projections, which would leave us without any map whatever, the imperfect projections have been accepted; and when their use can be defended as better than nothing, they are used with the knowledge of their imperfection.

This seems to me to be a rather startling turn of events in human history. We have not often so gently accepted such a large-scale compromise between theory and reality. But this well-known turn of events also prompts me to suggest that our experience with maps may well provide a useful metaphor for our search for wisdom. We have long sought the perfect characterization of the nature of wisdom, from Aristotle forward, without success. Therefore, perhaps we should be satisfied with a serviceable approximation—or better, several serviceable approximations—rather than continue to postpone our announcement of a precise and perfectly defensible representation of the nature of wisdom. The search for the perfect solution need not be abandoned—the search for a perfect map projection goes on—but workable solutions should not be rejected because of their imperfection.

Note how this approach to wisdom fits with Herbert Simon's approach to rationality; "the best is the enemy of the good," he proclaimed. And, as has been shown many times, we "satisfice" in most of our attempts at finding solutions when no specific easily identifiable empirical criterion is at hand.

Therefore, I propose that we use our experience with the search for a perfect map projection as a model for our attempts to discover with perfect accuracy the nature of wisdom. We should continue to develop theories of wisdom, but, as in the case of maps, we should now acknowledge that 3,000 or 5,000 years of trying is enough; and just as each map theory of the Earth carries its own distortions, each theory of wisdom carries its own distortions and thus its own compromise with reality, and we should and must accept the solution that best fits our specific situation.

We should not be embarrassed to relinquish our demand for perfection in our theory of wisdom; such a relinquishment of the demand for perfection is compatible with three great events in the history of science in the twentieth century. Palle Yourgrau has pointed out that the discoveries of the three great scientist–philosophers of the twentieth century, Albert Einstein, Kurt Gödel, and Werner Heisenberg, "each established a profound and disturbing limitation." That is itself a profound observation, for we are used to thinking of discoveries in terms of something (electricity, for example) that *removes* limitations, thus empowering us to do what we could not previously do rather than uncovers limitations. But Yourgrau, an established historian of science, tells us, "Einstein's theory of relativity set a limit—the speed of light—to the flow of any information-bearing signal. Heisenberg's uncertainty principle in quantum mechanics set a limit on our simultaneous knowledge of the position and momentum of the fundamental particles of matter. And Gödel's incompleteness theorem set a permanent limit on our knowledge of the basic truths of mathematics."[7]

Gödel's first incompleteness theorem can be seen as having nonmathematical ramifications and applications that are of special interest in justifying using both correspondence and coherence strategies. It states that within any given system of logic sufficiently sophisticated to describe arithmetic, there are always some propositions unprovable as either true or false using that system's own rules and axioms. Put more broadly, no self-contained logical system can contain all truths. Thus, to have access to all truths, one must use multiple systems. Dare it be said that this shows the ultimate flaw in using coherence alone and thus supports the utility of using both correspondence and coherence strategies with robust flexibility?[8]

Thus, we have two strong precedents from the history of science that may help us: the cartographers have shown us that much can be done with the acceptance of a compromise in relation to the achievement of a conceptual goal; and famous scientists (the physicist–philosopher Einstein, and the theoretical physicist Heisenberg, together with a mathematician–logician, Gödel) have shown us that scientific progress can be defined in terms of the discovery of limits in relation to physical phenomena.

There is a third precedent, easily overlooked, of what has often been called the "impossibility theorem," produced by the economist Kenneth Arrow, for which he received a Nobel Prize in 1972 for work in his doctoral thesis, published in 1951. Arrow showed that it was mathematically impossible to democratically order a set of conditions in such a manner as to reflect the desirability ranking of each individual in the collective.

When Arrow was introduced at the awarding of his prize, it was announced, "This conclusion; which is a rather discouraging one, as regards the dream of a perfect democracy, conflicted with the previously established welfare theory, which had long employed the concept of a social-welfare function." In short,

Arrow had shown that a critical feature of democracy was impossible to achieve—no small limitation. Nobel Prize aside, does it deserve the recognition accorded to Einstein, Heisenberg, and Gödel? I think it does.

So there is no need for embarrassment in acknowledging limitations in our efforts to find a single solution to the question of the nature of wisdom. As Arrow's work shows, the discovery, and appreciation, of such limitations is not restricted to the physical sciences.

History, Judgment and Decision Research, and the Search for Wisdom

How are these historical precedents in geography and cartography and physical and social science related to the field of judgment and decision making and our search for wisdom? That relationship can be understood by considering these precedents in relation to two major themes of judgment and decision-making research—the Brunswikian theme, as expressed by Gigerenzer, myself, and numerous colleagues that focuses on the correspondence competence of judgments, and Kahneman and Tversky's theme that focuses on the (limits to) coherence competence of judgments. For a person's wisdom will surely have to be considered in terms of its empirical quality—its correspondence with reality—and also the coherence of its logic. Despite the disputes among leading researchers, a half century of research in this field has led to a single conclusion: neither our correspondence competence nor our coherence competence is perfect. That result has been demonstrated—almost without exception—by numerous researchers.

Thus, there a strong similarity between the hard-won conclusions of Einstein, Heisenberg, and Gödel, as noted by Yourgrau ("each established a profound and disturbing limitation" in physical phenomena), and the equally hard-won conclusions drawn by Kenneth Arrow, and they are paralleled by the conclusions of the judgment and decision researchers: for they, too, have "established a profound and disturbing limitation" in the achievement of human subjects in learning under uncertainty.

Limits of Correspondence Competence

It was the Brunswikian researchers who conducted hundreds of studies of the correspondence competence of subjects learning under uncertainty during the latter part of the twentieth century. They all found that learners could not reach perfection, that is, could not learn to make perfectly accurate judgments under conditions of uncertainty—and they did so for much the same reason that map-makers discovered that they cannot make a perfect projection of a globe on a flat piece of paper—it is mathematically impossible. Many studies showed, however, that human subjects were capable of reaching the *limit of achievement* allowed by the uncertainty in the task.

That deserves a brief explanation. Suppose you create a task that requires someone to predict which of two lights will come on, a red one or a green one. Suppose you have arranged for the red one to come on 75% of the time and the green one to come on 25% of the time, each light appearing randomly within those limits. Now suppose you keep the ratio of the two lights constant at 75:25 but include randomness. Of course, the greater the randomness, the less predictable the appearance of the lights. Research shows that, with practice, people will get as many choices right as the randomness permits. Correspondence researchers have used much more complex situations than that, and the results are the same; subjects generally reach the greatest degree of accuracy mathematically possible, given the uncertainty or randomness in the task. Results like these tell us a great deal about people's correspondence competence under uncertainty.[9]

Limits of Coherence Competence

It was Ward Edwards, who, in 1954 began to pursue the question of our coherence competence in decision making. Edwards became famous for boldly (or foolishly, depending on your presumptions) suggesting that coherent intuitive decision-making behavior under uncertainty would be found to follow, or approximate, the results provided by a mathematical formulation known as Bayes's theorem.[10] To what extent people would follow the same process as implied by the form of the theorem was to be discovered by empirical research. The question then became: Are people "intuitive Bayesians," as Edwards claimed they (approximately) are? That is, if the same information is given to Bayes's theorem and to naive persons, will the latter intuitively reach the same conclusions that the theorem supported? (The reader should recall our discussion of the logic of comparing the results of an hourglass and a clock and inferring similar mechanisms on page 00, and ask if Edwards was led along this path.)

But in 1974, two psychologists, Daniel Kahneman and Amos Tversky, answered that question with a resounding no and thereby achieved even more fame than Edwards by claiming that Edwards was utterly wrong. Moreover, they did not merely argue but carried out numerous experiments that led them (and many others) to believe that people are not "intuitive Bayesians" and therefore suffer from limitations to the rationality of their decisions under uncertainty. (It is to Edwards's credit that one could achieve fame by disproving his theory.)

But Kahneman and Tversky's claim was broader than Edwards's; they believed that they had demonstrated that people had almost universally failed the test of rationality in relation to uncertainty, in their intuitive use of probabilities. Furthermore, they claimed that they had found *why* people failed to be rational in their use of probabilities. It is because people use "heuristics" that lead to "biases" (that is, errors of judgment), and that process created irrationality. It is this theme (and experimental results) from Kahneman and Tversky that led to the research of Sunstein and his colleagues. In 2002 the Nobel Committee announced that Daniel Kahneman (a psychologist) and Vernon Smith (an economist) were to be the joint recipients of the 2002 economics award. (Kahneman's colleague, Amos Tversky, a widely honored psychologist, died before the award was made.)

The study of human judgment, virtually nonexistent only a half century ago, was recognized by the granting of the Nobel Prize to students of human judgment Herbert Simon, Kahneman (and Tversky), and Vernon Smith. And they were honored for their discovery of the *limitations* in the ability of humans to achieve perfection in their intuitive judgments under uncertainty, precisely as Einstein, Heisenberg, Gödel, and Arrow had been honored for their discovery of limitations.

All this work, and the parallel work on the discovery of limitations to correspondence competence done by the Brunswikians, allows us to be more confident that our limitations regarding wisdom—and the metaphor of the Mercator projection—should be accepted. But we still need a theory of how wisdom is achieved, and to that we now turn.

The Author's Theory: A Synthesis That Leads to a Theory of Wisdom

The essential feature of the theory of wisdom to be developed here is the proposal that flexibility and robustness are fundamental characteristics of the human cognitive system and always have been. *Flexibility* refers to the ease with which cognition moves from intuition to analysis (and back) on the cognitive continuum; *robustness* refers to the capacity to match the properties of the cognitive processes to the properties of the task to which the judgment applies. That is, when a person begins a task by applying analytical cognition but fails to make successful judgments and then begins to apply intuitive judgments, she or he is exhibiting flexibility; if she or he has chosen correctly, that is, has applied intuition to an intuition-appropriate task, or analysis to the analysis-appropriate task, she or he will have demonstrated robustness. Thus, oscillation on the cognitive continuum that occurs in such a way as to match cognitive properties to task properties explicates the flexibility that is an essential part of wisdom. (See p. 277 for more on oscillation.)

The second criterion for wisdom and robustness is more difficult to describe inasmuch as the correspondence strategy and the coherence strategy imply two different forms of correctness. The first form is easy to see: high correspondence, that is, high empirical accuracy, obviously represents one form of robustness. That form carried us through millions of years of our evolution on the planet, as it has for so many other species, all by the same general process. But the second form of correctness—coherence—is harder to pin down.

The criterion for coherence competence can be readily achieved if the judgments are cast as a metaphor for a mathematical theorem, such as Bayes's theorem. And that is why that procedure became so frequently used. But once we move away from problems readily reduced to a simplified form of Bayes's theorem and toward more complex and more representative forms (for example, those with multiple intercorrelated indicators), trouble starts, the problem becomes intractable, and we lose our mathematical advantage. And that means we have to search for a criterion for the correctness for the coherence of our judgments, other than the mathematical formulas applied to simple problems.

The first place to turn, after mathematics, for a criterion for coherence is logic: We can ask if a judgment meets the criteria of logic. What are these? For that we can consult the dictionary; it will tell us that coherence is defined in terms of order or consistency, in short, noncontradiction. And that is what it all comes down to.

(Completeness—recall Gödel—is a second criterion, but we can overlook that for now.) Thus, in the absence of an empirical criterion, a person's judgment can be justified only in terms of consistency, the absence of contradiction. As a result, the criterion for coherence is hard to apply without slipping off into myths and unsupported beliefs to create the appearance of coherence.

We saw this happen when Alfred Wallace began his dispute with Charles Darwin. Wallace simply could not find—and his modern successors cannot find—a coherent explanation of selection that could compete with Charles Darwin's empirically based theory of natural selection, and so Wallace slipped from logic into spiritualism. Modern competitors such as creationism are also subject to the lures of mysticism, and "intelligent design" cannot seem to separate itself from religion. Yet attempts to supplement theories that are distasteful but coherent will continue not only to depose Darwinian evolutionary theory but theories of government as well. New proposals of new utopias will persist despite the disastrous consequences of trying to erect utopias in the twentieth century. That is the grave danger that faces the attempt to achieve coherence competence in the search for wisdom; we have seen some of the consequences, in which the search for utopia is aided by force, and thus goes astray.

So, while it is true that grave danger lies in wait, we should remember that there is no greater prize than the one that lies at the end of our scientific endeavor: the wisdom that could lead to a peaceful world.

Notes

INTRODUCTION

1. Amartya Sen, *Rationality and Freedom* (Cambridge, Mass.: Belknap, 2002), p. 4.
2. Alan Ryan, "The Way to Reason," *New York Review of Books*, December 4, 2003.
3. Rex Brown, "The Operation Was a Success but the Patient Died: Aider Priorities Influence Decision Aid Usefulness," *Interfaces 35* (2005), pp. 511–521.
4. Ibid., p. 513.
5. Personal communication with Rex Brown.
6. Elizabeth Kolbert, "Why Work? A Hundred Years of the 'Protestant Ethic,'" *New Yorker*, November 29, 2004, pp. 154–160.
7. Isaiah Berlin, *Freedom and Its Betrayal: Six Enemies of Human Liberty* (Princeton, N.J.: Princeton University Press, 2002), p. 43.
8. Ibid., p. 58.
9. *Bartlett's Familiar Quotations* (New York: Little, Brown, 1980), p. 292.
10. Richard Parker, *John Kenneth Galbraith: His Life, His Politics, His Economics* (New York: Farrar, Straus & Giroux, 2005), p. 601.
11. Eric Schlosser, "The Cow Jumped over the U.S.D.A.," *New York Times*, January 2, 2004, p. A19.
12. For a brief history of this development, see Kenneth R. Hammond, *Human Judgment and Social Policy: Irreducible Uncertainty, Inevitable Error, Unavoidable Injustice* (New York: Oxford University Press, 1996), pp. 3–7.
13. Ibid., pp. 294–299.
14. Robert Fogelin, *Walking the Tightrope of Reason: The Precarious Life of a Rational Animal* (New York: Oxford University Press, 2004).
15. For further reading on intuition, see Hammond, *Human Judgment and Social Policy*; Kenneth R. Hammond, *Judgments under Stress* (New York: Oxford University Press, 2000); William Goldstein and Robin Hogarth, *Research on Judgment and Decision Making* (Cambridge, Mass.: Cambridge University Press, 1997); and Robin Hogarth, *Educating Intuition* (Chicago: University of Chicago Press, 2002).
16. John Stuart Mill, *Autobiography* (London: Penguin, 1989), p. 114.
17. Janet Browne, *Charles Darwin: The Power of Place* (New York: Knopf, 2002), pp. 317–318.

18. Bob Woodward, *Bush at War* (New York: Simon & Schuster, 2002), p. 137.
19. *New York Times*, January 7, 2004, p. A1.
20. Mike Allen and David S. Broder, "Bush's Leadership Style: Decisive or Simplistic?" *Washington Post*, August 30, 2004, p. A1.
21. His February 5, 2003, speech at the United Nations may not have been his finest hour, but I am confident that his effort was genuine.

CHAPTER I

1. Isaiah Berlin, *The Sense of Reality: Studies in Ideas and Their History* (New York: Farrar, Straus & Giroux, 1996), p. 40.
2. Ibid., p. 47.
3. Vernon Smith, "Constructivist and Ecological Rationality in Economics," Nobel Prize lecture, Stockholm, 2002.
4. V. O. Key, Jr., *The Responsible Electorate: Rationality in Presidential Voting, 1936–1960* (Cambridge, Mass.: Harvard University Press, 1966), p. 270.
5. See Kenneth R. Hammond, *Human Judgment and Social Policy: Irreducible Uncertainty, Inevitable Error, Unavoidable Injustice* (New York: Oxford University Press, 1996).
6. For example, see Jared Diamond's highly acclaimed book *Collapse: How Societies Choose to Fail or Succeed* (New York: Penguin, 2005), p. 510.
7. See Hammond, *Human Judgment and Social Policy*, pp. 40–55, for a development of this approach based on the recognition of the duality of error.
8. Michael Ignatieff has written an excellent treatise on the problem of false positives and false negatives and civil liberties that thoroughly explores the philosophical and ethical issues involved but fails to address the role of uncertainty that clouds the treatment of these issues. See Michael Ignatieff, *The Lesser Evil: Political Ethics in an Age of Terror* (Princeton, N.J.: Princeton University Press, 2004).
9. See Hammond, *Human Judgment and Social Policy*, pp. 28 and 160, for detailed discussion of the development of mandatory sentencing.
10. Kenneth R. Hammond, "Measuring Attitudes by Error-Choice," *Journal of Abnormal and Social Psychology* 43 (1948), pp. 38–48.

CHAPTER 2

1. The *9/11 Commission Report* (New York: Norton, 2004), p. 344, states that although in 1941 the United States "had excellent intelligence that a Japanese attack was coming . . . these were the days of 'excruciating uncertainty.'"
2. Valerie Jameson, "Biggest Bets in the Universe Unveiled," New Scientist.com, August 26, 2004, http://www.newscientist.com/article/dn6331.html.

3. James Fallows, "Blind into Baghdad," *Atlantic Monthly,* February 2004, p. 53.
4. Edmund Wilson, *Patriotic Gore: Studies in the Literature of the Civil War* (New York: Oxford University Press, 1962); see also Louis Menand, *The Metaphysical Club: A Story of Ideas in America* (New York: Farrar, Straus & Giroux, 2001), for an intriguing account of Holmes's relations with C. S. Peirce, William James, and other intellectuals of his time in the "Metaphysical Club."
5. Menand, *Metaphysical Club*, p. 62.
6. *The Dialogues of Plato*, trans. Benjamin Jowett. Vol. 1 (New York: Random House, 1920 [1892]), p. 406.
7. Sheldon Novick, *Honorable Justice: The Life of Oliver Wendell Holmes* (New York: Little, Brown, 1989), p. 27.
8. Article about interview with Tim Russert, *New York Times*, February 9, 2004, p. A19.
9. Isaiah Berlin, "Notes on Prejudice," *New York Review of Books*, October 18, 2001, p. 12.
10. See Isaiah Berlin, *Personal Impressions* (New York: Viking Press, 1981), for his account of his life in Washington, D.C., and his impressions of famous people he knew. See also Michael Ignatieff, *Isaiah Berlin: A Life* (New York: Henry Holt, 1998), for a detailed personal biography. See also Ronald Dworkin, Mark Lilla, and Robert B. Silvers, eds., *The Legacy of Isaiah Berlin* (New York: New York Review Books, 2001).
11. Atul Gawande, *Complications: A Surgeon's Notes on an Imperfect Science* (New York: Metropolitan Books, 2002), p. 229.
12. George Packer, "War after the War," *New Yorker*, November 24, 2003.

CHAPTER 3

1. See my *Judgments under Stress* (New York: Oxford University Press, 2000), pp. 66–82, for the critical role of loss of constancy in the creation of stress.
2. Jeff Tietz, "On the Border: To Track Someone You Have to Learn to See Fine Disturbances," *New Yorker,* November 29, 2004, pp. 90–110.
3. John Keegan, *Intelligence in War: Knowledge of the Enemy from Napoleon to Al-Qaeda* (New York: Knopf, 2003).
4. See Ray Cooksey, *Theory, Methods, and Applications* (New York: Academic Press, 1996).
5. A similar situation occurred on United Airlines flight 232 when the hydraulic controls of the aircraft failed; I describe this situation in detail in *Judgments under Stress*, pp. 77–78.
6. Kenneth N. Gilpin, "Settlement Near for Insurer Accused of Overcharging Blacks," *New York Times*, January 10, 2002, p. C4.
7. James Franklin, *The Science of Conjecture: Evidence and Probability before Pascal* (Baltimore: Johns Hopkins University Press, 2001), pp. 164–165.

8. Ibid., p. 222.

9. Judith Miller, "A Battle of Words over War Intelligence," *New York Times*, November 22, 2003, p. A17.

10. Cynthia Grabo, *Anticipating Surprise: Analysis for Strategic Warning* (Washington, D.C.: Center for Strategic Intelligence Research, Joint Military Intelligence College, 1972). Reissued in 2002 by the Defense Intelligence Agency.

11. Thomas Shanker and Eric Schmitt, "Pentagon Weighs Use of Deception in a Broad Arena," *New York Times*, December 14, 2004, p. A1.

12. Jacques Barzun, *From Dawn to Decadence: 500 Years of Western Cultural Life, 1500 to the Present* (New York: HarperCollins, 2001), p. 434.

13. Richard Posner, *Public Intellectuals: A Study of Decline* (Cambridge, Mass.: Harvard University Press, 2001).

14. Frederick Schauer, *Profiles, Probabilities, and Stereotypes* (Cambridge, Mass.: Harvard University Press, 2003).

15. Christopher Drew and Ralph Blumenthal, "Arrested Men's Shaved Bodies Drew Suspicion of the FBI," *New York Times*, October 26, 2001, p. B4.

16. In his famous *Origin of Species*, he concentrated on natural selection.

17. See for example Cooksey, *Theory, Methods, and Applications*; Kenneth R. Hammond, *Human Judgment and Social Policy: Irreducible Uncertainty, Inevitable Error, Unavoidable Injustice* (New York: Oxford University Press, 1996); Hammond, *Judgment under Stress*; Kenneth R. Hammond and Thomas R. Stewart, eds., *The Essential Brunswik: Beginnings, Explications, Applications* (New York: Oxford University Press, 2001).

18. See, for example, David Buss, *Evolutionary Psychology: The New Science of the Mind* (Boston: Allyn & Bacon, 2004). For a more intensive focus on sexual selection, see Geoffrey Miller, *The Mating Mind: How Sexual Choice Shaped the Evolution of Human Nature* (New York: Doubleday, 2000). Also see David Buss and Neil Malumuth, eds., *Sex, Power, Conflict: Evolutionary and Feminist Perspectives* (New York: Oxford University Press, 1996).

19. Miller, *The Mating Mind*.

CHAPTER 4

1. Barbara Tuchman, *The Guns of August* (New York: Dell, 1962).

2. David Brooks, "The CIA: Method and Madness," *New York Times*, February 3, 2004, p. A27.

3. Douglas Jehl and David Sanger, "Powell's Case, a Year Later: Gaps in Picture of Iraq Arms," *New York Times*, February 1, 2004.

4. Dana Priest, *Washington Post*, "No Evidence CIA Slanted Iraq Data," January 31, 2004, p. A01.

5. I discuss the matter in more detail in chapter 10 of *Human Judgment and Social Policy: Irreducible Uncertainty, Inevitable Error, Unavoidable Injustice* (New York: Oxford University Press, 1996).

6. John Keegan, *Intelligence in War: Knowledge of the Enemy from Napoleon to Al-Qaeda* (New York: Knopf, 2003), p. 315.

7. Ibid., p. 319.

8. Prime Minister Blair's speech, reprinted in *The New York Times*, July 16, 2005.

9. Ibid.

10. See Peter Capella, *Independent Online* (South Africa), http://www.iol.co.za, July 25, 2005.

11. Sari Horowitz, "Police Chiefs Group Bolsters Policy on Suicide Bombers," *Washington Post*, August 4, 2005.

12. Ibid.

13. *New York Times,* January 17, 2006, p. 1.

14. Michael Bishop and J. D. Trout, *Epistemology and the Psychology of Human Judgment* (New York: Oxford University Press, 2005), p. 6.

CHAPTER 5

1. Michael Shermer, *In Darwin's Shadow: The Life and Science of Alfred Russel Wallace* (New York: Oxford University Press, 2002), p. 170.

2. Janet Browne, *Charles Darwin: The Power of Place* (New York: Knopf, 2002), pp. 317–318.

3. Browne, *Charles Darwin*, p. 56.

4. Jared Diamond, *Guns, Germs, and Steel: The Fates of Human Societies* (New York: Norton, 1997).

5. Ibid., pp. 268–269.

6. Ibid., p. 268.

7. Jack Goody, *The Interface between the Written and the Oral* (Cambridge, U.K.: Cambridge University Press, 1987); Goody, *The Logic of Writing and the Organization of Society* (Cambridge, U.K.: Cambridge University Press, 1986).

8. Goody, *Interface*, p. 25.

9. Diamond, *Guns, Germs, and Steel,* pp. 215–238.

10. Jack Goody, *The Power of the Written Word* (Washington, D.C.: Smithsonian Institution Press, 2000).

11. Ibid., p. 11.

12. Ibid., p. 12.

13. See Ray Cooksey, *Theory, Methods, and Applications* (New York: Academic Press, 1996).

14. Malcolm Gladwell, *The Tipping Point* (New York: Little, Brown, 2000).

15. Duncan Watts, *Six Degrees: The Science of a Connected Age* (New York: Norton, 2003), p. 20.

16. See, for example, pp. 195ff. and numerous places in the report of the 9/11 Commission.

17. Alan Wolfe, *Moral Freedom: The Search for Virtue in a World of Choice* (New York: Norton, 2001), p. 200.

18. Diamond, *Guns, Germs, and Steel*, p. 268.

19. Cass Sunstein, Daniel Kahneman, David Schkade, and Ilana Ritov, "Predictably Incoherent Judgments," John M. Olin Law & Economics Working Paper, No. 131, 2nd Series. University of Chicago Law School, 2001.

20. Ibid., p. 2.

21. Ibid.

22. Mark Lilla, "The Reckless Mind: Intellectuals in Politics," *New York Review of Books*, 2001.

23. Ibid., pp. 81, 198.

24. See Kathleen L. Mosier, "Automation and Cognition: Maintaining Coherence in the Electronic Cockpit," in Edward Salas, ed., *Advances in Human Performance and Cognitive Engineering Research 2* (New York: Elsevier Science, 2002), pp. 93–121; Kathleen L. Mosier and Shane McCauley, "Achieving Coherence: Meeting New Cognitive Demands in Technological Systems, in Alex Kirlik, ed., *Adaptation in Human-Technology Interaction: Methods, Models and Measures* (New York: Oxford University Press, in press), for research on this topic.

25. Gerd Gigerenzer and Peter Todd, *Simple Heuristics That Make Us Smart* (New York: Oxford University Press, 1999), p. 362.

26. Ibid., p. 364.

27. Ibid., p. 365.

28. Ibid.

29. Cass Sunstein, *Risk and Reason: Safety, Law and the Environment* (New York: Cambridge University Press, 2002), pp. 58ff.

CHAPTER 6

1. Ernst May and Philip Zelikow, *The Kennedy Tapes: Inside the White House during the Cuban Missile Crisis* (Cambridge, Mass.: Harvard University Press, 1997).

2. Michael Beschloss, *The Conquerors: Roosevelt, Truman and the Destruction of Hitler's Germany, 1941–1945* (New York: Simon & Schuster, 2002).

3. May and Zelikow, *Kennedy Tapes*, p. 701.

4. Ibid., p. 696.

5. Ibid., p. 701. See also the historian Gaddis's remarks about history's interest in particulars: John Lewis Gaddis, *The Landscape of History* (New York: Oxford University Press, 2002), pp. 62–106.

6. James Patterson, *Grand Expectations: The United States, 1945–1974* (New York: Oxford University Press, 1996), p. 508.

7. May and Zelikow, *Kennedy Tapes*, p. 30.

8. Ibid., p. 59.

9. Ibid., p. 480.

10. Ibid., p. 485.

11. Ibid., p. 491.

12. Ibid., p. 501.
13. Ibid., pp. 585–586.
14. For more on this, see Kenneth R. Hammond, *Human Judgment and Social Policy: Irreducible Uncertainty, Inevitable Error, Unavoidable Injustice* (New York: Oxford University Press, 1996), pp. 286–289.
15. May and Zelikow, *Kennedy Tapes*, p. 480.
16. May and Zelikow, *Kennedy Tapes*, pp. 479–480.
17. John Keegan, *Intelligence in War: Knowledge of the Enemy from Napoleon to Al-Qaeda* (New York: Knopf, 2003), p. 319.

CHAPTER 7

1. See Perry Link, "Wiping out the Truth," *New York Review of Books*, February 24, 2005, pp. 36–39, for the Chinese efforts to control information; See Edward Rothstein, Herbert Muschamp, and Martin Marty, *Visions of Utopia* (New York: Oxford University Press, 2003), for a thorough discussion of utopias and their inevitable demise.
2. Václav Havel, *Living in Truth* (London: Faber and Faber, 1989), p. 59.
3. Isaiah Berlin, *The Crooked Timber of Humanity: Chapters in the History of Ideas* (New York: Knopf, 1991), p. 15.
4. See the Perry Link reference in note 1 of this chapter for a description of China's effort to control the use of the Internet.
5. Cass Sunstein, *Republic.com* (Princeton, N.J.: Princeton University Press, 2001).
6. Ibid., p. 44.
7. Ibid., p. 67.
8. Todd Purdum, "So What Was That All About? The Impact of Dr. Dean," *New York Times,* February 22, 2004, Week in Review section, p. 1.
9. Jacques Barzun, *From Dawn to Decadence: 500 Years of Western Cultural Life, 1500 to the Present* (New York: HarperCollins, 2001), p. 797.
10. See Bernard Bailyn, *To Begin the World Anew* (New York: Knopf, 2003), for a discussion of the important role of *The Federalist Papers* in the American Revolution.
11. Link, "Wiping out the Truth."
12. Ibid., p. 67.
13. Ibid.
14. Mark Lilla, "The Reckless Mind: Intellectuals in Politics," *New York Review of Books*, 2001, p. 196.
15. Louis Menand, *The Metaphysical Club: A Story of Ideas in America* (New York: Farrar, Straus & Giroux, 2001), p. 62.
16. Edmund Morgan, *Benjamin Franklin* (New Haven, Conn.: Yale University Press, 2003), p. 314.
17. An excellent treatment of the role of coherent belief in the thought of Hitler and bin Laden can be found in Ron Rosenbaum, "Degrees of Evil: Some Thoughts on

Hitler, bin Laden, and the Hierarchy of Wickedness," *Atlantic Monthly*, February 2002, pp. 63–68.

18. See Isaiah Berlin, *The Sense of Reality: Studies in Ideas and Their History* (New York: Farrar, Straus & Giroux, 1996), for a brilliant treatise on the failure of utopias.

CHAPTER 8

1. William James, "Pragmatism: A New Name for Some Old Ways of Thinking," 1907, lectures (New York: Longmans, Green).

2. Garry Wills, *Inventing America: Jefferson's Declaration of Independence* (Garden City, N.Y.: Doubleday, 1978), p. 283.

3. For more on Jefferson and the role of his cognitive theory in government, see Kenneth Hammond, *Judgments under Stress* (New York: Oxford University Press, 2000); for more on the role of these cognitive processes in government, see Kenneth R. Hammond, *Human Judgment and Social Policy: Irreducible Uncertainty, Inevitable Error, Unavoidable Injustice* (New York: Oxford University Press, 1996).

4. For an example in which 11 task properties were listed, see Kenneth R. Hammond, Robert Hamm, Janet Grassia, and Tamra Pearson, "Direct Comparison of the Efficacy of Intuitive and Analytical Cognition in Expert Judgment," in William Goldstein and Robin Hogarth, eds., *Research on Judgment and Decision Making* (New York: Cambridge University Press, 1997), pp. 144–180.

5. Egon Brunswik, *Perception and the Representative Design of Psychological Experiments* (Berkeley: University of California Press, 1956). See also Kenneth R. Hammond and Thomas R. Stewart, eds., *The Essential Brunswik: Beginnings, Explications, Applications* (New York: Oxford University Press, 2001), pp. 260–264.

6. See Brunswik, *Perception,* pp. 90–93; and Hammond and Stewart, *The Essential Brunswik*, pp. 260–264, for reprinted pages and comment.

7. Hammond and Stewart, *The Essential Brunswik*, p. 263.

8. Ibid.

9. Ibid. See also Philip T. Dunwoody, Eric Haarbauer, Robert P. Mahan, Christopher Marino, and Chu-Chun Tang, "Cognitive Adaptation and Its Consequences: A Test of Cognitive Continuum Theory," *Journal of Behavioral Decision Making 13* (2000), pp. 35–54, for an empirical test of the utility of the concept of a cognitive continuum.

10. I have used *remote* as a substitute for the technical term *distal* used by perception psychologists. Brunswik used the term *distal aim* in his 1956 book to introduce the shift I have just described. The term *remote* (or distal) can be readily explicated in terms of time. That is, if I make a judgment about an event that will occur very soon, that judgment is directed at an event that is not remote from me, at least in time. If I make a judgment about an event that is distant in time, say, a student making a judgment about which college to attend, that event is more remote.

11. See Hammond and Stewart, *The Essential Brunswik*, pp. 135–162, for a description of this transition; see Hammond, *Human Judgment and Social Policy*, for a brief history of the development of judgment and decision making after Brunswik.

CHAPTER 9

1. I. H. Nagel, S. Breyer, and T. MacCarthy, "Panel V: Equality versus Discretion in Sentencing," Introduction by the Honorable Frank H. Easterbrook, *American Criminal Law Review 26*, 1989.
2. The phenomenon of oscillation has not been well documented in the scientific literature of cognitive psychology. However, Elise Weaver and George Richardson ("Threshold Setting and the Cycling of a Decision Threshold," *Systems Dynamic Review 22*, 2005, pp. 1–26) were successful in modeling oscillation by using a system-dynamics model of this phenomenon.
3. William Brennan, *Reason, Passion, and the Progress of the Law* (1987), p. 968.
4. Ibid., p. 958.
5. Antonin Scalia, *A Matter of Interpretation: Federal Courts and the Law* (Princeton, N.J.: Princeton University Press, 1997).
6. Ibid., p. 135.
7. Ibid.
8. Ibid., p. 25.
9. *New York Times,* June 21, 2002, p. A14.
10. Adam Cohen, "Psst . . . Justice Scalia . . . You Know, You're an Activist Judge, Too," *New York Times,* April 19, 2005.
11. Jean Stefancic and Richard Delgado, *How Lawyers Lost Their Way: A Profession Fails Its Creative Minds* (Durham, N.C.: Duke University Press, 2005).
12. Benjamin Sells, *The Soul of the Law: Understanding Lawyers and the Law* (Rockport, Mass.: Element Books, 1994).
13. Oliver Wendell Holmes, *The Common Law* (Boston: Little, Brown, 1923), p. 1.
14. Kenneth R. Hammond, *Human Judgment and Social Policy: Irreducible Uncertainty, Inevitable Error, Unavoidable Injustice* (New York: Oxford University Press, 1996), pp. 318–320.
15. Lawrence Tribe, a distinguished professor of constitutional law at Harvard University, in his "Comment" within Scalia's *A Matter of Interpretation* about Justice Scalia's thesis, p. 94.
16. Other illustrations are presented in Kenneth R. Hammond and Thomas R. Stewart, eds., *The Essential Brunswik: Beginnings, Explications, Applications* (New York: Oxford University Press, 2001); Hammond, *Human Judgment and Social Policy*; Kenneth R. Hammond, *Judgments under Stress* (New York: Oxford University Press, 2000).

17. John Yoo, Memorandum Opinion for Timothy Flanagan, the Deputy Counsel to the President, in Karen Greenberg and Joshua Dratel, eds., *The Torture Papers: The Road to Abu Ghraib* (New York: Cambridge University Press, 2005), p. 7.

18. Greenberg and Dratel, *The Torture Papers*, p. xvi.

19. Ibid., p. 223.

20. Ibid., p. xvii.

21. Brennan, *Reason, Passion,* p. 968.

22. Greenberg and Dratel, *The Torture Papers*.

23. Ibid., pp. 2–122.

24. Ibid., p. xix.

CHAPTER 10

1. Steve Lohr and Chris Gaither, "A Family Struggle, A Company's Fate. Hewlett-Packard's Plan for a Merger May Hinge on the Heirs of the Founders," *New York Times*, December 2, 2001, p. 1.

2. *New York Times*, May 28, 2002, p. D6.

3. Ian Buruma and Avishai Margalit, *Occidentalism: The West in the Eyes of Its Enemies* (New York: Penguin, 2004).

4. Robert Woodward, *Maestro* (New York: Simon & Schuster, 2000), p. 90.

5. Kenneth R. Hammond, *Human Judgment and Social Policy: Irreducible Uncertainty, Inevitable Error, Unavoidable Injustice* (New York: Oxford University Press, 1996).

6. James Holzworth, "Annotated Bibliography of Cue Probability Learning Studies, 1999," retrieved February 18, 2005, from the Brunswik Society Web site: http://www.brunswik.org/resources/mcplbib.doc.

7. See, for example, Gerd Gigerenzer and Peter Todd, *Simple Heuristics That Make Us Smart* (New York: Oxford University Press, 1999).

8. Obviously, there are many ramifications of the use of these models and their appearance in various situations; for further reading see Ray Cooksey, *Judgment Analysis: Theory, Methods, and Applications* (New York: Academic Press, 1996); Terry Connolly, Hal Arkes, and Kenneth R. Hammond, *Judgment and Decision Making: An Interdisciplinary Reader,* 2nd ed. (New York: Cambridge University Press, 2000); Gigerenzer and Todd, *Simple Heuristics*; William Goldstein and Robin Hogarth, eds., *Research on Judgment and Decision Making* (New York: Cambridge University Press, 1997).

9. See Dr. Jerome Groopman, *Second Opinions: Stories of Intuition and Choice in the Changing World of Medicine* (New York: Penguin, 2001).

10. Ibid., p. 126.

11. Ibid., p. 234.

12. *Wall Street Journal,* March 15, 2002, p. A10.

13. Sandra Boodman, *Washington Post,* December 3, 2002.

14. Christopher Landrigan et al., "Effect of Reducing Interns' Work Hours on Serious Medical Errors in Intensive Care Units," *New England Journal of Medicine* (October 28, 2004), p. 1838.

15. Atul Gawande, *Complications: A Surgeon's Notes on an Imperfect Science* (New York: Metropolitan Books, 2002), p. 224.

16. Shannon Brownlee, "Information, Please: Sounds crazy but One Way to Arrest the Spiraling Cost of Health Care Would Be to Figure Out What Treatments Actually Work," *Atlantic Monthly*, January/February 2004, p. 145.

17. Ibid.

18. Ibid.

19. See Kenneth R. Hammond and Thomas R. Stewart, eds., *The Essential Brunswik: Beginnings, Explications, Applications* (New York: Oxford University Press, 2001).

20. Philip Roth, *American Pastoral* (New York: Viking, 1997), p. 35.

21. Bob Woodward, *Bush at War* (New York: Simon & Schuster, 2002).

22. Bruce Hoffman, "Plan of Attack," *Atlantic Monthly,* July/August 2004, pp. 42–43.

23. Ibid., p. 42.

24. Ibid.

25. Although I treat this matter to some extent in *Human Judgment and Social Policy: Irreducible Uncertainty, Inevitable Error, Uunavoidable Injustice,* (New York: Oxford University Press, 1996), pp. 103–105, I offer a related argument here because of its importance.

26. National Commission on Terrorist Attacks upon the United States, *The 9/11 Commission Report: Final Report of the National Commission on Terrorist Attacks upon the United States* (New York: Norton, 2004).

27. Freeman Dyson, "A Meeting with Enrico Fermi: How One Intuitive Physicist Rescued a Team from Fruitless Research," *Nature* 427, no. 297, January 22, 2004.

28. Personal correspondence courtesy Robert Bateman and Freeman Dyson.

29. Freeman Dyson, *Disturbing the Universe* (New York: Harper & Row, 1979), pp. 55–66. See my *Human Judgment and Social Policy,* pp. 64–65, for further on scientists' and intuition, including reproductions of Feynman's diagrams.

30. See Hammond, *Human Judgment and Social Policy.*

CHAPTER 11

1. Thomas L. Friedman, *New York Times,* November 20, 2001, p. A19.

2. I classified this judgment as an analytical one because Friedman carefully points out the indicators he is using and states that it is these that lead him to conclude that it is democracy that makes the difference. Note also that he explicitly adds them up. But Friedman and all, or almost all, the rest of us can do more than that. Within the analytical process, we can multiply indicators, perform many mathematical operations, think of differential or integral calculus, and do far too many other operations to mention.

3. Jacques Barzun, *From Dawn to Decadence: 500 Years of Western Cultural Life, 1500 to the Present* (New York: HarperCollins, 2001), p. 202.

4. Barton Gellman, "U.S. Fears Al Qaeda Cyber Attacks," *Washington Post,* June 26, 2002.

5. Roger Lowenstein, *When Genius Failed: The Rise and Fall of Long-Term Capital Management* (New York: Random House, 2000).

6. Ibid., p. 149.

7. Robert Skidelsky, "The World on a String," *New York Review of Books 48,* no. 4 (2001), p. 12.

8. Fortunately, Soros is a frank and honest man who wrote a book to tell the world about his mistakes. For example, in 1998 he predicted the end of global capitalism, yet admitted in 1999, "I was wrong to predict disaster, and now I have some egg on my face." This mistake was a huge one; it was not only a cognitive mistake, it cost him a great deal of money. As Soros put it, "We had our head handed to us." How does Soros account for these failed judgments and predictions in the face of all the information, including judgments of other experts, he had at his disposal? The explanations are somewhat lengthy, but they come down to this: the "outlying phenomena" simply weren't "outlying," they were part of another coherent model. But no one knows exactly where that model is to be found.

9. Lowenstein, *When Genius Failed,* p. 235.

10. Ibid., p. 236.

11. Joseph Nocera, *New York Times,* October 1, 2005, p. B1; Nassim Nicholas Taleb, *Fooled by Randomness: The Hidden Role of Chance in Life and the Markets* (New York: Random House, 2005).

12. Mike McIntyre, "How Do Ferry Pilots Tell Speed? By Looking Out the Window," *New York Times,* October 19, 2003, p. 27.

CHAPTER 12

1. See Terry Connolly, Hal Arkes, and Kenneth R. Hammond, eds., *Judgment and Decision Making: An Interdisciplinary Reader,* 2nd ed. (New York: Oxford University Press, 2000); William Goldstein and Robin Hogarth, eds., *Research on Judgment and Decision Making* (New York: Cambridge University Press, 1997).

2. A little-known instance of a psychologist presenting an example of perceptual illusions to President Eisenhower in an unsuccessful effort to show him the value of psychological research in world politics is described in Kenneth R. Hammond, *Human Judgment and Social Policy: Irreducible Uncertainty, Inevitable Error, Uunavoidable Injustice* (New York: Oxford University Press, 1996), pp. 294–299.

3. Paul Thagard, Chris Eliasmith, Paul Rusnock, and Cameron Shelley, "Knowledge and Coherence," in Renne Eliot, ed., *Common Sense, Reasoning & Rationality* (New York: Oxford University Press, 2002), pp. 104–131. In short, intuitive cognition in search of coherence can be seen easily and obviously in the demonstrations of

perceptual illusions that often occur, as well as in the "biases" that now appear as selective memory, selective perception, social stereotyping, and in the ubiquitous appearance of conspiracy theories. Error appears in all of these as part of the effort to achieve coherence intuitively. Will this also be true in the psychology of judgment and decision making? Many think the answer is yes, and that this question is settled. But doubts remain about the way the problem has been studied, a matter to be discussed in this chapter.

4. See Connelly et al., *Judgment and Decision Making*, for descriptions of various studies.

5. Kristin Shrader-Frachette, "Methodological Rules for Four Classes of Scientific Uncertainty," in John Lemons, ed., *Scientific Uncertainty and Environmental Problem Solving* (Cambridge, Mass.: Cambridge University Press,, 1996), p. 18.

6. Note that evaluating the competence of correspondence judgments, however, is done by comparing the answer provided by intuition with the circumstances in the "outside world"; if the subject predicts rain, we look for rain. That contrasts with the method of comparing the answers produced by intuitive cognition and the product of an analytical method. In the case of correspondence competence we compare the subject's judgment with an empirical event rain or no rain. In the case of coherence competence we compare the subject's judgment with the product of an analytical process a statistical calculation. No inferences about the process can be directly confirmed in either case. But everyone is interested in the putative internal process, because it will tell us how we make our judgments. So we continue to try.

7. According to a September 12, 2005, report from Bloomberg, Secretary of State Colin Powell said the intelligence that led the United States to conclude Iraq was stockpiling weapons of mass destruction before the war "did not stand the test of time."

8. Isaiah Berlin, *The Crooked Timber of Humanity: Chapters in the History of Ideas* (New York: Knopf, 1991), p. 202.

9. Romanticism was the cognitive foundation of Adolf Hitler's dictatorship that resulted in one of history's greatest crimes against humanity, the deaths of tens of millions of Europeans and six million Jews. But did Berlin speak too soon when he refers to its "disintegrating influence"? Has the romanticism that led to "the sinister and destructive . . . totalitarianism" in fact "spent itself"? Or can it be seen to be playing a part in the approach to international relations taken by contemporary leaders? My answer is that romanticism indeed plays a significant role in international relations today, most importantly in the foreign policy of the Bush administration of the United States, and, of course, it can be found elsewhere. I will explain that answer.

10. For an excellent review of the current place of romanticism, see Gerald Holton, "The Rise of Postmodernisms and the 'End of Science,' " *Journal of the History of Ideas 61* (2000), pp. 327–341.

11. Louis Menand, "Nanook and Me: *Fahrenheit 9/11* and the Documentary Tradition," *New Yorker,* August 9 and 16, 2004, pp. 90–96.

12. Ibid., p. 92.
13. Berlin, *The Crooked Timber,* p. 202.
14. Bob Woodward, *Bush at War* (New York: Simon & Schuster, 2002), p. 137.
15. Ibid., p. 145.
16. *New York Times,* January 7, 2004, p. A1.
17. Richard Clarke, *Against All Enemies: Inside America's War on Terror* (New York: Free Press, 2004).
18. It is these cognitive circumstances that the intelligence agencies of the government will have to consider in its efforts to improve its dismal practices. It isn't simply that a new director is needed although some directors are undoubtedly worse than others; someone has to decide which cognitive approach is wanted. If the country elects romanticists to its highest office, the intelligence agencies will have to work with a romanticist, and as I have explained above, that will mean developing compatible methods—relying on intuition—for dealing with irreducible uncertainty. If, on the other hand, the country elects rationalists to its highest office, an approach to irreducible uncertainty will be required that is compatible with rationalism. Given our experience with George W. Bush, we know what to expect from a romanticist, but do we have a similar exemplar for rationalism? Yes, we do: Jimmy Carter was a rationalist president with a wide reputation for "micromanagement"; that is, examining every detail for its logical—not mere intuitive—coherence with other details. That is what micromanagement entails, and what rationalists appreciate. See Hammond, *Human Judgment and Social Policy,* for a report on my seminar at the Carter White House.

CHAPTER 13

1. See Terry Connolly, Hal Arkes, and Kenneth R. Hammond, eds., *Judgment and Decision Making: An Interdisciplinary Reader,* 2nd ed. (New York: Oxford University Press, 2000).
2. Oliver Wendell Holmes, *The Common Law* (Boston: Little, Brown, 1923), p. 1.
3. Louis Menand, *The Metaphysical Club: A Story of Ideas in America* (New York: Farrar, Straus & Giroux, 2001), p. 340.
4. Ibid., p. 342. This seems to be peculiar and unexpected behavior if you believe the justices engage in sober, rational thought that can only produce one correct answer, as in pure logic. Are those esteemed justices—supposedly the best in the land— arrogantly, willfully, insolently ignoring our trust in them by behaving in an irrational fashion—first deciding, then deducing? No. Menand explains it in this way: "When Holmes said that common law judges decided the result first and figured out a plausible account of how they got there afterward, the implication was not that the result was chosen randomly, but that it was dictated by something other than the formal legal rationale later adduced to support it." In other words, this "something other" is "experience." Menand explains that what Holmes meant by

" 'experience' we would today refer to as 'culture' " (ibid., p. 342). Menand also explains that this famous sentence does not "say that there is no logic in the law. It only says that logic is not responsible for what is living in the law. The active ingredient . . . is the thing called experience" (ibid., p. 341).

5. Holmes, *Common Law*, p. 1.

6. Edmund Morgan, *Benjamin Franklin* (New Haven, Conn.: Yale University Press, 2003), p. 294.

7. See Michael Ignatief, *The Lesser Evil: Political Ethics in an Age of Terror* (Princeton, N.J.: Princeton University Press, 2004), for a discussion of this principle.

8. Franz Kafka, *The Trial* (New York: Knopf, 1937). Can we fairly describe the maximizing that creates those long lines at the airport and similar undesirable situations as profane rationality? No; despite the above criticisms, the lines at the airport don't meet the criteria for that. Nor does insurance, which also is indifferent to the special needs of specific people; all members of a specific class are treated the same, a practice that seems quite democratic. So when does rationalism become profane? It becomes profane when its indifference to "due process" and the false positives it creates becomes more than common morality can accept. Of course, "common morality" is a shifting concept, as is acceptance, and can do as much harm as good. When I was 17 years old, I watched a lynching in San José, California. I remember being astounded when the crowd cheered and applauded as the two victims were hoisted in the air. I now see this cheering and applause as an expression of the "common morality," similar to the howling of German citizens at Hitler's ranting at the Nazi rallies.

9. See Kenneth R. Hammond, *Human Judgment and Social Policy: Irreducible Uncertainty, Inevitable Error, Unavoidable Injustice* (New York: Oxford University Press, 1996), pp. 176–177, for a brief history of mandatory sentencing.

CHAPTER 14

1. Robert Rubin, *In an Uncertain World: Tough Choices from Wall Street to Washington* (New York: Random House, 2003).

2. Ibid., p. x.

3. Ibid., p. xi.

4. Ibid.

5. Walter Isaacson, *Benjamin Franklin: An American Life* (New York: Simon & Schuster, 2003), p. 75.

6. Rubin, *In an Uncertain World*, p. xi.

7. Ibid.

8. Ibid., p. 373.

9. Ibid., p. 120.

10. Ibid., p. 214.

CHAPTER 15

1. For a brief overview of the development of the field of judgment and decision making, see Kenneth R. Hammond, *Human Judgment and Social Policy: Irreducible Uncertainty, Inevitable Error, Unavoidable Injustice* (New York: Oxford University Press, 1996); for a brief history of the concept of rationality, see Gerd Gigerenzer and Reinhard Selten, "Rethinking Rationality," in Gerd Gigerenzer and Reinhard Selten, eds., *Bounded Rationality: The Adaptive Toolbox* (Cambridge, Mass.: MIT Press, 2001), pp. 1–12. For an anthology of the introductory work on the "biases" in intuitive rationality, see Daniel Kahneman, Paul Slovic, and Amos Tversky, *Judgment under Uncertainty: Heuristics and Biases* (New York: Cambridge University Press, 1982). For a recent anthology with wide coverage, see William Goldstein and Robin Hogarth, *Research on Judgment and Decision Making* (New York: Cambridge University Press, 1997).

2. Paul Slovic and Sarah Lichtenstein, "Comparison of Bayesian and Regression Approaches to the Study of Information Processing in Judgment," *Organizational Behavior and Human Performance 6* (1972), pp. 649–744.

3. Kenneth R. Hammond, *Egon Brunswik's Psychology* (New York: Holt, 1966); Hammond, *Human Judgment and Social Policy*.

4. Edward Tolman and Egon Brunswik, "The Organism and the Causal Texture of the Environment," *Psychology Review 42* (1935), pp. 43–77; reprinted in Kenneth R. Hammond and Thomas R. Stewart, *The Essential Brunswik: Beginnings, Explications, Applications* (New York: Oxford University Press, 2001).

5. Charles Darwin, *The Origin of Species* (John Murray, 1902), pp. 669–670.

6. For more detailed examinations of Brunswikian research, see Hammond and Stewart, *The Essential Brunswik*, and Ray Cooksey, *Theory, Methods, and Applications* (New York: Academic Press, 1996).

7. Samuel D. Gosling, Sei Jin Ko, Margaret E. Morris, and Thomas Mannarelli, "A Room with a Cue: Personality Judgments Based on Offices and Bedrooms," *Journal of Personality and Social Psychology 82* (2002), pp. 379–398.

8. See Hammond and Stewart, *The Essential Brunswik*, for a collection of Brunswik's papers and a review of Brunswik's contributions.

9. James Fallows, "The Fifty-First State?" *Atlantic Monthly,* November 2002, p. 64.

10. Herbert Simon, *Models of My Life* (New York: Basic Books, 1991).

11. Gerd Gigerenzer and Peter Todd, *Simple Heuristics That Make Us Smart* (New York: Oxford University Press, 1999), p. vii.

12. Duncan Watts, *Small Worlds: The Dynamics of Networks between Order and Randomness* (Princeton, N.J.: Princeton University Press, 2003).

13. Ibid.

14. Ibid.

15. Ibid.

16. Stanislas Dehaene, *The Number Sense: How the Mind Creates Mathematics* (New York: Oxford University Press, 1997).

17. Ibid., p. 179.

18. Ibid., p. 237.

19. Paul Gordon, "Numerical Cognition without Words: Evidence from Amazonia," *Science* 15 (October 2004), pp. 496–499.

20. Ibid.

21. Marian Gomez-Beldarrain, Clare Harries, Juan-Carlos Garcia-Monco, Emma Ballus, and Jordan Grafman, "Patients with Right Frontal Lesions Are Unable to Assess and Use Advice to Make Predictive Judgments," *Journal of Cognitive Neuroscience 16* (2004), pp. 74–89.

22. Cass Sunstein, *Behavioral Law and Economics* (New York: Cambridge University Press, 2000).

23. Cass Sunstein, *Designing Democracy: What Constitutions Do* (New York: Oxford University Press, 2001).

24. Ibid., pp. 58ff.

25. Ibid., p. 59.

26. Ibid., pp. 50–66.

27. Lola Lopes and G. C. Oden, "The Rationality of Intelligence," in Ellery Eells and Tomasz Maruszewski, eds., *Probability and Rationality: Studies on L. Jonathan Cohen's Philosophy of Science* (Amsterdam: Rodopi, 1991).

28. Ibid.

29. See Kenneth R. Hammond, *Human Judgment and Social Policy,* p. 209; see also the interesting if somewhat oversimplified discussion of these differences in Steven Pinker's *The Clean Slate: The Modern Denial of Human Nature* (New York: Knopf, 2002), p. 302.

30. Robin M. Hogarth, "Is Confidence in Decisions Related to Feedback? Evidence from Random Samples of Real-World Behavior," in Klaus Fiedler and Peter Juslin, eds., *Information Sampling and Adaptive Cognition* (Cambridge, UK: Cambridge University Press, 2006), pp. 456–484.

31. Cass Sunstein, *Risk and Reason: Safety, Law and the Environment* (New York: Cambridge University Press, 2002), pp. 58ff.

32. Gerd Gigerenzer and Peter Todd, *Simple Heuristics That Make Us Smart* (New York: Oxford University Press, 1999), p. 18.

33. Laura Martignon and Kathryn Laskey, "Bayesian Benchmarks for Fast and Frugal Heuristics," in Gigerenzer and Todd, *Simple Heuristics.*

34. Peter Sedlmeier and Tillmann Betsch, *Frequency Processing and Cognition* (New York: Oxford University Press, 2002).

35. Gerd Gigerenzer, "In the Year 2054: Innumeracy Defeated," in Sedlmeier and Betsch, *Frequency Processing and Cognition,* p. 59.

36. For a counter example, however, see my comment on work by Nisbett and his colleagues, 1987, that shows that people are trainable, in Hammond, *Human Judgment and Social Policy,* pp. 204–206. It is worthy of note, however, that Nisbett states, "Previous theorists [he means Kahneman and Tversky and colleagues] may have been mistaken about trainability, in part because they misidentified the kind of rules

that people use naturally." Richard E. Nisbett et al., "Teaching Reasoning," *Science* 238 (1987), p. 625. The concept of natural frequencies has not gone uncriticized, however; see Thomas Gilovich, Dale Griffin, and Daniel Kahneman, eds., *Heuristics and Biases: The Psychology of Intuitive Judgment* (New York: Cambridge University Press, 2002).

37. Hammond and Stewart, *The Essential Brunswik*, pp. 135ff.

CHAPTER 16

1. See John Horgan, *The End of Science: Facing the Limits of Knowledge in the Twilight of the Scientific Age* (New York: Addison Wesley, 1996). See also Palle Yourgrau, *A World without Time: The Forgotten Legacy of Gödel and Einstein* (New York: Basic Books, 2005), for an excellent modern description of the struggle between empiricism and rationalism that illustrates how coherence and correspondence could not be reconciled in physics and mathematics.

2. *New York Times*, February 12, 2003, p. A35.

3. See my reproduction of the classical description by Karl Polanyi of the oscillating cognitive activity of mathematicians in Kenneth R. Hammond, *Human Judgment and Social Policy: Irreducible Uncertainty, Inevitable Error, Unavoidable Injustice* (New York: Oxford University Press, 1996), p. 194.

4. Oliver Wendell Holmes, "Codes, and the Arrangement of the Law," in Sheldon M. Novick, ed., *Justice Holmes: Complete Public Writings and Selected Judicial Opinions of Oliver Wendell Holmes* (Chicago: University of Chicago Press, 1870).

5. See, for example, Ray Cooksey, *Theory, Methods, and Applications* (New York: Academic Press, 1996).

6. Phillip K. Howard, *The Death of Common Sense: How Law Is Suffocating America* (New York: Random House, 1994).

7. Phillip K. Howard, *The Lost Art of Drawing the Line: How Fairness Went Too Far* (New York: Random House, 2001).

8. Cass Sunstein, "The Stifled Society," *New Republic,* July 9, 2001.

9. See also Hammond, *Human Judgment and Social Policy.*

10. Sunstein, "The Stifled Society."

11. Ibid.

12. Ibid.

13. Kenneth R. Hammond and Thomas R. Stewart, *The Essential Brunswik: Beginnings, Explications, Applications* (New York: Oxford University Press, 2001), pp. 55ff.

14. Gerd Gigerenzer and Peter Todd, *Simple Heuristics That Make Us Smart* (New York: Oxford University Press, 1999), p. vii.

15. Ibid.

16. See Kenneth R. Hammond, Robert Hamm, Janet Grassia, and Tamra Pearson, "Direct Comparison of the Efficacy of Intuitive and Analytical Cognition in Expert Judgment," in William Goldstein and Robin Hogarth, eds., *Research on Judg-*

ment and Decision Making (New York: Cambridge University Press, 1997), pp. 144–180, for an empirical demonstration of the use of these concepts.

17. See Cooksey, *Theory, Methods, and Applications*; Hammond, *Human Judgment and Social Policy*.

18. Cameron Peterson, Kenneth R. Hammond, and David Summers, "Multiple Probability-Learning with Shifting Weights of Cues," *American Journal of Psychology 78* (1965), pp. 660–663.

19. Kenneth R. Hammond, *Judgments under Stress* (New York: Oxford University Press, 2000), chapter 8.

20. See Hammond, *Judgments under Stress*, for an annotated bibliography and review of the literature.

21. Hammond, Hamm, Grassia, and Pearson, "Direct Comparison."

22. Hammond, *Judgments under Stress*, pp. 111–112.

CHAPTER 17

1. Dan Baum, "Battle Lessons: What the Generals Didn't Know," *New Yorker,* January 17, 2005.

2. Ibid., p. 47.

3. Bernard Lewis, *What Went Wrong?* (New York: Oxford University Press, 2002).

4. Isaiah Berlin, "The Concept of Scientific History," in Henry Hardy, ed., *Concepts and Categories* (New York: Viking, 1979), pp. 103–142.

5. Lewis, *What Went Wrong?*, p. 151.

6. For sharp, if not vicious, challenges to Lewis's thesis, see Edward Said's article in *Harper's*, July 2002, pp. 71–73.

7. Lewis, *What Went Wrong?*, p. 152.

8. Ibid., p. 159.

9. Ibid., p. 151.

10. Ibid., p. 73.

11. Herbert Simon, *Models of My Life* (New York: Basic Books, 1991), p. 361.

12. The question of the rational justification of when to stop the search will occasionally arise, but that topic is out of place here; see, however, Gerd Gigerenzer and Peter Todd, *Simple Heuristics That Make Us Smart* (New York: Oxford University Press, 1999), for detailed discussions.

13. William Dalrymple, "The Truth about Muslims," *New York Review of Books,* November 4, 2004, pp. 31–34.

14. Jared Diamond, "The Ends of the World as We Know Them," *New York Times,* January 1, 2005, p. A21.

15. See Jared Diamond, *Guns, Germs, and Steel: The Fates of Human Societies* (New York: Norton, 1997), pp. 18–19.

16. Ibid. p. 19.

17. Ibid., pp. 420–425.

18. Clifford Geertz, "Very Bad News," *New York Review of Books,* March 24, 2005, pp. 4–6.
19. Ibid., p. 4.
20. Ibid.
21. Richard Posner, *Catastrophe: Risk and Response* (New York: Oxford University Press, 2005).
22. Geertz, "Very Bad News," p. 6.
23. Ibid.
24. Jared Diamond, *Collapse: How Societies Choose to Fail or Succeed* (New York: Penguin, 2005), p. 19.
25. See the table in Kenneth R. Hammond, *Human Judgment and Social Policy: Irreducible Uncertainty, Inevitable Error, Unavoidable Injustice* (New York: Oxford University Press, 1996), p. 235, which shows the relationship between methodology and dispute.
26. Gordon Wood, "The Making of a Disaster." *New York Review of Books,* April 28, 2005, p. 34.

CHAPTER 18

1. Isaiah Berlin, *Personal Impressions* (New York: Viking, 1980), p. 145.
2. Richard Parker, *John Kenneth Galbraith: His Life, His Politics, His Economics* (New York: Farrar, Straus & Giroux, 2005).
3. Ibid., p. 664.
4. Ibid., p. 666.
5. Gerd Gigerenzer and Peter Todd, *Simple Heuristics That Make Us Smart* (New York: Oxford University Press, 1999).
6. Peter Sedlmeier and Tillman Betsch, *Frequency Processing and Cognition* (New York: Oxford University Press, 2002).
7. Christopher Wickens and John Flach, "Information Processing," in E. L. Weiner and D. C. Nagel, eds., *Human Factors in Modern Aviation* (New York: Academic Press, 1988), pp. 111–155.
8. See Kenneth R. Hammond and Thomas R. Stewart, eds., *The Essential Brunswik: Beginnings, Explications, Applications* (New York: Oxford University Press, 2001), for a description of Brunswik's career; see also Kenneth R. Hammond, *Human Judgment and Social Policy: Irreducible Uncertainty, Inevitable Error, Unavoidable Injustice* (New York: Oxford University Press, 1996), for examples of the application of Brunswik's methodology to social problems.

CHAPTER 19

1. Letter from Albert Einstein, August 2, 1939.
2. National Commission on Terrorist Attacks upon the United States, *The 9/11 Com-*

mission Report: Final Report of the National Commission on Terrorist Attacks upon the United States (New York: Norton, 2004), p. 323.

3. *Washington Post,* October 7, 2004, p. 1.

4. Richard Posner, "The 9/11 Report: A Dissent," *New York Times Review of Books,* August 29, 2004, p. 1.

5. Ibid., p. 9.

6. Benjamin DeMott, "Whitewash as a Public Service," *Harper's Magazine* October 2004, pp. 35–46.

7. Thomas Powers, "How Bush Got It Wrong," *New York Review of Books,* September 23, 2004, pp. 87–93.

8. Richard Clarke, *Against All Enemies* (New York: Free Press, 2004).

9. Irving Janis, *Groupthink: Psychological Studies of Policy Decisions and Fiascoes,* 2nd ed. (Boston: Houghton Mifflin, 1982).

10. See the 1992 edition of the *American Heritage Dictionary of the American Language.*

11. Kenneth R. Hammond, *Human Judgment and Social Policy: Irreducible Uncertainty, Inevitable Error, Unavoidable Injustice* (New York: Oxford University Press, 1996), p. 303.

12. Jared Diamond, *Collapse: How Societies Choose to Fail or Succeed* (New York: Penguin, 2005), p. 439.

13. Posner, "The 9/11 Report: A Dissent," p. 9.

14. National Commission on Terrorist Attacks upon the United States, "Institutionalizing Imagination: The Case of Aircraft Weapons," in *The 9/11 Commission Report,* p. 344.

15. Ibid.

16. See also, e.g., James Holzworth, "Annotated Bibliography of Cue Probability Learning Studies," retrieved from the Brunswik Society Web site (http://www. brunswik.org/resources/mcplbib.doc; 1999); Ray Cooksey, *Theory, Methods, and Applications* (New York: Academic Press, 1996); Hammond, *Human Judgment and Social Policy;* Kenneth R. Hammond, *Judgments under Stress* (New York: Oxford University Press, 2000); Kenneth R. Hammond and Thomas R. Stewart, eds., *The Essential Brunswik: Beginnings, Explications, Applications* (New York: Oxford University Press, 2001).

17. National Commission on Terrorist Attacks upon the United States, "Institutionalizing Imagination," p. 346.

18. For a detailed analysis of the putative efforts by the Soviet Union to deceive the United States during the Czechoslovac crisis, see Cynthia Grabo, "Soviet Deception in the Czechoslovak Crisis," *Studies in Intelligence,* Fall 2000.

19. National Commission on Terrorist Attacks upon the United States, "Institutionalizing Imagination," p. 346.

20. Ibid.

21. See also Hammond, *Human Judgment and Social Policy;* Hammond, *Judgments under Stress;* Kenneth R. Hammond and Thomas R. Stewart, eds., *The Essential Brunswik: Beginnings, Explications, Applications* (New York: Oxford University Press, 2001); and Cooksey, *Theory, Methods, and Applications.*

22. Michael Schrage, "What Percent Is 'Slam Dunk'?" *Washington Post*, February 20, 2005, p. B01.

23. David Sanger, "A Doctrine under Pressure: Preemption Is Redefined," *New York Times*, October 11, 2004. p. A10.

24. Ibid.

25. Elisabeth Bumiller, *New York Times*, June 8, 2005, p. A6.

26. Ibid.

27. Ron Suskind, "Without a Doubt," *New York Times Magazine*, October 17, 2004.

CHAPTER 20

1. James McPherson, "Friends of Abe," *New York Times Book Review*, November 6, 2005, p. 1.

2. Ibid.

3. Ibid.

4. Ibid.

5. Ibid.

6. Work by Robert J. Sternberg (Sternberg and Jennifer Jordan, eds., *A Handbook of Wisdom: Psychological Perspectives* [Cambridge: Cambridge University Press, 2005]) and Paul Baltes and Ursula Staudinger are current examples of this research in Europe and the United States.

7. Palle Yourgrau, *A World without Time: The Forgotten Legacy of Gödel and Einstein* (New York: Basic Books, 2005), p. 2.

8. Kurt Gödel, "Über formal unentscheidbare Sätze der Principia Mathematica und verwandter Systeme I" "On Formally Undecidable Propositions of Principia Mathematica and Related Systems"; *Monatshefte für Mathematik und Physik 38*, (1931), pp. 173–198. Translated in Solomon Feferman, ed., *Kurt Gödel: Collected Works, Vol. 1: Publications 1929–1936* (New York: Oxford University Press, 1986). For a layman-accessible, somewhat fantastical treatment of Gödel's incompleteness theorem and musings on related topics, see Douglas R. Hofstadter, *Gödel, Escher, Bach: An Eternal Golden Braid* (New York: Vintage, 1979).

9. See James Holzworth, "Annotated Bibliography of Cue Probability Learning Studies," retrieved from the Brunswik Society Web site (http://www. brunswik.org/resources/mcplbib.doc; 1999); and Ray Cooksey, *Theory, Methods, and Applications* (New York: Academic Press, 1996) for a review.

10. Ward Edwards, "The Theory of Decision Making," *Psychological Bulletin 41* (1954), pp. 380–417.

Bibliography

Baruma, Ian, and Avishai Margalit. *Occidentalism: The West in the Eyes of Its Enemies.* New York: Penguin, 2004.

Barzun, Jacques. *From Dawn to Decadence: 500 Years of Western Cultural Life, 1500 to the Present.* New York: HarperCollins, 2001.

Berlin, Isaiah. *The Sense of Reality: Studies in Ideas and Their History.* New York: Farrar, Straus & Giroux, 1996.

Browne, Janet. *Charles Darwin: The Power of Place.* New York: Knopf, 2002.

Brunswik, Egon. *Perception and the Representative Design of Psychological Experiments.* Berkeley: University of California Press, 1956.

Connolly, Terry, Hal Arkes, and Kenneth R. Hammond, eds. *Judgment and Decision Making: An Interdisciplinary Reader.* 2nd ed. New York: Oxford University Press, 2000.

Cooksey, Ray. *Theory, Methods, and Applications.* New York: Academic Press, 1996.

Dehaene, Stanislas. *The Number Sense: How the Mind Creates Mathematics.* New York: Oxford University Press, 1997.

Diamond, Jared. *Guns, Germs, and Steel: The Fates of Human Societies.* New York: Norton, 1997.

———. *Collapse: How Societies Choose to Fail or Succeed.* New York: Penguin, 2005.

Gigerenzer, Gerd, and Peter Todd, eds. *Simple Heuristics That Make Us Smart.* New York: Oxford University Press, 1999.

Goldstein, William, and Robin Hogarth, eds. *Research on Judgment and Decision Making.* New York: Cambridge University Press, 1997.

Goody, Jack. *The Interface between the Written and the Oral.* New York: Cambridge University Press, 1987.

———. *The Power of the Written Word.* Washington, D.C.: Smithsonian Institution Press, 2000.

Greenberg, Karen, and Joshua Dratel, eds. *The Torture Papers: The Road to Abu Ghraib.* New York: Cambridge University Press, 2005.

Groopman, Jerome. *Second Opinions: Stories of Intuition and Choice in the World of Medicine.* New York: Penguin, 2001.

Hammond, Kenneth R. *Human Judgment and Social Policy: Irreducible Uncertainty, Inevitable Error, Unavoidable Injustice.* New York: Oxford University Press, 1996.

————. *Judgments under Stress.* New York: Oxford University Press, 2000.

Hammond, Kenneth R., and Thomas R. Stewart, eds. *The Essential Brunswik: Beginnings, Explications, Applications.* New York: Oxford University Press, 2001.

Holzworth, James. "Annotated Bibliography of Cue Probability Learning Studies." 1999. Retrieved from the Brunswik Society Web site (http://www. brunswik.org/resources/mcplbib.doc).

Keegan, John. *Intelligence in War: Knowledge of the Enemy from Napoleon to Al-Qaeda.* New York: Knopf, 2003.

Lewis, Bernard. *What Went Wrong?* New York: Oxford University Press, 2002.

Lilla, Mark. *The Reckless Mind: Intellectuals in Politics.* New York: New York Review Books, 2001.

May, Ernst, and Philip Zelikow. *The Kennedy Papers: Inside the White House during the Cuban Missile Crisis.* Cambridge, Mass.: Harvard University Press, 1997.

Menand, Louis. *The Metaphysical Club: A Story of Ideas in America.* New York: Farrar, Straus & Giroux, 2001.

National Commission on Terrorist Attacks upon the United States. *The 9/11 Commission Report: Final Report of the National Commission on Terrorist Attacks upon the United States.* New York: Norton, 2004.

Novick, Sheldon. *Honorable Justice: The Life of Oliver Wendell Holmes.* New York: Little, Brown, 1989.

Parker, Richard. *John Kenneth Galbraith: His Life, His Politics, His Economics.* Farrar, Straus & Giroux, 2005.

Risen, James. *State of War: The Secret History of the C.I.A. and the Bush Administration.* New York: Free Press, 2006.

Rothstein, Edward, Herbert Muschamp, and Martin Marty. *Visions of Utopia.* New York: Oxford University Press, 2003.

Scalia, Antonin. *A Matter of Interpretation: Federal Courts and the Law.* Princeton, N.J.: Princeton University Press, 1997.

Shermer, Michael. *In Darwin's Shadow: The Life and Science of Alfred Russel Wallace.* New York: Oxford University Press, 2002.

Simon, Herbert. *Models of My Life.* New York: Basic Books, 1991.

Yourgrau, Palle. *A World without Time: The Forgotten Legacy of Gödel and Einstein.* Cambridge, Mass.: Basic Books, 2005.

Index

inferences
  about intentions, 56–61, 70–71, 269, 272,
    279–280
  inductive, 43–45, 258, 272
  inferential logic, 250, 251
  personal, 48–49, 157
  subjective, 251
  vicarious functioning and, 226
  vs. direct observation, 57–58, 59
inflection point, 87
information. *See also* indicators; intelligence
    agencies
  data mining, 67, 68–75
  false (disinformation), 48, 53–54, 61–62
  filtering of, 113–115
  information explosion, 22, 30, 67–68
  Internet, 113–115
  in natural vs. engineered environments, 37,
    38–39
  overload, 67
  passive use of, 22–23
  surface–depth continuum, 127–129
  thirst for, 30
insight, 154
instinct, 235–236. *See also* intuition
  George W. Bush's use of, xxii, 158, 181, 272
  Robert Rubin's use of, 193
insurance companies, 42
intellectuals, 95–96
intelligence agencies, 269–273
  CIA failures in intelligence, 181–182,
    269–273, 279–280
  judgments involving coherence competence,
    277–280
  judgments involving correspondence
    competence, 274–277
  military intelligence, 31–32, 46–47, 139–143,
    268
intelligent design, 79, 294
intentions, 55–64, 279
  to deceive, 61–62
  duality of error and, 59–61
  inferences about, 56–61, 70–71, 269, 272,
    279–280
  intractability of learning about, 62–63,
    101–109
Internet, 113–115, 167

interpersonal learning. *See* learning about the
    other
intuition, 58, 145–161, 173–183, 297n15
  compromise and, 223, 231
  dichotomy with analysis assumed, 123–124,
    125–126, 230–231
  in economic behavior, 214
  empirical accuracy and, 145–161
  intuition-inducing tasks, 124–125, 230
  intuitive cognition vs. "intuitive thought,"
    146–147
  intuitive learning, 154–155
  lack of retraceability, 133, 146, 147, 272–273
  in medicine, 149–154
  misperception, 156–158
  mysterious nature of, 145–146, 236
  in political judgments, 179–182, 272–273
  in probability judgments, 175–176, 264–265,
    292–293
  professionals, use by, 147, 149, 164, 229–230
  rationality and, 173–183
  robust flexibility and, 228–230
  romanticism and, 179
  science and, 160–161
  social policy and, 155–156
  speed and ease of, 133–134, 145–146, 149, 230
  on task continuum, 124–125
  thoughtless quality of, 146–147
  uncertainty, failure under, 215–217, 293
intuitive perception, 127
Iraq
  call for common sense in, 228
  justification of invasion, 177–178, 269, 279
  reconstruction of, 91–92
  U.S. involvement in, lessons to be learned,
    158–160
iris scans, 35
Irish Republican Army, 65
irreducible uncertainty. *See* uncertainty
Isaacson, Walter, 192
Islam, Bernard Lewis's study of, 247–253
"It's Not Who We Are, It's What We Do"
    (Kaplan), 65

James, William, 123
Janis, Irving, 271
Jefferson, Thomas, 123–124